Nationalism in Iran

U. S. S. R.
Caspian Sea
L. URUMIA
Tabriz
AZERBAIJAN
GILAN
Pahlavi
Rasht
MAZANDERAN
ELBURZ MTS.
Tehran
Qazvin
Mehabad
Mashhad
Hamadan
Kermanshah
DASHT KAVIR
KHORASAN
ZAGROS MTS.
IRAN
Isfahan
Yazd
DASHT LUT
Kerman
IRAQ
KHUZISTAN
Khorramshahr
Abadan
Shiraz
FARS
Bushire
AFGHANISTAN
PAKISTAN
BALUCHISTAN
N
SAUDI ARABIA
Persian Gulf

I·R·A·N

UPDATED THROUGH 1978

Nationalism in Iran

BY RICHARD W. COTTAM

University of Pittsburgh Press

Published by the University of Pittsburgh Press, Pittsburgh, Pa. 15260

Feffer and Simons, Inc., London
Manufactured in the United States of America

Library of Congress Cataloging in Publication Data

Cottam, Richard W
Nationalism in Iran.

Includes bibliographical references and index.
1. Nationalism—Iran. 2. Iran—Politics and government. I. Title.
DS318.C66 1979 320.9'55 78-12302
ISBN 0-8229-3396-7
ISBN 0-8229-5299-8 pbk.

CONTENTS

ACKNOWLEDGMENT

Most of the material for this book was collected during two very different sojourns in Iran: In 1951–52 I did research at the University of Tehran under a Fulbright scholarship, and in 1956–58 I served as a political officer in the American Embassy in Tehran. The first period was the apex of the Mossadeq era, and the Iran I saw had much verve but little order. The second period was one of royal dictatorship, and this Iran had much order but little verve.

Since a study of nationalism must focus on values and attitudes, personal interviews of Iranians of diverse views constitute a vital part of the source material of this book. I should like to acknowledge my debt to several Iranians who were particularly helpful. But Iran is a bitterly divided nation with followers of Mossadeq and royalists deeply and mutually suspicious. The analysis that follows is my own and includes sections—as any honest study must—which will displease both factions. And I would be naive not to reckon with the possibility that the governmental security agency might incorrectly ascribe parts of this analysis to specific individuals were I to mention names. Therefore, I must leave this part of the acknowledgment anonymous.

This book owes much to Professor Rupert Emerson of Harvard, as do so many other studies of nationalism published in recent years. My interest was first aroused in his course, and since then he has given me guidance and encouragement. My introduction to Iran came from a man with a profound grasp of its history, culture, and language, Professor Richard Frye of Harvard. In 1952 I first interviewed Professor T. Cuyler Young of Princeton, whose understanding of contemporary Iran is unsurpassed. Since then Professor Young has given generously of his time to my education. Both he and his colleague, Martin Dickson, read this manuscript and gave me many valuable suggestions.

The members of the United States Information Agency who

administered the Fulbright program in Iran did everything possible to support my research. Particularly helpful were Robert Steiner and Kate Gurney. Taylor Gurney, who is an institution in Tehran, opened many Iranian doors for my interviews. A grant from the Social Science Research Council permitted me to leave my teaching duties in order to write this book.

I should say a few words about the Persian source material used in this study. Political studies in Persian are, in general, weak analytically but reveal the attitudes, perspectives, and values associated with Iranian nationalism. For these I found political biographies particularly useful. Periodicals were of great value, especially for the years 1906–11, 1919–22, and 1946–53. Although press laws were often stringent, and at no time more so than in the Mossadeq era, they were only sporadically enforced during these periods. As a result magazines and newspapers mirrored the attitudes and values of their clientele, and for this reason they are an exceptionally good source. Even in the years of royal dictatorship much can be learned from the press. Propaganda lines utilized and areas of expression censored permit the analyst to reconstruct the propagandist's image of Iranian attitudes. The vigorous opposition press, printed clandestinely in Iran and openly in Europe and the United States, provides an excellent base of comparison.

INTRODUCTION

The year 1946 was a time of relief for most Americans. Responding to the overwhelming demands of the public, the United States government was breaking all speed records in demobilizing the huge World War II war machine; and in the back of the minds of both the public and the government was the unspoken wish to return to the uncomplicated pre-Hitlerian era when the United States could close its eyes to much of international politics. But in this same year obscure Iran and its unheard of northern province of Azerbaijan demonstrated beyond all doubt that a return to prewar mentality was impossible. In 1946 the Soviet Union made a dramatic demand for preeminence in the eastern Mediterranean and the northern Middle East. Not only Iran but also Greece and Turkey were threatened. In response to this challenge, the United States was compelled to face the fact that, as the greatest power of the noncommunist world, its responsibilities must now embrace the entire free world, including the Middle East. Having admitted this responsibility, the United States government stood firmly behind the Iranians, and the Soviets somewhat surprisingly retreated.

But this was only the beginning. Since 1946 United States involvement in Middle Eastern affairs has been extensive. What was called for in 1946 was simple determination and forthrightness in supporting the Iranian government. What has been called for in the intervening years is an accurate comprehension of the Iranian social and political situation in order to assess correctly the consequences of less dramatic but equally vital policy decisions. Although the United States can justly claim success for the comparatively simple policy decision of 1946, the ledger since that year is far less favorable. As with postwar United States foreign policy elsewhere in Asia, Africa, and Latin America, courage and determination were not the missing ingredients. Lack of success in the non-European areas must be attributed to failures of comprehension and political sophistication.

For these failures the American social scientists must share the responsibility. But it should be remembered that the neglect of the non-European world by social scientists prior to World War II was a universal phenomenon. Although a few isolated works of excellence had been written, much of the literature about this part of the world was produced by men untrained in the social sciences. The heritage of this literature consists largely of impressionistic clichés. The task, then, of the recent investigator has been made doubly difficult because not only must he begin from scratch in his empirical investigation, but he must devote much effort to exploding clichés that are as fallacious as they are tenacious.

The problem also has an aspect of the vicious circle. Gabriel Almond has commented on the compulsion of the American people to rationalize to a position of moral righteousness the various aspects of United States foreign policy; [1] and this observation applies to teachers and government officials as well as to the less informed general public. Its repercussions for scholarship concerning Iran and the Middle East are serious. The United States has made foreign policy errors concerning the Middle East because of faulty situational analyses. Having made these mistakes, Americans—the public, government officials, and academics alike—seem to feel compelled to prove that their actions were morally correct, even if an Orwellian rewriting of history is required to do so. The fallacious quality of the basic analyses cannot be admitted if the position of moral righteousness is to be maintained, and subsequent analyses will be distorted. Future foreign policy will suffer, because the most fundamental prerequisite for a successful foreign policy is an accurate situational analysis. In Iran the original error was made in regard to Dr. Mohammad Mossadeq and Mohammad Reza Shah. The distortions of the Mossadeq era, both in the press and in academic studies, border on the grotesque, and until that era is seen in truer perspective there can be little hope for a sophisticated United States foreign policy concerning Iran.

This study is based on an assumption that very few would dispute: that a major key to the understanding of Iranian attitudes and political behavior is to be found in the phenomenon of

[1] Gabriel A. Almond, *The American People and Foreign Policy* (New York, 1960), p. 52.

nationalism. However, a further assumption may find less ready acceptance: that a misreading of nationalism in Iran is responsible for many of the basic analytical errors regarding Iran. A case in point is the very common reference to Iranian nationalism as "negative nationalism." This phrase is a gross oversimplification of an exceedingly complex phenomenon, and it leads to the very common practice in both governmental and academic circles of seeing Iranian nationalists as a negative monolith. Many of the pages that follow are devoted to developing what is distorted by this simple phrase.

But the goal of this study goes beyond providing a better understanding of Iranian nationalism. The broader purpose is to furnish a case study of nationalism which, together with other case studies, can provide a more solid basis for general hypothesizing about this vital subject. Despite the fact that nationalism has been a strikingly pervasive phenomenon in the West since the French Revolution, our understanding of it is far from complete. The rapid progress made in many areas of the social sciences as a result of improved methodology has no parallel in the study of nationalism. Part of the explanation for this lag can be found in the fact that we have experienced this phenomenon so vividly. Hitler's Germany and Mussolini's Italy, where nationalism seemed to have reached the ultimate extreme, have led many in the West to look with favor on the indications that nationalism in the West has passed its climactic point. At the same time, many others view nationalism with approval and regard it as a desirable social sentiment. For these two groups of people agreement is impossible even on definition, and definitions of nationalism are as widely divergent as value judgments passed upon it.

Much of the disagreement results from a failure of qualitative analysis. Too frequently nationalism is spoken of loosely as an ideology without explaining how nationalism per se warrants such a classification. The definition of nationalism as used in this study is a belief on the part of a large group of people that they comprise a political community, a nation, that is entitled to independent statehood, and a willingness of this group to grant their community a primary and the terminal loyalty. Thus defined, nationalism which clearly insists on independence and dignity for the nation furnishes a part, but only a part, of the value system of the individual members of the community.

It is a major contention of this study that very little is to be learned about nationalism by viewing it in isolation from the other elements of a value system. Those who condemn nationalism frequently do so by confusing it, under the name of integral nationalism, with the complex political value system which characterized Hitler's Germany. Comparing this system, the dominant features of which related to leader adulation, racism, and nationalism, with the American value system, the dominant features of which relate to liberalism, democracy, and nationalism, it can be seen that nationalism is the constant and liberalism the primary variable. A rapid conclusion might even be that since nationalism is a constant it is therefore of a neutral hue and fails to give any normative coloring to the system. Such a conclusion overlooks the obvious fact that nationalism does generate a propensity to look to the community rather than to the individual and hence does reinforce and accentuate collectivist tendencies in any system. In a community in which liberal norms calling for a maximum of respect for the dignity of the individual personality are firmly entrenched, the collectivist propensity of nationalism is largely offset by the individualist propensity of liberalism. But in a community where these liberal norms are only weakly held, nationalist values can in fact be among the instruments used to destroy the hold of individualist values.

There is also substantial disagreement regarding the date of the appearance of nationalism on the world scene. Most authorities focus on the French Revolution as the critical era, but many others, particularly historians, are too much aware of evidence of national consciousness prior to that time to be able to accept the French Revolution as the beginning of the national era. This dispute is probably not a serious one since the two schools are really speaking from different definitions of nationalism. Yet the basis of the dispute needs to be spelled out if the real importance of nationalism is to be understood.

Men living in the society of other men will almost invariably include in their value systems a devotion to the welfare of one or several socio-political groups. Many years, even centuries, before the French Revolution there were men in England and France and elsewhere whose horizons were large enough to embrace an awareness of being a member of a people, and for some there was great pride in and loyalty to that people. To describe such men as nationalists is perfectly reasonable. But if the term "nationalism" is defined broadly enough to include this early period then those using such a definition must further refine their meaning to take into account the very substantial differences in the social and political impact of nationalism when it is a primary value of the very few and when it is a primary value of a large section of the population. Those who prefer to consider the French Revolution as the beginning of the nationalist era are defining nationalism as a phenomenon of mass politics in the era of the nation state. "Nationalism" in this study is used in the latter sense. Iran, in fact, is an excellent example of a state in which national consciousness can be clearly identified for many centuries. But the importance of nationalism as a primary determinant of Iranian attitudes and political behavior is largely confined to the twentieth century.

Iran is also an example of those states in which the participation in the political life of the state by a broad section of the population followed by more than a century the development of mass political participation in Western Europe and the United States. Therefore, at a time when nationalist values were central values for most Europeans and Americans, the concept of nationalism was an esoteric one for the vast majority of Iranians. There were, however, even in the late nineteenth century, Iranians who understood nationalism and held nationalist values regarding Iran which were in every sense comparable to the nationalist values of, say, contemporary Frenchmen toward France. These early nationalistic Iranians played an important role in Iranian political developments. Since their own political behavior was determined to a considerable extent by their nationalistic values, nationalism in Iran was an important determinant of political behavior and attitudes well before the development of mass political participation.

Not at all accidentally, those Iranians who constituted the early nationalists were also the men who could be classified as modernists. The objectives of a strong central government sincerely dedicated to ending the feudalistic landholding system, sloth and corruption in government, and the wholesale distribution of Iranian resources to foreigners were objectives closely related to the values of nationalism; they were also the universal objectives of Iranian modernizers. Nationalistic values therefore had an easy appeal for modernizers. But it would be a serious distortion to conclude that nationalism from the beginning was confined to the modernizers. This distortion is as common inside modernist circles in Iran as is the "negative nationalism" distortion among Americans concerned with Iran. Those Iranians who today call themselves "Nationalists" believe that they alone are the defenders of nationalism. In truth, however, most of the bitter enemies of the "Nationalists" include in their value systems nationalistic values.

Once introduced in Iran, nationalism carried a dynamic quality of its own. Traditional elements who hoped to preserve the status quo did not look upon nationalism as an ally of the enemy. On the contrary, nationalistic values gradually began to incorporate themselves in the value systems of traditional leaders; nationalism began to be a determinant of the political behavior of the traditional elements, even though it coincided far less with the self-interest of this group than with that of the modernists.

This study is an effort to describe and analyze the impact of nationalism on Iranian political behavior and political attitudes as Iran moves into the era of mass political participation. Since a basic theoretical assumption of this study is that the properties of nationalism can best be understood by observing the interaction of nationalist values with other values of any value system, no attempt will be made to theorize about Iranian nationalism in isolation. Instead, the generalizations that are suggested will deal with some consequences of the interaction of nationalist and other values.

Definitions of nationalism in the pre-World War I period, when nationalism was largely confined to states in which the populations were relatively homogeneous, very often called for the existence of a definite territory, a common and distinctive historical and cultural tradition, a common language, a common religion, and a belief in racial homogeneity. Today far too many examples can be found of nationalisms existing without several of these factors to include any of them in the definition. Even the territorial requirement had to be dropped, since the Jews can claim to have embraced nationalism before they had anything more substantial than a memory of territory. But the elimination of these requirements from the definition should not suggest a lack of importance. Any people who believe they are part of a community that deserves their terminal loyalty must be convinced that this community is distinctive. And strongly cohesive factors must be present if this belief is to persist. If none of the above listed factors were present, nationalism could not endure. Even if only territory and one other factor were present, as is largely true in Pakistan today, the hold of nationalism would be a tenuous one. Conversely, if all these factors were present the receptivity of a people for nationalism and the prospective longevity of nationalism would be greatly enhanced. Even here, however, the dynamic quality of nationalism asserts itself. Although the cohesive base for nationalism may be barely adequate, nationalism once introduced will alter it and usually, but certainly not always, will increase its cohesiveness. The essential starting point for a study of nationalism is, first, an exploration of these cohesive factors to gain an insight into the base of receptivity and, second, an investigation of the impact of nationalism once it appears on that base.

Even when most or all of the cohesive ingredients are present, there is no assurance that nationalism will find much receptivity. If, as was true in Iran at the turn of the century, only a tiny percentage of the population has a frame of reference broad enough to comprehend nationalism, then obviously receptivity is sharply limited. In Iran this point was accentuated because the small percentage which was politically aware was dominated by a basically traditional element; and although nationalistic values were eventually accepted by members of this group, they gained acceptance only after they had been thoroughly entrenched in the value systems of the modernizers. It is unlikely that nationalism could ever gain entrée to a people if the only channel open to it was the traditional elite structure which was contented with the status quo.

The early history of Iranian nationalism illustrates this narrow base of popular receptivity. But it illustrates as well the point that once nationalism gains a foothold within a people, a dynamic interaction occurs in which the base of appeal is sharply altered, usually in the direction of an expanded receptivity. An illiterate and politically inert peasant is denied an understanding of the nation of Iran simply because his horizons are too narrow. But once he is shaken out of his inertia and his traditional values are challenged, he easily absorbs nationalistic values. He leaves his village to seek economic opportunities in the city, and there he seeks a new group identification. With his broader perspective he can comprehend the nation, and at this point the nation can fulfill a basic psychological need. Thus the nationalistic politician has the opportunity of personifying the aspirations of the newly awakened citizen. As the politician's power grows, he will advocate policies to hasten the spread of political articulateness. Traditional politicians threatened in this way may, and often do, respond by seeking to outdo the modernists in utilizing a nationalist line, coupling it with an appeal to traditional values. The sum of the process is a rapid expansion of the popular base for nationalism.

There are significant elements of the Iranian population that are essentially nonnational; their terminal loyalty is to a unit other than the nation. In this study three such groups will be considered: religious minorities, the tribes, and the regional autonomists. In the prenationalist era these groups were able to maintain a good deal of autonomy. But their position must inevitably be changed with the infusion of nationalist values into the population. As the nation-state becomes increasingly an object of primary loyalty for the majority, the position of the nonnational groups will deteriorate. Even when an individual member of the majority couples liberal values with his nationalist values and is therefore tolerant of diversity, he is likely to express this tolerance in a willingness to see the integration of the nonnational group into the nation rather than in a continuance of an autonomous status. His antiliberal counterpart would almost certainly turn to persecution. Under the impact of nationalism, therefore, the nonnational groups seem to have only two alternatives. Either they can move in a direction of integration within the nation, in which case the nation for them would become a primary and the terminal loyalty, or they can move into an increasingly perilous isolation from the majority. The case of Iran should give some indication of the factors that would compel various nonnational groups to choose different alternatives.

This study may also be of value in general considerations of the relationship of religion and nationalism. Observers have long noted that the existence of a common, especially a unique, religion is a great source of strength for nationalism. At the same time, it is clear that an individual's religious values and his national values may stimulate different and sometimes conflicting behavior. Both sets of values satisfy basic needs and are likely to be held by a broad section of the population, including the least aware politically. Any conflict developing between the two sets of values would have the potential of being fundamentally disruptive. This picture is further complicated by the probable coexistence of religious and secular authorities for whom jurisdictional lines are blurred. As an overwhelmingly Moslem country, Iran adds to this picture adherence to a theology which offers no recognition of the concept of separation of church and state. If a conflict of the two sets of values is likely anywhere it should occur in Iran; and Iran should furnish a meaningful case study of the interaction of religious and national values.

When nationalism appeared on the Iranian stage at the turn of the century, an involved struggle for hegemony in Iran was taking place between England and Russia. Although Iran had a more than nominal independence, Anglo-Russian interference in Iranian affairs was extensive and largely overt. Furthermore, this interference was both tolerated and utilized by prenationalist Iranian regimes. The result was a bizarre situation in which a form of indirect colonial control existed in the hands of two imperial powers whose relative positions were in constant flux. Whereas prenationalist Iranian statesmen could view this situation casually, their nationalistic successors had a different perspective. Not surprisingly, neither the English nor the Russians recognized this altered perspective and its impact on Iranian attitudes and beliefs. But this impact was profound.

The situation was further complicated by the obvious preference of the pre-Bolshevik Russians and the British for the traditional-minded Iranian statesmen. External interference was therefore linked in the minds of many Iranians with the efforts of the traditional leaders to stave off the modernist challenge. The consequence was that the entire traditional elite structure was enveloped in a suspicion of treason. Although the Iranian case has many unique features, the nationalist response there to the alliance of the traditional class and the imperial power has features that are to be recognized wherever indirect rule was resorted to through traditional elements.

The final section of this book is an analysis of the general impact of nationalism on Iranian political developments in the twentieth century. A central proposition suggested by this section is that given optimum circumstances, nationalism can be a primary instrument for the inculcation of liberal norms in a rapidly developing nation, even though historically there is no liberal tradition. Optimum circumstances exist (a) when the modernizing forces in the country are numerically strong enough and well enough placed to constitute an alternative to the traditional elite structure; (b) when a dominant section of the modernizing forces accepts both liberal and national values; and (c) when awareness has appeared among a sufficiently large section of the hitherto politically inert so that this group can, when allied with the modernizers, provide sufficient strength to challenge successfully the dominant traditional elements, but before this group has become so large that a demagogue who might seek and win their backing would have the strength to overturn both the traditional and modernizing elite groups.

Without question those individuals who have recently become politically articulate will be more receptive to nationalistic values than to liberal values. Nationalistic values can be understood very easily, but comprehension of liberal values requires both a good deal of political sophistication and a real interest in the political process; the newly awakened are not likely to have either. Modernizing leaders, however, are natural allies of the newly awakened, who, although inarticulate, will almost always be dissatisfied with the status quo. Nationalism, coupled with programs of economic and social reform, therefore becomes the basis of the appeal of the modernizing leaders to the newly awakened. After achieving power, the modernizers will probably then proceed to establish a parliament and liberal institutions of free elections, political parties, and civil rights. In time these institutions will achieve symbolic significance and will become the means by which those individuals who are awakening politically can be channelled into the political process.

However, if the traditional elements are able to turn back the challenge of the modernists, the prospects for the inculcation of liberal values in the immediate future will be dim. The growth in political awareness is a trend of such force that it is doubtful that any government can do more than slow it down. The point will soon be reached at which the newly awakened need only find the requisite leadership to overturn the entire elite structure; and that leadership will be readily available in the form of demagogues for whom nationalism will certainly be a primary tool. To control this situation the traditional element must either turn to terror or provide the demagogic leadership for mass manipulation or a combination of both. In any case, the dynamics of the situation will destroy the old elite structure. If terror is utilized primarily, power will move steadily away from the traditional elements of government and toward the terror apparatus. If demagoguery and mass manipulation are relied upon, power will quickly gravitate into the hands of the demagogue and his allies. The triumph of liberalism in such a situation would require the accident of the appearance of a charismatic leader who was devoted to liberal values.

A basic assumption of this study is that nationalism was not a significant force in Iran prior to the 1890's. The roots of nationalism, of course, extend into the extraordinarily rich Iranian civilization down to and beyond the Achemenid period. Without question many insights could be gained regarding the quality of Iranian nationalism by a thorough exploration of this civilization. However, such an exploration is beyond the scope of this study and the competence of its author. Generalizations about Iranian history made in the pages that follow, therefore, refer only to the period of Iranian history from 1890 to the present.

Since this study follows a topical rather than a strictly chronological format, Chapter 1 is designed to give the reader who is not familiar with modern Iranian history a quick look at the most important political developments from 1890 to the post-Mossadeq period.

1

THE BACKGROUND

The little group of Englishmen who in 1890 were granted a concession to manage Iran's lucrative tobacco trade must have congratulated themselves most heartily. For over half a century and at an ever increasing tempo after 1872, Iran's kings had been doling out the resources of their domain to eager foreigners, mostly British and Russian. The tobacco concession was the latest, and potentially one of the most profitable, in a long series of concessions. The Qajar kings, and especially Nasr al-Din Shah, viewed the granting of concessions to foreigners as a simple way of bringing much needed revenue into the Iranian government coffers. Court expenses had been skyrocketing, especially since Nasr al-Din Shah's discovery of the joys of European voyages, and Iranian ministers were not squeamish about any revenue source. Besides, little real risk to Iran's independence was involved in this method of finance, at least as long as Iran's statesmen were careful to preserve an Anglo-Russian balance. But though neither the Court nor the British concessioners suspected it, the granting of the tobacco concession was a turning point in Iran's history.

In the long and sometimes glorious history of Iran there had been times when almost the entire civilized world looked with deep respect on the great empire of Persia. Even as late as the eighteenth century, an Iranian army led by Nader Shah Afshar had swept into India and plundered Delhi. But there had been other times in Iran's history when that ancient land lay at the mercy of foreigners. Nasr al-Din well understood that his own reign was one of those times. The dynamics of nineteenth-century Russian expansion into Asia had brought Russia to the borders of Iran, first on the Caucasus side of the Caspian and then on the Central Asia side. The deep yearning and stubborn drive of Russians, whether Tsarist or Soviet, for a warm water port is universally recognized, and the Persian Gulf has always been alluring to them. Why, then, should the Russians in the later nineteenth century have halted at the borders of Iran when apparently only the weak Qajar dynasty with its seemingly always sleepy subjects stood in the path of the Tsar's armies? There may have been Iranians who imagined that their mighty armies and clever statesmen had stopped the Russian southeastern sweep, but such men were not to be found in the Qajar Court. There it was clearly recognized that British fears for her trade routes to India and for India itself had prevented the Russians from swallowing Iran. Iran's independence was at the mercy of the two great powers. Neither power could advance further without risking a major war; indeed Iran's very existence hung on the continued peaceful rivalry of these two states.

Restricted as Russia and Great Britain were in the military field, the Anglo-Russian rivalry was expressed primarily in the economic realm. In 1872 a British subject, Baron Paul Julius von Reuter, was granted a concession for exploiting Iran's mineral resources which was of such breadth as to mortgage the country's future economic development. A year later this concession was withdrawn, not because of any mass revulsion on the part of Iranians, but rather because Russia viewed it as a threat. Other less elaborate concessions were granted and were not withdrawn because they did not seriously threaten the Anglo-Russian balance. The tobacco concession to a British company in 1890, involving one of the most important domestic items of trade in Iran, was inevitably the target of hostile Russian maneuvers, and even after the concession was granted Russian opposition continued. However, the British company could feel fairly secure, for the concession could not be cancelled without the Iranians' incurring a tremendous financial loss. Nevertheless, it was cancelled. The Russsians had helped bring about this setback to Great Britain, but their influence was not crucial. The greater role in the drama was played by an actor new to the Iranian stage, an actor that neither Nasr al-Din nor the British company dreamed existed, an outraged public opinion. The popular reaction was a primitive one and was evoked more by wounded religious sensitivities than by national pride; the people feared that their tobacco had been made impure by the handling of infidels. But nascent nationalistic forces did participate, and the course of Iranian history was from that time irrevocably altered. Six years after he granted the tobacco concesnion, Nasr al-Din Shah was assassinated.

The vast majority of Iranians—peasants, tribesmen, and urban laborers—were illiterate and politically inarticulate. They could only be stirred by a basic emotional appeal. But among the small layer of the articulate, three groups began to crystallize which, each for reasons of its own, stood in violent opposition to the policy of foreign loans and concessions. These groups were the clerical, the merchant, and the intellectual.

Nasr al-Din's son and successor, Mozaffar al-Din Shah, was a weak, luxury-loving ruler whose spendthrift ways resulted in the necessity of negotiating a new foreign loan. This he received from the Russians, but at the expense of mortgaging for many years the revenues from the state customs. For the clergy and for the merchants in particular, such conduct could not be tolerated, and in 1906 they staged an almost bloodless revolution.

Each of the three opposition groups wanted to see the influence of foreigners reduced, social reforms inaugurated, and an institutional check placed on the tyranny of the Court. To this extent they were united, and all three agreed that their objectives could best be achieved by forcing the Shah to promulgate a constitution which provided for a parliamentary system of government. Unfortunately, however, even among the revolutionaries such Western liberal democratic ideas were ill understood.

The clerical participants, without whom the revolution could not have succeeded, gradually came to understand that implicit within this new ideological complex was a stress on secularism which was entirely alien to Islamic thought. For most merchants the ideas per se were of little import; once their material demands had been met, their enthusiasm for the constitution waned. Finally, there was no tradition in Iran for intellectual participation in politics, and it was fairly easy for the intellectuals to drift back to their parlors and their interminable talk-fests. Beyond this, and ironically, in Iran as in most states with a feudalistic social organization, democracy had inevitably resulted in the domination of parliament by the very elements that sympathized least with liberal democracy. Added to the very small base of popular support and the waning enthusiasm on the part of the revolutionaries were the growing hostility of the Court, the army, a significant section of the clergy, and the landowners. The wonder is that this first burst of liberal, democratic nationalism endured from 1906 to 1912.

The appearance of Iranian nationalism posed a major problem for both the British and the Russians. But these were years of increasing uneasiness throughout the world, as Europe moved toward war. Whatever the ideological attractiveness of the new movement, especially to the British, the primary concern of both Britain and Russia was that Iran should not upset the delicate Anglo-Russian balance in the Middle East at a time when both were threatened by a challenge from Imperial Germany. The two powers sought to clarify and institutionalize their positions by the Anglo-Russian Agreement of 1907, which divided Iran into spheres of influence. That this treaty was effected in the period of the first constitutional regime is, no doubt, purely coincidental; but the budding nationalist movement could only view it as gross interference and unprincipled betrayal. The overall Anglo-Russian objective for Iran was internal stability, and in the early days of the constitution both powers believed this stability could appear only if the Shah were to make his peace with the nationalistic modernizers. British and Russian diplomatic representatives repeatedly urged him to do so. Gradually, however, the two powers began to see in the nationalist movement a disruptive force which threatened to produce civil war and, in the process, to upset the Anglo-Russian balance. This attitude hardened to such a degree that it was a British-supported Russian ultimatum delivered in December 1911 which overthrew the constitutional regime and replaced it with a virtual Anglo-Russian condominium.

The British and Russians were not without domestic allies in their battle against the nationalists. Many influential Iranians had never been reconciled to the 1906 revolution and wanted nothing more than the restoration of the status quo ante. Mozaffar al-Din Shah died shortly after the promulgation of the constitution and his son, Mohammad Ali Shah, a strong-minded despot who bitterly resented the constitutional limits to his rule, was determined to overthrow the constitution. He had in his control the Russian-officered Persian Cossacks, a formidable weapon against which the nationalists could throw only their untrained volunteers. Mohammad Ali failed in his first major attack on the nationalists, mainly because of his own indecision. The second attack, in 1908, succeeded in Tehran but failed in Iran's second city, Tabriz, in the rich northwestern province of Azerbaijan.

The city of Tabriz and the Turkish-speaking province of Azerbaijan were the heroes of the year 1908–09. While many of the intellectual fathers of the nationalist movement cheered from abroad, having fled Iran convinced that the time was not yet ripe for a democratic regime, Tabriz defeated numerous government attempts to capture the city. A blockade proved more effective, however, and eleven months after the beginning of the siege, the resistance of Tabriz began to crumble. Even so, Mohammad Ali was denied the city. The Russians, who feared the looting of foreign property and the loss of foreign lives by a hungry populace, marched into Azerbaijan and occupied Tabriz.

Although deprived of personal victory, the citizens of Tabriz could take solace from the fact that their resistance had given heart to constitutionalists in other areas. The city of Rasht, a few miles from the Caspian Sea, rose against the Shah and sent a small army to attack the capital. From the old Safavid capital of Isfahan, a Bakhtiari tribal chief led a contingent of his tribesmen to join the Rashtis. In July 1909, despite Anglo-Russian efforts to dissuade them, the constitutionalists occupied Tehran and sent Mohammad Ali into exile in Russia. The glory of this victory is marred for the Iranian nationalists because few nontribal Iranian Moslems were among the attackers. The Isfahan force was largely tribal, and the Rasht force was predominantly Armenian and Caucasian.

There followed two and one-half years of parliamentary rule during which the nationalists began to learn how difficult it was to find solutions for the country's ills. Outside of Tehran there was no security. Tribesmen and robber bands roamed at will, and both Tabriz and Mashhad, the principal city of the northeastern province of Khorasan, were occupied by Russian troops. The nation's financial situation was deplorable. Taxes could not be collected, and without revenues order could not be restored. On the political plane, the divergent interests of the landlords and the emerging urban middle class had to be reconciled, and social reforms were needed.

Despairing of finding solutions to these accumulating problems, the government decided to turn to foreign technical assistance. The Majlis, the Iranian lower house, authorized the hiring of an American financial expert and staff. The American State Department recommended Morgan Shuster, a New York banker, for this task, and their choice was in many respects an admirable one. Shuster arrived in 1911, quickly won the confidence of the leaders of parliament, and began to make visible progress. Some taxes were collected; a Swedish-officered gendarmery for establishing order and collecting taxes was inaugurated; and some system was given to the nation's finances. The spirits of Iranian nationalists had declined during the past two years of internal disorder, but when gains, small though they were, were registered under Shuster's tutelage, a new wave of hope swept the country. And when Mohammad Ali Shah suddenly appeared in Iran with Turkoman tribal support, he was soundly defeated. But Shuster had committed the unforgivable sin of refusing to recognize the division of Iran as outlined by the Agreement of 1907. A Russian ultimatum of 1911 demanded his dismissal, and Russian troops compelled compliance. With Shuster's departure, Iranian nationalist morale collapsed.

It is widely believed that nationalism appeared suddenly in Iran with the premiership of Dr. Mohammad Mossadeq in 1951. The roots of Iranian nationalism go far deeper than that. In order to understand the Mossadeq period, it must be realized that much of the character of Iranian nationalism had already been determined during the formative years of 1906–12.

The years between the departure of Shuster and the entrance of Turkey into World War I were characterized by a hopeless inactivity in Iran. Insecurity was so widespread that the Shuster-organized gendarmery could make no headway against it. The British were compelled to bring their own troops to guard Britons in Isfahan and in Shiraz, the capital of the southwestern province of Fars. World War I merely compounded misfortune for Iran. Although the government declared its neutrality, Russian troops occupied Azerbaijan, which borders Turkey, and Iran inevitably became a Russo-Turkish battleground. Germany tried to woo Iran over to her side, and she certainly had the propaganda advantage. The liberal nationalist leadership, loosely organized in the Democratic Party, was strongly pro-German, and when the Central Powers set up a headquarters in the city of Kermanshah, not far from the Iraqi border, many Iranians joined them. But Russia was in actual control of much of the country, and the British South Persian Rifles, organized and headed by Sir Percy Sykes, occupied the southern centers. The government had no choice but to maintain a fiction of neutrality and to do the Russo-British bidding.

When one of the two powers that had been exercising virtual colonial control over Iran suffered a revolution and then announced its intention of withdrawing from Iran, the reaction was enthusiastic. The Iranians, who had convinced themselves that all their ills could be laid at the door of foreign interference, expected that the departure of the Russians would magically restore their country's health. They were soon disillusioned. Complete anarchy reigned wherever British or Turkish armies were not in occupation; the four northern provinces of Khorasan, Mazanderan, Gilan, and Azerbaijan were virtually beyond the control of the central government; and government finances were in complete disorder. There were still the British to blame, however, and a major reason for the inability of the central government to reestablish control was the conviction on the part of local leaders that it was under British control.

This was the moment that the British chose to offer Iran a "very generous treaty,"[1] the Anglo-Persian Treaty of 1919. By the terms of this treaty British specialists would reorganize the government services, British officers would organize and train the Iranian army, a loan would be granted, and roads and railroads would be constructed. This treaty was the brainchild of Lord Curzon, who with such other friends of Iran as Sir Percy Sykes, assumed that Iranians would recognize the treaty as a sincere effort to help the country's recovery. They were shocked at a flare-up of violent popular antagonism. The Iranians can hardly be blamed for seeing

[1] Or so British observers saw it; see for example Sir Percy Sykes, *History of Persia*, II (London, 1930), 520–22.

such bounty as suspiciously similar to colonial generosity. For the second time liberal nationalism raged with an intensity sufficiently strong to reverse the course of Iranian history.

The years 1919–21 were comparable to the 1909–11 period in that governments genuinely responsive to public opinion were frequently in power in Iran. These governments, however, had no more success in solving the overwhelming internal problems than had their predecessors of the previous decade. As a result there was a good deal of disillusionment with democracy. But this conclusion should not be drawn too tightly. British interference in governmental affairs continued, at times crassly. A Soviet army landed in the province of Gilan in pursuit of a British-White Russian force, but very quickly engaged in an effort to subvert the province and overthrow the Tehran government. Consequently, the Iranian reaction was less one of simple disillusionment with democracy than a realization that Iranian democracy could not deal with internal difficulties and at the same time cope with Anglo-Russian interference.

Almost total paralysis characterized the Iranian government by 1921, and few were surprised when a *coup d'état* brought into power a new, strong-minded leader, Sayyed Zia al-Din Tabatabai. Sayyed Zia immediately inaugurated a vigorous program of social reform and dealt with the inevitable landlord opposition by jailing a number of grandees. But he had moved too quickly. In order to carry out his *coup d'état,* Sayyed Zia had allied himself with an ambitious and equally strong-minded colonel of the Persian Cossacks, Reza Khan, who received as his reward the position of commander-in-chief of the Cossacks. Having antagonized the landowning element and the Court and being unable to attract nationalist support because of the nationalists' conviction that the *coup d'état* was actually a British maneuver,[2] Sayyed Zia found himself three months after the *coup* totally dependent on Reza Khan's Cossacks. Reza Khan, who was not the simple soldier Sayyed Zia imagined, soon forced Sayyed Zia into exile in the British mandate of Palestine, where he remained until the British permitted him to return to Iran during World War II. Reza Khan had begun his climb to absolute power.

[2] See Chapter 12 for a full discussion of this point.

For a period of more than a year Reza Khan satisfied himself with the position of minister of war. Prime ministers came and went, but not until 1923 had he so established his power, largely by consolidating his control over the Cossacks and gaining control over the gendarmery, as to compel a reluctant Majlis to accept him as His Majesty's first minister. As prime minister, Reza Khan was able to consolidate the national police with the army and the gendarmery. From the time he first attained high office, Reza Khan had attacked the problem of internal security with vigor, and by the time he became prime minister, Iran had security such as had not been known for over a century. The tribes were severely disciplined, and the border provinces were brought under control. Reza Khan utilized his newly consolidated security force to establish his authority over Khuzistan, the southwestern oil-rich province which had been a virtual autonomous sheikhdom under British protection.

Reza Khan was a fierce nationalist, although his nationalist values were little influenced by the liberalism of the earlier nationalist leaders, most of whom remained in sullen opposition until 1941. His was more the nationalism of an Ataturk; in many respects the Reza Khan and Ataturk regimes were parallel. Reza Khan deeply admired the Turkish dictator and modeled many of his reforms on those of Turkey. He quickly discovered, however, that there were solid differences between the two countries. His attempt in 1924 to emulate Ataturk by establishing a republic resulted in a stinging setback. He had underestimated the power of the clergy, which, as a group, feared the secular example of republican Turkey above all things. Clerical opposition was so strong that Reza Khan was actually driven to resign, although he well understood that his absolute control over the security force would bring him quickly back into power.

Having abandoned the idea of a republic, Reza Khan in 1925 ousted the Qajar dynasty and had himself enthroned as Reza Shah Pahlavi. During his reign, which lasted until 1941, he sought to westernize Iran as rapidly as that country's resources and the psychology of its people would permit. Education, industry, transportation, communications, and the army were greatly improved. Cities were forcibly westernized, and many of the traditional items of dress were eliminated, including the veils of women. His reign did a great deal to unify and stabilize Iran, but, as was true with Ataturk, his solutions were too often superficial. The West was industrialized; so Iran had to be industrialized. There was little rationality in the process, and the really important agricultural base of the Iranian economy was largely ignored.

In 1941 forces from Britain and Russia again entered Iran, arguing that the pro-German policies of Reza Shah left them no alternative. Actually, they were more interested in establishing a vital supply line from Britain to Russia; Iran was again the victim of her strategic location. The Iranian people, powerless to resist, sat bewildered while their supposedly mighty army collapsed. Reza Shah had become increasingly tyrannical as his regime progressed, and at the time of his overthrow was widely hated. The Iranian press greeted his abdication in favor of his son, the present Shah, with unrestrained relief, but the fact that the overthrow was at the hands of Iran's most feared enemies was not a pleasant one.

Reza Shah did much to make of Iran a national state in the Western sense. But he neglected one important aspect in equipping Iran with the attributes of an independent state—the development of a politically mature people. Reza Shah's dictatorship was as absolute as the inefficient and individualistic Iranian social order permitted. Although formal education was advanced considerably, political education deteriorated. The press was severely censored, and freedom of thought and speech restricted. The legacy of this neglect was seen in the caliber of Iranian leadership during and after World War II. At a time when dynamism and imagination were essential, neither was to be found; and not until the premiership of Ahmad Qavam in February 1946 did strong leadership appear.

The termination of World War II, far from freeing Iran from foreign control, found her deeply involved in a struggle for existence. Considering the long history of Anglo-Russian rivalry, it was perhaps inevitable that Iran should quickly become a Cold War battlefield. Even before World War II had ended, the USSR had launched an involved campaign to separate the province of Azerbaijan and the Kurdish tribal area from Iran. The defeat of the Soviet maneuver in 1946 was due less to nationalist reaction in Iran (although that reaction was intense) than to divided Soviet aims, American support for Iran, and good luck.

After the Soviet defeat, the Iranians focused their sights on what they regarded as the primary imperial agent in Iran, the Anglo-Iranian Oil Company. The ensuing struggle was climaxed in 1951 by the most exciting and tragic period in modern Iranian history —the two and one-half years under the premiership of Dr. Mohammad Mossadeq. It is no exaggeration to say that for the first time in Iran's very long history a national leader had appeared who enjoyed the respect, devotion, and loyalty of the vast majority of politically aware Iranians. Few movements and few individuals are so poorly understood in the West as are the Iranian Nationalist movement and Dr. Mossadeq. A major part of the last section of this book is devoted to that period. Here it is important to note only that the Mossadeq government, despite massive popular support, was unable to achieve its often-stated goal of developing a stable liberal democracy capable of pursuing an independent course in world affairs. Obsessed with his struggles against foreign imperialism, Mossadeq failed to develop a constructive approach to Iran's problems. His overthrow in 1953 was a direct result of this failure, but in the minds of his followers it was caused by an Anglo-American conspiracy.

The young Shah, whose throne was almost lost in 1953, not only returned to his constitutional prerogatives but within a year and a half had established virtual dictatorial control. Of the prime ministers who served under him only one, Dr. Ali Amini, who occupied the office in 1961–62, had any real independence. Since 1954 Iran has absorbed huge oil revenues and United States financial support and as a consequence has undergone an economic and social transformation. The literacy rate is rapidly rising, and the numerical growth of the middle class is impressive. At the same time, the Shah's governments have been incapable of attracting substantial support from this newly emergent element. Acquiescence and apathy are more descriptive of their general attitude than is enmity; but with regard to the politically most interested and active members of the middle class, in effect those who constitute most of the modernizing elite structure, their predominant attitude is hostile.

2

COHESIVE BASE FOR NATIONALISM

For all its stark beauty, Iran is the victim of a formidable geography and a harsh climate. The massive mountains and desolate deserts stand as gigantic barriers to easy communications. In all but a narrow belt along the Caspian Sea the populace is constantly in danger of a ruinous drought. Inevitably, every aspect of the Iranian social organization and social psychology is deeply influenced by this geography and climate.

Geographically viewed, Iran presents to the world a large triangle that in the pre-aerial age was very difficult to breach. The northwest apex of this triangle is the beginning of two mighty mountain ranges. The Zagros Mountains form the southwestern leg of the triangle, and the Elburz Mountains the northern leg. Both ranges commonly rise to 11,000 feet in altitude, and Mount Demavend in the Elburz range rises to 18,600 feet. They are young ranges and hence have few of the deep canyons that could make for easy transit. Both of these legs of the triangle are reinforced for a part of their lengths by large bodies of water. The Elburz range borders on the Caspian Sea, and the southern section of the Zagros range is on the Persian Gulf. The third leg of the triangle, the eastern leg, is the most forbidding of all. It comprises the great deserts of Iran, the Dasht Kavir and the Dasht Lut. This leg of the triangle is no narrow line. One-third of the territory of Iran is included in its oppressively barren, life-defying expanse.

The triangle has proved to be most vulnerable at the point at which the desert meets the Elburz Mountains. Here it is possible to enter the Iranian plateau by skirting along the southern foothills of the mountains to the north of the great deserts. This has been the classic invasion route of the Turkic and Mongol peoples. Iran has been invaded many times in its history and for a total of many centuries has been subject with varying degrees of intensity to foreign control. However, the fact remains that in spite of these invasions, an exclusive Iranian national character, culture, and history have survived. It is difficult not to agree with Dennison Ross when he says, "To her isolation is no doubt in great measure due the preservation of her peculiar national characteristics and her national independence."[1] Although at times the waves of human invaders could not be contained, the geography and climate of Iran made for easy defense, and only the most powerful of invasions were successful. Were it not for this geography, countless minor forays might have occurred which would have disrupted or destroyed the cultural and historical continuity of Iran.

Geographical isolation, of course, did not give rise to nationalism, but there are few factors that strengthen the nationalism of a people more than the belief that they are culturally and historically unique in the world. To the extent that geography was responsible for the uniqueness of Iranian character, culture, and history, it helped create a national particularism which in turn served as a catalytic force for the growth of nationalist sentiment.

The same climatic and geographical conditions that aided the growth of nationalism in Iran, from another point of view hindered this growth. The impregnable triangle served to isolate from the plateau areas those sections of Iran that lie outside the legs of the triangle. Khuzistan, the Caspian coastal area, Khorasan, Sistan, and Iranian Baluchistan—all located outside the triangle—could disregard the central government to a considerable degree. Furthermore, the barriers to travel presented by the terrain worked against any widespread acquaintance of the people of the peripheral areas with the state of Iran as a whole. For them a local, rather than a national, cultural, and political, orientation was the natural result of this situation.

Even within the protected Iranian plateau, geography and climate conspired against the imposition of control from Tehran and against the acquisition by provincial dwellers of a primary national loyalty. Distances were great betweeen cities and villages, and the low rainfall of the plateau, combined with a legacy of centuries of overgrazing, made the intervening territory extremely arid and difficult to cross. Before the time of Reza Shah, whose rise

[1] E. Dennison Ross, *The Persians* (Oxford, 1931), p. 20.

to power began in 1921, travel was mainly by camel caravan and hence was prohibitively slow and costly for most city or town dwellers. Also, the proximity of the mountains and deserts, which were ideal retreats for depredating tribal or robber bands, permitted frequent raids on caravans, a prospect which added nothing to the attractiveness of travel.

The difficulty of travel in Iran helped accentuate a very striking feature of Iranian nationalism: the fact that until the 1950's nationalism was the property of the very few. The difficulty of the terrain made travel unthinkable for the vast majority of illiterate and poverty-stricken peasants. But for the literate minority travel was not totally ruled out. The merchant was likely to have business interests that would periodically compel him to visit other cities. The clerical leaders could be expected to have visited and very likely to have lived in the Mesopotamian religious center of Najaf and Karbala and in the Iranian holy cities of Qom and Mashhad. The intellectual, too, in many cases would have the desire and the means to visit the ancient historical and cultural centers of his country. Consequently, the world of these groups was not confined to one particular town or city, but encompassed much of Iran, and therefore their receptivity to nationalism was considerably enhanced.

The sum effect of the geography of Iran, then, has been to help generate national particularism, but to hinder the growth of nationalism for all but the very few. In the last thirty years, however, the influence of geography and climate on the character of nationalism has declined precipitately, and nationalism itself has had a great deal to do with that decline. The strong nationalists were anxious that Iran should assert herself in the world scene. To do so, they realized that Iran must be modernized and that the first step of any plan of modernization was an improvement in communications. Once roads and railroads were built, the geographical barriers that had helped create localism were progressively neutralized.

With Reza Shah lies much of the credit for establishing a communications system which, though far from being complete, has permitted even villagers to gain a new and national perspective. The relative ease and the declining cost of transportation have reduced the number of self-sufficient villages and cities, and merchants and farmers are becoming aware of the world as it exists outside Iran. Although the average peasant or laborer may himself not travel, many of his associates do. With an increasing tempo, the popular base of receptivity to nationalism is widening.

Historical Consciousness

In addition to geography and climate, there is much that divides the Iranian people, including linguistic differences and social incompatibilities; but the people's awareness of and tremendous pride in Iran's great history serve as strong cohesive forces to help counter the many divisive factors. Few Iranians would agree and most would emphatically disagree with the selection of 1890, the year Nasr al-Din Shah awarded the tobacco concession, for the beginning of a discussion of nationalism. In their eyes the days of Iranian national greatness have long since passed, and if the nation is to be seen in true perspective, a description of its present humble position in the society of nations must be balanced by an account of its past imperial greatness under the Achemenid, Sassanid, and Safavid dynasties and under Nader Shah.

However, the definition of nationalism chosen for this study restricts the application of the term to societies in which there is large-scale popular political participation; and no one claims that such characterized any of the periods of Iranian imperial greatness. Yet, historical greatness has a major role to play in the study of Iranian nationalism because the consciousness of this history has done much to give nationalism its present strength and vitality. A highly developed historical consciousness among educated Iranians is readily apparent. Iranian poetry of the first decades of the twentieth century demonstrates a heavy stress on history. Likewise, the press of the past fifty years is replete with references to the days of Iranian supremacy; hardly an issue of any newspaper can be found that fails to refer to Iran's past.

Less easily demonstrated is the extent to which historical consciousness pervades the uneducated element. In the absence of a relevant sociological study, views on this point range from the bald assertion by two American missionaries, longtime residents of

Iran, that the uneducated have no idea of Iranian history,[2] to a commonly expressed view of the nationalists that the "poorest Persian lad gloats over the history of the conquest of India by Nadir Shah or over the doings of the old heroes of Ferdowsi."[3] There is little apparent reason to expect that the illiterate element of the population would have much knowledge of, or interest in, Iran's national status or history. In the more remote villages and tribes this expectation is probably correct; and even the peasant of the larger or more accessible towns may have no clear idea of the concept of a nation. However, the reference to the great epic poet Ferdosi is significant. The *Shahnameh,* or *Chronicle of the Kings,* a vast epic written about 1000 A.D., blends actual Iranian history with romantic mythology. It is immensely appealing to Iranians of all classes, and, as one Iranian wrote, "It was and is sung before battle, recited in villages, tribes, coffee houses, community centers."[4] For the politically unaware, whose horizons are too limited to comprehend national history, much less nationalism, the *Shahnameh* creates a predisposition for a rapid infection with genuine nationalism.

Not only are all of the various Persian-speaking provinces able to identify themselves with this single history, but Turkish-speaking Azerbaijan can think of itself as "one of the most important cradles of Iranian civilization."[5] Here too the *Shahnameh* is sung and strengthens the feeling of oneness with Iranian history. Even the separatist-minded Kurds consider themselves as descendants of people who historically have always been closely tied to the Iranians.[6] Iranian nationalists have clearly understood the importance of historical consciousness in spreading a nationalist sentiment; and in his campaign to strengthen national unity, Reza Shah made especially heavy use of the awareness of a great history.

Despite this strong feeling for tradition, a minority of the early

[2] Dr. Livingstone Bentley, Reverend Mr. William Muller, interview, Tabriz, March 1952.

[3] "Letters to the Editors," *The Near East,* July 26, 1912, p. 356.

[4] Issa Sadiq, "Ferdousi," *Iran and the United States of America,* February 1947, p. 13.

[5] Arani, "Azerbaijan," *Farangistan,* September 1, 1924, pp. 247–48.

[6] Arshah Safrastian, *Kurds and Kurdistan* (London, 1948), pp. 18–27.

nationalists regarded the long history of Iran as a source of shame rather than pride. On the first anniversary of the constitution, the influential newspaper *Habl al-Matin* commented: "This day is the day that the nation of Iran was delivered from under the burden of 6,000 years of despotism."[7] For the early nationalists, deeply devoted as they were to liberalism and democracy, there was little cause for pride in Iran's history. But as time passed and the Western ideological complex was better digested, the Western-minded Iranian discovered that much in his history had contributed to world civilization, though not to liberalism or democracy, and today condemnations of Iran's past are rarely heard.

Cultural Consciousness

Iranians complain bitterly and with much justification that their magnificent cultural heritage and their cultural preeminence in the Middle East and South Asia, far from being appreciated, are not even recognized in the West. Iranian literature occupies an especially stellar position not only in the minds and hearts of Iranians, but also in the cultural heritage of educated men throughout Islam and India. Sa'di, Hafez, Ferdosi, Rumi, and Nezami, to mention only a few outstanding poets, are read and quoted throughout Iran to an extent that is astonishing to an American. And familiarity with Iran's great poetry is not limited to the educated elements. Many Iranians who cannot sign their names can quote at length from this great literature.[8]

With the striking exception of Ferdosi's *Shahnameh,* however, the golden age of Iranian poetry does not directly add to or substract from nationalism. The great poets were not much concerned with the native land. Even in Ferdosi, whose poetry does extol the Iranian nation and race, there is little to bring comfort to the modern Iranian nationalist. Ferdosi's poetry, in the words of Professor Browne, is ". . . always of the triumphant, victorious and imperialistic type, while of the more subtle and moving patriotic verse of the conquered and helpless nation . . . which can only strive to maintain its spiritual life under the more or less galling yoke of the foreign invader, and must sustain its sense of na-

[7] July 23, 1907, p. 1.
[8] Richard N. Frye, *Iran* (New York, 1953), p. 22.

tionhood by memories of a glorious past and hopes of a happier future, there is hardly a trace in Persian or Arabic until this present century." [9] Iran's great poets were cosmopolitan in their orientation, and they sought the universal truths. Their role for Iranian nationalism is somewhat akin to that of Schiller and Goethe for German nationalism. The Iranian people could be proud that their country produced such genius, and when Iran suffered the degradation of foreign control Sa'di and Hafez could offer escapist refuge.

The Iranian's consciousness of his cultural heritage has an importance for nationalism closely paralleling that of his historical consciousness. Both are strongly unifying forces which help mitigate the many disruptions to national unity. His cultural consciousness permits the Iranian to view himself as one of a people deserving of the respect and admiration of international society. Such a feeling of uniqueness aids mightily in the integration of nationalism in the popular mind. Beyond that, it combines with nationalism, once established, to provide an incentive for greater national achievements. As one young Iranian wrote, "Can you understand what our music, our poetry means to us? Firdausi is not a poet long dead. He lives. He is part of our life, his couplets tell us to be great Persians again, to cultivate the best ideas of Zoroaster, to cease to submit to Russia, to England, to know and love our own country." [10]

Nationalism, when it arrived in Iran, brought with it a curious dialectical dilemma. The concept of nationalism itself is a product of Western thought, and the Iranians who first became infected with it were those who felt most strongly the cultural impact of the West. But nationalism calls for stressing and glorifying the uniqueness of one's own culture. What then should be the Iranian nationalist's attitude toward the other phases of Western thought and civilization? There were some among the nationalists who felt that the old Iranian civilization could in no way compete with the more dynamic civilization of the West: the old should be discarded

[9] Edward G. Browne, *The Press and Poetry of Modern Persia* (London, 1914), pp. xxxii–iii.

[10] O. A. Merritt-Hawks, "Firdausi, the Persian Epic Poet," *Asiatic Review,* April 1935, p. 349.

and a new Western civilization should be adopted *in toto*. Others took the opposite extreme view: Iran's cultural greatness demands that it not be sullied by contact with other lesser breeds; Iranians must reject everything foreign (excluding the idea of nationalism of course) and reestablish the pristine quality of their own culture.

Much of both tendencies could be found under Reza Shah. He ripped down sections of cities, ruthlessly destroyed mosques and other edifices mellow with the charm of age, and replaced them with broad, tree-lined but incongruous boulevards. But at the same time he launched a fierce campaign to remove all the foreign influences from the Persian language. Both reactions have the aura of the convert, the evangelist. Once nationalism has established itself securely in Iran, a more relaxed attitude toward the outside world is to be expected. Then a synthesis of Iranian and Western civilizations can materialize.

Language

Many past definitions of nationalism included as a necessary ingredient the existence of a common language. Scholars usually hastened to add that this requirement was not an absolute one, as Switzerland and Canada demonstrate, but that the exceptions were rare. Now, however, the fantastic linguistic diversity of India, Pakistan, Ceylon, Indonesia, and other states where nationalism has appeared demonstrates the need to modify the stress on linguistic unity. It would be a major error to disregard this factor, because nationalism still requires a people to think of itself as a unique entity, and the existence of a common language among them helps generate such a view. When the citizens of a state speak a wide diversity of tongues, persuading them that they are unique becomes a difficult task indeeed.

The wide linguistic diversity in Iran seems to lead to the conclusion that for Iranian nationalism, too, this poses a major problem. There are no reliable statistics as to the percentages of the Iranian people in various linguistic groupings, but the generally accepted view is that a majority speak Persian.[11] Still, Iran's most important province, Azerbaijan, is Turkish-speaking, as are the

[11] Donald N. Wilber, *Iran: Past and Present* (Princeton, 1950), p. 183.

Qashqai, Turkoman, some of the Khamseh, and many lesser tribes, plus scattered villages. Arabic is common in the southwestern province of Khuzistan and all along the Persian Gulf; Kurdish, a cousin of Persian, is spoken by the large and powerful Kurdish tribal group; other dialects of Persian, such as Luri, Tabari, Gilaki, are spoken in local areas; Armenian and Syriac are the languages of the Christian minorities; and the Jewish element, which in the past has spoken its own brand of Persian, is now turning to Hebrew.

However, any comparison of the linguistic difficulties faced by Iranian nationalism with those confronting Indian nationalism would lead to the conclusion that the problem for Iran hardly exists. That Persian is the predominant tongue in Iran has never been seriously questioned. Furthermore, it is not acquiescence to the popular predominance of the Persian-speaking element that produces the Turkish-speaking educated Azerbaijani's willingness to see Persian the primary language. On the contrary, the educated Iranian everywhere speaks and reads Persian and deeply loves that beautiful tongue. He knows and is able to recite at length Persian poetry, and he almost always reads one or more Persian-language newspapers. The educated Iranian's great pride in the Persian language does much to offset the problem of diversity.

For the illiterate, however, the situation is different. Few Turkish, Arabic, or Kurdish-speaking illiterates know Persian. The love of the beauty of the language is unlikely to extend far beneath the literate minority, even in the Persian-speaking areas. Linguistic diversity, then, does seriously inhibit the spread among the illiterate element of the belief that they are part of a single people. Consequently, language, along with geography, tends to make nationalism in Iran mostly the property of the educated elite.

The various Persian dialects are probably not much of a divisive force. As education becomes more pervasive and travel more common, they should be no more than a slight inconvenience for spreading the base of nationalism. Arabic and Turkish in Iran present a special problem, since these languages, in addition to being very different from Persian, are the national languages of important nearby states. That foreign powers would attempt to pry the non-Persian-speaking elements from Iran was demonstrated strikingly by the Soviet-sponsored Azerbaijan separatist movement. Some Iranians are enough alarmed about the potential for disunity inherent in the linguistic diversity to favor a systematic plan for its eradication including the resettling of linguistic minorities.[12] Even liberal Iranians favor compulsory education in Persian and the banning of publications in the local languages.

Racial Consciousness

Today, while the memory of Hitlerian Germany is still warm, no one needs to be convinced of the interrelationship of a belief in the racial uniqueness of a people and nationalism. Nationalism can, of course, exist and be extremely strong without such a belief. But a belief in racial uniqueness ranks along with beliefs in historical, cultural, and linguistic uniqueness in furnishing the cement that can give a degree of stability to nationalism.

Iranian and Western historians agree that the inhabitants of modern Iran are descendants of the Indo-European Aryan peoples who began occupying Iran as long ago as 3,500 years. However, whereas Western historians agree that the succeeding years have seen a great deal of ethnic intermixing in the area, some Iranian nationalists claim that Iranians today are of a pure racial stock. Dr. Afshar, who was an outstanding nationalist thinker, did not claim complete Aryan racial purity for Iranians, but he did minimize very much the extent of admixture of the Aryan with the Turkic, Mongol, and Arab invaders.[13] With this view there is wide agreement in Iran.

Although the Nazis made a strong appeal to Iranian racial consciousness in their propaganda in World War II, evidence of their results is lacking. References to the Iranian race in periodicals are fairly widespread, but the concept of racial uniquenesss was not stressed by the more responsible elements of the Iranian national movement. Only the fascistic Pan-Iranist movement treated race as if it were of primary concern. Nevertheless, racial consciousness does appear to furnish an element of cohesion for Iranian nationalism and one capable of a good deal of development in the years to come.

[12] Afshar, "The Problem of Nationalism and the Unity of Iran," *Ayandeh*, Spring 1927, pp. 566–67.

[13] *Ibid.*, pp. 560–61.

3

SOCIAL BASE FOR NATIONALISM

The picture that is emerging of the cohesive base for Iranian nationalism is a fairly bright one. Culture and history give exceptional support; racial consciousness helps; and even geography and language must be rated as more beneficial than detrimental. Compared with the nationalism of a state such as Pakistan or with Arab nationalism, the Iranian base is more solid. When we move to the sociological scene, however, the bright picture begins to change, for in this realm Iran compares less favorably with some of its neighbors.

The Peasantry

Nothing would be easier than to ignore the Iranian peasant in a study of nationalism in Iran. Since his world and his loyalties center around village, clan, and family, the peasant's horizons are much too narrow to permit more than the vaguest conception of Iran. Nationalism in the West is capable of arousing even the least informed citizenry and hence is the ideal tool of the demagogue; in Iran it is esoteric, at least when viewed in relation to the entire population. Certainly, it is far too removed from the peasant to be comprehensible to him. Yet failure to discuss the peasant in connection with nationalism in Iran would be a major error. He may be generally apolitical, but still he has given the basic coloring to every socio-political phenomenon that has occurred in Iran, including nationalism. There is a simple explanation for this impact. The peasantry and the tribesmen comprise over 80 per cent of the population, and inevitably such a large percentage of the population affects every social trend.[1]

[1] Lewis V. Thomas and Richard N. Frye, *The United States and Turkey and Iran* (Cambridge, Mass., 1951), p. 183.

Since the peasant is usually both docile and politically inarticulate, he most commonly serves as a willing tool for the village landowner. But he is not so bovine as to be impervious to all outrages; there are traditional limits within which the landowner must act. Furthermore, peasants are not all of one variety. There are even some small independent landholders among them, although the percentage of these is not large. Most of the peasants live in villages owned by one or more landowners, but many live in villages owned by the Crown, and many others in church-owned villages. Traditionally profit is divided five ways: a fifth each goes for labor, animals, seed, water, land. If the landowner, for example, in addition to the land provides the water, animals, and seed, his return will be four-fifths. Trouble appears when the routine is upset and greater demands are made on the peasant.[2]

As a positive actor in the struggle for and against nationalism in Iran, the peasant has made an unenlightened, sporadic, and contradictory appearance. When the Bakhtiari force marched from Isfahan toward Tehran to overthrow the tyrannical Mohammad Ali, they included a number of peasant participants, and the peasantry from the Isfahan area gave their heartfelt support.[3] But nationalism had not suddenly become alive and meaningful for these people: the peasantry in the Isfahan environs had been subjected to a very heavy and ruthlessly enforced land tax. They joined the march on Tehran to overturn this tax. Again, in the early 1920's Reza Khan received some enthusiastic peasant support in his effort to establish control over all Iran, not because the image of Iran had become beautiful but because tribal raids and robber depredations were being halted.[4] Shortly after, Reza Khan, now Reza Shah, was confronted with isolated rebellion from some villages and sullen resistance from most. The change in attitude came from peasant opposition to conscription.[5] That conscription would bring unity and strength to the motherland mattered not at

[2] For an excellent account of land ownership in Iran see Ann K. S. Lambton, *Landlord and Peasant in Persia* (London, 1953).

[3] Great Britain, Accounts and Papers, *State Papers 1909, Persia No. 2* (London, 1909), pp. 46–47. Hereafter cited as *State Papers . . . .*

[4] Ebrahim Khajenuri, *Bazigar Asr Talai: Sepahbod Amir Ahmadi* (Tehran, n.d.), pp. 8–9.

[5] Mirza Firuz Khan, "Persia," *The Near East and India*, December 9, 1926, p. 671.

all. The peasant saw it only as a new and unwarranted interference in his ancient routine.

If the peasants have had little direct influence on nationalism, their indirect influence has been great. In 1906 the nationalist leaders envisioned a new Iran which would emerge in a few years—a prosperous country, able to defend itself against foreign interference, and fully devoted to liberal democracy. Six years later these leaders were bitter, disillusioned men who believed that their cause had been destroyed by foreigners. They should have looked to the peasant as the chief source of villainy. With the granting of a constitution in 1906 the peasant had acquired the vote, but he lacked both interest in and awareness of the meaning of his new privilege. Bewildered, he marched obediently to cast his vote for the candidate of his landowner. The peasants placed in the Majlis avowed enemies of liberal democracy who had not yet understood and accepted nationalist values. The chief consequence of the political activity of the peasants in the formative years of Iranian nationalism was to deny the movement the support or understanding of the majority of the population. Thus nationalism became the property of a fairly narrow elite. Beyond this, the overwhelmingly complex problems of land reform and agricultural improvements, issues that must play a role in any real effort to bring prosperity to Iran, were enough to dampen the greatest enthusiasm.

Until very recently the picture of the peasants as a major bulwark of the monarchy was illusory. The peasant probably did have a vague loyalty to the almost mystical father-figure of the Shah, but this loyalty had yet to be expressed in any positive manner. The peasant's chief influence was to furnish the economic means by which the grandees retained their social and political position, and to the extent that these gentlemen supported the Shah, the peasant was something of a support, but little more.

But the potential, positive and negative, of the peasantry for influencing Iranian nationalism is explosive. The peasantry cannot forever be denied direct entry into the political scene. Given more time, the agricultural reform program of Dr. Mossadeq might very well have produced this entry. With the inauguration of a major land redistribution program in 1962 the peasantry is clearly on the threshold of political activity, but it is much too early to conclude whether they will give support to liberal democratic nationalism, to an antiliberal nationalism, or to communism.

Labor

The worldwide trend toward urbanization has not bypassed Iran. The twentieth century has seen a steady and accelerating influx of peasants into Tehran and the major provincial cities. Inherent in this phenomenon are the seeds that will change the social and political complexion of Iran. The new arrivals in the urban centers fall inevitably into the general category of "labor," but in several respects this terminology is misleading. Most of the new arrivals are intermittently employed at various unskilled jobs, the remainder finding employment as domestics or as unskilled help for shopkeepers or artisans. These people are, mentally at least, transplanted peasants. Inevitably, merely by travel and by dwelling in centers in which foreigners are concentrated, the unskilled laborer has his horizons broadened; but any claim that he hence becomes politically articulate is an absurdity. A common sight in the frenzied days of 1951–52 was a wildly cheering bus load of demonstrators driving past groups of unskilled laborers who were barely curious enough to lift their heads and gaze.

Yet, ironically, the unskilled laborer has been far more influential politically than his better educated, better organized brothers who are employed as factory laborers and who are on the border line of political awareness. The influence of the unskilled laborer has been exercised in favor of and in opposition to nationalism, sometimes both at the same time. It would be fruitless to seek an explanation for this apparent vacillation in events that altered the unskilled laborer's thinking. In truth, with the inevitable few exceptions, he has had no real political orientation, and to understand his actions one must turn to those who lead him. The only times in the past when the unskilled laborers themselves burst forth into political activity were when they rioted in periods of bread shortages. Such riots occurred both under reactionaries and under liberal nationalists; [6] the unskilled laborer was impartial.

[6] For a running account of the innumerable bread riots, see the British diplomatic correspondence for the period. *State Papers,* 1909–1914.

Whatever ideological consistency there has been in political demonstrations and rioting by unskilled laborers has been due to the influence of religious leadership. The village mullah, or religious leader, is an influential figure, to whom the villagers turn for advice and guidance as well as for religious ceremonies. But politically the village mullah rarely challenges the leadership of the landowner. Once the peasant moves to the city, he looks to his neighborhood mullah for guidance. Here, however, the mullah need not be subservient to any political leader, and he is able to and frequently does cajole the unskilled laborer into political activity that the laborer hardly attempts to comprehend. As will be discussed later, religious leaders are usually on both sides of major political questions, and their illiterate followers loyally give them the numerical support they need.

Along with the mullahs and frequently closely allied with them are professional mob leaders. These men typically center their activities in a varzeshgah (athletic club). There are many varieties of varzeshgahan, some of them respectable clubs which not only serve as centers for athletics, but also for other valuable group activities. But the varzeshgahan of the mob leaders are centers for athletic young toughs, known as chaqu keshan, who can be hired for any kind of corrupt or terroristic activity. Generally, also, the mob leader will control a number of brothels and gambling houses. He and his men are for hire by politicians, and when a sizeable political demonstration is desired the mob leaders purchase the participation of large numbers of unskilled laborers. In 1952 observers claim to have seen workers demonstrating for the communists, for the royalists, and for the Mossadeqist National Front on successive days.[7] However, no more basic mistake could be made—and it is frequently made, particularly by British observers—than to adopt the cynical view that all Iranian mobs have been purchased. Both the Mossadeq and the Communist forces had genuine and widespread support from people who volunteered to enter the streets and do battle with their opposition.

The chaqu keshan mobs are most frequently purchased by rightist and royalist politicians. The mob that appeared from the

[7] Remarks made to the author by several Iranian observers considered by the author to be reliable.

slums of South Tehran on August 19, 1953, and presented the rightist Army generals with victory over Mossadeq were mullah- and chaqu keshan-led.[8] Herein lies both the strength and the weakness of the Shah today. Although it is probably true that most unskilled laborers share with the peasantry a vague loyalty to the Shah, this loyalty will not find expression in overt political support without instigation from the mullahs and/or chaqu keshan. The typical laborer is incapable of sustained political interest. Consequently, the Shah must depend on mullah and chaqu keshan support. The latter and much of the former can be purchased. But there is a growing dissatisfaction among many of the more enlightened and sincere religious leaders, and this dissatisfaction is a real threat to the Shah. When the majority of religious leaders feel strongly about a political issue, as they did for a time in favor of Dr. Mossadeq, the chaqu keshan will be wary about demonstrating against them, regardless of the price paid.

There is reason to believe that a good deal of the growing dissatisfaction of religious leaders reflects the early beginnings of an appearance of political awareness on the part of the unskilled laborers. As is true with the peasant, the unskilled worker will certainly begin demanding a direct political role. That he is becoming dissatisfied already may well explain the clerical attitude of growing dissatisfaction, since the mullahs, like leaders of men everywhere, must never fall out of harmony with their flocks. Whether the unskilled worker will be a source for radical, possibly communist, support depends upon government efforts to bring about urban social and political reform.

The industrial workers, new to Iran, appeared as a consequence of Reza Shah's industrialization policy. Iran is still far from being an industrialized state, and this group, although it is growing rapidly, is not yet large. The Abadan refinery employs about 60,000 Iranians, and there are a number of industrial workers in Isfahan, Tehran, and in the northern provinces of Azerbaijan, Gilan, and Mazanderan. As a recent arrival on the social scene the industrial worker lacks any genuine group traditions. However, he is easily organized and is a natural political target. Already he is more articulate than is the unskilled worker, but his political edu-

[8] See Chapter 13 for a full account.

cation remains deficient. In the early stages of industrialization a large percentage of the labor leaders either were chaqu keshan types themselves or were in close alliance with them. They cared little for the interests of the worker and were largely concerned with using him. Prior to the fall of Dr. Mossadeq, however, genuine and dedicated labor leadership was beginning to appear. One of the chief parties of the Mossadeq coalition, the Toilers Party, based its support on the industrial worker, and although the chaqu keshan-type leader was prominent in the Toilers, there were also many sincerely prolabor leaders, such as Khalil Maleki. The extent of communist inroads into the labor movement is unknown but is believed to be great, especially in the oil fields and in the refineries.

The present government's stated policy is dedicated to the proposition that genuine labor unions are desirable. In fact, labor has been virtually abandoned to the leadership of the chaqu keshan, and little effort has been made to disguise the unrepresentative character of these men. For the Shah's government this is a major gamble. By compelling the workers to submit to such leadership, the government is destroying the likelihood that moderate nationalist leaders will be able to compete with radical demagogues or communists if a political upheaval occurs in Iran.

Intelligentsia

When an Iranian and an American speak of the "intellectuals," their meanings are broadly different. The American usually refers to a narrow group of individuals who are deeply concerned with thought, with the arts, and with scholarship for its own sake. The Iranian, on the other hand, refers to the most highly educated people, including almost the entire professional class. Inherent in this disagreement is much of the difference between the social attitudes of Iran and the United States, in particular the attitude toward the commercial element. In Iran this group, far from occupying a central prestige position as in the United States, has not been quite respectable. This attitude is rapidly breaking down, and Iranians are beginning to speak of a middle class that includes business people, white-collar workers, bureaucrats, professional people, and what in America is meant by "intellectuals." A study of nationalism in Iran, however, must consider the professional, highly educated group separately from the commercial element because the Iranians have done so.

Nationalism appeared in the West at a time when the middle class was sufficiently strong to make a bid for political power. The doctrine proved to be remarkably well suited for this middle class, and in a startlingly short period it became firmly established wherever the middle class was strong. The speed with which Western states suddenly became nations was due in large part to the fact that receptivity to the idea of nationalism preceded the appearance of the idea. In Iran the reverse was the case, except for a very small merchant group. As indicated above, the vast majority of the Iranian people were totally unprepared for the idea of nationalism. A small group, however, was receptive to it, along with liberalism and democracy, and once the idea was established among this narrow group it exercised a dynamic quality of its own. Those infected by nationalism seemed compelled to follow a course of action that would broaden popular receptivity.

That the intellectuals served as the vehicle by which nationalism entered Iran and other Asian states would seem to be only natural and too often is accepted as a matter of fact. Actually, this study questions that conclusion. Of the three groups involved in the nationalist constitutional revolution of 1906—the clergy, the merchants, and the intellectuals—the last group played, demonstrably, the least important role. After commenting on the role of the European intellectuals in the development of European nationalisms, William S. Haas, in his excellent book, *Iran,* says: "In Islamic countries there was no such development. Religion and tradition held thought in their spell and kept the new ideas and discoveries from expanding their creative energies into the sphere of general culture." [9] Although evidence is abundant to indicate that by 1906 the Iranian intellectuals thought about and talked about nationalism and politics a great deal, the tradition of non-participation in politics prevented their playing a more important role in the 1906 revolution.

Once the revolution had been won, however, the intellectual threw himself into the constitutional movement with enthusiasm.

[9] William S. Haas, *Iran* (New York, 1946), p. 103.

His was the role of educator. Liberal, democratic, and nationalist values were only slightly understood by even the articulate citizenry, and it fell to the intellectual to explain these concepts, although it must be admitted that in many cases he himself only poorly comprehended them.

Still, with a habit of nonparticipation in politics and with only a new, badly understood political ideology to rely upon, the intellectual had difficulty maintaining his enthusiasm. As unforeseen ideological and power conflicts developed among the former religious, merchant, and intellectual allies, as the reactionary forces recouped their strength, and as the immensity of the problem of reconstructing old Iran into a modern nation became apparent, disillusionment spread. Spirits fell when Mohammad Ali's troops closed the Majlis, and they soared when Tabriz resisted so fiercely that Mohammad Ali tottered and fell. The same cycle repeated itself in the following years, but when Morgan Shuster was compelled to leave Iran intellectual enthusiasm seemed to collapse.

The years 1919–21 revealed much about the strength and the weakness of the nationalist intellectuals. Opposition to the proposed Anglo-Persian Treaty of 1919 was led forcefully and with imagination by intellectuals, and much of the explanation for the eventual rejection of this treaty lies with the intellectual opposition.[10] Though they proved themselves capable of waging and winning a negative battle, the intellectual nationalists were too weak numerically, too lacking in power, and too unconcerned with developing a dynamic program to prevent the collapse of liberal democracy.

Up to the time of the appearance of the Reza Shah dictatorship, the intellectual was far weaker in the realm of power than in the realm of ideology. Consequently, Reza Shah confronted the intellectuals with a major dilemma, a dilemma that so divided them that to speak of the intelligentsia as a political unit from 1921 to 1941 is to speak of a fiction. Reza Shah wished to unify, modernize, and industrialize Iran. His natural opponents were the clergy and landowners, who wished to maintain the status quo. His natural allies were the commercial and intellectual elements. They

[10] The best account of this is to be found in Abdollah Mostofi, *Tarikh Ejtemai va Edari Dore Qajarieh,* 4 vols. (Tehran, 1945–47).

had the same goals for Iran, and without question Reza Shah added greatly to the numerical and political strength of both elements. The middle class attained such eminence that Arnold Wilson writing in 1932 concluded: "The middle class, though numerically small, is today predominant in every walk of life. Its members form an oligarchy which controls elections, manages all public affairs, and in the last resort, by constitutional or other methods, exercises a decisive influence in national policy." [11] Much of the intelligentsia, however, had deeply believed in liberalism and democracy as well as in nationalism. For these people the tyranny of Reza Shah, even though nationalism was firmly established, was intolerable, and they remained in silent opposition throughout his reign.

After the abdication of Reza Shah, upper-class political predominance returned. The present Shah, Mohammad Reza Pahlavi, lays claim to being a liberal democratic nationalist as well as an intellectual. But whereas his father, who had no such pretensions, attracted the support of many intellectuals in the early days of his regime, the present Shah, ironically, has elicited little enthusiasm from this group. Today the intellectuals have returned to the sullen quiescence which is their tradition whenever a hostile regime is in power. They participate in the economic life of the state but without enthusiasm. A few have accepted seats in the Majlis, but they usually lose their influence in the intellectual community because of this participation. Some others are engaged in underground opposition activities, and although the extent and effectiveness of these activities are unknown, they are not presumed to be great.

The great champion of the intellectuals was, of course, Dr. Mossadeq, and the years of his premiership were the period of greatest intellectual predominance. In the National Front coalition probably the strongest party was the Iran Party, headed by the former Iranian ambassador to the United States, Allahyar Saleh. This party, about which more will be said later, symbolized intellectual political participation.

The intellectual element not only predominated in Mossadeq's coalition, it also predominated in the Tudeh Party, the political

[11] Arnold T. Wilson, *Persia* (London, 1932), p. 45.

party arm of communism in Iran. Although the Shah's security forces have destroyed the Tudeh organizational apparatus within Iran, many of the leaders have fled abroad, and a new organization is certain to be waiting, vulture-like, for its opportunity to return to Iran. In such an event it is virtually certain that a large percentage of the intellectuals will join its ranks, regardless of the well-demonstrated antinationalist aims of communism for Iran.

Commercial Middle Class

Just as nationalism suited European middle-class elements admirably, so did it conform almost precisely to the interests of the small but assertive mercantile element in Iran. The merchants in the late nineteenth century, who were striving desperately to expand their activities, were confronted with two very different but equally imposing restrictions. First, the social base in which they sought to operate approximated the feudalistic and was hopelessly decentralized. National communications hardly existed, there was no internal security, and provincial governors, far from seeking to establish central control, helped perpetuate the localism that the landowning system generated. To operate effectively, the merchants needed a stable, unitary state, and nationalism, which demanded a view of Iran as a unit, had for them a strong natural appeal. Second, the merchants saw in the increasing number of concessions being granted foreign business elements the destruction of their own commercial prospects. Since nationalism called for national independence and the elimination of foreign interference, the merchants again were easily attracted. The ideas of liberalism and democracy had a less natural appeal, but the merchants favored them because they were anxious to place an institutional control over the ability of the Court to give away Iran's economy to foreigners, and liberal democratic institutions could provide such control.

As early as 1890 a delegation of merchants had protested to the Shah against the granting of the tobacco concession,[12] and opposition to external and internal governmental policy mounted after that. In the revolution of 1906, which resulted in the promulgation of the constitution, the merchants played a major role, co-

12 Edward G. Browne, *The Persian Revolution: 1905–1909* (London, 1910), p. 49.

equal with that of the clergy and much stronger than that of the intellectuals. By taking bast (refuge) in the British Summer Embassy grounds to the number of 14,000, the merchants were able to paralyze the commerce of the city and to bring the government to its knees.[13] In the following six years the merchants remained generally faithful to the constitution, although the intensity of their attachment visibly declined. The liberal democratic minority in the Majlis was composed largely of merchants; and when Mohammad Ali Shah attempted to circumvent or destroy the constitution, the bazaar invariably reacted by closing in protest.[14] The merchants had much to gain from the success of the nationalist movement in Iran. In an orderly, unified, and truly independent state they could expand their commercial activities.

After Shuster's expulsion the already waning enthusiasm of the merchants vanished, and in the years that followed, internal security, even when established by foreign troops, appeared to be the primary objective of the merchant. He was never again to play the predominant role in the nationalist movement that had been his in the constitutional period. In the first months of that period the merchant was almost a monolithic force. Iranian merchants were members of tightly organized and controlled guilds which acted with a near unanimity in favor of the constitution. With the advent of Reza Shah, however, a development that had begun earlier was accelerated. The larger, more imaginative, and more westernized merchants began to leave the covered bazaar and the discipline of the guilds and locate in modern shops in the new commercial centers of towns. For nationalism the repercussions of this move were manifold.

Many of those who moved became strong supporters of Reza Shah, for they profited greatly from his efforts to unify and revitalize the state and also from his encouragement of commercial activities. The smaller merchants remaining behind in the bazaar, on the other hand, opposed Reza Shah (then still Reza Khan) to the point of openly demonstrating and closing the bazaar. They did so, however, not because they had been offended at his tyranny, but because the clergy, who were highly influential in the bazaar,

[13] *State Papers 1909, Persia No. 1*, pp. 4–5.
[14] Ahmad Kasrevi, *Tarikh Mashrutah Iran* (Tehran, 1951), p. 210.

hated and feared the secularism of Reza Khan. At the same time that the bazaar was registering its opposition, several hundred well-to-do merchants participated actively in a demonstration favoring the establishment of a new Pahlavi dynasty.[15] Nationalism per se was not at issue here, but the type of nationalism favored by the modern merchants and that favored by the bazaar merchants varied sharply. The former wanted strong central control and cared little about attendant political tyranny. The latter, reflecting the view of the clergy, favored an independent Iran but did not wish to see the secular trend devour the traditional clerical power.

Not until early 1951 did the merchants again act with near unanimity. There were very few Moslem merchants not caught up in the nationalistic enthusiasm that enveloped Iran in the first weeks and months of the premiership of Mossadeq. The smaller bazaar merchants were closely associated with the religious arm of nationalism which was led by the ruthless, colorful Ayatollah Abolqasem Kashani and which exercised much influence over National Front policy. But the larger, more westernized merchants lacked organization, and, though some individuals among them did gain major policy-making positions, as a group their influence was not great. Their moderating force was not felt as strongly as might have been the case had they been better organized. Furthermore, as the battle against the Anglo-Iranian Oil Company progressed and Iran was suddenly confronted with a loss of foreign exchange, the large merchants, most of whom depended on the import trade, felt the financial pinch and were among the first to move into Mossadeq's opposition.

This split appears to exist today. The bazaar remains a center of pro-Mossadeqist sympathy, but many of the larger merchants, who profit from the lax foreign exchange controls and the mammoth oil income, favor the present government.

Landowners

The lingering prejudice of the intellectuals against commerce is due in part to the drift of sons of the aristocracy into the intelligentsia. Although there is no question of the overall hostility

[15] Hossein Maki, *Tarikh Bist Salleh Iran* (Tehran, 1945–47), III, 395.

of the upper class to liberal nationalism, individuals not only have joined the nationalist movement, but have furnished it with some of its most impressive leadership. The most spectacular example of this is, of course, Mossadeq himself, a product of the aristocracy and now the symbol of Iranian nationalism.

The typical large landowners at the turn of the century were not offended by the overweening foreign influence in Iran. They associated more with the Russian aristocracy than they did with their own people, and a common observation of the period was that much of the Iranian aristocracy identified more with their Russian counterparts than with the nation of Iran.[16] Like the Russian nobility, Iranian aristocrats failed to check the concentration of power in the hands of the monarch. Very frequently a shah who had become jealous of the wealth and power of a feudal lord would confiscate the lands of that unfortunate grandee and reduce his family to penury. Conversely, royal favor sometimes permitted members of even the lowest class to break into the highest feudal order. The class situation, therefore, had a certain fluidity, and the feudal contract, so important in the evolution of Western political institutions, did not play a comparable role in Iran. The legacy of social mobility had important results in the development to nationalism, all centering around the Iranian upper class's failure to develop an *esprit de corps*.

The Iranian landed aristocrats were the natural allies of the embattled Qajar monarchs in the early twentieth century, just as the French aristocrats were the allies of the Bourbons when the French middle class was making its bid for power in 1789. There were inevitable grievances against the Qajars among the landowners, but by and large the status quo was favorable, and the preceding century had given ample demonstration that a feudalistic society would be overturned if the middle class predominated. Nevertheless, the landed aristocracy gave at best passive support to the Qajars, and the explanation appears to lie largely in this lack of any real feeling of class solidarity.

On the surface the ability of the constitutionalists to maintain themselves in power in this period appears to be inexplicable. The Shah despised the constitution and worked openly to destroy it.

[16] Kasrevi, p. 147.

He had under his control the only armed force of any importance, and as an increasingly important section of the clergy turned against the constitution, the liberal nationalists could no longer count on their ability to control the city mobs. Then, as a final irony, the majority of Majlis deputies, the very heart of the constitution, opposed or were unenthusiastic about the entire movement. Even though Tehran and Tabriz were overrepresented in the First Majlis, the landowners and their selectees predominated. That the constitution could endure in the face of such strength is best explained by a combination of indecision on the part of Mohammad Ali Shah and a lack of class solidarity on the part of the aristocracy.

At this point, Mohammad Ali chose as his first minister one of the few reactionary aristocrats with courage, determination, and decisiveness, a man known as "the Atabak." This shrewd politician very quickly perceived the extraordinary weakness of the nationalist position and moved to exploit it. He negotiated with the reactionary clerical leaders and persuaded them to bring out mobs of supporters as a show of strength. The Russian-officered Cossacks maneuvered ominously to further emphasize the power of the Court. Then when the revolutionary leaders demanded the dismissal of the Atabak, their protests were disdainfully disregarded, in spite of popular demonstrations. With such a show of strength, the landowner majority in the Majlis, like a frightened turtle, at first timidly and then with more determination stuck out its neck and expressed its solidarity with the government. But just when the battle appeared to be won, the Shah and his Court and the landed representatives in the Majlis suddenly abandoned the field and retreated back to their old position of giving lip service to the constitution as the expression of the popular will. This startling reversal came as the result of a single act by an unknown nationalist merchant from Tabriz—the assassination of the Atabak.

The members of the landowning class were running true to form. They saw in the nationalist movement a threat to their privileged position in society, and they much preferred the loose organization of a feudal-type state to the strong central control demanded by the nationalists. But they lacked the class spirit and loyalty necessary for energetic resistance. When it became clear that the merchants and clergy really meant to change the old order, the landed gentry accepted the constitution and attempted to use their position in the Majlis to check any radical alteration of their privileged position. With the Atabak in command and with the reactionary clergy as allies, the aristocracy cautiously moved backward; but with the assassination of the Atabak they bowed again to the national will. This timidity was the pattern throughout the 1906–12 period, and the landed aristocracy emerged from the constitutional period largely unscathed and with most of their privileges intact. But they had gained the scorn of the nationalists, who believed that the grandees would prefer to accept foreign control of their country rather than submit to the will of their own people. This view of the aristocracy characterizes Iranian nationalism to this day.

The aristocracy did not escape so easily from their next encounter with nationalism. In the early constitutional period the Court and the landowners had shared a hostility to nationalism, but in the Reza Shah period the Court was the advocate of a fierce, all-encompassing nationalism. This spirit, combined with Reza Shah's tightly centralized government, was anathema to the aristocracy, and from the beginning they recognized the threat to their position. They were not without allies. The clergy was increasingly monolithic in its opposition, and the element of the intelligentsia that valued liberalism saw in Reza Shah's tyranny a betrayal of the very essence of their ideology. Together with these allies, the landowners were in firm control of the Majlis. With strong leadership, with more determination, and, above all, with class spirit the landowners might have defeated Reza Shah. Indeed, in 1924 the dictator was very close to defeat. But the Majlis had permitted him to gain control of the security forces, and he used this weapon to rig elections in his favor. Later, after gaining full dictatorial control, Reza Shah attacked the landowners directly; he had many of them murdered, and confiscated a great many villages. But he did not strike at the root of landowner power, as he could have done by a program of land reform. Consequently, when Reza Shah abdicated, the remaining landowners reasserted their power.

The post-Reza Shah governments until 1951, without exception, included representatives of the landowner mentality. However, the profound social revolution which was so important in the early constitutional period had been encouraged by Reza Shah, and it had progressed to the point where a more fundamental challenge to the landowning class could be made. This challenge came from the National Front of Dr. Mossadeq. The landowners were overwhelmingly predominant in the Sixteenth Majlis, and Mossadeq and his supporters numbered only a handful of the total membership. Yet when Premier Ali Razmara was assassinated in 1951, the landowner deputies reacted just as their predecessors had done at the time of the Atabak's assassination. They bowed to the popular will and voted unanimously for nationalization of the oil industry and overwhelmingly for the premiership of Dr. Mossadeq.

Under Mossadeq, the landowners' behavior adhered to the familiar pattern. They were bitterly opposed to the middle-class predominance of the period, and clearly understood that the Mossadeq agricultural program could destroy their power. Since direct opposition could have brought about their immediate elimination, they preferred to follow the traditional policy of using their Majlis strength to chip away at the opposition and to enter into intrigues for a *coup d'état.* In this policy they were successful. However, if the landowners expected to return to the status quo ante Mossadeq, they were due for a sad awakening. Social revolution had gone too far for that. The middle class had become a formidable force, and the darling of that class had been Mossadeq. The successor government had only two choices: to win the middle class or to control it by force. Either method would spell doom for the old, leisurely status quo.

The Shah has chosen the latter method, and his regime has inevitably taken on the complexion of the police state. Confronted with the subsurface hostility of the politically articulate middle class, he has countered by constructing a secret police organization. But if there is any rule that has validity with regard to a feudalistic society, it is that the aristocracy always abhors a one-man dictatorship. On the part of the old landowners in Iran today there is a striking lack of enthusiasm for the Shah's dictatorship. But theirs is no choice at all. The alternatives to the Shah or another rightist dictatorship are at best the nationalists and at worst the communists, and under either the destruction of the rural social base of the landowning system would proceed apace. Furthermore, the landowners themselves are changing. Most have accepted nationalist values both implicitly and explicitly, and many have dropped all their prejudice against commerce and are investing their money in business, particularly in luxury real estate. As they do so, they acquire a vested interest in the present government, and now even their memory of the good old feudal days grows thin.

4

NATIONALISM AND THE TRIBES

There is only one safe generalization to be made about the tribes of Iran: that no generalization is valid. Some tribes are almost totally nomadic, others have settled in permanent villages, and there is every degree of difference between them. Tribal loyalties vary greatly, ranging from the intense to the lukewarm. This very diversity in tribal structure, tribal loyalty, and the extent of nomadism is of great importance for the development of nationalism in Iran. One-sixth to one-fourth of the Iranian population are members of tribes.[1] In a land in which the vast majority of the population are politically inarticulate, internal political developments can be determined by a mere handful of men. Should even a small percentage of the one-sixth of the population that are tribal have decided to act in concert to dominate Iran politically, they could very likely have done so. It was the diversity among the tribal groups and the particularistic orientation within the various tribes that protected nationalism in its infancy.

At the beginning of the nationalist era the individual tribesman resembled the individual villager. Both were illiterate and ignorant, and both had limited horizons. For the villager life revolved around one or a few small villages. The tribesmen's orbit consisted of the small section of his tribe with which he had daily contact. If either had any realization that his village or tribe was part of Iran, that realization was vague; and neither was capable of comprehending nationalism. Generally, the tribesman was less receptive to nationalism than the peasant, for his loyalty to the tribe was stronger than the peasant's loyalty to the village and hence more of a barrier to the acquisition of a higher loyalty to the state.

The tribes usually inhabited mountainous territory or plains that were better suited for grazing than for farming. The severity

[1] John Murray, ed., *Iran Today* (Tehran, 1950), p. 29.

of the winter in the mountains and the lack of sufficient year-round feed in the warm lowlands necessitated migration between summer and winter quarters. Close cooperation was necessary for these semiannual migrations—just as it was needed to carry out the tribal custom of supplanting income by robberies and raids. Of necessity, the tribes had to be organizationally self-contained. The khans, or chiefs, were virtual dictators of the basic tribal units; they collected taxes and, together with the mullahs, carried out the functions of the courts, both civil and criminal. There was little left for the central government to do and little reason for the tribesmen even to think of an external authority. However, as agricultural methods improved there was a trend toward permanent settlements. Most tribes broke into sections, one remaining nomadic and tending the livestock, the other producing whatever crops the land would yield. This trend gave greater freedom for individual initiative and reduced the differential between tribesman and peasant.[2]

At the turn of the century, the most important of the tribes, politically speaking, were the Kurds, the Qashqais, the Lurs, the Bakhtiaris, the Khamseh complex, the Shahsevans, and the Turkomans. (The Kurds are a special case and will be considered in the next chapter.) All of the tribes recognized the suzerainty of the Shah and his prerogative to name the tribal leadership. But actual interference in tribal affairs was rare, and most tribes remained indifferent to the central government as long as they were left alone.[3] Nevertheless, the tribes played a significant, possibly decisive, role in the growth of nationalism in Iran.

Early Constitutional Period

Acknowledging the suzerainty of the Shah is not the same thing as having a loyalty to Iran. Rather, the typical tribal response to

[2] The Turkomans were an example of this pattern. The khans were far less effective in controlling the sedentary sections of their tribes. See *State Papers 1912, Persia No. 3*, p. 147.

[3] For the Arab tribes see Yanel B. Mirza, *Iran and the Iranians* (Baltimore, 1913), p. 104. For the Qashqais see Oliver Garrod, "The Nomadic Tribe of Persia Today," *Journal of the Royal Central Asian Society*, January 1946, p. 39. For the Turkomans see George N. Curzon, *Persia and the Persian Question* (London, 1892), pp. 189–98.

the central government varied directly with the strength of the central government. If the government was strong and effective, tribal raids and depredations would be at a minimum. If the government was weak, tribal raiding on travelers, villages, and even cities would increase. For the vast majority of tribes the 1906 revolution meant that a relatively weak government had been replaced by one that was even weaker. It is most unlikely that more than a fraction of the tribesmen understood that provincial control in 1906–08 was weakened because the Shah and the nationalists were preparing for a showdown battle in Tehran. Tribal raiding increased, as it always had when control weakened.[4]

In 1907 the Turkoman tribe broke into revolt and engaged in an orgy of raiding and depredation.[5] For the individual tribesmen and lesser chiefs the objective must surely have been loot. However, at the beginning of the revolt the ilkhan (supreme khan) demanded as a condition for peace that the Shah discard the constitution and reassume the old royal prerogatives. The revolt was put down, but it had been a serious portent for the future. There was little reason for the Turkomans to be dissatisfied. Governmental interference had declined, and surely there had been no kind of anticonstitutional agitation on the part of the politically inarticulate tribesmen; yet the ilkhan of the Turkomans wished to see the constitution overturned. Whether this wish was motivated by his personal loyalty to the Shah, to his ideological disapproval of democracy, or to pressure from the Russians is not known. But this revolt demonstrated that the political attitude of a tribal chief could have a great bearing on political developments in the capital.

The tribes were far from being a complete asset to the royalists. After the Majlis had been closed in 1908, the absolutist government of Mohammad Ali suffered from the same tribal lawlessness that had oppressed the earlier constitutional regime. But of infinitely more importance was the decision on the part of important Bakhtiari khans to give support to the liberal nationalists. Sardar Asad, a brother of the Bakhtiari ilkhan Samsam al-Soltan-

[4] Agnes Hamilton, "The Persian Crisis," *Fortnightly Review*, August 1908, p. 205.

[5] Abdolsamad Khalatbari, *Zendegani Sepahsalar Azam* (Tehran, 1948), pp. 26–27.

eh, returned to Iran from Europe in 1908 a proclaimed believer in liberal democracy and an outspokenly enthusiastic nationalist.[6] Mohammad Ali Shah, partly as a reaction against Sardar Asad, used his prerogative to select the tribal ilkhan by replacing Samsam with his chief rival.[7] He could scarcely have made a more foolish move. Very much as a result of the Shah's actions, Samsam al-Soltaneh and Sardar Asad determined to join forces with the pro-nationalist force from Rasht and march on Tehran. The Bakhtiari tribal force led by Sardar Asad was a decisive element in Mohammad Ali's defeat.

During this period Turkoman and Shahsevan tribes opposed nationalism, and the Bakhtiari tribe supported it. The individual Bakhtiari tribesman certainly had no more or no less feeling for Iran than had his Shahsevan opposite number. But because of the political ideology of one chieftain and the thwarted personal ambitions of another, the Bakhtiari tribesmen helped the nationalist movement triumph. Following this victory, both Sardar Asad and Samsam al-Soltaneh became leaders of the national movement, and each periodically served as premier. Their tribesmen helped garrison Tehran and maintain the government in power. It was a symbiotic relationship. In return for services rendered, the Bakhtiari leaders achieved national prominence, and the Bakhtiari tribe was not only permitted to keep the taxes collected in its territory, but also received a portion of military tax revenue.[8]

For the most part, however, the tribes in the 1909–12 period continued their raiding and virtually halted communications between Tehran and the provinces. In 1911 the southwestern province of Fars shows in microcosm the confusion and turmoil the tribes created and also explains their basic weakness.[9] Fars had enjoyed relative tribal tranquillity prior to 1911. There had been much raiding and the highways were unsafe, but at least the question of tribal leadership had been temporarily resolved. The dominating figure in the province was Qavam al-Molk, who had established himself in power through the support of the Turco-

6 This is asserted by Mostofi, I, 387 and Khalatbari, p. 49.

7 David Fraser, *Persia and Turkey in Revolt* (London, 1910), p. 87.

8 J. M. Balfour, *Recent Happenings in Persia* (London, 1922), p. 99.

9 See for this account *State Papers 1911, Persia No. 1,* pp. 18–20.

Arab Khamseh tribal complex. The Khamseh cooperated with him because they gained thereby a predominant position among the tribes of Fars and, with this position, special privileges. Nor was this Qavam's only source of power. As the ally of the vigorous Bakhtiari tribal khans, Qavam seems to have been in a particularly strong position. Also, many Iranians are convinced that he was in a close alliance with the British, who had extensive commercial interests in Fars. Yet, despite this position of strength, in 1911 Qavam was severely challenged by the increasingly powerful and ambitious ilkhan of the Turkish-speaking Qashqai tribe, Solet al-Doleh.

Solet's ambitions were not confined to Fars. He was intensely jealous of Samsam al-Soltaneh and the latter's predominance in Tehran. Therefore, Solet launched a campaign to wrest the control of Fars from Qavam and the Bakhtiari-dominated central government. Thus far it could be concluded that this was a simple power struggle between individuals and their tribal backing; but any such conclusion would be an oversimplification. Power struggle it was, but not simple, and no one should be surprised to learn that neither side won a clear-cut victory. In the struggle that followed, a rival Qashqai khan joined with the Khamseh-Bakhtiari coalition against Solet. But this gain was countered by a defection within the Bakhtiari tribal complex in which several subtribes allied themselves with Solet. Other features of the struggle included the following: Solet persuaded the ferocious Boir Ahmadi tribe to attack Qavam's forces, which they did, but having tasted battle and the fruits of victory, they refused to be restrained and devastated wide areas; [10] Solet reportedly instigated an anti-Semitic riot in Shiraz, the capital city of Fars, to demonstrate to Tehran (and to the British) that Qavam could not maintain order in Shiraz; [11] rival religious factions backed the two contestants, the most prominent Isfahan clerics supporting Solet's Qashqai rival.[12] From a study of such tribal conflicts the conclusion that is important from the point of view of progress of nationalism in Iran is

[10] *State Papers 1911, Persia No. 1*, p. 19.
[11] *Ibid.*, p. 112.
[12] *Ibid.*, p. 95.

that not only were the tribes incapable of uniting to form a common front, but even the strongest were incapable of maintaining intratribal unity.

Tribal lawlessness had important consequences for nationalism. First, a severe financial strain resulted from the denial of provincial revenues and from the cost of the feeble efforts made to restore order. Second, by isolating the provinces the tribes made certain that nationalism would evolve as primarily a Tehran affair, a situation that had an important influence on its coloring. Third, the inability of a liberal regime to establish internal security raised a doubt in the minds of many that Iran was prepared for liberal democracy; thus the ground was laid for nationalist acceptance of the Reza Khan dictatorship. Fourth, the insecurity in Iran and the inability of the central government to maintain control made inevitable British and Russian intervention on behalf of their own commercial interests.

1912–21

After the expulsion of Shuster, which tore the heart from the nationalist movement, the tribal situation did not change. Raids and robberies and inter- and intratribal conflicts continued at undiminished tempo except where prevented by foreign control.[13] In Tehran the Bakhtiari khans and their military contingent remained prominent even though most of the dynamism had been drained from the liberal nationalist movement which they once supported. Iranian nationalists today, in fact, have difficulty admitting that there was any sincerity in the nationalism of Sardar Asad and Samsam al-Soltaneh.

Since they were fundamentally opposed to the establishment of the type of strong nation-state that nationalism demands, the Iranian tribes must be regarded as an essentially antinationalist force, in spite of service by some khans to the nationalist movement. But if the tribes opposed the creation of a strong national government, they were even more violently opposed to the establishment of tight foreign control in Iran. The Azerbaijani Shahsevan tribe, for example, had consistently opposed the constitu-

[13] See *State Papers 1912, Persia No. 5; State Papers 1913, Persia No. 1; State Papers 1914, Persia No. 1.*

tionalists and had been a major source of support for Mohammad Ali Shah. When Azerbaijan was occupied by Russian troops, however, the Shahsevans fought against them bravely and unceasingly. Undoubtedly included in their motivation for opposing the Russians was the traditional resistance of a tribal group to any force, foreign or domestic, which is capable of establishing a strong central control. But xenophobia and religious hatred were surely involved also. The Shahsevan khans swore to fight the infidel Russians as long as they could and then to flee to Turkey. They sent this message to Tehran: "Do not send any more Mussulman soldiers against us. We do not care to kill our Mussulmen brethren, but send all the Russians you can. We will settle our accounts with these yellow dogs." [14]

Most Iranian nationalists would contest any statement that the tribes were antiforeign. They would argue that far from being anti-British, the various tribal khans in the British area of influence were in fierce competition for British support in their tribal rivalries. The British are believed to have controlled the tribes by a sophisticated divide-and-conquer technique. From their complete files on tribal personalities, they understood the complexities of intra-tribal competition, and when one khan got out of control, they would throw their support to his rival. In this manner they could protect their commercial supply lines and oil fields. British "support" is said to have consisted of heavy subsidies to their friends, who in turn provided them with tribal units through which recalcitrant khans could be disciplined. This portrait of British procedure cannot be documented, although many Iranians will swear to firsthand knowledge of its truth. That the British did deal directly with the tribes is admitted in British diplomatic correspondence; and that oil subsidies were paid to Bakhtiari tribal khans is an established fact. Furthermore, since the Iranian government was incapable of protecting British lives and property, it is not unreasonable to conclude that there is truth in the Iranian explanation.

However, the Iranians go far astray in their analysis of the tribal motivation behind this cooperation. In their emphatic con-

[14] Mirza Firuz Khan, "The Shahsevans and the Cossacks," *The Near East,* August 2, 1912, p. 383.

demnation of the cooperating tribal chiefs, the nationalists reveal an interesting and very natural dichotomy in thinking. Nationalist ideology calls for complete independence from foreign interference, but the political facts of life in Iran include foreign interference to an extent that is far beyond nationalism's point of tolerance. Fully infected with nationalism and yet confronted with the necessity of dealing with foreigners who wield great power inside Iran, the nationalists even today damn their countrymen who have worked with foreigners; but at the same time they will seek foreign support to aid their own rise to power. Consequently, the nationalist equates the close working relationship between tribal khans and the British with treachery.

A fairer assessment should be made. The relationship of the khans and the British paralleled that of the khans and a strong central government. In both cases, the khans recognized an external force that was too strong for them to defeat. As a result, a working relationship developed that was sensitive to every increase or decrease in the strength of the force, whether British or Iranian; and the extent of tribal raiding depended on this strength. Likewise, in the interminable inter- and intra-tribal rivalries all sides attempted to make use of external forces. When control by the central government deteriorated, the tribes expanded their raiding until the British felt compelled to provide internal security. At this point the tribes began dealing with the British much as they had dealt with the government.

It is easily demonstrable that the tribes were almost unanimous in their wish to be free of British control. During World War I the Germans dispatched agents into the tribal areas, where, initially, they met with spectacular success in their anti-British recruitment. The Lur tribes in west central Iran harassed the British and also sent contingents to join with Kurdish elements in Kermanshah to fight with the Turks, Germans, and Iranian nationalists against the Russians and British.[15] But it was the Qashqai tribe in Fars that fought the British and in one major battle—of which Iranians are eternally proud—defeated them.[16] When the British

[15] "Notes from Persia," *The Near East,* February 20, 1914, p. 504; Yahyah Dolatabadi, *Tarikh Moaser, Ya Hiyat Yahyah* (Tehran, 1948–52), II, 351.

[16] Sir Percy Sykes, "Persia and the Great War," *Journal of the Royal Central Asian Society,* October 1922, p. 180.

began emerging as the inevitable victors in World War I, the tribal khans bowed to reality and accepted their old relationship with them. However, they had demonstrated a determination to seize every opportunity to oust the hated British.

The Pahlavi Dictatorship

The romantically inclined visitor from the West has often been charmed by the life of the Iranian tribesman.[17] The Iranian nationalist has never beeen susceptible to these blandishments, and in 1921 he found the tribes especially unalluring. Admittedly, they had occasionally resisted foreign invasions, and in the first two decades of the twentieth century they had been more willing to fight than to cooperate with foreigners. But the nationalist ledger was weighted very heavily against the tribes. They had brought chaos, suffering, and death to Iran; and they stood as a formidable roadblock in the path of unification, financial solvency, and modernization. Furthermore, their primitive fighting qualities were no longer an effective barrier against the mechanized armies of the West. It was clear that tribal activities must be severely curtailed if Iran were to become a national, Western-style state.

Indeed, probably no single aspect of the program of Reza Shah had more appeal for nationalists than his policy of disciplining the tribes. Also, nothing in the twenty years of Reza Shah's dominance in Iran is so revealing of the native shrewdness and the extreme ruthlessness of the man. No program to subdue the tribes was announced; nor in all likelihood did Reza Shah carefully calculate a plan for the destruction of tribal power. He wanted absolute power in a unified and controlled state, and the autonomy of the tribes had to be destroyed for the achievement of this goal. Instead of launching a highly advertised program, which might have united the tribes against him, Reza Shah proceeded to establish central authority wherever and whenever it was challenged. An example will demonstrate the effectiveness of his approach.

When Reza Khan took responsibility for internal security in 1921, a contingent of Bakhtiari tribesmen was still part of the governmental armed force. Obviously, the situation was intolerable; Reza Khan must eliminate this independent contingent in order to

[17] William O. Douglas, *Strange Lands and Friendly Peoples* (New York, 1951).

gain complete control over his security forces. But Reza Khan shrewdly avoided an early showdown with the powerful Bakhtiari khans. Instead, he made full use of their contingent in his effort to restore central authority in Khorasan—and he must have been pleased when they fared badly and had to be reinforced by his own Cossacks. Reza Khan then proceeded to strengthen his own position by chastening one section of the Kurdish tribe and by bringing Gilan, Mazanderan, and Azerbaijan under Tehran's control. In the meantime, he waited for the inevitable incident. It came in 1922, when a Bakhtiari tribal group, probably acting on its own, staged a brutal ambush and robbery. Public opinion was highly incensed, and with its full approval Reza Khan removed many Bakhtiari officials, officers, and tribal units from Tehran.[18]

The action was typical of his tactics: wait until a tribe revolts or commits some outrage which will arouse public opinion—then, and only then, punish it. In these early years he was careful that the punishment was not so out of proportion to the crime as to alienate public opinion, which meant that each tribe had to be disciplined several times. Typically, he would refrain from making a frontal assault on the tribe as a whole and would limit his disciplinary measures to the erring section. But with each governmental foray the tribe would be weakened. Many warriors would be killed, weapons would be captured, and the most hostile leaders would be executed or brought to Tehran for forced exile. Thus in 1922 an army subdued foraging elements among the Lurs, and in 1924 when the Lurs rose again, they were easily crushed. Likewise, in 1923 Reza Khan began the first stage in the destruction of the Qashqai and Shahsevan power.

The Bakhtiari still presented the most delicate problem. Reza Khan first legally separated the two chief divisions of the Bakhtiari, the Chahar Lang and the Haft Lang. When a subtribe made the mistake of opposing Reza Khan's military campaign to overthrow the pro-British ruler of oil-rich Khuzistan, the entire tribe was widely condemned. Reza Khan was then able to deliver a crushing military defeat to the tribe with full public approval. In 1924 the Turkomans had their turn. By the time of his coronation in 1925 Reza Khan had broken the back of tribal resistance. He

18 "Persia," *The Near East,* October 19, 1922, p. 500.

had done so without losing popular support or alarming the tribes into unity.

Incidents of tribal rebellion occurred after this time, but never again were the tribes a serious challenge. A revolt of Arab tribes was easily and ruthlessly put down in 1927.[19] The revolts of the still-dangerous Qashqai tribe in 1929 and 1932 [20] were more serious, but they, too, were crushed, and the ilkhan Solet al-Doleh was forced to move to Tehran where he died. Many believe he was murdered.

Other aspects of Reza Khan's (as Shah) program were even more effective than military action in destroying the tribal potential. The railroad and new road system enabled the army to patrol formerly inaccessible tribal areas and to ensure the collection of taxes. Enforced conscription took away many tribesmen of fighting age and forever reduced their tribal attachment by giving them a broader view of Iran. Almost as bitterly resented as conscription was the order for every adult male in Iran to wear the so-called Pahlavi hat. Since tribal distinctiveness is demonstrated by headgear, the enforced abandonment of their own headgear in favor of the same hats as those worn by rival tribes and effete townsmen was, and was meant to be, supremely humiliating.

After Reza Khan won virtually absolute power, he ceased to be concerned with public opinion. The typical nationalist still believed the tribes had to be brought under central control, but he did not necessarily approve of the increasing brutality of Reza Shah's methods. Many khans met with mysterious ends, until tribal leadership had been decapitated. Examples of the sadistic methods of terrorizing whole tribes are only too common.[21] But probably the most brutal, though least spectacular, of Reza Shah's methods was compelling the tribes to establish permanent settlements. Nothing is more successful in destroying the independence of a tribe than to force the tribesmen to become sedentary. Reza Shah ordered the tribes to settle without adequately preparing them for their new life and without ensuring that their villages would be agriculturally self-sustaining. His policy resulted in ter-

[19] "Persia Without and Within," *The Near East,* January 26, 1928, p. 100.
[20] "Persia," *The Near East,* July 4, 1929, p. 8.
[21] For an easily accessible example see Douglas, pp. 104–09.

rible suffering and the pauperization of the tribes, and liberal nationalist writers have roundly condemned him for it.[22]

Post-Reza Shah

The extent to which Reza Shah's tribal policy had succeeded was dramatically revealed in 1941 when the Anglo-Russian invasion occurred. Iran's army evaporated, and the fleeing soldiers sold their arms to the eager tribesmen. Nevertheless, with only one major exception, the tribes did not return to their pre-Reza Khan practices.

The major exception was the Qashqai tribe. With the abdication of Reza Shah, Solet al-Doleh's sons returned to the Qashqai tribe and were widely accepted. The Qashqais acquired arms and reverted to their old nomadic way of life. Their neighbors, the Boir Ahmadi, a minor tribe but a fierce anachronism even in the tribal milieu, attacked and completely defeated a battalion of Iranian troops in 1943. In 1946 the Qashqais engaged in open rebellion against the trouble-beset government of Ahmad Qavam. The tribe demanded greater representation for Fars in the Majlis, a provincial council, the right to appoint its own officials, and a railway. They also demanded the ousting of three Tudeh Party cabinet ministers.[23] This last demand was accepted. Some writers believe that the chief purpose of the revolt was anticommunism; others believe that the British instigated the rebellion to place heavy pressure on Qavam.[24] Whatever their attitude toward communism, the Qashqais disliked strong central control, and there is every reason to believe that a desire to be more free of these controls was a strong motivation for their rebellion.

Despite the obvious facts that the tribal power had been hopelessly crippled, that the trend toward permanent settlements was continuing, that with the removal of their judicial functions the chiefs had lost their dictatorial potential, the nationalists during the Mossadeq period remained highly suspicious of the tribes. Both British and Americans were constantly accused of intriguing with

[22] For example see Arsalan Khalatbari, "Political Sins From Sharivar 1320 and Afterward," *Ayandeh*, September 1944, pp. 282–83; and Mostofi, III, 308–10.

[23] A. C. Edwards, "Persia Revisited," *International Affairs*, January 1947, p. 59.

[24] Douglas, p. 136; Christopher Sykes, "Russia and Azerbaijan," *Soundings*, February 1947, p. 48.

the tribes.[25] Such was the legacy of past interference. But, incongruously, the tribe that retained the largest potential for mischief, the Qashqai, supported Mossadeq more or less faithfully and has suffered grievously for doing so. Because of the alleged murder of their father, the Qashqai khans are bitterly hostile to the rule of the Pahlavi dynasty. This hostility is clearly understood by the Shah, and His Imperial Majesty has ordered frequent and continuing persecutions of the Qashqais. In the Nineteenth Majlis elections, for example, the Shah's government ordered the selection of a member of a rival Qashqai clan from a Qashqai district.

With the eclipse of the Qashqais—and it should be noted that the present Shah has not acted with anything approaching the ruthlessness of his father—the focus of tribal attention (other than on the Kurds) is once more on the Bakhtiari. The Shah's second wife, the ex-Queen Soraya, is the daughter of a Bakhtiari chieftain, and as long as she was queen the Bakhtiari presence, and probably influence, in the Court was great. Even more important, General Timur Bakhtiar, the Shah's ex-chief of SAVAK, the Iranian Gestapo, was for a time probably the second most powerful man in Iran and is still a possible future rightist dictator. General Bakhtiar, a strong-minded, shrewd leader, is a member of a leading Bakhtiari family. However, the Bakhtiari should not be viewed as a monolithic force. There are countless units of power among the Bakhtiari, and some of the most prominent Bakhtiaris were and still are pro-Mossadeq. Dr. Shapur Bakhtiar was a leading Iran Party member, and may again become a prominent figure in a future nationalist government.

Conclusion

By helping to ward off foreign invasions, the tribes can lay claim to having helped Iran acquire and retain a unique history and a distinctive culture—elements that have been extremely useful for the integration of nationalism. On the other hand, they have bitterly resisted the imposition of the central control that is essential for any modern nation-state. In the actual nationalist struggle for

25 For some examples in the free press of the Mossadeq era see *Besu Ayandeh,* February 1, 1952 (communist); *Ettelaat,* January 20, 1952 (centrist); *Azad,* October 17, 1951 (nationalist); *Atesh,* October 10, 1951 (rightist); *Tolu',* January 9, 1952 (rightist).

power, the tribes fought on both sides. Nevertheless, in spite of this mixed picture, a tribal system of the type found in Iran prior to Reza Khan is an anachronistic force that can find no place in the modern nation-state. Nationalism demands a primary loyalty to the state; the exclusiveness of tribal loyalty as it was in Iran before the 1920's precluded such a loyalty. As nationalism became established, it inevitably demanded that Iran become a nation worthy of the respect of other nations, with a national army, an adequate communications system, and a broad extension of education. All of these developments tended to destroy tribal isolation and autonomy. Furthermore, tribal raids and depredations could not be tolerated by a modern nation-state, and the government crushed by military action the tribal potential for such raids. Probably few, if any, of the tribal leaders foresaw the forces inherent in nationalism that would be destructive of tribal independence. Had they done so, possibly they would have presented a more united front against its growth. But the vital fact is that they did not, and nascent nationalism was never confronted with the overpowering monolith of tribal unity.

It would be an error to conclude that as nationalism becomes more pervasive the tribes must disappear in their entirety. Loyalty to the nation can exist along with a multitude of other loyalties and that to a tribe can be one of them. But loyalty to the nation must be the terminal and a primary loyalty, and in the tribal system as it existed in the past, this could not have been so.

5

KURDISH NATIONALISM IN IRAN

The Kurds, among the most colorful and distinctive of Iranian tribal people, present a major problem for nationalism. In many respects the Kurd closely resembles other Iranian tribesmen. When nationalism first appeared in Iran, the average Kurd was ignorant, illiterate, and a blind follower of his khan. He had no more understanding of world politics or of his own citizenship in the state of Iran than did other tribesmen. Prior to 1921, his khan dispensed justice and proclaimed law for the tribe as did other tribal leaders. The Qajar dynasty occasionally asserted its authority over the Kurds by refusing to agree to the leadership of a particularly powerful khan, but in general they were left alone and had to submit to a minimum of interference from the central government. For the Kurd, as for other tribesmen, the concept of Iranian nationalism did not exist.

There are, no doubt, ways in which the Kurd differs from other tribesmen of Iran. Curzon writes that cohesion within the Kurdish tribe is firmer than in most nomadic tribes and the attachment to the chief stronger.[1] Hay and Mostofi paint a different picture. They assert that the Kurd gives up nomadic life more quickly than many other tribesmen if the opportunity presents itself and soon comes to dislike his chief's greedy exactions.[2] Whatever the truth of this question, the really important difference between Kurds and the other Iranian tribes lies elsewhere—the Kurdish people number nearly three million. Statistics are unreliable in Iran, and those having to do with tribes grossly so, but a commonly accepted figure for the number of Kurds in Iran is 700,000.[3] In the mountains of Turkey and Iraq that are contiguous to the chief

1 Curzon, p. 99.
2 Mostofi, IV, 299; W. R. Hay, *Two Years in Kurdistan* (London, 1921), p. 47.
3 Safrastian, p. 91.

Iranian Kurdish area in western Azerbaijan, and in the Syrian plains to the west, there dwell approximately 2,300,000 Kurds. Furthermore, an indeterminate number of these Kurds believe that the Kurdish people constitute a nation—a nation whose destiny includes independent statehood.

The existence of a unique history, as we have seen, can help give cohesion and meaning to nationalism, and Kurdish nationalists claim for their people a particularly proud heritage. They trace Kurdish history back to the ancient kingdom of Gutium in the twenty-fourth century B.C.; they see themselves as the descendants of the ancient Medes who served as the military vanguard for the great Achemenid dynasty; and they claim their ancestors were the military protectors of the great Sassanian dynasty.[4]

Throughout their history the Kurds were noted for military valor. In later years they served both the Turkish sultans and the Iranian shahs in return for booty and for noninterference in Kurdish affairs. Beginning in the nineteenth century the Turks placed tighter restrictions on the Kurds until, in 1877, taking advantage of a Turkish defeat by the Russians, the Kurds living in Turkey vainly revolted.[5] Three years later the first attempt to unite the Kurds of Turkey (then including Iraq) and Iran was made. Led by the fiery chieftain Sheikh Obeydolleh, an armed force attempted to bring Iranian Kurds into a united Kurdistan under Turkish suzerainty. Obeydolleh was defeated, but his actions served to spread a consciousness of being Kurdish to more of his people.[6]

The accuracy of the historical account of Kurdish nationalists is not of prime importance for a consideration of Kurdish nationalism. The important point is the extensiveness of its acceptance. Clearly, the Kurds believe that they have a proud and distinctive history, and this belief gives cohesion to their nationalism. In the history itself, however, there are two disturbing features for nationalism. First, the Kurds have not since ancient times formed a stable state of their own. Second, the Kurds have been in close alliance with Iran for much of their history. These two features

[4] *Ibid.*, pp. 17–30.
[5] *Ibid.*, pp. 51–62.
[6] G. W. Prothero, ed., *Armenia and Kurdistan* (London, 1920), p. 25.

would seem to incline the Kurd less toward independence than toward a loose autonomy under Iranian suzerainty. Historically-minded Iranians, very much aware of the intimate connection between their own and Kurdish history, insist that the past demonstrates that all Kurds, not only those in Iran, are really Iranian.[7]

Since they are aware of the importance of a distinctive culture in giving strength to nationalism, Kurdish nationalists in the twentieth century have worked diligently to resurrect and record past cultural achievements. It has not been a rewarding task; at the very best, the Kurdish culture is meager. It may please the uneducated tribesman, but it will hardly be satisfactory for the educated, intellectual Kurd. For those Kurds who live in Iran and receive an education in Iranian schools, the contrast between the exquisite, highly developed Iranian culture and the barren Kurdish culture is sharp and cannot help orienting them toward Iran.

If Kurdish history, language, and culture serve to draw the Kurd toward Iran, religion pushes him away. Ninety per cent of Iranians are of the Shiite sect of Islam; the vast majority of Kurds adhere to the orthodox Sunni sect. Iranian nationalism gains great inner strength from having a vast majority of the people members of a single sect, but for those outside of the Shiite orbit, identification with this nationalism is more difficult. According to Curzon, the religious antagonism between Shiite and Sunni was instrumental in Sheikh Obeydolleh's preference for Turkish rather than Iranian suzerainty over a united Kurdish people.[8] This difference of religion is not a minor matter. The conflict is mitigated somewhat because a minority of Kurds is Christian and another minority is Shiite,[9] a religious diversity which makes a certain amount of tolerance necessary and prevents the Kurds from establishing a solid anti-Iranian front on religious grounds. Also, many Kurds are Moslems in name only and care little for orthodoxy of any variety. Still, religion is a major divisive factor which tends to separate the Kurds from Iran and thereby aids Kurdish nationalism.

From the sociological point of view, Kurdish nationalism is a caricature of Iranian nationalism in that it is a movement of the

7 Afshar, "The Realm of the Persian Language," *Ayandeh*, April 1945, pp. 406–07.
8 Curzon, pp. 550–53.
9 Frederick Millengen, *Wild Life Among the Koords* (London, 1870), pp. 209–10.

few. For the ignorant tribesman, whose particular tribe is his world, Kurdish nationalism is only slightly less inconceivable than Iranian nationalism. Any participation in the Kurdish national movement by these tribesmen can come only at the behest of their khans, and their services for Kurdish nationalism will parallel those of Sardar Asad's Bakhtiaris for Iranian nationalism—they will neither favor nor oppose nationalism but will fight for it because they are commanded to do so. The settled Kurdish peasant will find nationalism no more comprehensible than will the tribesman. The only Kurds who can be expected to have the attributes necessary for nationalism are the educated urban dwellers, and these constitute only a tiny percentage of the total Kurdish population. Furthermore, there are indications that these educated Kurds have had difficulty identifying with their nomadic brethren. Frederick Millengen, writing of his experiences with the Kurds, says that in 1870 the city Kurds would have been insulted if asked if they were Kurds, an appellation used by the educated Turk or Iranian comparable to the American "hayseed." [10]

It is true that since Millengen wrote, nationalism has appeared in the Middle East, and for those who adhere to Kurdish nationalism the term "Kurd" is now a source of pride rather than opprobrium. But many of the intellectual Kurds living in Iran have chosen Iranian over Kurdish nationalism, and the attraction of Iranian history and culture remains strong. In addition, the Kurdish and the Iranian economies are closely linked. Tobacco is a major Kurdish crop that finds its market in the Iranian urban centers. The Kurds who are engaged in the production and sale of tobacco would presumably find independence within Iran less appealing.

Kurdish Separation prior to World War II

There is little to distinguish the activities of the Kurds during the constitutional period from those of other major tribal groupings. The Kurds reacted to the relaxation of central control due to the nationalist revolution in the same manner as all other tribes, i.e. they expanded their raiding activities. However, one incident does point to a commonly held view in Iran of Kurdish distinctiveness. In 1907 a number of Kurdish tribesmen from Turkey sud-

[10] *Ibid.*, p. 149.

denly invaded Iranian Azerbaijan and laid waste large areas. Iranian nationalists in Azerbaijan and Tehran saw in these unusual raids a sinister plot between Mohammad Ali and the Turkish Sultan Abdul Hamid II to overthrow the Iranian constitution.[11] Anti-Kurdish sentiment flared, and there was rioting against members of the Sunni sect. There is no verification for the Iranian belief in the Sultan's culpability, but the incident is significant because of the willingness of the Azerbaijanis to condemn the Kurds. They viewed the Kurds as distinctive and suspect simply as a result of their living on both sides of the border and of their adhering to Sunni Islam.

Although the Iranian Kurds were easy targets for Turkish propaganda in World War I, the appeal of the Sultan's call for a jehad (holy war) was probably of less importance than their hatred of the Russian forces which had been occupying Azerbaijan since 1909. Besides, they found the Turkish invitation to plunder Armenian and Assyrian villages most attractive. The cooperation of the Iranian Kurds with the Turks and Germans paralleled the close cooperation of the Lur tribe, which was unambiguously Iranian, with Central Powers. This parallel belies any conclusion that Iranian Kurds favored Turkey because of a feeling of oneness with Turkish Kurds.

At the close of the war, however, two very different drives for an independent Kurdish state did shake the tranquility of Kurdistan. One of these was a tribal revolt led by Sheikh Mahmud.[12] This movement was in the primitive tradition of an ambitious chief seeking to establish predominance over other clans and subtribes. The other movement, led by intellectual Kurdish nationalists, was far more sophisticated.[13] When the Treaty of Sevres restored peace between Turkey and the Allies, the Kurdish nationalists, with British support, were able to include in the terms a promise of independence in one year for the Kurds in the former Ottoman Empire if they proved they wanted it. Sheikh Mahmud's plans died a natural death at the hands of the intra-tribal rival-

11 Kasrevi, p. 478.

12 For accounts of this revolt see *The Near East,* June 6, 1919, p. 518; July 11, 1919, p. 30; March 18, 1920, p. 382.

13 For an account of this see General Sherif Pasha, *Memorandum on the Claims of the Kurd People* (Paris, 1919).

ries, and the rise of Mustafa Kemal in Turkey destroyed the dreams of the Kurdish intellectuals. Both Sheikh Mahmud and the intellectuals wanted an independent Kurdistan, but the political entities envisioned by each differed as much as the Middle Ages and the twentieth century. This absolute difference in perspective has characterized the Kurdish tribal and intellectual power foci ever since.

Reza Khan's epical Kurdish opponent was the colorful and courageous tribal leader Aqa Ismail Smitqu. In his early search for prestige, Reza Khan saw in Smitqu a primary target. For the Iranian nationalists the Kurdish chief symbolized the lawless raiding and arrogance of the tribes. Ebrahim Khajenuri, a favorable biographer of Reza Khan, describes Smitqu as that "wicked, vicious cannibal in every respect a traitor to his country and a tool in the hands of the enemies of Iran." [14] When the Iranian Cossacks won a decisive victory over Smitqu, celebrations with fireworks and illuminations were held all over Iran. But Smitqu was in no sense a traitor, since Iran had no claim on his loyalty. His goal was total freedom for the Kurdish tribes. Although he called for an independent Kurdistan, he would have been only slightly more pleased with a strong Kurdish government that controlled the tribes than he was with Reza Shah.

Smitqu was not finally defeated until 1930. He joined with the Pishtadari Kurdish tribe which had for many years migrated at will back and forth across the Turkish-Iranian boundary. Such behavior was equally abhorrent to the intense nationalisms of Reza Shah and Ataturk, and they regarded the complete subjugation of the Pishtadari as essential. This cooperative endeavor was no easy task, but it is significant that in the final battles the Iranian army was joined by other Kurdish tribes which were only too pleased to see their militant brethren forever silenced.

Mehabad Republic

Reza Shah's policies of improved communications, more widespread education, and enforced settlement were no less effective in the Kurdish areas of Iran than in other tribal areas. The balance of power between the settled and nomadic Kurds shifted sharply

[14] Khajenuri, p. 45.

in favor of the former as the nomadic chiefs were weakened and as the urbanized, educated base of the Kurdish population was widened. In the other areas of Iran this type of development widened the base of receptivity to nationalism and hence resulted in a significant strengthening of Iranian nationalism. The popularity of the Mehabad Republic in 1946 indicates that there was no such result in the Kurdish areas. More people embraced nationalism, but the majority, at least of those who remained in Kurdistan, chose Kurdish rather than Iranian nationalism.

The Kurds had long presented a dilemma to Soviet policy makers.[15] Both the Kurdish intellectuals and tribal chiefs were unhappy with the political divisions that separated the Kurds of Iran, Iraq, Turkey, and Syria. Furthermore, many of these would have cooperated readily with the Soviet Union if the latter had been willing to aid in the unification of Kurdistan. Here was a ready-made device for establishing a USSR-oriented wedge in the heart of the Middle East. Although the temptation to support an independent Kurdistan was great, it was always counterbalanced by the Soviet realization of the deleterious consequences for the USSR among the Turks, Iranians, and Arabs.

The temptation was compounded by wartime developments in the Middle East which brought Soviet occupation troops onto the borders of the Kurdish areas. In the summer of 1943 in Mehabad, an important urban center in the Kurdish area of Iran, a secret Kurdish nationalist society, the Kumelah, was formed.[16] The program it advocated called for political and cultural autonomy within Iran, but followers were attracted in Turkey, Iraq, and Syria as well. Iranians quite naturally feared autonomy as the first step in a move toward separation and then amalgamation with Kurds from other lands under Soviet sponsorship. The Soviets, who had long before inaugurated an infiltration of the Kurdish national movement, accelerated this program. Then in 1945 Soviet agents persuaded a highly respected leftist, Qazi Mohammad, to accept leadership of the Kumelah. Qazi incorporated in the Kume-

[15] See George Agabekov, *O. G. P. U.: The Russian Secret Terror* (Binghamton, New York, 1933), p. 95.

[16] For accounts in English see Archie Roosevelt, "The Kurdish Republic of Mehabad," *Middle East Journal,* July 1947; and Douglas, pp. 57–64.

lah program demands for land and social reform and a promise of close working relations with the Soviet-sponsored Autonomous Republic of Azerbaijan.

The cities and towns of Kurdistan could furnish leadership and rank and file recruits for the nationalist movement, but, like the Iranian nationalists in the 1906–12 period, they could not provide Kurdish nationalism with armed support. Such support could come only from the tribes. In early 1946, Qazi Mohammad issued a proclamation announcing the virtual independence of the Iranian Kurds, and several important chiefs joined in signing his proclamation. They had done so, however, only at the insistence of the Soviet occupation forces and actually had little or no enthusiasm for the new Mehabad Republic.[17] The Kurdish tribal khans had a historical hatred of Russians, and they regarded the republic as Russian sponsored. Furthermore, submission to an urban-based government, even though Kurdish, had little appeal. Consequently, when Qazi called for armed support from the tribes, little was forthcoming.

Support did come and from an unexpected quarter. An Iraqi Kurdish tribe, the Barzani, which had fled into Iran from Iraq, furnished the requisite armed force. The Barzani leader, Mullah Mostafa, had a long history of conflict with the Iraqi government over the question of Kurdish independence. In his demands of the Iraqi government, he called for a federation of Kurdish tribes into a Kurdish province, a Kurdish minister in the Iraqi cabinet to handle Kurdish affairs, and educational and cultural independence for the Kurds.[18] This is not the program of a Sheikh Mahmud or a Smitqu, but reveals Mullah Mostafa as a tribal leader in the Sardar Asad tradition—fully capable of comprehending and supporting nationalism. The Barzani supported the anti-British Rashid Ali government in 1941 and resisted British efforts to pacify the area after Rashid Ali was defeated and sent into exile. Finally, in 1945, after four years of warfare they crossed into Iran. That Mullah Mostafa should have joined forces with Qazi Mohammad was perfectly natural under the circumstances, and does not in itself demonstrate any more attraction toward the USSR than his ear-

[17] Roosevelt, p. 255.
[18] *Az Mehabad Khunin* (Tehran, 1949), p. 33.

lier collaboration with German-supported Rashid Ali indicated an attraction toward Hitlerian Germany.

A good indication that the Mehabad regime actually represented Kurdish nationalism is given by the contrast in popular reaction in Tabriz and in Mehabad when the two Soviet-supported regimes were overturned by the Iranian army in 1946. When Iranian troops marched into the Azerbaijan Autonomous Republic and expelled the Pishevari government, they were greeted with wild enthusiasm,[19] while the troops that entered Mehabad were greeted coldly.[20] In Tabriz a spontaneous rising of the population against the pro-Soviet regime and a slaughter of the communist government officials preceded the arrival of the Iranian forces. The people of Mehabad awaited the Iranian troops sullenly.

Furthermore, the name of Pishevari is a synonym of Soviet imperialism among nationalists in Azerbaijan, but the grave of Qazi Mohammad, who was executed by the Iranian authorities, is, according to Justice Douglas, now a Kurdish shrine.[21] The Qazi Mohammad government had been reformist and only mildly oppressive. As a result it had achieved some popularity among the urban population. Such was not true among the tribes, however, and with the approach of the Iranian army, the chiefs quickly deserted the Mehabad cause. Archie Roosevelt, who served as a representative of the American diplomatic service in Mehabad, reported that only two small tribes remained loyal to the Mehabad Democrats.[22] This accounting does not include the Barzani tribe, however, which resisted strongly and eventually escaped into the Soviet Union.

Kurds since Mehabad

Were it not for the ominous Soviet presence on Iran's northern border, a prediction could be made that the Kurds would eventually be incorporated into the Iranian nation, although not without great difficulty. After the Iranian army reestablished its authority in the Kurdish areas, Kurdish autonomy was dealt with severely. Many of the nationalist and tribal leaders were executed or imprisoned, the Kurdish printing press was destroyed and books in

19 See Chapter 9 for a full account.
20 Roosevelt, p. 267.
21 Douglas, p. 64.
22 Roosevelt, p. 265.

Kurdish were burned, and the old ban against the teaching of Kurdish was reimposed.[23] Political activity gradually resumed in these areas, but strictly within the Iranian framework. Still, when the Mossadeqist National Front was in power, several of its most prominent leaders were Kurds, and these men gave testimony to the possibility of attracting the Kurdish intellectuals into an advocacy of Iranian rather than Kurdish nationalism. As education in Persian becomes more widespread and as more and more Kurdish youths begin attending Iranian universities, the already strong attraction of Iran for Kurds will be strengthened.

However, the fact remains that Iran does border on the Soviet Union, and any prediction of Kurdish-Iranian integration could be upset overnight as a result of Soviet maneuvering. The appeal of Kurdish nationalism will remain for some time and with it a potential for Soviet exploitation. This potential has beeen compounded since July 1958, when the late Premier Qasem achieved power in Iraq. Probably as a peace gesture to the Kurds, Qasem permitted Mullah Mostafa and his Barzani tribesmen to return to Iraq from the USSR and allowed them much more autonomy. In the Kirkuk rioting of July 1959, however, strong evidence was given of communist influence among the Kurds. Relations between Qasem and the Kurds deteriorated until a state of open rebellion resulted. Mullah Mostafa is the leader of the rebellion, which has persisted since Qasem's overthrow. There is little reason to doubt that it has elicited a favorable response among Kurds in Iran whose receptivity for Kurdish nationalism is considerable. At the same time, the prediction can be made with some confidence that most Kurdish tribal chiefs in Iran will regard Mullah Mostafa's uprising more with alarm than pleasure. In any case, should the rebellion continue, the result is certain to be a slowing down of the integration of Iranian Kurds into the Iranian nation.

[23] *Ibid.*, p. 267.

6

NATIONALISM AND THE NON-MOSLEM MINORITIES

Well over 95 per cent of the inhabitants of Iran are Moslems, a near unanimity that has characterized the country for several centuries. For the tiny percentage of Zoroastrians, Christians, and Jews such a situation would seem to be unbearable; that they have been able to endure largely unmolested speaks well for the tolerance of Islamic Iranians. To be sure, in this long history many instances of violence and discrimination have occurred, but the overall record is one for which Iranians, comparatively speaking, need feel little shame.

With the arrival of nationalism in Iran a change in this easy tolerance was inevitable. Since nationalism requires a feeling of oneness among those people embracing it, the acquisition of such a feeling apparently would be easier for the Shiite Moslem who had a community of interest with the majority of Iranians than for the Christian or Jew who had long been aware of the exclusive position of his people in the country. On the other hand, nationalism is inherently a secular movement and can bring together members of many different religious sects in a common loyalty. Furthermore, the sentiment of nationalism did not arrive alone and naked in Iran. It was clothed in the garb of Western liberal ideals—ideals that called for respecting the right of an individual to his own religious beliefs. The position of the religious minorities was certain to change as the result of the appearance of nationalism in Iran, but the direction of this change was not easily predictable.

The Armenians

When viewed in outline, the problems for emerging Iranian nationalism posed by the Kurds were repeated by the Armenians. The Armenians, too, lived on both sides of Iran's northern and western borders. They had a distinctive religion, language, culture, and history; and the development of Iranian nationalism coincided with the development of Armenian nationalism just as it did with that of Kurdish nationalism.

However, those forces working against the incorporation of Armenians into the Iranian nation were stronger than were their counterparts for the Kurds. Armenian history was long and proud and, unlike that of the Kurds, not an appendage of the Iranian past. Armenian culture, far richer than Kurdish, was more distinct from the Iranian. Although the Armenian, Kurdish, and Persian languages were all related, Armenian differed profoundly from the other two and was written in a different script from the Arabic used by both Iranians and Kurds. Finally, the Armenians were Christians, and the gulf between Iranian Moslems and Armenian Christians was certainly far greater than that separating the Iranian Shiite from the Kurdish Sunni. In addition, a larger proportion of the Armenian population than of the Kurdish was educated, had had contact with the West, and was hence receptive to nationalism. As a result, Armenian nationalism had a much broader base of support. Nevertheless, the Kurds have always been far more of a problem for Iranian nationalism than the Armenians have been, simply because they outnumber the Armenians in Iran by more than ten to one.

The Armenian population of approximately sixty thousand[1] is concentrated in three areas—Azerbaijan, the environs of Isfahan, and Tehran. Each of these communities has its own history and traditions. The Azerbaijan community, which has been in existence for centuries, was in close association with Armenian communities in the south Caucasus and eastern Anatolia prior to World War I. The Armenians near Isfahan are descendants of people imported by Shah Abbas in the sixteenth century to provide an industrious artisan and mercantile element for his capital city. The Tehran community is composed primarily of recent arrivals, mainly refugees from Turkey and the Soviet Union. There is little communication among the three communities, and unity of action is even more difficult than mere physical separation would warrant.

[1] Thomas and Frye, p. 207.

The social organization of the Armenians in comparison with that of the Kurds also makes for a more tranquil relationship with Iranians. The settled Armenian communities did not confront the government with ready-made, semimilitary forces as did the Kurdish nomadic tribes.

Somewhat incongruously, considering the elements working against unity with Iran, the Armenians not only participated in the early Iranian national movement, but they played an extremely important role in it. Armenian intellectuals helped bring Western ideology to Iran and assisted in inculcating many Moslem Iranians with these ideals. But the Armenians did far more than give intellectual stimulus to liberal nationalism. They supported it and fought for it. Among the Tabriz defenders of liberal nationalism against the onslaughts of Mohammad Ali's tribal mercenaries were many Armenians.[2] Within the insurgent forces that marched from Rasht and, together with the Bakhtiaris, liberated Tehran, Armenians were prominent. In fact, the leader of the Armenian contingent, Yefrem Khan, was given responsibility for internal security after Mohammad Ali's abdication; and since the government had no force of its own, he guarded the second constitutional regime with his own Armenian contingent and the Bakhtiari tribesmen.

Yefrem Khan led this strange, un-Iranian coalition to victories over a reactionary force from Tabriz in 1909, Mohammad Ali's Turkoman-supported invasion in 1911, and Salar al-Doleh's Kurdish-supported challenge throughout the period. It was during a decisive battle with Salar al-Doleh shortly after the expulsion of Shuster, that Yefrem Khan was killed. News of his death was received with despair by the nationalists, and his funeral was the occasion for a gigantic Armenian-Iranian nationalist demonstration of solidarity. Thousands lined the streets to pay homage; his funeral was attended by government dignitaries and Armenians and Iranians of all classes.[3]

This early Armenian prominence in the Iranian nationalist

[2] Kasrevi, p. 685; *State Papers 1909, Persia No. 1*, p. 178; *State Papers 1909, Persia No. 2*, p. 11.

[3] *The Near East*, July 5, 1912, p. 266; July 26, 1912, p. 356; Arthur J. Funk, "The Missionary Problem in Persia," *Moslem World*, April 1920, p. 139.

movement is not difficult to explain. Many Armenians were merchants or artisans and shared with their Iranian colleagues an antagonism to the old regime because of its feudalistic base and its willingness to give Iran's resources to foreigners. More important for understanding the Armenian role in the development of Iranian nationalism, however, is the fact that disproportionately large numbers of Armenians had contact with the West. Christian missionaries, especially the French, focused much of their attention on Armenians and enrolled many of them in their schools. Also, Armenians who were in contact with their kinsmen in Russia were influenced by the Revolution of 1905. In order to understand this Armenian attitude, the reader should keep in mind the value system that Armenian intellectuals supported. At least as important as its nationalist aspects were its features of liberalism and democracy. Since the intellectual Iranian nationalist believed firmly in liberalism and democracy, the Armenian nationalist could find much in common with him. Furthermore, a primary goal of nationalism for both the Iranian and Armenian was to destroy foreign domination, a domination that both resented.

Obviously, however, Iranian nationalism and Armenian nationalism had different and conflicting objectives, and it was inevitable that these would reveal themselves. As far as their value system was concerned, the Iranian liberal nationalists may have been capable of accepting Armenians as brothers, but there was little likelihood that the easily aroused resentment against Armenians among their more ignorant Moslem neighbors would permit any growth in brotherhood.

Even in the earliest days of the constitutional movement, there were signs that the divisive factors separating Armenians from Iranian nationalists could not be ignored. Several Iranian merchants were killed by Armenians in the Caucasus in 1906, and anti-Armenian sentiment flared in Tabriz. The nationalist leaders maneuvered this public reaction into a demonstration against the oppressive regime of Mohammad Ali, then heir apparent and governor of Azerbaijan.[4] The following year, after the Anglo-Russian Agreement of 1907 was announced, anti-British and anti-Russian demonstrations took on an anti-Christian flavor, and both

[4] Kasrevi, pp. 163–67.

Armenians and Assyrians suffered.[5] But these were minor matters and were confined to the least enlightened of the supporters of the constitution. As education became more widespread, they could presumably have been overcome.

However, the overthrow of the constitutional regime in late 1911 and the subsequent death of Yefrem Khan spelled the end to Irano-Armenian cooperation. In this period the Armenians, like the Iranians, had organized a number of societies for the purpose of advancing nationalism. The international Dashnaksutuin was the most prominent of the Armenian societies. As long as the Iranian liberal nationalists maintained their struggle against reaction and foreign control, the Armenian Dashnaks found no difficulty in associating their cause with the Iranian. But after Shuster's expulsion only the shell of liberal democracy remained. In 1912 the Dashnaks announced that since liberal democracy had been betrayed, they were withdrawing their support from the government. The Armenian contingent in the national security force, once so proudly led by Yefrem Khan, refused to fight further.[6]

In a future liberal regime the Armenian and Iranian nationalists might have worked together. But before such could materialize, international developments forced the Armenian and Iranian nationalists into opposite camps and spelled out so clearly the conflict inherent in the two nationalisms that a future union was made impossible. In the eyes of the Armenians, no greater enemy existed than Turkey. In their view, Armenians had been the victims and the Turks the executors of one of the most vicious examples of genocide the world had yet seen. Not content with the murder of Armenians inside Turkey, the Turks after 1890 had urged Iranian Kurds to raid, plunder, and massacre Christian villagers, both Armenian and Assyrian.[7] The Russian troops in occupation of Azerbaijan after 1909 frequently came to the support of the Christians. Consequently, when war broke out, the Armenians gave strong support to Russia, and in the fall of 1914 the Armenians in Tabriz staged a major pro-Russian demonstration.[8] The Iranian nationalists, on the other hand, saw in Russia evil incarnate; their

[5] Yonan H. Shabaz, *The Rage of Islam* (Philadelphia, 1918), p. 38.
[6] *State Papers 1913, Persia No. 1*, pp. 55, 173, 276.
[7] Prothero, p. 25; Shabaz, p. 38.
[8] Mirza Firuz Khan, "Persia," *The Near East*, November 6, 1914, p. 6.

sympathies were overwhelmingly with the Central Powers. They viewed the Armenian support of Russia as clearly traitorous. Many Armenians were killed by Moslem Iranians, and many more fled to Russia.[9] The breach was irreparable.

There were reports that Sayyed Zia hoped to utilize Armenian support in his power struggle with Reza Khan in 1922.[10] No show of strength occurred, but if these reports were true, it is likely that Sayyed Zia had not fully comprehended the changed circumstances brought on by World War I. To use Armenians against an Iranian national force would not have been the best plan for a man already regarded as a foreign agent. Reza Shah clearly understood that Armenians were considered an antinational force and could be dealt with harshly. In the 1930's he took steps to suppress all manifestations of Armenian distinctiveness, including closing Armenian schools and presses.[11]

Just as Armenian pro-Russian sentiment in World War I destroyed, probably forever, the possibility that Armenians living in Iran would be integrated into the nation of Iran, so does pro-Russian sentiment on the part of a significant number of Armenians today work against tranquility for the Armenian communities inside Iran's borders. Since many Armenians view communist-governed Soviet Armenia as their homeland, the communist ideology has become appealing to many of them. In any event, a disproportionate number of Armenians in Iran have embraced communism, and the Soviets have made heavy use of Armenians as their agents in Iran.[12] The Armenian communist involvement, of course, has done little to endear Armenians to Iranian nationalists. In particular, the support given the Azerbaijan Autonomous Republic by the Christian element in Azerbaijan infuriated Iranians, whose convictions that Armenians are basically traitorous were thereby reinforced.[13]

9 *The Near East*, January 15, 1915, p. 285; January 22, 1915, p. 319; April 21, 1916, p. 675.

10 Maki, I, 206.

11 Elgin Groseclose, *Introduction to Iran* (New York, 1947), p. 115.

12 Agabekov, p. 95; George Lenczowski, *Russia and the West in Iran* (Ithaca, 1949), p. 232.

13 For an account of this attitude see *Farman*, January 26, 1952.

However, for a sizeable section of the Armenian population in Iran, "the Armenian homeland" is now an enslaved land held against the will of the populace by the Russian communists. The intensely nationalistic Dashnak organization despises both the USSR and communism and works for Armenia's eventual liberation. Fierce struggles occur between the pro- and anticommunist Armenians, but neither group is much concerned with Iran. When Iranian liberal nationalism was again in full bloom in the early Mossadeq days, the Armenians remained aloof and disdainful, unable to find among the Iranian Moslems any political development worthy of respect. They remain much the same today. Only those Armenians who adhere to communism work in close cooperation with their Iranian colleagues.

Early indications that nationalism would be the vehicle for Armenian assimilation into Iranian society were not borne out by events. International developments over which neither Iranians nor Armenians had control have destroyed any possibility that Armenians might embrace Iranian nationalism. The likelihood is that these developments merely hastened the arrival of the day in which Armenians and Iranians will understand that the loyalty Armenians have for Armenia is much too strong to allow fidelity to Iranian nationalism.

The Assyrians

The other Christian minority in Iran are the Nestorian Christians, a ragged remnant of a once-numerous people who call themselves Assyrians and claim descent from the ancient Assyrians. For many centuries and despite periodic severe persecutions, they have doggedly clung to their separate religion, language, and traditions. The Assyrians dwell both in Iran and in adjacent states, but there are only two regions in which they live in appreciable numbers: the Lake Urumia area of Iran and the Mosul district of Iraq. They number in Iran only about thirty thousand,[14] and the entire world total cannot be much over one hundred and fifty thousand. The really significant difference between the Armenians and the Assyrians in Iran is that the former aspire to independent

[14] Thomas and Frye, p. 207.

nationhood, whereas the latter hope only to live peacefully with their neighbors. The Assyrians are too small a minority to aspire to independent nationhood.

The history of the impact of Iranian nationalism on the Assyrians reads like that of the Armenians, only in minor key. The vast majority of Assyrians were ignorant peasants and hence outside the zone of receptivity to Western ideas. However, since the missionaries, particularly the Americans, concentrated their efforts on the Assyrians as well as on the Armenians, a surprisingly high percentage had contact with the West. Some Assyrians joined the Armenians in an advocacy of Western ideas, but there is little in recorded history to indicate a parallel participation in the military defense of the Iranian constitutionalists.

Because of their location on the Turkish border and in the midst of Kurdish villages, the Assyrians suffered even more from the Turkish and Turkish-inspired Kurdish raids than did the Armenians. Their suffering became so severe that they despaired of ever again living in peace in Urumia, and a large number fled toward Iraq and British protection.[15] More than one-half are said to have perished on the journey. The story of their flight is one of those epical human tragedies that cries for a great novelist to record. After the war many Assyrians returned to Urumia, but many others stayed at or near the city of Kermanshah.

Based on this brief account, the natural conclusion is that Assyrian incorporation within the Iranian nation is even less likely than Armenian incorporation. The Assyrians participated much less than the Armenians in the early days of the constitution and suffered much more in World War I. And they, no less than the Armenians, were pro-Allies when the Iranian nationalists were overwhelmingly in favor of the Central Powers. But there is evidence that Assyrians are not regarded as an antinational force. Dolatabadi, a writer who generally reflects nationalist attitudes, refers to Armenians as traitors and exonerates the Turkish massacres but expresses deep sympathy for the plight of the Assyrians during the war.[16] More significant, the bylaws of the Kurdish nationalist society, the Kumelah, restrict membership to pure-

[15] Frederick A. Coan, *Yesterdays in Persia and Kurdistan* (Claremont, 1939).
[16] Dolatabadi, IV, 84.

blooded Kurds with only one exception: the mother can be Assyrian.[17] An American missionary, a longtime resident of Iran, has stated that a minority of Assyrians were genuinely loyal to Iran—a condition only rarely found among Armenians.[18]

This divergence should not be too surprising. The Armenian has great difficulty accepting Iranian nationalism because his loyalty to his own nation is too intense. The Assyrian, while strongly attached to his people, cannot seriously hope to see the establishment of an independent Assyria. Consequently, he is much more inclined to accept Iranian citizenship as permanent and, perhaps, even to become proud of it. The Soviets, however, are doing their best to upset any such developments. Assyrians have been a primary Soviet propaganda target, and with a fair amount of success. A disproportionately high percentage of Assyrians joined the Tudeh Party.[19] Still, the prospects are much brighter for the eventual incorporation of Assyrians into the Iranian nation than of Armenians.

The Jews

The Jewish community in Iran dates its history back continuously for over two thousand years. That such a tiny group, estimated by Frye as about forty thousand,[20] but probably double that number, could survive in an overwhelmingly Aryan society gives strong support to the claims of individuality of the Jewish people. Scattered among various Iranian cities, the Jews inevitably lost most of their cultural distinctiveness. Until very recently the Jews spoke a form of Persian distinguishable only by a peculiar accent from the language spoken by Moslem Iranians. However, the Jews often used the Hebrew script in writing Persian. They knew and loved Iranian literature, and their historical and cultural oneness with Iran inevitably found expression in affection for and loyalty to Iran. Offsetting these ties, however, was a history of discrimination which, though rarely violent, was always humiliating.

Individually some Jews were active in the early constitutional movement, but as a people the Jews neither supported nor resisted

17 Roosevelt, p. 250.

18 Reverend Mr. Hugo Muller, interview, Tabriz, March 1952.

19 Lenczowski, *Russia and the West in Iran,* pp. 117, 232.

20 Thomas and Frye, p. 207.

the advent of Iranian nationalism. Some recognized in nationalism a movement that would be disruptive of internal security and tranquility, and a number from south Iran left for Jerusalem in the early constitutional period.[21] Their fears were justified. The Iranian nationalists prior to Reza Shah had been true to their liberal creed and refused to exploit anti-Semitism as a means of gaining popular support from the unsophisticated. But from 1906 to 1921 anti-Semitic riots did occur in Isfahan, Kashan, Shiraz, and Kermanshah. The most serious of these were in Isfahan, where a reactionary Moslem leader directed a campaign of discrimination and humiliation against the Jews,[22] and in Shiraz, where the rioting instigated by the Qashqai ilkhan resulted in an orgy of destruction that left 5,000 Jews destitute.

Reza Shah dealt with the Jews as with all other minorities. He attempted to obliterate any evidence of their distinctiveness by destroying their books and closing their schools. Given time, he might have turned to other measures. One report claims that he was considering establishing pales of the old Russian order and restricting the Jews to three cities in Iran.[23]

Zionism and Naziism in combination have probably destroyed, at least for many years, the possibility that Iranian Jews can become adherents of Iranian nationalism. As Jewish settlements in Palestine increased in numerical strength until finally the independent Jewish state of Israel established itself, the deep group loyalty of many Iranian Jews evolved into Jewish nationalism. For those Jews in Iran who see in Israel an object of primary loyalty, the possibility of ever becoming Iranian nationalists is very slight. Today Hebrew is taught in Jewish schools and is replacing Persian as the spoken language in Jewish homes. At least 47,000 Jews have already left for Israel, and several thousand more plan to leave, thus giving those left at home a greater tie to Israel.[24] These factors are driving a deep wedge between Iranian Moslems and Iranian Jews—a wedge that is all the stronger since the overwhelming majority of Iranians sympathized deeply with the Arabs in their war

[21] *State Papers 1909, Persia No. 1,* p. 21.

[22] *Ibid.,* p. 20.

[23] *Great Britain and the East,* June 16, 1938, p. 662.

[24] Figures from the Information Service, Jewish Federation, Pittsburgh, August 1960.

against Israel and agree with Arab nationalists that Israel is in actuality an arm of Western imperialism.

Naziism also helped in separating the Jews from the Iranian nation. Early nationalism in Iran had been liberal and as such tolerant of religious diversity, but as it extended downward in the population past the middle class, which is rarely guilty of gross discrimination in Iran, it began embracing people with a traditional hatred of the Jews. The former liberal coloring of Iranian nationalism with regard to race and religion began to change. This change was accelerated a good deal by the anti-Jewish Nazi propaganda. Note, for example, a sentence from a front page article in the March 1952 (New Year's) issue of *Pan-Iranism:* "Arise, workers oppressed by the chains of the Jewish capitalists, and free yourselves." It must be concluded that with the widening popular base for nationalism, latent anti-Semitism will be given greater expression and the possibility of Jews ever becoming an integral part of the Iranian nation will become more remote.

The Zoroastrians

The Zoroastrian community in Iran, numbering only 15,000,[25] presents a very different picture from those discussed above. Zoroastrians believe that they differ from Moslem Iranians only in being more purely Aryan. Many Zoroastrians live in India and maintain close contact with their coreligionists in Iran. But there is no resultant Zoroastrian attraction to India comparable to the Armenian attraction to Russia. On the contrary, the Parsees, as they are called in India, are strongly drawn toward Iran.[26]

The great kings of the Achemenid and Sassanian dynasties were Zoroastrian, as were most of their Iranian subjects, and it is to these eras in Iranian history that the nationalists point with the most pride. Since the Arab invasion in the seventh century A.D., the feeling of historical oneness of Moslem and Zoroastrian Iranians has been marred. Sharing the same language and the same culture helps offset the memory of such periods of fanaticism as that of the early Safavid kings. However, the religious differential is a divisive factor of no mean force, expecially where, as in Islam,

[25] Thomas and Frye, p. 207.
[26] Afshar, "The Problem of Nationalism and Unity in Iran," pp. 560–61.

the two-sword concept of church and state is unknown. When such an overwhelming majority of the Iranian people adhere to one church, membership in another and often bitterly hostile church, makes identification with the majority difficult.

The Zoroastrians as a group did not figure prominently in the early nationalist movement, although a few individuals among them did. Many Zoroastrians were merchants and as such should have felt the same repugnance toward the old regime and attraction toward the new as were felt by the Moslem merchants. However, most of the Zoroastrians lived in Yazd and Kerman, cities in the south and southeast of Iran which were somewhat isolated from the national movement. A report by the British consul in Kerman in 1911 claimed that the Zoroastrian merchants in the area hoped for British intervention.[27] This claim is not as damning as might first appear, for the Yazd and Kerman area had suffered more extensively than had other Iranian sections from tribal raiding due to a relaxation of central control. The Zoroastrian merchants might well have been choosing between evils.

In 1907 a Zoroastrian merchant in Yazd was murdered by a Moslem. Few Zoroastrians expected to see the murderer punished, since Zoroastrians, as infidels, were often considered fair game. When the liberal Moslem leader in Tehran, Sayyed Mohammad Behbehani, sent a telegram urging local priests not to oppose punishing the murderer,[28] the Zoroastrian community was surprised and immensely pleased. This act was symbolic of the improvement in the Zoroastrian position that the advent of nationalism would bring. It was not just the liberalism of the early nationalists which resulted in this improvement. The Zoroastrian position improved even faster under the reign of Reza Shah, and no one has accused Reza Shah's nationalism of being diluted with liberalism. The really basic reason for the improvement lies in the inherent secularism of nationalism. As loyalty to the nation of Iran grew in intensity, the feeling of being distinct from Zoroastrians, who were in every respect Iranian, declined precipitately. In fact, a not insignificant group of ostensibly Moslem Iranian nationalists began to glorify the Zoroastrian religion as a genuine Iranian

[27] *State Papers 1912, Persia No. 4,* p. 131.

[28] *State Papers 1909, Persia No. 1,* p. 19.

religion and to deprecate Islam as a foreign, forcibly imposed religion.[29] There are indications that Reza Shah shared this sentiment.

In his article "The Problem of Nationalism and the Unity of Iran," Dr. Afshar states that the Armenians and Jews are forever excluded from the nation of Iran, but he accepts the Zoroastrians without reservation.[30] This view appears to be general in Iran, but the Zoroastrians have not yet been completely assimilated politically. Like the Jews and the Christians they have their own representatives in the Majlis, which underlines their distinctiveness, and by law no non-Moslem can be prime minister. The advent of nationalism in Iran has done much to integrate the Zoroastrians into the community and many of them have embraced Iranian nationalism, but Zoroastrians are far from being completely satisfied with their political position.

The Bahais

The extraordinary difficulty of dealing accurately with the followers of the Bahai religion is suggested by the various population estimates made regarding the Bahais in Iran. The son of a Bahai leader says 10,000 is a fair figure; [31] Frye writes that there are 200,000; [32] and an Armenian professor at the University of Tehran estimates that there are over 1,000,000.[33] But all agree that the Bahais are the most badly treated minority in Iran.

In no sense can the Bahais be regarded as constituting a separate nation. Although a number of Jews have been converted, the majority of Bahais are descendants of Moslem Iranians and hence have the same language, culture, and history as their Moslem brothers. The Bahai religion, which today calls for universal peace and brotherhood and claims to be "the sublime idea in which all creeds converge," [34] evolved directly from the Shiite sect in the nineteenth century. The founder of Bahaism (although it was a very different sect in his day) was Sayyad Mohammad Ali, a native of Shiraz. He and most of his followers were originally

29 Arnold T. Wilson, "The Outlook in Persia," *The Near East and India*, June 30, 1927, p. 781.

30 Afshar, p. 561.

31 Mr. Fuad-Rohani, interview, Tehran, June 1952.

32 Thomas and Frye, p. 207.

33 Professor Haknezarian, interview, Tehran, June 1952.

34 Haas, p. 91.

Shiite, and this accounts for the present hatred of the Bahais. The Jews, Christians, and Zoroastrians can be forgiven because their faiths preceded the coming of Mohammad, but the Bahai religion is a Moslem heresy and as such cannot be tolerated.

When reactionary religious leader Sheikh Fazlollah needed an epithet for the constitutionalists, he called them "infidels and Bahais." [35] The phrase indicates why Bahais prefer to remain incognito. Besides being regarded as heretics, they are accused of consistently serving foreign interests. The most frequent charge against them is that they are servants of the British, but they are often linked with the Russians as well. They are given no representation in the Majlis and can hold no public office. The Bahais are in constant danger of persecution, and as late as 1955 a vicious campaign was waged against them. The dome of their handsome temple in Tehran was replaced by a tin roof, and the building was converted into the headquarters of the military governor of Tehran. The Shah had used reactionary religious leaders in overturning Dr. Mossadeq, and now he was compelled to permit their attack on the helpless Bahais. Official sanction was given to the campaign when the Shah's own chief-of-staff swung the first pick against the Bahai temple dome. Iran received very bad international publicity as a result of this outrage. The Shah is now strong enough to resist the demands of the clergy and a recurrence of this attack is unlikely. It is significant that no such attack occurred during the emotionally nationalistic Mossadeq period.

To what extent Iranian Bahais adhere to nationalism is, of course, impossible to determine. T. Cuyler Young writes that the universalist principles of Bahaism run counter to the demands of national particularism.[36] However, members of the Iranian Bahai community insist that Bahais are the most devoted of Iranian nationalists. They claim that since an Iranian was chosen to be the Bahaollah, the manifestation of God on earth, the Bahais believe that the Iranian nation has a glory above all others. Probably there is truth in both opinions. It is unlikely that the Bahais, Iranian as they are in language, culture, and history, could be immune to the force of nationalism. But their intense persecution,

[35] *State Papers 1909, Persia No. 1*, p. 47.
[36] T. Cuyler Young, *Near Eastern Culture and Society* (Princeton, 1951), p. 136.

together with their universalist outlook, will drive them in the other direction.

Conclusion

A clear pattern emerges from this consideration of the impact of Iranian nationalism on the religious minorities of the country. Where the minority think of themselves as being part of another nation and grant that nation a primary loyalty (as with the Armenians and the Jews), their position in Iranian society deteriorates as Iranian nationalism becomes more pervasive. Conversely, when the religious minority are ethnically Iranian and identify themselves with Iran (as with the Zoroastrians), the growth of Iranian nationalism can help integrate the minority into the Iranian nation.

The Assyrians fall in between. Ethnically they are not Iranian, yet neither do they regard themselves as belonging to another nation. Indications are that Iranian nationalism will bring about the gradual assimilation of the Assyrians into the Iranian nation. However, much depends on two other factors if this prediction is to be fulfilled. First, if the Soviets choose to exploit the historic attraction of the Assyrians to the Russians (and they can do so only at the price of offending Iranian nationalists), they can reverse the trend toward assimilation of Assyrians into Iranian society. Second, if Iranian nationalism again drops its alliance with liberalism, there is a strong possibility that minorities such as the Assyrians will be attacked, just as German nationalism under the Nazis suddenly turned on the Jews, who were being rapidly assimilated into German society.

The Bahais should fall into the same category as the Zoroastrians. That they do not is due largely to the fact that Iranian nationalism is still under the influence of Shiite religious leaders. However, the failure of the strong religious element in the Mossadeq alliance to persuade the National Front to permit an attack on the Bahais is a significant and encouraging sign. As a secular movement, nationalism in Iran should, and apparently does, minimize the religious differential. The recent attack on the Bahais occurred when most of Iran's Nationalists had no voice in the determination of policy. The pervasive belief that the Bahais are traitorous will require time to overcome, but after a few years under a liberal nationalist government this atavistic or totally mythical belief should fade away.

One institutional change that could help accelerate the integration of Zoroastrians and Assyrians would be to eliminate their separate representation in the Majlis and to permit them to vote for the district candidates. If deputies from Yazd, Kerman, and Tehran, for example, had to compete for the Zoroastrian vote and campaign contributions, they would be much more likely to pay attention to the wishes of the Zoroastrian community than they do now. Of course, such a reform would be meaningless at present, when elections are rigged by the Shah, but if free elections are held in the future this institutional change could be of great value.

7

NATIONALISM AND LOCAL PARTICULARISM

The visitor to Iran would be ill-advised to take seriously a Tehrani's description of his fellow countrymen. The Tehrani will insist, and only in part with tongue-in-cheek, that the Tabrizi is hard-working and courageous, but something of a clod; that the unfortunate Rashti is hopelessly dull-witted; that the Isfahani, though cunning and clever, is unscrupulous; that the Shirazi is soulful and romantic, but not practical. Such generalizations are usually 90 per cent fallacious under any circumstances, but the frequency and the determination with which they are made in Iran indicate that the Iranians believe each of their cities and provinces is unique. Without question there is a basis for this belief. Until recently the masses of the people were compelled by geography, poverty, and poor communications to remain in the locale of their birth all their lives. In a city such as Yazd, for example, surrounded by barren deserts and forbidding mountains, the average citizen was hardly aware of the existence of other cities. Local customs and habits of thought and speech were unmitigated by contacts with other parts of Iran. This local outlook is inhibitive to the development of nationalism, which requires an ability to see one's country as a whole.

Theoretically, nineteenth-century Iran lived under a unitary, highly centralized governmental system. There was no such thing as local government, but rather a hierarchy of centrally appointed officials. Ordinarily, such centralization would produce a national orientation. But this was not true in Iran because the formal centralized structure did little more than camouflage an informal structure which institutionalized local control. A governor was appointed for each province, and the office of the governor was open to the highest bidder. Obviously anyone willing to pay a big price for a governorship hoped to purchase something of value. Part of the reward was the prestige of the office, but the overwhelming majority of governors purchased their positions with the primary object of making a financial killing.[1] The governor was given the responsibility for tax collection, but the central government in Tehran understood that only a fraction of the revenue collected would reach them after passing through the hierarchy of officials. For the governor, then, the success or failure of his mission would be measured in monetary terms. He had to get back his purchase price and then some. Furthermore, every governor knew that although he would be given almost total latitude in his position, he would receive almost no support in the form of security forces. To collect the maximum of taxes, therefore, he had to establish a harmonious working relationship with the landowners and the tribal chiefs who controlled the area.[2] The shrewd governor would throw his support now to one rival chief or landowner and then to another. Although this tactic helped in the collection of taxes, its ultimate result was a reinforcement of the local feudalistic or anarchic tribal status quo rather than an assertion of the power of the central government.

Sometimes the landowners or chiefs in power would refuse to pay any taxes. At this point the central government would be compelled, reluctantly and only after months and even years of hesitation, to send in a force of Cossacks or mercenary tribesmen to assert its authority. Local leaders understood this pattern and therefore were to Tehran what Curzon aptly describes as "negatively loyal." [3] No one expected any provincial Iranian to be devoted to the government that administered its provinces in this way. Rather, the governmental system engendered cynicism and repugnance and was viewed by the articulate element of the population as one of those unfortunate aspects of life about which, like poverty, one could do nothing. It is understandable that the provincial intellectuals should have been apolitical and should have sought refuge in profound discussions on religion.[4]

1 Curzon, p. 181.
2 Dr. Khan Baba Birjani, *Tarikh Iran* (Tehran, 1938), pp. 255–57.
3 Curzon, p. 218.
4 Young, pp. 136–37.

Although the sentiment created by the governmental system was one of disgust, the results for nationalism were more neutral than deleterious. If the provincial Iranian disliked the Tehran government, he disliked it because it helped perpetuate locally a distasteful status quo. There was no loyalty to a local governmental apparatus to stand in the way of loyalty to the central government. There wasn't even interest. The intellectually-inclined provincial Iranian loved the culture, the history, the traditions, and the language of Iran. He also loved the area in which he lived, its people, customs, and physical appearance. There was no reason why he should see any necessity of choosing between Iran and his province, and there is no evidence to indicate that he did so.

Provinces prior to Reza Shah

Because most liberal religious leaders and a large percentage of the merchants of Iran lived in Tehran, the capital city was the focal point of the liberal movement, and the revolution of 1906 was largely a Tehran affair. When the provincial liberal religious leaders, merchants, and above all intellectuals learned the results of the establishment of the constitution, they were shocked and surprised. Governmental corruption and the total dominance of the feudal element were not after all unhappy aspects of life simply to be endured! Men to whom the thought of engaging in political activity had never occurred suddenly found themselves participating in government. The intensity and depth of the approval of the new government, however, varied greatly from province to province. Generally speaking, the northern urban areas embraced the movement wholeheartedly; in the southern cities there was only a slight stirring of interest; in the villages there was, typically, no response at all. There is an easy explanation for such diversity. Support for the constitution varied in direct proportion to the size of the middle class, and the thriving commercial centers of the northwest boasted a much larger middle class than did the southern cities.

Mostofi claims that the caliber of the governors appointed by the new government was much higher than that of their predecessors.[5] This assertion is probably correct, although the reactionary

[5] Mostofi, III, 315.

Court still had a good deal to say about the choices. But the major change in provincial government resulting from the revolution lies in the first appearance of genuine provincial councils. These councils were the end result of the spontaneous political activity of the largely middle-class constitutionalists. Even before the revolution a few secret societies had been formed in the provinces mainly just for talking about how bad things were. After the revolution these societies, called anjumans, came above ground, and their membership and number greatly multiplied. They did much more than serve as discussion groups. In the constitutional period liberal elements made an effort to institutionalize provincial anjumans as the centers of provincial government,[6] and in many instances they did become the actual governing body of the city and sometimes of the province. Thus, once nationalism triumphed, it willingly granted real power to local governing bodies despite the normal predisposition nationalism generates for greater centralization. This action appears incongruous only if the close association of liberalism and nationalism at this time is forgotten. The dynamics of a nationalism acting alone might have been to work for greater rather than less centralization, but a liberal concern with the position of the provinces in Iran called for greater decentralization.

The most outstanding anjuman was in Tabriz; it dominated that city and much of the province of Azerbaijan from 1906 until the arrival of Russian troops in 1909. Anjumans were also in control of the cities of Rasht and its port, Enzeli (now called Pahlavi), commercial centers for the trans-Caspian trade to Baku; in the cities of Mianeh and Zanjan, commercial centers on the Tabriz-Tehran routes; and in Qazvin, which is a trade center for both the Tabriz-Tehran and Rasht-Tehran routes.[7] The cities of Isfahan and Mashhad in west central and northeastern Iran were less dominantly commercial, and, although anjumans were formed in both, they were not able to gain complete control. In both places power had to be shared with the clergy; and in Mashhad, where the clergy

[6] For the best account in English of the anjuman movement see Browne, *The Persian Revolution.*

[7] *State Papers 1909, Persia No. 1,* p. 5; Kasrevi, pp. 227, 264, 385, 518, 599; Browne, *The Persian Revolution,* pp. 130–31.

was uncompromisingly reactionary, paralysis was the result. In Isfahan the predominant clerical leader, Mohammad Taqi Najafi, a moderate in politics and able to work with the anjuman to a degree, eventually gave the liberal nationalist movement his support.[8]

The southern commercial center of Shiraz included proconstitution elements but was virtually taken out of the constitutional arena by the tribal dominance of Qavam al-Molk and later by the struggle for control between the Khamseh and the Qashqai tribal groups. Although Yazd and Kerman in the south central and southeast were largely isolated by tribal and robber raids, proconstitution committees were formed in both. The city of Kermanshah gained a weak constitutional movement, but the landowners of the area overpowered and smothered it.[9]

In 1908, however, almost without any resistance, the constitutional movement in the provinces seemed to fade away. There were a few demonstrations and some outraged telegrams sent to Tehran, but with the striking exception of Tabriz the provinces acquiesced to the destruction of the constitution without a struggle.[10] In the north there was genuine sorrow, but in the south the dominant emotion is better described as relief. This phenomenon can be explained much more satisfactorily than by saying, as the West traditionally does, that the Iranian population is fickle. Fickle it may be, but no more so than other people. The central point is that besides not accepting the constitution, the people of the provinces did not understand it. Only a veneer of the population understood and gave rational support. The rest, as always, followed authority and hoped that their situation would improve.

The first two years of the constitution may have been intellectually satisfying to the provincial liberal nationalist, but they were hardly satisfying in any other way. Reactionary landowners refused to follow the orders of liberal governors or the anjumans, and no force could be gathered to compel them to accept author-

8 *State Papers 1909, Persia No. 1*, pp. 5, 24, 93, 102, 142, 162; Kasrevi, pp. 266, 310, 385, 517, 600; Browne, *The Persian Revolution*, pp. 130–31; Dolatabadi, II, 348.

9 *State Papers 1909, Persia No. 1*, pp. 27, 30, 93, 108, 122, 174; Kasrevi, pp. 281, 517, 518, 545, 600; Browne, *The Persian Revolution*, pp. 130–31.

10 *State Papers 1909, Persia No. 1*, p. 174; Kasrevi, pp. 677, 815; Dolatabadi, II, 346.

ity. As central control relaxed, the provincial cities were increasingly isolated, trade fell off, and lives were in constant danger. Faced with this insecurity, only the strongest-minded could remain true to their faith. For the unsophisticated, the new government, which they had followed only because it could exercise authority and might improve a bad situation, had failed and no longer carried authority. Consequently the constitutionalists in most areas were reduced to a few individuals.

Likewise, when the Mohammad Ali government proved to be no more successful in restoring internal security than the constitutionalists had been, the mass willingly turned again to constitutional leadership. The situation was not exactly the same, however. The governors sent out by Mohammad Ali were of the old variety—greedy and oppressive—and the memories of even the inarticulate were awakened by their exactions. In January 1909 the Bakhtiaris were able to join with the small liberal nationalist element and with many peasants in Isfahan to oust a particularly obnoxious governor and prepare for the march on Tehran.[11] The Rasht anjuman regained control in February 1909 and began negotiations with the Isfahan group.[12] These were the historically important uprisings. Others, of less significance, followed and were successful in Qazvin, Mashhad, Hamadan, Astrabad, Shiraz, Bushahr, Bandar Abbas, and even Torbat-Heydari near Iranian Baluchistan. Although Tabriz, Rasht, and Mashhad were soon removed from the political scene by Russian occupation,[13] the provincial uprisings brought down the reactionary government and deposed Mohammad Ali. The 1906 revolution may have been confined to Tehran, but by 1909 the constitutionalists had enough support in the provinces to upset a strongly entrenched reactionary government in Tehran.

There is no need to spell out the next phase of the cycle. Once again enthusiasm for the constitution was rapidly replaced by de-

[11] *State Papers, 1909, Persia No. 2,* pp. 16, 18, 19, 46–47; Browne, *The Persian Revolution*, p. 266; Abdolsamad Khalatbari, p. 35.

[12] *State Papers 1909, Persia No. 2,* p. 44; Browne, *The Persian Revolution,* p. 292.

[13] *State Papers 1909, Persia No. 2,* pp. 29 (Astrabad), 48 (Hamadan), 65 (Bandar Abbas), 67 (Bushahr), 70 (Bushahr), 84 (Hamadan, Shiraz), 124 (Torbat-Heydari), 126 (Hamadan); Browne, *The Persian Revolution,* p. 292.

spair, and once again the constitutionalists were reduced to a handful. Reports of robbery, conflict, and chaos were received from every city in Iran not under Russian occupation. The reforms Morgan Shuster attempted to inaugurate might have reversed the trend and restored provincial support. His plan to establish a gendarmery capable of maintaining security and collecting taxes would have struck at the basis of provincial disaffection. However, the enthusiasm Shuster generated in the capital was not equalled in the provincial centers, although enough life did return to the provinces to create some headaches for the British and Russians. In Tabriz there was a surge of opposition to the presence of Russian troops in the fall of 1911.[14] In Shiraz in December of 1911 the leading cleric ordered a boycott of British goods and a refusal to sell anything to British troops.[15] Rasht and Enzeli followed with a boycott of Russian goods, and the Isfahan clergy ordered the citizens to join both boycotts. The bazaar of Kerman was closed in sympathy with these boycotts; and in Mashhad large numbers of people took refuge in the great mosque as a protest against the Russians.[16]

This popular upsurge against foreign interference, however, was a temporary enthusiasm generated by the hope that Shuster inspired and fanned by the foreign interference that ousted him. Considering the weakness of the base of popular support for the proconstitution liberal nationalists, the enthusiasm was destined to die, as it had before, and the provinces soon settled down to a routine of tribal depredations, central government lassitude, and foreign intervention.

Up to this point nothing had appeared in the provinces to indicate that in any area provincial loyalty would become so intense as to preclude a primary loyalty to Iran as a nation. The provincial opposition to nationalism was tribal, aristocratic, and religious; it was based on a desire to preserve the old status quo rather than on any strong provincial loyalty. Liberal nationalists sought to institutionalize provincial self-government, but this in no way

[14] *The Near East,* November 1, 1911, p. 638.

[15] *State Papers 1912, Persia No. 4,* pp. 115–17.

[16] *Ibid.,* pp. 139–40 (Rasht); *State Papers 1912, Persia No. 5,* pp. 34, 79 (Rasht), 79, 114 (Isfahan), 114 (Kerman); *The Near East,* April 19, 1912, p. 783 (Mashhad).

conflicted with a primary and terminal loyalty to Iran. The separatist movements that occurred at the close of World War I will be considered in the following chapter.

Provinces under Reza Shah

The provincial picture confronting Reza Khan in 1922 was not a pretty one. Three of Iran's economically most important provinces, Gilan, Azerbaijan, and Khorasan, were or were about to become embroiled in serious separatist movements; oil-rich Khuzistan was an autonomous, British-sponsored sheikhdom; and tribal and robber band activity in the remainder of the country was so widespread that no road was safe. This situation could not be endured by an intense nationalist and a would-be dictator: Reza Khan set out immediately to remedy it. Within the startlingly short period of three years, internal security characterized all but the most isolated areas. The separatist movements were destroyed, and Khuzistan was an integral part of Iran.

Having established central control, Reza Khan confronted the problem of reorganizing the provincial governments. Obviously the system of turning the provinces over to governors as their virtual fiefs could not be maintained. But the critical question was to what extent should the governor be subject to the control of the provincials. This problem had presented the liberal democrats of the first constitutional period with a dilemma, since any application of the democratic principle would have turned the provinces over to men for whom liberalism, democracy, and nationalism were equally undesirable. For Reza Khan there was no such difficulty. Since his nationalism was of the uncomplicated variety, it was clear to him that the governors should be subject to rigid central control. To remove any possibility of their acquiring independent power, he took from them the right to collect taxes and gave this power to special financial agents from Tehran.[17]

Reza Shah revised the administration of the provinces several times in his attempt to insure central control, and later in his reign he took the logical step of destroying the old provincial boundaries. Ten new ostans (provinces) were created which differed enough from the old provinces in boundary to give the im-

[17] Arthur Millspaugh, *The American Task in Persia* (New York, 1925), pp. 191–93.

pression of being new units rather than the old provinces under new names.[18] As had been his purpose in ordering a new uniform national headgear and national dress, Reza Shah established new administrative units in order to erase forever any feeling of provincial, tribal, or sectional distinctiveness.

But the real destruction of the vital base for any future provincial autonomy movement was administered by Reza Shah in his economic policy. He designated Tehran as the clearing house for Iran's economy and the center of commerce. The government operating in Tehran took control over foreign trade and made government monopolies of the sugar, tobacco, and opium industries. The purchase of government supplies was centralized in Tehran, and supplies were sent out to the provinces from there.

When the trans-Iranian railroad was built, Tehran alone of Iran's major cities was given rail access to both the Caspian and the Persian Gulf. As a result there was a mass exodus of merchants and other middle-class elements from the provinces to Tehran. The reforms of Reza Shah served to dislocate and obstruct the commercial life of Iran and tended "to concentrate business more and more in Tehran to the detriment of the traditional commercial centers such as Tabriz and Isfahan . . . the merchant class in Persia . . . [was] practically ruined and the activity of great trading centers . . . paralyzed." [19] Reza Shah attempted to compensate for the ill effects of his reforms by placing industries in various parts of the country; but commercially the provinces have not yet recovered.

Post-Reza Shah

The effects for nationalism of Reza Shah's provincial policy were not clearly seen until after his abdication. Without question, Reza Shah's great contribution to Iranian nationalism was to provide it with a solid popular base of support. By expanding commerce, education, the government service, and the army, he gave depth to the middle class which was to be the mainstay of nationalism. At

[18] Ann K. S. Lambton, "Persia," *Journal of the Royal Central Asian Society,* January 1944, p. 14.

[19] Violet Conolly, "The Industrialization of Persia," *Journal of the Royal Central Asian Society,* July 1935, pp. 459, 462.

the same time, his policy of concentrating governmental and commercial activities in Tehran resulted in the moving of this nationalistic middle class to Tehran. Reza Shah had murdered some landowners and stolen the land from many more, but he had not launched the kind of agricultural reform program that would have destroyed their power potential. When he abdicated he left the provincial basis of right wing power virtually intact. Since the provincial middle class, which had given such strong support to nationalism, had departed, nationalism outside of Tehran had actually been weakened. When Reza Shah's son, Mohammad Reza Pahlavi, chose to base his regime on the upper rather than middle class, the former by virtue of its dominance in the provinces had no difficulty gaining complete control of the Majlis. Conversely, with the concentration of the politically articulate in Tehran, the major political decisions made by popular force were and are made there. It was Tehran that twice compelled the Court to accept Dr. Mossadeq; it was Tehran that finally ousted him.

Symbolic of this development, the formerly vibrant provincial press has become a mere shadow. The two largest Tehran papers outsell by far the local newspapers in Tabriz, Rasht, Isfahan, and Shiraz. What this decline of the provincial middle class means in the political scene was shown clearly by the Seventeenth Majlis elections in 1952. Dr. Mossadeq insisted that these would be the first free elections in Iran's history, and by and large he succeeded. But the question arises, what is a free election in a country of Iran's economic and social development? Does freedom require that the landowners be free to instruct their peasants how to vote and to herd them to the polls? Dr. Mossadeq apparently believed it did. The results for the Nationalists were disastrous. Tehran, of course, voted overwhelmingly for National Front candidates; Tabriz and other Azerbaijan cities likewise returned followers of the National Front. But from rural provincial areas, district after district saw the election of men who, though willing to give lip service to Mossadeq, were known to want nothing more than the destruction of his government. Confronted with the inevitability of defeat unless he utilized the traditional rigging devices of his predecessors and successors, Mossadeq halted the elections after a quorum had been elected. Of the major cities, Tehran, Tabriz,

Kermanshah, Qazvin, Rasht, Kashan, and Kerman returned nationalist deputies; Yazd and Hamadan sent rightists to the Majlis; and the vote was never held in the crucial centers of Mashhad, Isfahan, and Shiraz. Thus the Mossadeq forces were not even capable of controlling all the major provincial cities, and the smaller centers returned an overwhelmingly anti-Mossadeq delegation.

Even in the city of Tabriz, the elections were far from satisfactory for the liberal nationalists. Clearly a sizeable number of people in this area were politically aware and felt the Seventeenth Majlis election was meaningful; the 72,000 votes cast compared with a high of 38,000 in the previous election.[20] But when the votes were counted, five of the nine deputies elected from the area and three of five from Tabriz itself were candidates of the clerical wing of the national movement. Furthermore, the two top vote getters, Ebrahim Milani and Angaji, were mullahs.

These returns reflected the social transformation of Tabriz resulting from Reza Shah's rule. With the exodus of much of the middle and upper-middle class, the influence of the lower-middle class had grown greatly. This group, which is very religious and very much under the influence of religious leaders, was in 1952 the dominant political force in Tabriz. Had elections been held in Mashhad, Isfahan, and Shiraz in 1952 and had the Nationalists triumphed, there is reason to believe that clerical representation from these cities would have been equally predominant. The front-running Nationalist candidates in these cities were all clerical.

Since Mossadeq's fall, the elections in the provinces, as in Tehran, have been predetermined in the Court and consequently are meaningless with respect to a continuation of this analysis from 1953 to the present. However, the Tabriz elections did indicate that nationalism in the provincial cities would have less of a secular flavor than nationalism in Tehran.

[20] Figures given the author by United States Consul Burdett in Tabriz, March 1952.

8

SEPARATIST MOVEMENTS

Reza Shah's program of centralization reversed a trend toward decreasing central control that had been in force, despite periodic reversals, ever since the early days of the Qajar dynasty. Prior to the victory of Iranian nationalism in 1906, the centrifugal tendencies in Iran were due primarily to the increasing predominance of powerful landowners and tribal chiefs. But the nationalist victory raised the question of whether nationalism itself could not now take over as the chief force for disintegration. Those supporting this view could argue that local nationalisms developing in several of Iran's provinces were stronger than Iranian nationalism. For evidence they could point to a series of separatist movements that occurred in the provinces of Gilan, Khorasan, Khuzistan, and Azerbaijan. It is to the first three of these that we now turn. Azerbaijan separatism will be discussed in the following chapter.

Gilan

If genuine local nationalist movements were to appear anywhere in Iran, the tiny province of Gilan was a likely candidate. Geographically, Gilan is separated from the Iranian plateau and Tehran by the mighty Elburz range which rises from sea level to a height of 11,000–18,600 feet. To the north lies the Caspian Sea and across it Russia. In climate Gilan stands in striking contrast to the Iranian plateau. The plateau is stark and barren and pathetically dependent on the few inches of annual precipitation; in contrast Gilan has difficulty controlling its rain forests. Along the narrow plain that separates the Elburz from the Caspian, a surprisingly high percentage of Iran's agricultural produce is grown, thus giving Gilan an agricultural surplus and economic independence. In addition, Gilan's position astride the Tehran-Baku trade route means that the port city of Enzeli (Pahlavi) and the provincial capital of Rasht have been among the most important commercial centers in Iran. As a result, merchant and middle-class elements in Gilan comprise a fair percentage of the population. Finally, the language of the province is Gilaki, which, though a dialect of Persian, is sufficiently different to lend an aura of uniqueness to the people of Gilan. In the years immediately following World War I Gilan was ruled independently of Tehran and there was some concern that this separation might become permanent. Gilan had geographic isolation, economic self-sufficiency, linguistic distinctiveness, and a middle class large enough to give backing to a local nationalism. But as noted in Chapter 8, Gilan had served Iranian nationalism well prior to World War I. Rasht, along with Isfahan, had sent an armed contingent which helped depose Mohammad Ali and to restore the nationalist regime. Still, the Iranian nationalist revolution had not progressed as Gilan's constitutionalists had hoped and the question could be asked if Gilan would now turn to its own nationalism.

The leader of the Gilan movement, Kuchek Khan, was a moderately well-to-do landowner and a liberal intellectual—an ideal prospective leader for a local national movement. Kuchek Khan was a nationalist, but his primary loyalty was directed toward the nation of Iran, never toward Gilan. This little man, so often described today by Western writers as a communist quisling, was highly religious, highly moral, and highly patriotic; and the story of his political career and of the movement he led is a tragedy.

In 1915 Kuchek Khan met in Tehran with a small group of like-minded men and drew up a program of reform for the Iranian nation. The program called for total independence for Iran, land and social reform for the downtrodden, and Islamic unity.[1] Standing in the way of the achievement of this program were primarily the foreigners and secondarily the landowners and tribal chieftains. In the eyes of Kuchek Khan and his followers, the Tehran government by 1915 had lost its independence and was now no more than an unhappy servant of the British and Russian overlords. There is no reason to conclude that by disavowing this gov-

[1] Lenczowski, *Russia and the West in Iran,* p. 54; Nasrollah Fatemi, *Diplomatic History of Persia* (New York, 1952), p. 219; Dolatabadi, IV, 93.

ernment Kuchek Khan and his men were committing treason. On the contrary, in their eyes it was a patriotic duty to disavow the Tehran government and establish an alternate government in the forests of Gilan and its sister province of Mazanderan.

The record of the next few years does nothing to alter this analysis. Kuchek Khan and his men, called Jangalis (Forest Men), fought alike all the enemies of a strong Iranian nation. They fought the Russians and, when the Russians fell back, the British. When a German-Turkish force threatened to advance into their area of control, the Jangalis announced their intention to fight these troops as well.[2] Nor did the internal enemies of a united nation fare any better. The Jangalis campaigned against the tribal units and robber bands that threatened internal security.

After the Bolshevik Revolution, however, this clear picture became blurred. The Tehran government was no longer a mere lackey of foreigners; British influence remained very great, but some independence of action was possible. Should the Gilan movement disband and its leaders join the Tehran government? This choice of action was a strong possibility until the terms of the Anglo-Persian Treaty of 1919 became known. Kuchek Khan shared the general nationalist view that the treaty made of Iran a British protectorate and that its negotiator, Prime Minister Vosuq al-Doleh, was little more than a British servant. Kuchek Khan announced, "My purpose and that of my friends is the independence of the state and the reforming and strengthening of the central government." [3] He publicly deplored the separation of Gilan from the rest of Iran and promised that as soon as the central government had reformed and had rejected the treaty, Gilan would return to its jurisdiction.

There is nothing in Kuchek Khan's early record to offend the Iranian nationalist, and it is noteworthy that Iranian authors write of him as basically a good nationalist. However, at the next crossroads in the history of his movement, Kuchek Khan, from the Iranian nationalist point of view, made the wrong turn. A British expeditionary force that had occupied Baku in a vain effort to keep that city out of Bolshevik hands was forced to retreat across the Caspian

[2] Mostofi, III, 9; Dolatabadi, IV, 143.
[3] Maki, I, 318.

to Enzeli. The Bolsheviks came in pursuit. During the next weeks a series of encounters between the two forces raged in Gilan. This situation confronted Kuchek Khan with four choices. He could fight everyone; he could reunite with Tehran and hence side with the British; he could cooperate with the Russians; or he could shun the entire battle. Consistency called for choosing the first alternative. But there were among Kuchek Khan's followers many men who thought they saw in Bolshevism a genuine approach to a problem Russia and Iran shared in common—upper class and imperial control. The Jangali second-in-command, Ehsanollah Khan, had become a communist and thus a firm advocate of an alliance with the Soviet. Kuchek Khan reluctantly concurred, and an agreement with the Bolsheviks was concluded.[4]

From this point on, the noose tightened and the gallant little man who once fought under the banner of "Unity of Islam" now was forced to sanction a brutal antireligious campaign. Fatemi claims Kuchek Khan was quickly disillusioned, quarrelled with his masters, and gave them less than enthusiastic support.[5] This judgment may well be true, but the fact that he gave any support is sufficient to tarnish his reputation and to make his death at the end of Reza Khan's hangman's rope seem less unjust in the minds of the nationalists.

Shortly after making their deal with Soviets, the Jangalis began losing public support. Land was distributed to peasants in a few areas, and they willingly accepted; but no enduring support could be expected from this ignorant and politically inarticulate group. War refugees flooded the urban areas, where some support was at least theoretically possible, and presented an insoluble economic problem to Kuchek Khan and his supporters.[6]

Soviet agents chose this inauspicious moment to launch an antireligious campaign. In Gilan such action alienated many and attracted almost none. The highhanded Russian actions, which became increasingly brutal as hostility rose among the people, reminded the Gilanis of their long history of Russian invasions.

4 Dolatabadi, IV, 143; Mostofi, III, 170. For a typically distorted view see Carl Brocklemann, *A History of Islamic Peoples* (New York, 1947), p. 503.

5 Fatemi, pp. 220–36.

6 *Ibid.*, p. 231; Khajenuri, p. 64.

Middle-class elements in particular were appalled by the violence, the disrespect for property, and the open foreign control of the movement. Kuchek Khan's patriotic words sounded cold and barren against the background of a government dominated by the historic Russian enemy.

Finally, the Soviets were confronted with the same type of dilemma that they faced when formulating policies toward the Kurds, the Armenians, and the Assyrians. Should the Soviets try to break off a section of Iran and thus incur the eternal enmity of the Iranian nation, or should they concentrate on winning the central government? Here, as in every other instance, the Soviets chose to drop Kuchek Khan and try for bigger game. They left him leading a wretched little band of men marching toward Qazvin under a red banner. His force was easily destroyed, and the Gilan movement came to an inglorious end.

The Kuchek Khan movement began as a branch of Iranian nationalism and ended as a pathetic tool of the Soviets, but still advocating an Iranian nationalist line. Even at the height of Soviet control, however, the Gilan movement did not call for independence or even autonomy. The Kuchek Khan government called itself the "Persian Socialist Soviet Republic." [7] Far from giving evidence of separatist or even autonomous tendencies in the Caspian provinces, this movement argues the opposite. In origin it resembled very much the revolt against the central government in Rasht in 1909, although in that instance, the nationalists recognized the Russian troops as their primary enemy.

Khorasan

The province of Khorasan and its principal city, Mashhad, were never leading actors in the constitutional movement. Although Khorasan borders on Russian territory in Central Asia, trade has not been brisk over this route for several centuries. Consequently, Mashhad did not develop a strong, vibrant middle class that could win the city for the constitution. There was a small middle-class group, but its influence was more than offset by that of the clergy. Since Mashhad is, along with Qom, the most important religious center in Iran, clerical influence has been extremely

[7] Fatemi, p. 221.

strong there. Why the Mashhad clergy should have been under reactionary control while their brothers in Tehran and in the Iraqi holy cities were under liberal control can be explained in part by the church's mammoth landholdings in Khorasan. With large numbers of villages under their control, the clerical administrators of the properties are likely to adopt the landowner point of view and to influence, in turn, the clergy of Mashhad. There have been and are liberal clerical leaders in Mashhad, but the overall record is on the reactionary side.

Although the social base for nationalism was weak in Khorasan, the geographical basis for autonomy was strong. Khorasan is a large, economically self-contained area which is a long distance from Tehran. The maintenance of central control was traditionally difficult because of the problem of communications. Either Khorasan was to be reached by crossing the harsh desert that licked the southern foothills of the Elburz or by crossing the Elburz and approaching Mashhad via the east Caspian. Either way presented difficult access.

The liberal nationalist newspaper *Bahar,* published by one of the few outstanding thinkers of the nationalist movement, was a Mashhad journal. *Bahar* demonstrated a deep devotion to Khorasan, but a primary loyalty to the Iranian nation. The two sentiments, expressed in the journal's extravagant style, were intertwined: "Khorasan! That piece of glittering gold in Iran. That Ka'bah of the hopes of Iranians. Khorasan! Khorasan glitters like gold in the reflection of the great leadership and distinguished services of its sons in the early days of the constitution when their blood was expended in war with Iran's enemies both internal and external." [8] *Bahar* was filled with demands for better governors, for a program of national reform, for less corruption in Tehran, for less subservience to foreigners. But there was no cry for autonomy or separation.

Khorasan had suffered at the hands of avaricious governors, just as had every other province, with only a brief respite in the constitutional period. In 1919, however, Ahmad Qavam, one of the outstanding men of recent Iranian history, became governor of Khorasan. Qavam deserves a good, objective biography, and un-

[8] *Bahar,* August 21, 1917.

til one is written he will remain an enigma of Iranian politics. In the Khorasan autonomy movement of 1922 and in its background, Qavam, typically, is part hero and part villain. As governor from 1919–21 he was mostly hero. He worked with the liberal nationalist element in the province and attacked energetically an overwhelming problem of tribal and robber band depredations. However, Qavam was something of a prima donna and did not respond to Sayyed Zia's efforts to gain tight control over the provincial governors following the latter's *coup d'état*. In his typical blunderbuss manner, Sayyed Zia ordered Colonel Taqi Khan, commander of the Khorasan gendarmery, to arrest Qavam.[9] The colonel executed the order and then became acting governor. But within a matter of weeks in Sayyed Zia's recent position as premier was none other than Ahmad Qavam.

Colonel Taqi Khan was destined to be the leader of the Khorasan revolt, and a less likely choice for an autonomous Khorasani movement can hardly be imagined. A native of Azerbaijan and only a recent arrival in Khorasan, Taqi Khan had an impressive record as an Iranian nationalist. During World War I he had distinguished himself fighting alongside other Iranian nationalists at Kermanshah. Iranian historians and biographers agree that Taqi Khan, like Kuchek Khan, was a sincere and devoted nationalist of the liberal variety.

If Ahmad Qavam had made surprising progress against tribal depredations in Khorasan, Taqi Khan was spectacularly effective in dealing with this problem. He brought tranquility to the countryside and inaugurated a number of important reforms. The contrast with past governorships, even Qavam's, was great, and Taqi Khan's popularity, immense.[10]

Then came the bombshell. At the very height of Taqi Khan's popularity, the government of Ahmad Qavam, apparently with Reza Khan's concurrence, ordered the colonel to surrender his position and return to Tehran. At the urging of the gendarmery and with the overwhelming support of the politically aware in Khorasan, he refused. The explanation for his recall and his refusal is complex and in keeping with the personality-orientation

9 Maki, I, 161–62; Mostofi, III, 343; Dolatabadi, IV, 270.
10 Maki, I, 199; Dolatabadi, IV, 269–70.

of Iranian politics. There is, however, very little support for the opinion of those who see in this movement an expression of sentiment for autonomy or separation on the part of the people of Khorasan.

Qavam's motivation is clear. He bitterly resented his arrest, especially since the arresting officer, Taqi Khan, had had the effrontery to make such a record for himself as governor of Khorasan as to deglamorize Qavam's own achievements. Now was his chance to strike back. Reza Khan's motivation was also mainly personal. He was engaged in a nationwide campaign to gain control of the gendarmery, a control he knew was essential for his own power climb. Reza Khan saw Taqi Khan's insubordination as part of his struggle with the gendarmery, and as such it could not be permitted to stand unpunished. Besides, Reza Khan had no desire to see a rival military figure with popular appeal appear on the scene, and Taqi Khan's record had had an impact even in Tehran.

For Taqi Khan the recall order was a gross injustice and a personal affront. If he returned to Tehran, he could be certain of a career of minor posts and early retirement. By resisting the order, he could join the struggle of the gendarmery against Reza Khan, who, it should be remembered, was a long way from his goal of absolute power. If he were victorious, Taqi Khan could be virtually certain of becoming a national figure.

The people of Khorasan presented their list of grievances and demands to the central government. They requested that a permanent Khorasan gendarmery be established, officered by men with provincial approval; and they asked for a greater voice in the selection of governor. Finally, they asked that Taqi Khan be permitted to go abroad for two years. Reza Khan refused these terms.[11]

In the campaign to bring Taqi Khan to heel, Qavam and Reza Khan first used the old technique of inciting a tribal force against him, this time the Qochan tribe. Failing in this venture, they sent Samsam al-Soltaneh's Bakhtiaris, but these too were defeated.[12] Then Reza Khan sent his Cossacks to reinforce the Bakhtiaris, and Taqi Khan was defeated and killed.

[11] Malek al-Shoara' Bahar, *Tarikh Mokhtasar Ahzab Siassi Iran* (Tehran, 1942), pp. 145–46.

[12] Dolatabadi, pp. 274–76.

When news of his defeat and death reached Mashhad, a period of mourning was declared. The city's population turned out to honor their hero, and the newspapers were filled with eulogies of him. The Tehran press also was filled with odes to Taqi Khan. Justly or unjustly, he was regarded as a martyr to liberal democracy, then under strong attack from Reza Khan. Every eulogy and every ode refers to Taqi Khan as an Iranian patriot. Nowhere is reference made to a demand for self-government or autonomy in Mashhad.[13]

Both Maki and Bahar attest that the merchant and intellectual elements of Mashhad were the core of the popular support for Taqi Khan. Since previous rebellions against central control had been led by landowners, religious chiefs, and tribal chiefs, this shift is of great significance. The element of the population that is generally most receptive to nationalism rebelled against a strongly nationalist regime in Tehran. There are many explanations for this seeming paradox. Reza Khan was still suspect of owing his power to British favor, and nationalists in Khorasan in 1922 may be pardoned for not recognizing his nationalism as genuine. In any case, the Tehran regime was illiberal, and many intellectuals opposed it for this reason. But the fundamental explanation for their support of Taqi Khan lies in his record of accomplishments.

Khuzistan

Like Gilan and Khorasan, Khuzistan is located beyond the central triangle of the Iranian plateau, and because it is more remote from Tehran communications prior to the days of Reza Shah were even more difficult. Khuzistan is located in the southwestern corner of Iran and consists of the lowlands between the Zagros Mountains to the north and east and the Iraqi frontier and the Persian Gulf to the west and south.

Khuzistan, or Arabistan, presented a very different problem for Iran than did Gilan or Khorasan. The inhabitants of the latter provinces are of Aryan descent, speak the Persian language, and identify themselves with Iranian history and culture. The inhabitants of Khuzistan at the turn of the century included a popular

[13] Maki, I, 294–97.

majority of Arabic-speaking people, mostly nomadic tribesmen, who in no way identified themselves with Iran. Both socially and geographically, Khuzistan resembled Baluchistan. There was no large commercial center in the province, and a middle class was almost nonexistent. There was no participation from either of these provinces in the constitutional movement; indeed, there was neither comprehension nor interest. But destiny would not permit Khuzistan to remain beyond Iranian control. Khuzistan happened to be the province in which most of Iran's known oil resources lay. Also, because of its position on the upper Persian Gulf, Khuzistan inevitably became the southern outlet and inlet for Iranian trade.

Much of Khuzistan, including the area in which the Anglo-Iranian oil refinery would later be constructed, was under the control of the man who held the normally hereditary position of Sheikh of Mohammarah, always a great Arab chieftain whose power compared with that of his counterparts in Kuwait and other Persian Gulf Arab sheikhdoms. As a great feudal lord the Sheikh of Mohammarah was always happiest when the government in Tehran was unable to exert more than a minimum of interference; by no means must it ever become strong enough to collect taxes from him. The harassed governments that ruled in Tehran prior to Reza Khan had no alternative but to permit the perpetuation of the status quo. Occasionally Tehran mediated a dispute between the Sheikh and a section of the Bakhtiari tribe, but nothing more. This was not the case with the British. With the discovery of oil, their interest in Khuzistan was suddenly intense. There is no reason to believe they would not have preferred dealing with the Tehran government regarding the maintenance of security in the oil-producing area, but they fully understood that Tehran exercised no real control there. The British therefore made a treaty with the man who did exercise control, the Sheikh of Mohammarah. In return for his promise to maintain internal security and not to interfere in the oil extraction, they guaranteed support against any external attack and in addition paid the Sheikh a handsome annual stipend.[14]

There is no evidence suggesting that the Arabic-speaking peo-

[14] Mostofi, IV, 471; Brocklemann, p. 504.

ple of Khuzistan resisted central control from Tehran because of an adherence to Arab nationalism. On the contrary, the vast majority of these people were socially too primitive to be seduced by the allure of any nationalism and certainly not by the Arab nationalism just beginning to stir in Beirut and Damascus. The Iranian nationalists bitterly resented their inability to establish control over Khuzistan and regarded the British treaty with the Sheikh as a national humiliation. The early nationalist governments were too weak even to give serious thought to Khuzistan (oil had just been discovered and was not yet important in nationalist thinking), but when Reza Khan seized power the situation in Khuzistan was to be altered.

If the accounts of Iranian historians [15] regarding the Sheikh of Mohammarah in 1921 are at all accurate, this man was an anachronism—an oriental despot of the old school. Sheikh Khazal is said to have murdered or blinded many of his brothers in order to acquire a secure hold on his position. Once firmly established, he ruled with almost unparalleled brutality and oppresssion. Even when allowance is made for exaggeration, it is safe to conclude that the Sheikh was interested only in the preservation of his predominant position.

But his record also demonstrates that he was shrewd and perceptive. From the very first he recognized the threat to his position inherent in Reza Khan and proceeded energetically to protect himself. His tactics were to approach the problem in four different and mutually contradictory ways. First, he sought to persuade the chieftains of the Lur, Bakhtiari, and Khamseh tribes that they and he had a common interest in preventing Reza Khan from becoming too powerful.[16] Had he been successful, the Zagros could have been converted into an almost impregnable fortress. But, of course, he failed. It would have taken more than the pleadings of Sheikh Khazal to convince these tribal chiefs to work together. Second, he sought to cement his relations with Ahmad Shah. Posing as the most loyal of the defenders of the Qajar dynasty, he implored the Court to stand firm against the ambitious upstart,

[15] Maki, III, 204; Dolatabadi, p. 326.
[16] Mostofi, IV, 478; Vincent Sheean, *The New Persia* (New York, 1927), pp. 47–48.

Reza Khan.[17] Here again he failed. Life had already departed from the house of Qajar. Third, Khazal allied himself with the Majlis opposition to Reza Khan. In a number of letters to the opposition leader, Modarres, the Sheikh revealed himself as an old and staunch constitutionalist, a devoted Iranian nationalist, and a liberal whose very soul had been offended by Reza Khan's illiberality. The opposition somewhat nervously accepted the alliance.[18] They had no illusions about the Sheikh's real motives, but they were ready to make an alliance with the devil in their struggle against Reza Khan. Still they were defeated. Fourth, the Sheikh sought to enlist British support. Now he was the defender of Islam and the Shariat (holy law) against Iranian secularism. His people, he suddenly discovered, were really recent immigrants to Khuzistan who had no real ties to the people of Darius. The Arabs of Khuzistan could easily be separated from Iran, he hinted broadly.[19] In his desperate bid to retain control, Sheikh Khazal was willing to assume a garb of any coloring.

His only real hope lay with the British. But when forced to choose between the Sheikh and Reza Khan, the British did not hesitate. Their previous dealings with the Sheikh were due to the failure of Tehran to establish its own control in Khuzistan. Now that a government existed in Tehran that was capable of establishing control, the British were not going to stand in its way. They allowed their treaty with the Sheikh to expire. Reza Khan promptly launched a three-pronged military attack, and Khuzistan was subdued in a matter of hours, with almost no loss of life.[20]

Reza Khan made the most of this campaign. Since Sheikh Khazal was pictured as a British tool, Reza Khan's attack on him was described as incredibly courageous. The drive down the Zagros into the Khuzistan plains was compared with the great drive of Nader Shah down the Hindu Kush onto the Indian plateau. The ancient role of Khuzistan and its current importance to Iran were

[17] Mostofi, IV, 474; Maki, III, 179.

[18] Maki, III, 158–80. This citation includes the Sheikh Khazal-Sayyed Modarres correspondence.

[19] *Ibid.*, III, 244.

[20] Mostofi, IV, 470; Maki, III, 260–77; *The Near East*, December 25, 1924, p. 658; January 22, 1925, p. 87.

widely advertised.[21] The campaign and the propaganda were extremely successful. In every major city of Iran celebrations were held; when Reza Khan returned to Tehran his reception, by several accounts, was tumultuous and unprecedented.[22] There is nothing to indicate that there was corresponding enthusiasm in Khuzistan, and none should have been expected. No element of the population at that time could have been receptive to nationalism.

Sheikh Khazal was a relic of the prenationalist era. He had been able to remain in power so long because of a combination of an ignorant local populace, a weak central government, geographic isolation, and foreign interference. His pleadings for British aid to preserve the Arabs of Khuzistan from ungodly Iranian oppression were no more sincere than his prayers of devotion to Iranian nationalism. As it did to his Persian-speaking feudal counterparts, nationalism, whether Iranian or Arab, represented a threat to Khazal's happy status quo and was hence to be abhorred.

However, with the integration of Khuzistan into Iran, with further development of the oil fields, and with the growth in size and importance of port and refinery centers such as Khorramshahr and Abadan, political awareness developed among the inhabitants of Khuzistan. As more and more Arabic-speaking Khuzistanis became educated and moved into middle-class status, their receptivity to nationalism steadily increased. The nationalism that many of them embraced was Arab. For Iran, the problem posed by the growth of a virile Arab nationalism in Khuzistan gave by contrast the prenationalist struggle against Sheikh Khazal even more of a comic opera appearance. As early as 1927 Dr. Afshar had fully realized the dangerous implications for Iran to be found in the siren call of Arab nationalism drifting across the Khuzistan border from Iraq. His remedies were drastic: eliminate Arabic as a spoken language in Iran, redistrict the provinces in order to erase the name and boundary of Khuzistan, and transplant some Arab tribes to other parts of Iran.[23] Reza Shah was in full sympathy with these views, but the problem of Arab nationalism in Khuzi-

21 Maki, III, 219.

22 See for example *The Near East*, February 12, 1925, p. 165.

23 Afshar, "The Problem of Nationalism and Unity in Iran," p. 567.

stan did not become acute until after his abdication. Even today, for historical and social reasons, few Iranians understand how potentially acute their problem is.

Following Reza Shah's abdication, the Arab tribesmen returned to their old dress and nomadic customs. In 1946, at the height of the Qashqai rebellion, several Arab chieftains called for Khuzistan's incorporation into Iraq.[24] These developments caused apprehension among nationalist elements in Tehran, and during the Mossadeq period newspapers frequently expressed fear that Khuzistan would be separated from Iran. But in every case these articles assumed that the stimulus for separation would come from abroad—either directly or indirectly from the British.[25] Herein lies the explanation of why Arab nationalism per se in Khuzistan was of little concern to the Iranian Nationalists. It probably did not occur to them that the chiefs who had called for Khuzistan's incorporation into Iraq were Arab nationalists. In 1946, when the chiefs had made their declaration, there was danger that northern Iran would be seized by the USSR, and many Iranians were convinced—and they remain so—that the British were prepared in such an event to insist on the partition of Iran, with the south going to Britain. How much safer for the British if the oil of Khuzistan were in the hands of the pro-British Iraqi government! Thus in the nationalists' eyes the actions of the chiefs were merely a typically subtle British maneuver which had nothing to do with Arab nationalism.

Again during the Mossadeq period, Iraq was feared not as an entrée for Arab nationalism into Khuzistan, but as a pliant British tool. Iranian Nationalists believed that since the British would go to any lengths to regain their control of Iran's oil, it was only reasonable to expect that they would make full use of their Iraqi servants in waging this battle. Few Iranians, either of the right or the left, ever have doubted that the late, many-times premier Nuri al-Said and the late crown Prince Abdolillah of Iraq were British agents. The former was respected by many as a man of force, in-

[24] George Lenczowski, *The Middle East in World Affairs* (Ithaca, 1952), p. 175.

[25] See for example *Tolu'*, May 8, 1952 (rightist); *Atesh*, September 19, 1951 (rightist); *Pan Iranism*, May 20, 1952 (extremist Nationalist); *Nabard Bayard*, May 5, 1952 (centrist); *Zelzeleh*, April 10, 1952 (Fedayan Islam); *Novid Azadi*, February 1, 1952 (communist).

telligence, and even honesty, but hardly as a man around whom Arab nationalism could rally. Consequently, however much influence Iraq might have exerted on Khuzistan in 1951–53, Iranian Nationalists felt confident that Arab nationalism was not a part of it.

After the Asian-African Conference in Bandung, however, Arab nationalism gained a new rallying point in President Nasser of Egypt. The electric attraction of this man throughout the Arab world has not bypassed Khuzistan. That there is pro-Nasser Arab nationalism in Khuzistan today is beyond question, but its depth and the force of its attraction for Arabs outside of the small intellectual and middle-class element cannot be gauged. Since Iran is a dictatorship, the expression of pro-Nasser sympathies by an individual would certainly result in his coming under official suspicion, if not in his actual arrest. But even today the threat of Arab nationalism in Khuzistan is badly understood by Iranians. Iranian Nationalists who supported and still sympathize with Dr. Mossadeq think Nasser is fighting their battle. His enemies, the Western imperialists, are their enemies. Far from being a figure to be feared, Nasser is a hero to large numbers of Iranian Nationalists. Compared to the larger struggle against imperialism, the possible clash of interest between Iranian and Arab nationalism in Khuzistan is insignificant. Propaganda attempts by the government to stir fear of Nasser have failed.

The Shah and his followers, of course, do not share the pro-Nasser sentiments of the Nationalists. To them Nasser symbolizes the triumph of the middle- and lower-class elements that are challenging their government. They recognize the sympathy of the Iranian middle class for Nasser as Nasser's greatest threat against the Shah. Whatever inroads Nasser is making in Khuzistan are, by comparison, an insignificant problem. However, the fall of the Shah's close allies in Iraq in 1958 and their replacement by General Qasem gave the situation in Khuzistan a new and sinister complexion. The variety of support General Qasem commanded was not clear, but it seems to have been more lower class than middle class. Since most of the Khuzistani Arab workers are employed as unskilled labor, it may be that Qasem's appeal overshadowed that of Nasser, and that communism rather than nationalism predominated among the Arabs of Khuzistan. With Qasem's assassination in 1963 this development was at least temporarily allayed.

Very important factors are counterbalancing this Arabic pull on Khuzistan. Foremost of these is the fact that a majority of the population is now said to be Aryan.[26] One of the fondest programs of the post-Mossadeq governments has been a gigantic Khuzistan redevelopment scheme which provides for the irrigation of large areas of the province. If these expectations materialize, Khuzistan will be able to absorb a much larger population, and most of the new arrivals will be Persian-speaking. Furthermore, Persian-speakers predominate already in the vital middle-class element of the population. Most of the white-collar workers and the engineers employed in the oil fields and refineries are Persian-speaking. Consequently the Arabs form a small minority of the population that is currently receptive to nationalism.

Since education is in Persian, the Arab children who enter the educated segment of the population will read and speak Persian and be fully acquainted with the history, culture, and traditions of Iran. Many of those capable of going on to higher education will attend the tuition-free Iranian universities. There they will be in contact with intensely nationalistic Iranian students. Inevitably many of the educated Arabs will be absorbed into Iranian nationalism. But many others, probably the majority, will not be, and barring the absorption of Iran into the communist world, Arab nationalism in Khuzistan will yet be a major headache for Iran.

[26] D. L. Lockhart, "Khuzistan, Past and Present," *Asiatic Review*, October 1948, p. 412.

9

AZERBAIJAN: PROVINCE OR NATION?

To Stalin in 1946, Iranian Azerbaijan must have resembled a ripe plum already plucked and begging to be devoured. Soviet troops were in occupation; a puppet government was set up; the British and Americans were in the process of frantic demobilization; and Iran was powerless to do more than mildly protest. The incorporation of Azerbaijan into the Soviet empire, in fact, seemed to present fewer problems than did the incorporation of several Eastern European states.

Since the language spoken by the majority of the peoples of Iranian and Soviet Azerbaijan is identical, Soviet policy makers may have concluded that a desire for a closer fraternal association with their cousins in the Caucasus, if not already present, would be easy to develop in Iranian Azerbaijan. If these were their thoughts, Soviet officials were not the first to have reasoned that the dissociation of Azerbaijan from Iran as a result of linguistic disharmony was inevitable and would only require mild external prodding. Since Azerbaijan also borders on Turkey, many a Turkish advocate of pan-Turanism included Azerbaijan in his dreams of a great Turkic-speaking empire. There have been several separatist movements in Azerbaijan in the nationalist era, and an investigation of these events should determine if there is much basis for Soviet or Turkish expectations that Iranian Azerbaijan would willingly break away from the Iranian nation.

The attitude of the Iranian nationalist toward Azerbaijan is clear enough: to him it is an integral and vital part of Iran. Economically, Azerbaijan is the source of much of the grain needed to feed Iran's cities. Called the breadbasket of Iran, Azerbaijan receives enough rain in good years to produce a winter and spring wheat crop from dry farming. When Azerbaijan has a drouth all

Iran suffers. Strategically, Azerbaijan occupies the northwestern apex of the Iranian defense triangle and stands as a massive barrier to aggression from Iran's traditional enemies, the Turks and the Russians.

The claim of Iranian nationalists that Azerbaijan is an integral part of Iran by virtue of historical and cultural oneness may be subject to challenge. But their contention that the people of Azerbaijan think of themselves as Iranians is supported by the early history of the liberal nationalist constitutional movement. Because of its agricultural surplus and home industries and even more because of its importance as a gateway to Russia and Turkey and, through them, to the West, Azerbaijan became a commercial center of prime importance. A thriving mercantile element appeared, and prior to Reza Shah Azerbaijan could have claimed the largest middle class, both by numbers and by percentage, of any province. The direct relationship between the size of the middle class and the strength of nationalism gave Azerbaijan a potentially decisive role in the early history of Iranian nationalism. The question was not whether the politically aware population would be nationalistic but rather would they embrace Iranian nationalism.

Even before 1906 there were indications that the Azerbaijanis would indeed become Iranian nationalists. Tabriz was the most vigorous of Iranian cities in adhering to the tobacco boycott, and it led the way in the campaign in 1900 to force the removal of Belgian customs agents.[1] Then when the 1906 revolution succeeded and elections were held for the First Majlis, the twelve deputies elected from Tabriz formed the core of the liberal, nationalist faction in the Majlis.[2] The Tabriz anjuman was the most energetic in the nation and the most intransigent in its devotion to liberalism and nationalism; it was able to solicit a subscription for a proposed national bank that equalled Tehran's subscriptions.[3] Having suffered for many years under the harsh governorship of Crown Prince Mohammad Ali Mirza, Azerbaijan was his most

[1] T. E. Gordon, "The Reform Movement in Persia," *Proceedings of the Central Asian Society,* March 1907, p. 20; Kasrevi, p. 30.

[2] Browne, *The Persian Revolution,* p. 146; Mostofi, II, 457.

[3] Browne, *The Persian Revolution,* p. 132.

hostile and suspicious opponent when he became Shah. Whenever the reactionaries attempted to outmaneuver the liberal minority in the Majlis, the Tabriz delegation, led by the young and highly respected Hassan Taqizadeh, solicited the support of the proconstitutionalist Tehran crowd standing outside the doors of parliament. Whenever the Shah seemed to be preparing a military force to overthrow the government, the Tabriz anjuman would offer to send a contingent of its own to meet the threat. It was one such contingent, though small, that helped defeat Mohammad Ali's first serious effort to forcibly replace the government.[4]

When Mohammad Ali finally succeeded in ousting the nationalist government and closing the Majlis, the Iranian liberals were in despair. Their disillusionment threatened the entire constitutional movement. Few expected any real support from the provinces, and in most of the provinces the movement died easily. In each province a little performance was repeated, comic, yet tragic in its implications. There would be a furious march to the local telegraph office, a violently-worded telegram composed and dispatched—and then the little group would disband and disappear into the narrow walled alleyways and the refuge of centuries of political passivity. In Tabriz, too, the hard core of the anjuman sent the usual telegram, and many there also argued that wisdom demanded disbanding the anjuman and waiting for more auspicious days. Marling, the British minister, claims that only stupid maneuvering on the part of the reactionary clergy and fear of retaliation prevented the acceptance of this advice.[5] Possibly this assessment is true, but the subsequent resistance argues for a more basic analysis. Even at this time the British had difficulty admitting that a public opinion could exist in the backward Middle East.

The siege of Tabriz lasted ten months, and a maximum of 10,000 Tabrizis stood off a besieging force which ranged in size from 15,000 to 30,000.[6] Two extraordinarily courageous and energetic men, Sattar Khan and Baqer Khan, assumed the leadership of the defenders and gave life to the movement. Even here, however,

[4] *Ibid.*, p. 165; Kasrevi, pp. 516–19.
[5] *State Papers 1909, Persia No. 1*, pp. 176–77.
[6] *Ibid.*, p. 178; Kasrevi, p. 751.

British observers refuse to attribute anything to the patriotism and idealism of the Iranian people. Accounts by British diplomats, correspondents of *The Times of London* and of the *Near East,* and private British observers are unanimous in denying even the slightest heroism. One chronicler, after ridiculing Iranian martial qualities, wrote: "So much for the brave Persians who were giving their lives for the Constitution. Without the Caucasians, Armenians and Georgians one would like to know how much fighting there would have been at Tabriz." [7]

It is quite true that Armenians and others from the Caucasus area fought actively for Tabriz and that they, being more warlike, were frequently the star performers in the battle lines. But the heroism of the average Tabrizi constitutionalist should not be discounted. It may be a different kind of courage when men and their families suffer starvation and material loss for a cause than when a man risks his life, but it is courage nonetheless; and this kind of courage is evidence of the strength of Tabrizi sentiment for a liberal nationalist government.

In any event, the resistance of Tabriz revitalized the liberal nationalists everywhere in Iran and was indirectly responsible for Mohammad Ali's abdication. Tabriz helped give the nationalists two and one-half additional years—years in which more men could be infected more deeply with the spirit of nationalism and thus gain the endurance to maintain their convictions during the 1912–19 period of virtual colonial control.

For Tabriz, however, the show was over. When Russian troops arrived in 1909, they were greeted with relief. The blockade was lifted, and, since troops of a great power rather than Iranians occupied the city, the honor of Tabriz was unimpared.[8] A few months later the Russian troops were bitterly resented, all the more so because the Russians chose to rule through a detested reactionary royalist, Shoja' al-Doleh.[9] The city was largely demoralized and, except for brief but violent demonstrations, politically

[7] Fraser, p. 74.

[8] *Ibid.*, p. 79; Browne, *The Persian Revolution*, p. 274.

[9] Fraser, p. 79; Browne, *The Persian Revolution*, p. 274; *State Papers 1910, Persia No. 1*, p. 22.

quiet. Was the disillusionment with Iranian liberal nationalism in Tabriz so great that henceforth the eyes of Azerbaijan would turn inward and embrace a local nationalism?

Azadistan

Nowhere in Iran was the Bolshevik Revolution greeted with more enthusiasm than in Azerbaijan. This reaction had no ideological overtones. The Bolshevik Revolution meant that at last Azerbaijan would be free of the Russian troops that had been in occupation since 1909. Pro-German and Turkish sympathies had been so strong in 1914 that even the presence of Russian troops and their reactionary puppet Shoja' al-Doleh could not prevent the staging of demonstrations in favor of the Central Powers.[10] Although Turkish troops had occupied Tabriz during the war, their behavior had destroyed much of the city's pro-Turkish sentiment.[11] What was desperately desired in 1917 was the withdrawal of all foreigners. With the departure of the Russians, Azerbaijani hopes seemed to have materialized.

In December 1917 a Tabrizi group sent a telegram to Tehran demanding the removal of the Russian-selected governor, new elections for the Majlis, and a return of anti-Russian political exiles. From the very weak Tehran government no positive response was to be expected, and none came. The departure of the foreign troops left a political void in Azerbaijan which the Tehran regime lacked the energy even to attempt to fill.

In the absence of directives from Tehran, Sheikh Mohammad Khiabani assumed leadership in Tabriz. Khiabani had been a member of the liberal nationalist minority faction in the Majlis, the Democrats, and was regarded as an ideologically convinced democrat and Iranian patriot. He was a cultured man with a deep love for Iranian history and traditions, and nothing in his early career suggests that he had ever entertained any Azerbaijani separatist ideas.[12] Yet Khiabani was caught in the same dilemma that eventually destroyed Kuchek Khan in Gilan. Could the govern-

10 *The Near East,* July 31, 1914, p. 452; July 9, 1915, p. 269.
11 *No Bahar,* January 12, 1915; Dolatabadi, IV, 77, 86.
12 Mostofi, III, 171; Maki, I, 16; Fatemi, p. 247.

ment of Vosuq al-Doleh, which negotiated the Anglo-Persian Treaty of 1919, be considered the legitimate government of Iran? Khiabani decided it could not be. On April 10, 1920, he openly broke with the Tehran government over the issue of this treaty.

There are no grounds for suspecting Khiabani of engaging in foreign intrigue. He opposed Turkish efforts to annex Azerbaijan in 1918 and issued a strongly-worded statement condemning all foreigners—Turks, Russians, and English. Nor was he attracted by Bolshevik efforts to woo him into an alliance with Kuchek Khan.[13] On the contrary, he issued a statement roundly condemning Kuchek Khan for having entered into relations with the Bolsheviks. But Khiabani went much farther along the road to total separation from Iran than had either Kuchek Khan or Colonel Taqi Khan. Calling his domain Azadistan—land of freedom—he refused to accept Tehran's control even after Vosuq al-Doleh had been replaced as premier by men whose Iranian patriotism was beyond question. Khiabani had been a popular leader in Tabriz, and his refusal to accept the Anglo-Persian Treaty added to that popularity. But his continued unwillingness to deal with Tehran, even when the government was headed by patriots, apparently lost him support. When the central government dispatched a force against him, he received little help from the populace. He was easily defeated and banished.[14]

Two years later Azerbaijan again broke with Tehran. This time it is even clearer that Azerbaijan separatism was not at issue. The second insurrection was another aspect of the campaign Reza Khan was waging to destroy the independence of the gendarmery and to bring it under his control. But Lahuti Khan, the leader of the gendarmery in Azerbaijan, was no Taqi Khan. Despite his vigorous efforts to convince the Azerbaijanis that the gendarmery was the true defender of the Iranian nation, he attracted virtually no popular support. Significantly, the gendarmery made no appeal to Azerbaijani separatism. Maki, the defender of Taqi Kahn and no friend of Reza Shah, writes that when Reza Khan's Cossacks arrived in Tabriz, they were greeted with enthusiasm and were

[13] Fatemi, p. 247.
[14] Mostofi, III, 176–79.

joined by many liberal nationalists who then fought against the gendarmery.[15] Lahuti Khan fled to the Soviet Union and remained there until his death.

There were in Azerbaijan in the Azadistan era men who favored independence for Azerbaijan, and presumably such men are still to be found there. This point is granted. But the evidence offered by the Azadistan episode and even more so by the brief gendarmery revolt strongly supports the conclusion that those favoring separation for Azerbaijan were a small minority. Even the case for Khiabani as a separatist is not strong. The Tehran government had little appeal for a man whose strongest compulsion was to fight imperialism. At times sincere patriots did occupy the office of premier, but Khiabani knew that even then the views of the British general in Tehran could prevail. When Sayyed Zia and Reza Khan finally established a strong regime, a common view in Iran was that this government was British in inception and support. Khiabani cannot be blamed for sharing this opinion. Indeed, Khiabani's belief may well have been that Tehran was not likely to be free in the near future. The case was not a clear-cut one, but whatever Khiabani's personal convictions, history demonstrates that he was unable to convince more than a tiny group of Azerbaijanis that freedom for Azerbaijan was the only way to avoid the foreign yoke.

The Autonomous Republic of Azerbaijan

Although the post-World War I years demonstrate that only a few of the politically articulate Azerbaijanis wanted to see Azerbaijan separated from Iran, nothing that happened prior to 1946 indicates positively that the majority of the population identified themselves with Iran. These were lean years for Azerbaijan. Reza Shah's policy of centralizing commerce in Tehran hit Tabriz particularly hard. The city lost its commercial preeminence, and the most active and vital of its citizenry moved to Tehran. Their departure emasculated Azerbaijan as a political center. The situation was worsened by the Soviets, who in the 1920's periodically discontinued their trade with Iranian merchants, thus bringing extreme distress to exporters, importers, producers, and retailers.

[15] Maki, II, 17.

During one of these periods the notoriously antinationalist and pro-Tsarist Tabriz correspondent for the British journal *Near East and India,* Mirza Firuz Khan, wrote that separatist thinking was sweeping Azerbaijan.[16] His views, hotly denounced in the letters-to-the-editor column,[17] were probably greatly exaggerated. Dissatisfaction was intense—to this day a strong conviction exists in Azerbaijan that the province was discriminated against by Reza Shah—but the conclusion that more than a small group of citizens favored leaving Iran cannot be supported by any solid available evidence.

Nevertheless, the strong dissatisfaction plus whatever separatist sentiment existed helped create the impression that influenced Soviet policy makers in the latter days of World War II. In Tabriz and in every other Azerbaijan city of any size, a communist coterie existed, ready and willing to assume the leadership of a separatist movement. Support could be expected from much of the Christian element; the Iranian army could easily be neutralized by the Soviet occupation forces; land and social reforms should produce acquiescence, if not sympathy, from the huge peasant and illiterate worker population; and because of general dissatisfaction, little opposition could be expected from the small layer of Iranian nationalists.

A strong case has been made by Robert Rossow, Jr. for the hypothesis that the Soviet move in Azerbaijan was part of an aggressive Middle East policy which had as its primary objective the reduction of Turkey.[18] This and other possible explanations will be considered in a later chapter dealing with Iran's foreign relations. Whatever the motivation, separating Azerbaijan from Iran was clearly a well-thought-out, carefully planned Soviet project. The first move came in 1944, when Mohammad Pishevari, the Soviet candidate for the leadership of a puppet regime, issued his manifesto of the newly formed Democratic Party of Azerbaijan.[19] It was obvious that this party was a new name for the Azer-

[16] Mirza Firuz Khan, "Russo-Persian Trade Relations," *The Near East and India,* July 29, 1927, p. 118.

[17] *The Near East and India,* September 1, 1927, p. 265.

[18] Robert Rossow, Jr., "The Battle of Azerbaijan," *Middle East Journal,* Winter 1956, pp. 17–32.

[19] Nejafqoli Pesian, *Morg Bud Bazgasht Ham Bud* (Tehran, 1949), pp. 20, 61–63.

baijan branch of the Tudeh Party and the closest working relations were always maintained between the Democrats and Tudehites. But Pishevari had suddenly discovered that Azerbaijan had a destiny of its own. His manifesto stressed the unique language and took great pains to find other aspects of Azerbaijan culture and history that were unique. He made no demand for independence, but the manifesto insisted on provincial autonomy and a larger Azerbaijan delegation in the Majlis. Obviously, if the Azerbaijanis were as distinct a group as Pishevari claimed, a separate communist party was called for.

The next move came in 1945. A communist-dominated group seized control of the Azerbaijan agricultural center of Mianeh. Simultaneously, the Iranian army garrison in that city was confined to its barracks by Soviet occupation forces and then disarmed.[20] This pattern was repeated in the next few weeks throughout Azerbaijan. The Soviets wished to remain as much as possible in the background, probably to avoid antagonizing the local population—certainly the outside world would not be deceived. In two instances they were compelled to reveal their hand, but in neither case because of the resistance of Iranian nationalists. Russian troops had to give open support to the Democrats in Ardebil when the Shahsevan tribe joined the local gendarmery in resisting the communist take-over.[21] And the newly formed Democratic army, trained, supplied, and no doubt led by the Soviets, had to be dispatched to the Lake Urumia area, where Shiite Iranians fought Assyrians, Armenians, and Kurdish partisans of Pishevari.[22]

The Pishevari government immediately inaugurated social and economic reforms and promised to begin a land distribution program. Even strongly anti-Pishevari residents of Tabriz admitted that more improvements were made in the city of Tabriz in one year of Democratic rule than in the twenty years under Reza Shah. Because of these accomplishments, the regime attracted significant support from the populace. But the elements of the population that gave support were the very groups that understood politics

[20] *Ibid.*, p. 27.
[21] *Ibid.*, pp. 82–87.
[22] *Ibid.*, pp. 81, 115–16.

the least—the peasants and illiterate laborers.[23] Large numbers of these people willingly served in the Democratic army and accepted Russian uniforms and Russian equipment. The propaganda line fed these soldiers reveals that the Democrats had learned something since Pishevari's original manifesto. Most of the propaganda was personal, as well it should have been for men with little political awareness. The soldiers were promised rapid promotions, high pay, and the best treatment. But whatever political propaganda was included, the idea of an independent Azerbaijan was never stressed. Rather, the soldiers were told that they were in the vanguard of a crusade against the antinational Iranian government and were to restore a democratic, patriotic rule in Tehran.[24]

An important lesson is to be learned from Tabriz, as much by American as Soviet policy makers, regarding the impact of reforms and material improvements. Tabriz demonstrates that man is not yet so crassly materialistic that he will be won by this type of program alone. For the Iranian nationalists among the Azerbaijan population, the Pishevari government was a national humiliation that was no less undesirable because streets were paved, schools constructed, and hospitals built. A brief but bloody uprising occurred in Tabriz in which disarmed Iranian soldiers (mostly Azerbaijanis) and private citizens fought a pathetically futile battle against Soviet troops.[25] Small though this engagement was, it gave evidence of the failure of the Soviet experiment. By the end of a year even the peasants were disillusioned. The Pishevari government apparently decided that the support of landowners was at least temporarily necessary and a surprisingly high percentage of landowners did cooperate. The price was the sacrifice of Pishevari's land distribution program. Christopher Sykes writes that 100,000 people migrated from Azerbaijan during the year of Pishevari's rule.[26] The figure is improbable, but there was a great deal of economic dislocation as well as political dissatisfaction, and no doubt large numbers did leave.

The failure of Pishevari to attract and maintain any real sup-

[23] *Ibid.*, pp. 79–80; Christopher Sykes, "Russia and Azerbaijan," p. 48.
[24] Pesian, pp. 128–42.
[25] *Ibid.*, p. 120; Mostofi, IV, 135.
[26] Christopher Sykes, "Russia and Azerbaijan," p. 48.

port for his movement may have been part of the reason for the Soviet decision to withdraw from Azerbaijan and to leave Pishevari to his fate. Pishevari's failure was one factor, but only one, in this very complex case which will be discussed in Chapter 13. From the point of view of an analysis of the strength of Azerbaijani separatism, it is important to discover what kind of support Pishevari could attract in Azerbaijan once the Iranian army was free to restore central control. Here the evidence is complete and overwhelming. Sykes writes as follows: "I was in the first car which travelled north from Mianeh after the campaign, and I was in Tabriz twenty-four hours before the army arrived. Except in France in 1944 I have never seen such violent and spontaneous enthusiasm. . . . Mob hysteria is catching in towns but not in villages, and it was in the villages that I saw the wildest excitement over the turn of events. I believe there was the most genuine pleasure possible on the part of the people at the termination of the Russian-sponsored regime." [27] In Tabriz itself prior to the arrival of the army the populace rose and executed all the Democratic officials they could lay their hands on. Rossow says five hundred is a conservative figure of those murdered, and many more were subsequently hanged after being condemned by court of law.[28]

General Ali Razmara, addressing the officers and men of the army advancing into Azerbaijan, said the troops were restoring "the soul of Iran" to the nation.[29] This remark set the tone for the Iranian reaction to the return of Azerbaijan. Writers and orators sought to outdo each other in poetic and highly emotional protestations of love for Azerbaijan and in denunciations of the wickedness of the crime of separating Azerbaijan from the rest of the country. When news of the capture of Tabriz reached Tehran, popular demonstrations occurred which Mostofi insists were spontaneous.[30] The anniversary of the liberation of Azerbaijan became a major national holiday.

Without question, the Soviets erred very badly in their estimate

[27] *Ibid.*, pp. 51–52.
[28] Rossow, p. 31.
[29] Pesian, p. 237.
[30] Mostofi, IV, 214.

of separatist sentiment in Azerbaijan. Their propaganda line to the Democratic army indicates that even those of the population who were attracted by reform measures had no interest in separation and rather needed to be told that the Democrats were actually working in the interests of Iran. Possibly had Pishevari had more time and the strength to distribute land to the peasants, he might have gradually convinced the primitive workers and peasants that Azerbaijan should be independent. But evidence indicates that the politically aware population resented the Soviet-imposed regime and hated the police-state rule that went with it.

Of course, there is no positive proof that Azerbaijan separatism did not exist. It can be argued that all that is proved is that Azerbaijanis prefer Iranian to Soviet domination. However, the case against the existence of separatist sentiment becomes much stronger if the Pishevari regime is compared with the Kurdish Mehabad Republic. In the latter instance, the Soviets were able to work with and through a genuine nationalist party, the Kumelah. If a grass-roots separatist sentiment had existed in Azerbaijan, the Soviets would probably have been able to deal with it, just as they did with the Kumelah, and thereby would have gained popular backing for their puppet.

Azerbaijan since 1946

After the liberation of Azerbaijan, the status quo ante returned. Turkish books and the Turkish press were destroyed, and the Persian language was once again taught; the Army and feudal landowners again controlled the Azerbaijan Majlis delegation; and the general policy of sloth, corruption, and neglect returned. But in 1951, when Dr. Mossadeq became prime minister, the entire political complexion of Azerbaijan changed. No other province joined more completely in the Mossadeq movement. There was a bitter election conflict in Tabriz in 1952, but not between Mossadeq Nationalists and royalist conservatives; the contest was between competing elements of the Mossadeqist National Front. Even some of the smaller Azerbaijan cities fell under Nationalist domination, and Ayatollah Kashani was able to swing several rural districts over to the Nationalist side. Although there was more freedom of expression in Iran in the years 1951–52 than at any time since the days of the Tabriz anjuman, no separatist movement of any significance appeared.

Tabriz, like most other provincial centers, preferred the Tehran newspapers *Ettelaat* and *Keyhan* to the local press, which consisted of small circulation journals designed to advance the political fortunes of individuals. The qualitative poverty of these papers is not to be explained by a charge of governmental control. The local papers were often bitterly critical of the Mossadeq government, to the extent of accusing it of treason. Surely it is not unreasonable to conclude that the failure of a vibrant press to appear calling for separation or autonomy is good evidence that such an appeal would have attracted no customers.

The makeup of the Azerbaijan garrisons of the Iranian army gives further evidence of a lack of Azerbaijani separatism. Because of the expense of transportation and the linguistic problem, the soldiers in the Azerbaijan garrisons are recruited or conscripted in Azerbaijan, and a disproportionately large number of the officers are local residents. Were a desire for independence at all pervasive, the manning of the Azerbaijan army bases by Azerbaijanis would be folly.

Heavy emigration from Azerbaijan to Tehran is likely to tie Azerbaijan even more closely to Iran. This emigration is from all classes, not just from the merchants, and Turki can be heard spoken by many of the laborers in the capital city. Consequently, an increasingly high percentage of Azerbaijan families will have branches in Tehran and through them a personal means of identification with Iran.

A number of Tabriz residents were interviewed in 1952 in connection with this study, and it was their unanimous view that there is no real separatist sentiment in Azerbaijan. However, there is a great deal of dissatisfaction, and frequent demands are made for better and more locally controlled provincial government. But no demands have been advanced that would give Azerbaijan anywhere near the independence of an American state.

Several Tabrizis recounted how difficult it was for Azerbaijani students to handle lectures during the Pishevari regime. At this time all lectures had to be delivered in Turki in order to accentuate the feeling of distinctiveness from Iran, but the students had not learned how to read or write their mother tongue and hence had to translate the lectures simultaneously into Persian in order to take notes. This is not to argue that there is approval among the intellectuals in Azerbaijan for the policy of suppressing Turki. In fact this policy is generally resented, but apparently not enough to cause any significant disaffection. Efforts to create linguistic homogeneity have characterized many youthful nationalisms, beginning with the French Revolution, and the followers of these movements in linguistically diverse areas have apparently submerged any resentment they may feel.

The conclusion is inescapable that Azerbaijani separatism is not an important sentiment in Iran and without gross foreign interference is not likely to become one. On the contrary, in the two periods of democratic nationalist control of Iran, in the early constitutional period and under Dr. Mossadeq, Azerbaijan was the most enthusiastic provincial stronghold. The chief danger that separation will become important appears to lie in the increasing pervasiveness of political activity. As long as the only political influence was wielded by the educated element, which is literate in Persian, the divisive strength of the language differential was minimal. However, as more and more illiterate Azerbaijanis who know no Persian become politically active, the possibility of successful demogogic appeals to separatism grows. These are the people who listened to Pishevari, and there is reason to believe they would listen to his successor.

Pan-Turanism

Dr. Afshar advocated for Azerbaijan the same policy he advanced for Khuzistan: prohibiting the speaking of Turkish, transferring part of the Turkish-speaking population to Persian-speaking areas, and obliterating the name and boundary of Azerbaijan.[31] He advocated this drastic policy not because of a fear of Azerbaijani separatism, but because he feared a major and successful effort by Turkey to woo Azerbaijan away from Iran. Although evidence indicates a basis for Dr. Afshar's suspicions of Khuzistan, there is no parallel support for his sensitivity about Azerbaijan.

[31] Afshar, "The Problem of Nationalism and the Unity of Iran," p. 562.

Unlike the Arabic-speaking Khuzistani, the Turki-speaking Azerbaijani adheres to the same sect of Islam as does the Persian-speaking element and shares with the latter common culture, traditions, and history—a history, by the way, which includes many ferocious battles with Turkey. As the province to suffer most from contact with the Turks, Azerbaijan has a vivid memory of Turkish depredations.

If ever pan-Turanism was to triumph in Iranian Azerbaijan, the period of World War I was the propitious time. The Young Turks in command in Turkey were advocates of a Turkish-speaking empire stretching from the Aegean Sea to the Great Wall of China. Furthermore, pro-Turkish sentiment in Azerbaijan was at an all-time high. Thanks to the long and bitterly resented occupation by Russian troops, the Azerbaijanis looked to the arrival of the Turkish army as a liberation. The Iranian government, hopelessly weak and discredited, offered no obstacle. Many Turkish agents argued that Azerbaijan should first declare its independence from Iran and then unite with Turkey. The sweetness of this siren call was more than offset by the conduct of the Turkish troops in Tabriz. Their behavior, in no sense that of liberating brothers, restored dim memories of past plundering and looting by Turkish invaders.[32] Apparently very few Azerbaijanis were persuaded to support pan-Turanism, and, as mentioned earlier, the most powerful and popular of Azerbaijani leaders led the fight against the Turkish plan. An effort to attract the Turkoman tribes of Khorasan to the pan-Turanism banner was even more of a failure. These people were far too tribal-oriented to feel any attraction for pan-Turanism.

After Ataturk seized control, there was a reaction in Turkey against the cosmopolitanism of the Ottoman Empire and the pan-Turanism of the Young Turks. Pan-Turanist leaders were dropped, and the teaching of pan-Turanism was forbidden. These were wise moves. The feebleness of pan-Turanism outside of a small Turkish intellectual circle was manifest, and Ataturk had more than enough of a challenge within Turkish boundaries. With the passing of interest in pan-Turanism, the movement died. It is unlikely to be revived in Azerbaijan. In World War II the

[32] Dolatabadi, IV, 77, 86; *The Near East,* December 28, 1917, p. 693.

Germans made some half-hearted exploratory proddings of pan-Turanist sentiment in Azerbaijan but were rebuffed there and violently denounced in the Iranian press.[33]

Logic would argue that Iranian Azerbaijanis should be more attracted by suggestions for union with the inhabitants of Soviet Azerbaijan. The language is identical and the culture still very similar. Yet even when Azerbaijan declared its independence of Russia after Brest Litovsk there is no evidence of any strong mutual attraction of the two Azerbaijani peoples. Religious differences and a long historical separation are probably important divisive factors. Soviet officials in Iranian Azerbaijan during World War II included many Soviet Azerbaijanis, but this did not strengthen appreciably the attractiveness of the Soviet-sponsored separation. When the Tabriz residents interviewed in 1952 were asked about sentiment for union with Azerbaijanis now in the Soviet Union, their reactions underlined a conclusion of no attraction. Their unanimous response was one of incredulity.

[33] *Darya,* June 18, 1944.

10

RELIGIO-NATIONALISM AND PAN-ISLAM

Shiite Islam differs from Sunni Islam, among other ways, in its belief that the prophet Mohammad was succeeded as bearer of the faith by his son-in-law Ali and by a direct male line of descent after Ali. There are many variations within the Shiite world, but the sect that is generally adhered to in Iran asserts that this direct line of descent extended down to the twelfth in line. However, the Twelfth Imam disappeared and is believed to be wandering the earth, at some unknown moment to return and to assume Islamic leadership. It appears incongruous that this doctrine of lineal Semitic descent appeals to the Aryan Iranians, while most of Mohammad's fellow Semitic Arabs prefer the Sunni sect. In fact, however, there is reason to believe that a strong sense of being a unique and culturally superior people was instrumental in the Iranians' acceptance of the Shiite sect.

No attempt will or could be made here to explain why Iran responded so naturally and warmheartedly to this sect. That task would require a team of poets and social psychologists. But one aspect of the total explanation is relevant to Iranian nationalism. Iranian Shiites believe that Hossein, the son of Ali, married the daughter of Yazdgerd III, the last Sassanian monarch, and that the subsequent imams were the descendants of the union. In this way the line of imams was symbolically Aryanized, and the humiliation of the Arab invasion and the suppression of a native Iranian religion, the Zoroastrian, was somewhat mitigated. The importance granted this aspect of Shiite belief is indicative of the historical strength of Iranian particularism. In addition, the very adherence to a sect that was not dominant in Islam probably reinforced the Iranian's feeling of independence.

Ninety per cent of the Iranian people are Shiites; and the consequences of this statistic for nationalism are manifold. The minority 10 per cent that are either non-Moslem or members of another Moslem sect have a deeply ingrained feeling of being different from the rest of the population. Nationalism demands an identification of an individual with the community as a whole, and for the 10 per cent such an identification has often been impossible to achieve. Conversely, for members of the 90 per cent identification with the community is relatively easy. The bond of a common religion was sufficiently strong, Browne concludes, that no one prior to the twentieth century had suspected that loyalty to the state of Iran and loyalty to the Shiite sect were two different loyalties.[1]

It is in this close association of religion and nationalism that Iranian nationalism appears to be most anomalous. Nationalism was conceived in the Christian world, and it matured there as an inherently secular force. The appearance of nationalism was directly related to the decline in clerical power and the diversification of religious sects. Religion could no longer serve as a primary bond in the West tying together the large majority of the people and the state, and nationalism could furnish the needed cement.

Much is made of a basic theological difference between Christianity and Islam involving the separation of church and state. In Islam the two-sword concept does not exist; all aspects of social life, including the political, are subject to the holy law, the Shariat, based on the Qoran. Theoretically, this difference is fundamental, and its implications for nationalism should be very great. In fact, however, this point is probably overstressed. Far too many logical conclusions are drawn from it without the proper empirical investigation. More is to be explained by a study of the relative power, position, and political policies of the clergy in the Christian and in the Moslem states than by a study of the theological differences between them. For example, in France the church identified itself with an intolerable status quo at the time of the French Revolution, and the grievous blow it suffered followed naturally. In Iran, on the other hand, leading clerical figures not only opposed the status quo, but were among the most energetic advocates of revolution. Whereas the emerging nationalism in France could be unabashedly secular, the same reaction could not be expected in Iran. Yet nationalism, if it means anything, demands that loyalty to the

[1] Edward G. Browne, *A Literary History of Persia,* IV (London, 1930), 14.

nation be a primary loyalty. Since the nation of Iran includes non-Shiites, the nationalist government that emerged from the revolution had to be somewhat independent of the predominant sect in order to command the loyalty of all the people. Furthermore, both liberalism and democracy, which came along with nationalism to Iran, had secular implications. Democracy demanded that the people, not the mullahs, be the legislators; and liberalism called for religious tolerance and respect for individual differences.

The secular implications of the new ideology being embraced in Iran were not understood. This is not surprising, for such understanding asks too much of man's prescience. The Iranian clerical and lay leaders were allies in a battle against foreign encroachments, official sloth, corruption, and increasing tyranny. Men confronted with such a struggle rarely look beyond to the implications of victory. The secular implications were there, however, and the problems resulting from them have not yet been resolved.

In the waning years of the nineteenth century the world had difficulty remembering the past greatness of Islam. The Ottoman Empire was crumbling, and as it weakened, the Christian West advanced closer to the Anatolian heartland. Iran was caught in a spiral of corruption and decay that seemed to be leading toward total foreign control. Central Asia was fast succumbing to Russian manifest destiny, and farther east, the Moslems of India, Indonesia, and the Philippines had long since passed under the control of the Christian powers. Little solace was to be gained from a view of the magnificent intellectual and cultural past of Islam. The society and culture of the Christian West was clearly the more dynamic and its victory over the Islamic world seemed assured.

That the Moslem world did not bestir itself earlier was due in part to the unspectacular nature of the West's advance. No great armies ravaged the countryside, Genghiz Khan-like, bringing with them fear and hate. No Christian overlords established themselves for the villagers or poor urban dwellers to see and to hate. In some areas there were Christian soldiers and efficient Christian administrators, but there was little oppression. True, there were Christian missionaries who tried to convert, but most of their activities were absorbed in medical and educational work. For the village mullah there was no real danger that his flock would suddenly desert and seek a Christian priest. In fact, very few Moslems were converted to Christianity. Viewed from the eyes of the peasant and his mullah, Western penetration had little meaning or interest. Among some religious leaders there was a feeling of deep dissatisfaction coupled with an intense drive to restore some of the lost grandeur of Islam, but this feeling was confined to the educated few.

For those who cared there were three possible directions in which to respond to the Western challenge. They could surrender unconditionally and accept Western culture as rapidly as it could be absorbed; they could struggle against the Western challenge in all its manifestations; or they could retreat to a more defensible position. In fact each of these alternatives had its advocates in Iran. Among religious leaders only the first alternative was universally rejected.

Islam resembles Judaism in its unwillingness to grant formal religious authority to an institutionalized clergy. A clergy exists in Iran and the laity willingly grants them considerable authority, but since theological doctrine denies to any man religious preeminence over his brother, the hierarchical structure borders on anarchy. For example, there is no religious body vested with the authority to grant a particularly outstanding clergyman the title "ayatollah." When a clerical leader achieves a certain eminence, his followers may begin to call him "ayatollah," and if enough of the respected theologians accept the title, it sticks. But there will almost always be men who deny his right to the title. The political significance of this top level anarchy is that it has prevented the church from ever presenting a vast, monolithic front. Had such a front existed in opposition to the tender bud of the early liberal democratic nationalism in Iran, there would never have been the blossom of the constitutional period.

Prerevolutionary Leadership

There was in Islam in the late nineteenth century a great liberal religious leader, Jamal al-Din al-Afghani. Today Iran and several other Islamic states claim Jamal al-Din as their own, and each state has a right to claim him. Jamal al-Din was a citizen of Islam. No man was more appalled than he at the political, economic, and cultural inroads being made by the West into all of the Moslem states, and his life was dedicated to the task of halting this advance. Of the three alternate responses outlined above, Jamal al-Din was the supreme advocate of the third. He reasoned that conservative tradition rather than theological doctrine was responsible for the decay that threatened to smother all Islam. To him nothing in the Qoran stood to preclude the acceptance of some of the liberal and humanitarian values of the West. On the contrary, were these to be accepted and translated into governmental programs of social and political reform, not only would Islamic society greatly benefit, but the basis of much of the attractiveness of the West would be destroyed.[2] Jamal al-Din felt that a first step in any effort to halt Western imperialism had to be the reinvigoration of the governments of the few remaining independent Islamic states.[3] What he called for resembled very closely the modern nation-state concept. Those modern-day nationalists in Iran, in Turkey, and in the UAR who claim Jamal al-Din do so with more justice than he would have admitted. In his own mind Jamal al-Din was in no sense a nationalist.[4] Much of what appalled him about the West was the growing primacy of secularism and the eclipse of the power of religious authorities. But nationalism, a vibrant sentiment in the West, was taking hold in the Islamic world. Jamal al-Din was too realistic a thinker to cast aside such a weapon. He clearly understood that the national differences within Islam were deep and not easily to be bridged, so he adopted an attitude toward nationalism that closely resembled that of Lenin. Nationalism was a potent force that could be used in the process of gaining the desired end, but in itself it was not a part of that end. Jamal al-Din wished to desecularize nationalism and then use it to combat the inroads of the West. Once this battle had been won, he wished to discard nationalism and replace it with a pan-Islamism which would unite all Islam into a progressive state in which the Shariat would remain the basis for all law.

The fact that the Western challenge was cultural, economic, and

[2] For a very good summary of Jamal al-Din's thinking see Browne, *The Persian Revolution*.

[3] See the discussion in H. A. R. Gibb, *Modern Trends in Islam* (Chicago, 1947), pp. 27–29.

[4] Browne, *A Literary History*, IV, 420.

political rather than theological made of pan-Islam an essentially political movement. Although Jamal al-Din and other pan-Islamists were religious leaders, their primary goal was a political one: the elimination of Western imperialism from Asia. So pre-occupied were they with this goal that they failed to confront the obvious problem of distinguishing between ultimate objectives for the Moslem peoples of Asia and the non-Moslems.

In Jamal al-Din's writings, appeals for pan-Islamism alternated with appeals for freedom for all the peoples of the East.[5] What emerges is a distant and only slightly developed view of a pan-Islamic community, a more concrete demand for ousting the West from Asia, and a very specific concern for revitalizing the governments of the Middle Eastern states, including Iran. Jamal al-Din died before the 1906 revolution, but no man was more responsible for its success. The vital religious leadership of the constitutional movement owed its inspiration to him.

Nasr al-Din Shah made the great mistake of persuading Jamal al-Din to come to Iran. In all likelihood Nasr al-Din was sincerely attracted by the fervent drive for Islamic dignity that Jamal al-Din symbolized; but the Shah and his Court with their extravagant tastes and dull sense of national honor did not realize that they were too much a part of the decay of Iran not to become the primary target of Jamal al-Din. Jamal al-Din's outspoken attacks soon had attracted a strong and dedicated following among the clerical intellectuals. The most noted of his converts were Sayyed Mohammad Tabatabai and Sayyed Abdollah Behbehani, who became the most prominent of the religious leaders in the revolutionary period.[6] Jamal al-Din was forced to leave Iran, but he continued his criticism from Istanbul. In one letter to Nasr al-Din he roundly condemned the Shah's first minister for "selling the realms of Islam and the abodes of Mohammed and his household . . . to foreigners." [7]

So far Jamal al-Din's appeal had been confined to the clerical intellectuals, but he saw in the tobacco concession granted the British a weapon that could reach even the most illiterate of mul-

[5] Browne, *The Persian Revolution,* p. 28.
[6] Kasrevi, pp. 35–108.
[7] Browne, *The Persian Revolution,* p. 19.

lahs. Since the highly orthodox Moslem believed that by merely passing through the hands of Christians tobacco would become impure, he could easily be attracted to a campaign against granting a tobacco concession to infidels. This campaign, sparked and prodded from Istanbul by Jamal al-Din, finally culminated in a religious dictum from Haji Mirza Hassan Shirazi, generally recognized as the leading theologian in Iran, calling for an absolute boycott of tobacco.[8] By 1905 enough men were convinced of the necessity of a basic change in Iran that the informal intellectual-merchant-religious coalition was formed to demand a halt to Western penetration. The members of the coalition agreed upon three basic aims: stopping the granting of concessions and negotiating foreign loans, establishing some popular check on the powers of the Court (later to become an advocacy of the parliamentary system), and engaging in a broad program of social and economic reform. The religious leaders had one more basic aim, the return to closer adherence to the Qoran as a model for society. Included in this aim were the acceptance of the Shariat as the basic law of the land and the insistence that any man-made law be interpreted by a board of ulema (respected theologians) to ascertain that it was in accordance with the Shariat. These conditions were willingly accepted by the other members of the coalition, who fully understood the immense power the clergy exercised by virtue of their ability to lead the politically inarticulate masses.

For the next year a large number of mullahs in the Tehran area engaged in a campaign of agitation. Their theme, always anti-foreign, ranged from the sophisticated doctrinal and philosophical arguments of Sayyed Mohammad and Sayyed Abdollah to the elemental xenophobia of their illiterate allies. Twice the reformist leaders took bast (refuge) during the immediate prerevolutionary period. The first time they protested against the exile of a liberal theologian in Kerman and against the sale of an Islamic school and cemetery to the Russian bank.[9] Large crowds gathered in the streets of Tehran in their support, and the government gave way. Next, the timely arrest of one leader and the murder of an-

[8] *Ibid.*, pp. 49–57; Kasrevi, pp. 15–18.
[9] Kasrevi, pp. 52–73.

other led to a more spectacular taking of bast in the city of Qom, ninety miles to the south. Thousands of Tehranis accompanied the clerical leaders in their march south.[10] This action amounted to a withdrawal of religious sanction for the regime and thus challenged its legitimacy. In Tehran the merchants struck their blow at this time by taking bast in the British Summer Embassy grounds and bringing economic paralysis to the city. Thus by utilizing the time-honored, almost sacrosanct, institution of bast the merchants and clergy were able to force their demands for a constitution upon the government.

The 1905–06 agitation was markedly different from the campaign against the tobacco concession. In 1891 the entire country joined in the campaign; in 1905–06 Tehran was the scene of the struggle. The explanation is not difficult to find. The leaders in Tehran were intellectual, convinced liberals who understood and fully supported Jamal al-Din's thesis that basic reforms must be undertaken if Islam was to meet its challenge. For the majority of mullahs, especially those in the provinces, these ideas were too sophisticated to be understood. A campaign against foreigners—especially those who handled their tobacco—was comprehensible, and with it the illiterate mullah could sympathize. There were, however, a significant number of intellectual mullahs who understood the liberal ideas of the constitutional leaders and who stood in basic opposition to them. For these reactionary mullahs, the status quo was not an unhappy one, and they feared the secular implications of the innovations of the reformists. A clash between the two soon followed.

A House Divided

Tabriz, always the most enthusiastic supporter of the constitution in the provinces, gave its first elected delegation to the Majlis a grand send-off. The climactic moment came when the new deputies took a solemn oath on the Qoran to defend their country and their religion.[11] A year later this same delegation was leading a fight against sectarian influence in government affairs. As a wire

[10] *Ibid.*, pp. 95–107; *State Papers 1909, Persia No. 1*, p. 2.
[11] *State Papers 1909, Persia No. 1*, p. 17.

from the Tabriz anjuman to the Majlis stated the issue, "We want the law of the constitution . . . not the Shariat." [12] For the first time a significant group had chosen to stand in open opposition to clerical influence. The explanation for this radical stand lies in the violent conflict between the ruling Tabriz anjuman and the Islamiya (clerical anjuman), which after a fierce struggle resulted in the triumph of the liberal element and the expulsion of several mullahs from the city.[13]

The liberal triumph in Tabriz, followed by the open espousal of secularism by the ruling body of that city, spelled out for the few capable of understanding it the secular implications of nationalism. Many mullahs in Tehran and the overwhelming majority of educated provincial mullahs did not like what they saw. In 1907 Haji Sheikh Fazlollah Nuri arrived in Tehran from Najaf to assume the leadership of the reactionary opposition. Sheikh Fazlollah regarded himself as the most brilliant thinker in the Shiite world, and many theologians apparently agreed. He bitterly resented the primacy of Sayyed Abdollah, Sayyed Mohammad, and the third of the proconstitution triumvirate, the Imamjomeh of Tehran, all of whom he regarded as distinctly inferior. The issue was thus more than ideological; it involved bitter personal and factional power struggles. But the battle was fought, as personal power struggles often are, on the ideological plane. The issue raged around the question of the constitution. Sheikh Fazlollah insisted that the constitution by its very existence contravened the Shariat, which does not recognize the validity of man-made law. His liberal opponents argued that as long as a board of ulema could have the final say regarding the basic harmony of the Shariat and legislation approved by the Majlis, there was no contravention.[14]

As would be expected, this doctrinal struggle poured over into the political arena. Sheikh Fazlollah and the reactionaries joined forces with Mohammad Ali Shah and were able to bring with them large numbers of illiterate followers. The liberal mullahs found their natural allies in the liberal but moderate Tehran delegation

12 Kasrevi, p. 322.
13 *Ibid.*, pp. 131, 239–46, 300–22.
14 See the newspaper *Nedaye Vatan*, July 23, 1907, p. 6 for this view.

to the Majlis. They, too, were able to bring illiterate and uncomprehending supporters to the defense of their side. But the liberal alliance was the weaker. To begin with, there was the constant pressure from the Tabriz anjuman and the Tabriz delegation to the Majlis to beware of treachery from the clergy. Most Tehran liberal leaders saw no major contradiction in the values of liberalism, nationalism, and Islam and believed that the Shariat and the constitution could be combined. They well understood that their alliance with the liberal clergy was essential to the victory of the constitution, and they resented the doctrinaire approach of the Tabrizis.[15] But suspicion of the clergy was endemic with the liberal intellectuals, and the Tabrizi argument found its mark in many a Tehran target. Furthermore, there were stirrings of dissension within the liberal Moslem group. Sayyed Abdollah and the Imamjomeh proved to be consistently more conservative and more jealous of clerical prerogatives than was Sayyed Mohammad.[16]

In the summer of 1907, despite the rapid weakening of their position, the constitutional moderates and the liberal clerics were in the ascendancy. The fruits of their victory are to be seen in the second article of the constitution:

> Article II. The National Assembly had been founded with the help of the Twelfth Imam, the bounty of his Islamic Majesty, the watchfulness of the mujtahids and the common people. The laws passed by it must never in any age be contrary to the sacred precepts of Islam, and the laws laid down by the Prophet. It is obvious that the decision as to whether the laws passed by the Assembly are in opposition to the precepts of Islam rests with the Ulema. It is therefore officially decreed for all ages a committee composed of five persons, who shall be mujtahids and religious doctors and who shall be acquainted with the requirement of the Shariat be elected. . . . The committee shall discuss and thoroughly investigate the bills brought in by the National Assembly and reject every one of the bills that is contrary to the sacred precepts of Islam in order that it may not become law.

But the position of Sheikh Fazlollah and his followers was more consistent than that of the liberals and less likely to lead to weak-

15 Kasrevi, p. 220. The Kasrevi book gives a fairly complete account of religious attitudes. It is a biased account, however, and there are few sources available that present different views.

16 *State Papers 1909, Persia No. 1*, p. 27.

ening disagreement. They stood firmly against any secular trend. Within the liberal camp the already smoldering disagreement burst into flame. The issue in question was the granting of equal political rights to non-Shiites. For the Imamjomeh and Sayyed Abdollah Behbehani this was carrying liberalism too far; it appeared to justify many of Sheikh Fazlollah's arguments that the new ideological creed of the constitutionalists would destroy the prerogatives of the clergy and the high place of the Shariat. Sayyed Mohammad, no doubt with his eye on the 90 per cent Shiite predominance in Iran, saw no such danger and threw his support to the more radical wing of the constitutionalists. This dispute had become severe enough that by mid-1908, when the Shah made his assault on the constitutionalists, the liberal clerical wing could not present a united front.[17]

In his moment of triumph Sheikh Fazlollah overplayed his hand by sanctioning the execution of some highly respected religious laymen. This exhibition of personal vindictiveness shocked many Shiite leaders living in the holy Mesopotamian cities of Najaf and Karbala, beyond the reach of Mohammad Ali's wrath. There were deep disagreements among these divines, who included in their number some of the best known figures in the Shiite world, and sharp conflicts took place with the more liberal faction eventually triumphing. The victorious group immediately issued an edict excommunicating Sheikh Fazlollah[18]—an edict which, although it carried no doctrinal authority, did immense damage to Sheikh Fazlollah's position among theologians. Further, the group issued this statement: "The Shah has committed an act of killing Moslems and therefore we say positively that it is important to strengthen the constitution for the purpose of protecting the religion." [19] To Mohammad Ali they sent this telegram: "God has cursed the tyrants; you are victorious for the moment, but you may not remain so." [20] British observers claim that this stand of the Najaf theologians was a shot of adrenalin for the constitutionalists and helped bring about Mohammad Ali's downfall.[21]

17 Kasrevi, pp. 619–60.

18 Kasrevi, p. 729; *State Papers 1909, Persia No. 1,* p. 173.

19 Dolatabadi, II, 367.

20 *State Papers 1909, Persia No. 1,* p. 210.

21 *State Papers 1909, Persia No. 2,* p. 29.

After the abdication of Mohammad Ali, Sheikh Fazlollah was hanged; the triumph of the liberal clerics was again complete. But the secular-sectarian conflict flared almost immediately, and under the impact of growing radicalism even the constitutional-minded mullahs moved further into the more conservative camp. The climax came when the radicals, grossly overestimating their own strength, assassinated Sayyed Abdollah. Popular reaction in Tehran was swift and severe. Hassan Taqizadeh, the Tabriz leader, was forced to flee Iran,[22] even though no evidence existed that would tie him to the murder. During the 1907–12 period, the mullah deputies to the Majlis consistently opposed reform measures that they feared would increase secular power. But on the issue of national independence their position was unassailable. They fought with great determination the Russian efforts to oust Morgan Shuster and did much to give life to Iran's heroic resistance in December of 1911.[23]

During World War I German agents in Iran let it be known that Kaiser Wilhelm and much of the German nation had embraced Islam.[24] That such an extravagant propaganda line should have been thought effective by the Germans is typical of the gross overestimation by Westerners of pan-Islamic sentiment in Iran. Such Iranians as Malek al-Shoara' Bahar, the brilliant Mashhad editor of *No Bahar,* argued for the concept of pan-Islam; but to intellectuals of this variety the German propaganda line could only have been ludicrous. Those whose ignorance would make such a rumor believable were at the same time incapable of embracing pan-Islam because they understood nothing of the world beyond their narrow confines.

The nationalism of much of the liberal constitutional element was inextricably interwoven with a devotion to Islam. But the battle being waged by these people was against domestic reactionaries, including many clerics. They were fighting for liberal democracy in a politically independent Islamic Iran. Their goal, then, was a national goal, and although their nation and their religion were regarded as indivisible, their loyalty to their re-

22 *State Papers 1911, Persia No. 1,* p. 81; Dolatabadi, III, 126–28, 137.
23 *State Papers 1912, Persia No. 4,* pp. 119–20.
24 Sir Percy Sykes, *History of Persia,* p. 443.

ligious brothers, particularly the Sunnis outside Iran's borders, was vague and ill-defined.

Reza Shah and the Triumph of Secularism

Reza Shah was no political theorist. He had no careful plan for rebuilding Iran and no scheme by which he would dispose of the secular-sectarian dilemma. Reza Shah had two overriding goals that were for him so inseparable as to be one and the same thing. He wished to restore some of the greatness of Iran and to establish for himself absolute power within the reconstructed nation. His pursuit of these goals was determined and ruthless; any force that stood in the way of his achievement was mercilessly attacked and, so far as possible, destroyed. Thus the independence of the tribes, the strength of the landowners, the Qajar Court, and liberal, democratic ideas—all were subject to his attacks. Inevitably, clerical power, too, had to be reduced.

Even before Reza Khan launched his first salvo against clerical power, some of the more astute clerical leaders recognized in his bid for dictatorial control a great challenge to their own prerogatives. The dynamic and forceful leader of the clerical bloc in the Majlis, Sayyed Hassan Modarres, saw the danger signs and was more responsible than anyone for preventing Reza Khan's achieving the premiership in 1922–24.[25] But fate willed a very real assist to Reza Khan. In 1922 the British expelled two Shiite leaders from Iraq as troublemakers. This British action united Iran as few things could have: for the sophisticated it was another example of arrogant imperialistic behavior; for the unsophisticated it was the kind of concrete affront that could stir elemental xenophobia. Reza Khan had an almost unerring instinct for doing the politically expedient. Far from attempting to salve the open wound, he cut deeper by giving full diplomatic support to the ousted clerics and by permitting them to roam throughout the country. Since they proved to be rabble rousers par excellence, anti-British rioting because of this incident continued for an entire year; [26] and Reza Khan's stock with much of the Shiite leader-

[25] Maki, II, 191; Dolatabadi, IV, 288.

[26] *The Near East,* December 7, 1922, p. 727; August 27, 1923, p. 192; August 30, 1923, p. 217; October 25, 1923, pp. 424–25; Dolatabadi, IV, 288; Maki, II, 247–58; M. Bahar, pp. 352–60.

ship was high. The year was a crucial one for Reza Khan. He was occupied winning his battle with the gendarmery, a victory which would give him the power to challenge anyone.

Prior to 1924 the fifteen clerical members of the Fifth Majlis fought a rear guard action against Reza Khan's efforts to consolidate his power. They attempted to keep together the grotesque alliance of socialists, liberals, reactionary landowners, and tribal chiefs, but with steadily diminishing effect. Then in 1924 Reza Khan, possibly overly confident because of his victory in finally gaining the premiership, launched a direct assault on the Qajar dynasty and called for a republic. Around this issue not only could all of Reza Khan's victims unite, but even the urban illiterates could be stirred momentarily. Their view of the Shah was that of a vague father image, and the mullahs were able to paint this latest move as akin to patricide. The mob formed. The bazaar closed tightly, resisting police efforts to reopen it. Reza Khan rushed personally to the Majlis to disperse a mob that had gathered there, only to be greeted with booing, jostling, and even stoning. Decisive as always, he marched into the Majlis and denied emphatically any desire to establish a republic. Next he wired the Shiite leaders in Qom expressing his deep love for Shiite Islam; and then he issued a manifesto to the people in which he claimed eternal devotion to the dual goals of the greatness of Islam and the independence of Iran. Last, dramatically, he resigned and permitted the Army to maneuver ominously and demand his return to power.[27]

Reza Khan barely survived this crisis; any significant defection the part of the Army would have toppled him. Once again the religious leaders had demonstrated, as they did in 1891, that if they could unite on an issue their strength would be overpowering. This was a bitter lesson for Reza Khan, but he learned it well. He had to discard his republican goal, and for some time he was careful to do nothing to antagonize the religious leadership as a group. He made a pilgrimage to Najaf and Karbala and showed every sign of being personally devout.[28] But he continued his struggle against clerical influence, though less openly. Although the better

[27] M. Bahar, pp. 206–08; Maki, II, 321–43, III, 14–15; Dolatabadi, IV, 332; Mostofi, IV, 417–28; *The Near East,* May 1, 1924, pp. 451–52; Mohammad Essad-Bey, *Reza Shah* (London, 1938), pp. 90–107.

[28] Maki, III, 23–31; Mostofi, IV, 443–46; Dolatabadi, IV, 365.

educated religious leaders understood that their battle had seen only partial victory, there was no new incident around which they could rally primitive support. They associated themselves with the popular sentiment against conscription, but this issue did not carry them very far. Eventually quarreling factions appeared even among the educated mullahs, and effective political resistance collapsed. Reza Shah, not yet satisfied and recognizing that much of the educated middle class was like himself indifferent to religion, spurred the growth of this element and gave it increasing political power. He thereby nurtured the development of a class that could be counted on to give him popular support in any future conflict with the clergy.

Finally, with the political power of the clergy at low ebb, Reza Shah launched a three-pronged propaganda offensive in the controlled press. Journal after journal began depicting the clerical leaders as political and social reactionaries opposing reforms that would bring a better life to the people. The press implored the mullahs to give up their superstition and to recognize that reform programs were fully consonant with the teachings of Ali. All of these articles were prepared in a lofty, scholarly vein which indicates that the target of the campaign was the educated middle sector.[29]

The second prong of the attack was also directed at the educated: every effort was made to glorify the pre-Islamic history of Iran, the Zoroastrianism of the Achemenid and Sassanid dynasties being frequently noted. The idea was stressed that the Arabs had humiliated Iran in the seventh century and compelled or tricked Iranians into accepting a new religion.[30] The third prong was aimed at a less politically sophisticated audience. Here the government portrayed the mullahs as a group of men ever willing to sell their country to the foreigners, especially the British. This line was particularly effective, for it reinforced a conviction already held by many.[31]

Reza Shah understood that a great deal of the elemental appeal of the religious leadership lay in the mullahs' control of many traditional symbols such as the great religious holidays and cere-

[29] See for example *Eqdam,* February 4, 1926; *Iran,* August 11, 1925.
[30] Wilson, p. 781.
[31] *The Near East and India,* April 7, 1927, p. 399.

monies. He therefore began an attempt to reduce their ceremonial role. Included in a 1928 law standardizing dress throughout the land was a provision regulating the use of religious robes and the turban.[32] Many self-ordained and theologically ignorant mullahs were thus deprived of their turbans, and government control over the others was deepened. In 1929 an edict from the Shah removed from public view the practice of self-flagellation indulged in by the fanatical during the most intense of the religious holidays of Iran, when the Shiites mourn the martyrdom at Karbala of Ali's son Hossein.[33] By this edict Reza Shah tore the emotional heart from this most important of holidays and reduced it to a tame observance. The few mullahs who had the temerity to object were banished. With the decline of the religious holidays, Reza Shah created new symbols such as civic holidays, including his own birthday, in which there was mass participation in parades and ceremonies. Boy and girl scouts were organized; athletic programs were scheduled; and the historic Iranian interest in polo was revived. The most spectacular move came in 1935 when women were forbidden to wear the veils upon which religious leaders had insisted.[34]

Even more devastating to clerical power, however, was the reduction in their judicial prerogatives. In 1927 a new civic code was promulgated with the object of reconciling the Qoran and the Code Napoleon.[35] This new code provided a uniform basis for applying the Shariat by eliminating the possibility of broad interpretation by the mullahs, reduced the influence of Islam in criminal procedures, transferred the verification of property titles to secular authorities, and restricted the activity of the mullahs to such matters of a personal nature as marriage, divorce, and wills. Within a few years these latter fields were invaded by the government, and the clerical judges, then paid a salary by the state, had exclusive jurisdiction over only purely religious questions.[36] The ground had been laid for the complete destruction of reli-

[32] Henry Filmer, *The Pageant of Persia* (New York, 1936), pp. 368–69.

[33] Mirza Firuz Khan, "Reforms in Persia," *The Near East and India,* April 4, 1929, p. 426.

[34] Filmer, pp. 371–73.

[35] Bruce Hopper, "The Persian Regenesis," *Foreign Affairs,* January 1935, p. 298.

[36] Filmer, p. 367.

gious influence in state affairs, but Reza Shah's downfall came too soon for the rout to be complete.

Other events of the period add to the conclusion that pan-Islamism was a relatively unimportant sentiment in Iran at this time. In August 1925 the fundamentalist Wahhabis of Saudi Arabia bombarded the great mosque at Medina, and the entire Islamic world recoiled in horror at this ultimate in blasphemy. The press of Iran was filled with vigorous demands for action. Two papers went so far as to call for the formation of a single Moslem state with a unified army which could be equipped and dispatched to punish the Wahhabis.[37] Sayyed Hassan Modarres stated: "Today the nation of Iran is a part of the organization of Islamic nations." [38] This was the high point of Iranian identification with Islam. But the same Modarres who claimed to be an uncompromising Iranian nationalist had, three years before on a trip to Turkey, called for the brotherhood of Iran and Turkey and had expressed a very strong dislike of Arabs. Thus the same individual called for Iranian nationalism, an anti-Arab campaign, and pan-Islamism. Every man has his loyalties and prejudices that are inconsistent and even contradictory. But the fact that Modarres, a leader of pan-Islamism, would publicly flaunt his anti-Arabism indicates that for him and his followers pan-Islamism was far too weak and unimportant to have inspired much real thought.

Of course, Reza Shah was not in favor of pan-Islamism, but he did aspire to what Essad-Bey calls "pan-Asiatism." [39] Realizing that most of Asia shared a political goal in opposition to imperialism, he favored a loose alliance of the entire continent. What is remarkable is the close resemblance of this openly secular plan and the pan-Islamism of Jamal al-Din, Modarres, and Kashani. The conclusion is thus strengthened that pan-Islamism was far more a political than a religious response and, in any case, not to be taken seriously.

Revival of Religious Power

Almost as if some magic button had been pressed, the veil returned to Iranian women when Reza Shah fell from power. But

[37] *Qanun,* August 9, 1925; *Iran,* August 9, 1925.
[38] Maki, III, 367.
[39] Essad-Bey, p. 200.

it was a different type of covering. In place of the grim, sexless veil of the pre-Pahlavi days, there appeared the ghost-like and sometimes even graceful chador, which, though designed to cover the body completely, can be worn so that it does not deprive the wearer of all individuality. This change symbolized the results of the Pahlavi reform. Much of the substance of Reza Shah's antireligious campaign had taken hold. Most of the legal reforms were retained, although the law permitting the sale of religious endowments was overturned.[40] But the antireligious atmosphere evaporated, and religious exiles, among them the colorful, politically powerful Sayyed Abolqasem Kashani, returned to Iran and political activity.

In March 1951 the premier upon whom the West had staked many hopes, Ali Razmara, fell before the bullets of a religious assassin, and stunned Iran fell into the emotional release of the Mossadeq period. Khalil Tahmasabi was the murderer. Overnight he became a national hero and a year later made this statement: "If I have rendered a humble service, it was for the Almighty in order to deliver the deprived Moslem people of Iran from foreign serfdom. My only desire is to follow the doctrines of the Qoran." [41] Tahmasabi was a member of a small group of religious fanatics, the Fedayan Islam, numbering at most a few thousand. Theologically, the Fedayan sought a return to the caliphate in which the secular and sectarian would blend into one compound.

It is ironic that a member of such an organization should have inaugurated the Mossadeq era of extreme nationalism. The entire concept of nationalism was foreign to the advocate of Fedayan Islam, and the strengthening of the secular arm of the government and the refusal to take guidance from religious leadership which accompanied Mossadeq's rise quickly threw the Fedayan Islam into opposition. A year after Razmara's death a Fedayan gunman wounded Dr. Hossein Fatemi, a leading Mossadeqist. The gunman proclaimed that Mossadeq had been his first target.

Many Iranians insist that there is no sincerity in the Fedayan Islam and that the organization will sell to any buyer, foreign or

[40] Lawrence P. Elwell-Sutton, "Iran and the Modern World," *Journal of the Royal Central Asian Society,* April 1942, p. 124.

[41] *Bakhtar Emruz,* February 25, 1952.

domestic. This view cannot be proved and is probably exaggerated. But the Fedayan Islam as an organization has at times been used by others, and no doubt individual members have frequently been paid for services by various interested groups. Kashani claims to have helped instigate the Razmara murder. Following Razmara's death, however, Kashani and the Fedayan broke, and in a matter of weeks the Fedayan made him their primary propaganda target.[42] The cynical say that this antagonism appeared when Kashani ceased paying the Fedayan a handsome subsidy for their support. But Fedayan antagonism could be explained on ideological grounds alone; the absolutism of the Fedayan doctrine made the political Kashani a natural target.

Of far greater significance than the Fedayan was the Majlis delegation of religious leaders, generally regarded as the parliamentary instrument of Kashani. This delegation was the Majlis spearhead of an organization called Mojahadin Islam, ostensibly headed by a spellbinding political opportunist, Shams Qanatabadi. Kashani and his followers were usually described as fanatical nationalists—in a sense a true appraisal. But in another sense Kashani's goal was far removed from what is in the West understood as nationalism. Since he allied himself with the liberal nationalist lay element, the supposition would seem to be valid that Kashani was the modern-day equivalent of Sayyed Mohammad or Sayyed Abdollah. However, the only real basis of the Mossadeq-Kashani alliance lay in their having common enemies. Both regarded the Razmara government and most of its predecessors in postwar Iran as little more than instruments of an unholy British-landowner alliance. Beyond this agreement, their values and aspirations differed far more fundamentally than did those of the landowners and the Mossadeqists.

For Kashani there was no distinction between the spiritual and the temporal. As he put it, "Islamic doctrines apply to social life, patriotism, administration of justice and opposition to tyranny and despotism. Islam warns its adherents not to submit to a foreign yoke. This is the reason why the imperialists try to confuse the minds of the people by drawing a distinction between religion and government and politics. In Islam religious leaders are to guide

[42] See the issues of *Zelzeleh*, 1951–1953.

the people in social affairs." [43] Kashani admitted that legislation is permissible so long as it conforms with the Shariat, and he stood for election to the Majlis. But he favored the repeal of all of the secular laws of Reza Shah and advocated very few laws of a reformist nature. Unlike his constitutional predecessors, Kashani was in no sense a liberal. His ideological rejection of the West was, except for nationalism, complete and absolute.

Among Shiite theologians, Kashani was regarded as a political mullah. He was not highly thought of as a theologian and was not even compared with the great Shiite thinkers of the day. Like their Christian counterparts, most of these religious doctors had acquiesced in temporal control of state affairs and were primarily apolitical, occupying their time with considerations of moral and theological problems. It is probably indicative of an overwhelming drive on Kashani's part for personal political power that he was less of a theologian than his fellows but more fanatically devoted to the concept of Shariat predominance.

The same conclusion emerges from Kashani's pan-Islamism. Kashani claimed to be an advocate of pan-Islam, and occasionally he sounded as if he really were. For example, he exhorted the West to "allow the Moslem countries to lay a foundation for their defense by creating a united bloc to serve as a balancing factor between the western and eastern blocs." [44] But the reason for his pan-Islamism appears to be more tactical than ideological. More frequently his statements took another approach: "I am preparing the ground for the unity of not only the countries of the Middle East, but of the whole of Asia, so that a new and powerful bloc will be created between the Soviet and Anglo-American blocs." [45] This pattern is typical of all the pan-Islamists in Iran. Their goals are essentially political, and their pan-Islamism appears to be little more than an ineffective propaganda line.

The liberal nationalist members of Dr. Mossadeq's coalition were aware of the divergence between their own and Kashani's aims for Iran. As the organ of the Iran Party editorialized, "We are in turn threatened by the possibility of military dictatorship and

[43] *Bakhtar Emruz,* March 6, 1952.
[44] *Bakhtar Emruz,* February 3, 1952.
[45] *Atesh,* December 1, 1951.

the rule of the clergy." [46] But the Mossadeqists needed Kashani. As he had demonstrated very clearly in the Tabriz election, Kashani and his religious followers could defeat their liberal nationalist opponents by virtue of their greater appeal to the lower-middle class, lower class, and peasant elements. In the major pro-Nationalist demonstrations throughout 1951–52 Kashani supporters almost always predominated.

Both sides viewed a clash between Mossadeq and Kashani as inevitable, and after 1952 the only question was when it would occur. Kashani was probably confident of victory, since it was he who precipitated the open split in 1953. It is one of the great lessons of the Mossadeq period that he was defeated so overwhelmingly as to sink from number two man in Iran to obscurity. Traditionally, Kashani's militant support had come from the covered bazaar, but when the time came to stand up and be counted the dominant wing of the bazaar unhesitatingly chose Mossadeq.[47] Most of the Majlis clerical delegation, including the important Tabriz delegation, sided with Mossadeq. Only the corruptible Shams Qanatabadi and a few others joined Kashani.

Nothing demonstrated more dramatically than this shift in allegiance that Mossadeq had ceased being just another Nationalist leader. He had become the symbol of Iranian nationalism; anyone daring to strike at this symbol must suffer the consequences. But the conclusion should not be drawn that secular nationalism of the Western pattern had at last emerged victorious over the strange religio-nationalism that had established itself in Iran in 1906. What had been defeated was a strong effort by a religious demagogue to seize control of the Nationalist movement. Kashani's defeat no doubt weakened the religious element within the National Front coalition; but religious leaders remained in the National Front, and their influence was considerable up to the day of Mossadeq's fall.

Although Mossadeq won in the Majlis and in the bazaar, Kashani had his revenge. None of the religious leaders who remained with Mossadeq had the type of organization that could at a mo-

[46] *Jebhe Azadi,* February 20, 1952.
[47] *The New York Times,* April 16, 1953, 8:3.

ment's notice mobilize a large mob of uncomprehending illiterates. This organization had been Kashani's major contribution to National Front success; there was no one to replace him. Bazaar leaders and loyal mullahs continued to bring out mob support, but not in numbers that compared to the Kashani multitudes. The hard core of Mossadeq support lay in the educated middle class, which is not the element of the population that does much demonstrating after it graduates from high school or the university.

The weakened Kashani organization was ready to serve the royalists, who were working night and day for Mossadeq's overthrow. But the royalists could not rely on this force alone. Their chief source of mass support was the son of Sayyed Abdollah Behbehani, who, ironically, played a role almost exactly parallel to that of Sheikh Fazlollah in support of Mohammad Ali. Ayatollah Behbehani presided over a fairly extensive religio-political organization in south Tehran and was willing to utilize it in order to bring down Dr. Mossadeq. Behbehani's motives are not clearly understood. His supporters insist he was convinced that the Tudeh would seize power if Mossadeq were not to fall. His detractors claim he was well paid for his decision, and they speak knowingly, if vaguely, about "Behbehani dollars" which were used to bring out the mob.

Whatever the motivation, there is no doubt that the mob that appeared on August 19, 1953, and toppled Mossadeq from power was a conglomeration of south Tehran illiterates collected by Behbehani's organization with the assistance of Kashani, other lesser mullahs, and a wide assortment of chaqu keshan leaders. The mob screamed pro-Shah slogans, and no doubt some individuals did so with conviction; but sustained royalist support could not be expected from this quarter. In no sense was the mob antinationalist; it lacked the sophistication to be either for or against nationalism. However, some Mossadeqists are being unfair when they refuse to admit that Behbehani and other mullahs were acting out of loyalty to Iran. Without question, the chaqu keshan leaders were performing a service for which they had been paid, and many mullahs were very likely doing the same. But the inability of Mossadeqist Nationalists to realize that for some of the participating mullahs devotion to the Court and fear of communism were motivating forces helps make a solution to Iran's current political problems more difficult.

In any event, the mullahs once more demonstrated their influence over the lower and lower-middle classes. Their activity strengthened the general conviction that the mullahs by and large are an essentially antinationalist force. It is most unlikely that religious influence on Iranian nationalism will ever again reach the proportions it exercised in 1951–52. However, there are included among the most active members of the pro-Mossadeq underground both mullahs and highly religious laymen. Their presence and their very real services should do much to prevent an open break between the temporal and the spiritual should the middle-class Nationalists again triumph politically.

For the time being, however, reactionary mullahs occupy all politically significant religious positions, largely because of governmental favor. These men no longer bring out mobs, except for carefully organized state celebrations and elections. Khalil Tahmasabi and other Fedayan Islam leaders have been executed, and Kashani ceased being a figure of importance long before his death in 1962. Kashani could not remain in alliance with a government that reestablished close relations with the British. Whether he really despised the British or not, his public image was that of a fanatical Anglophobe, and he could not hope to regain his lost standing if he remained in alliance with an openly Anglophilic government. So Kashani withdrew to his dwindling band of loyal supporters.

The values of nationalism are secular values, and the doctrine of Islam implicitly denies exclusive secular values. Yet this study demonstrates clearly that a devotion to the nation of Iran and a devotion to Islam can coexist in the same individual. When clashes occur they are likely to be the result of jurisdictional conflicts between secular and temporal authorities which are given doctrinal rationalizations. If the Iranian clergy had been organized into a rigid hierarchy, quite conceivably the conflict might have been more severe. But leading clerics throughout this century have accepted both liberal and national values and have carefully interpreted the latter so that they do not clash with Islam. Others have denied both liberal and national values, and the big majority of lesser clerics have taken no stand. The secular, intellectual nationalist typically looks down on the mullah as standing in the path of progress and accepting alms from agents of imperialism. But the dominant modernist leaders know that a head-on clash with the clergy is neither wise nor necessary. Nevertheless, despite the lack of a prolonged conflict, there seems little doubt that a long-term trend is in motion in the direction of granting national values precedence over religious values.

11

EARLY IMPERIALISM: THE GENESIS OF NATIONALIST MYTHOLOGY

Britain and Russia in Iran: Uncontrolled Rivalry Prior to 1907

Although Iran and Afghanistan remained independent, at least to a degree, in the nineteenth and early twentieth centuries when much of Asia and Africa was falling under foreign control, the freedom of these countries cannot be attributed to the courage and devotion of their inhabitants. Nor was their independence due to geographical obstructions, which by the nineteenth century were already beginning to lose their effectiveness. The reason for their continued independence was that Iran and Afghanistan occupied a geographical belt at which the dynamics of Russian expansion and British expansion met. Neither Britain nor Russia could have gained and solidified control there without risking a major war.

Of the two imperial powers, Russia was the more to be feared. As early as 1723 Russian armies under Peter the Great had occupied parts of Azerbaijan and Gilan. Although Iran recovered all the lost territories within twelve years, it had been placed on notice that it stood directly in the path of the Russian southward drive. Iranians realized their need and they were receptive to Napoleon's overtures when he tried to bring them into an alliance against Russia. When the French alliance failed to materialize they were only too anxious to negotiate with the British. The Russian victory over Napoleon upset the balance in Russia's favor, and in the Treaty of Gulistan in 1813 the Iranians gave the Russians whatever claim they had to Baku and much of eastern Transcaucasia, Georgia, and Daghestan. In 1828, by the Treaty of Turkomanchai, Iran surrendered its claim to Armenia, and the Araxes River was fixed as the northwestern boundary with Russia. Between 1864 and 1885 the Russian advance in Central Asia moved with accelerating momentum to the borders of Khorasan. Iran was confronted with the force of a giant, semimodern state whose expansion was motivated by an intense historical drive for a warm water outlet.

British statesmen were watching the Russian advance with a degree of alarm. Iran did not hold the same allure for the British that it did for the Russians. A minority of British statesmen and colonial officers wished to expand into this area, but prior to the discovery of oil the overwhelming British interest in an independent Iran was strategic. Iran lay astride the life line to India, and the British were suspicious that the Russians' goal was India.

For Iran the response was obvious: a precarious independence could be maintained only if the Russians and British were balanced against each other. The type of subtle game necessary to balance the two great powers was naturally suited to the Iranian mental process, but in such a precarious situation even the Iranians sometimes moved too far in one direction or the other.

Since neither power wished to resort to arms in Iran, competition moved onto the economic plane. The Treaty of Turkomanchai had compelled Iran to accept a system of capitulations by which the foreign businessman, instead of being subject to Iranian courts, would have any litigation to which he was a party handled by his own country's consular representatives. The effect of this procedure was to remove the foreign businessman from the plethora of red tape and restrictions under which the Iranian merchant labored. This gave the foreigner a freedom of action which when added to his superior financial resources gave him a substantial advantage over his Iranian competitor. The British and Russian governments worked energetically to advance the commercial interests of their nationals in Iran. The primary foreign policy task of the Iranian government, in fact, became one of balancing concessions granted the businessmen of the two great powers.

H. J. Whigham's *The Persian Problem,* published in 1903, puts this rivalry in clear perspective. Whigham's book also suggests the attitude of the foreign commercial interests toward Iranians. He wrote, "In China and Corea we admire many characteristics of the people while we condemn the corrupt systems of government. In

Persia—apart from the lawless tribes, who have their rude qualities—we are face to face with a people at least as corrupt as its Government, and nothing worse could be said than that. Such a people and such a Government cannot much longer escape the salutary rod of foreign control. It is merely a question as to whether the rulers will be single or many." [1] Whigham wrote at a time when proconstitutional sentiment was gathering force, and his total unawareness of that movement appears to have typified the reactions of his British and Russian colleagues. More than any other factor, including the intellectual impact of the West, the anger and humiliation aroused by these foreign economic inroads led to the rise and triumph of Iranian nationalism—and Iranian nationalism was a consequence of their economic rivalry that neither power anticipated.

Anglo-Russian rivalry was not confined to a competition for economic concessions. The diplomatic missions of both powers sought to gain influence over individual Iranians whose position or potential position could be utilized. The extent to which the Russians and British actually controlled influential Iranians—one of the most important problems in a study of Iranian nationalism and the most difficult to handle objectively—can never be accurately documented. The British State Papers of the period make it clear that they exerted some control. Most Iranians are sure that entire factions of politicians were owned body and soul by either the Russians or the British. Consequently, in Iranian folklore a clever first minister in planning his cabinet would balance Russian agents with British agents—unless he were trying to gain a concession, and in this case he would overload his government with agents of the rival power. Without question, the Iranians exaggerated the extent of foreign control, but the reader would do well not to discount this conviction. The important point for understanding nationalism is that the Iranians were convinced that foreign intervention was a daily occurrence on all levels.[2]

Imperialist economic rivalry was not without its advantages for

[1] H. J. Whigham, *The Persian Problem* (London, 1903), p. 391.

[2] This point is quickly apparent in the first few pages of any of the major Iranian references but nowhere so apparent as in Mahmud Mahmud's study of Anglo-Iranian relations, *Tarikh Ravabet Siyasi Iran va Engelis dar Qarn Nuzdahom,* 4 vols. (Tehran, 1949–50).

Iranians. The Qajar Court under Nasr al-Din Shah and later under Mozaffar al-Din Shah soon recognized the financial advantages to be gained from playing the two powers against each other. Regardless of the Court's indebtedness, there was almost no likelihood that either power would permit the other to use the debt as an excuse for armed intervention. Furthermore, the Court could feel confident that the powers would try to outbid each other whenever it requested a loan. It mattered not at all to the Court that an ever higher percentage of Iran's resources came under foreign control as more concessions were granted and more loans were accepted.

By 1906 Russia had made great economic inroads. It had established a powerful bank; it owned important mining and communications concessions; and it controlled the sugar, match, and fishing industries.[3] In addition, the final omnibus loan granted Mozaffar al-Din by the Russians gave Russia a major share of the revenue from customs and actual control of much of the customs administration. Belgians were selected to administer the customs, but their chief, M. Naus, and his assistants were universally regarded as employees of the Russians.[4] The British, too, had major concessions, especially in south Iran, but prior to the discovery of oil the Russian commercial and political inroads were unquestionably the greater.

Reasoning from this predominance and the known preference of the Iranian Court and aristocrats for the Russians, most articulate Iranians concluded that the Court and its far rightist supporters were under Russian influence. In spite of the Revolution of 1905, the image of Russia current in Iran was one of black reaction. Russia symbolized despotism, and was assumed to be determined that this form of government should predominate in Iran. Much credence was given this belief by the willingness of the Russian-officered Persian Cossacks to give full support to the Court. It was inconceivable to the Iranian that the Russian Legation could be in anything but total agreement with this policy.

The Iranian image of the British was quite the opposite. As the

[3] Kasrevi, p. 12; Mostofi, II, 81.
[4] See for example Mostofi, II, 74–75.

liberal nationalist newspaper *Habl al-Matin* wrote in 1901: "Most of the statesmen of the world who have studied political science and have written books on that subject have concluded that the best form of government is one founded upon the same principles as is the government of England." [5] With a tradition of liberalism and democracy behind them, surely the British in Iran would favor the liberal faction of Iranian politicians and the movement to establish a constitution. This Iranian image of Britain was so strong that during the 1906 revolution the constitutionalists turned to the British for support.

The Western reader may conclude that nationalism could not have been very deeply ingrained among the constitutionalists if they were willing to seek foreign support against their own countrymen. However, by 1906 the belief in foreign interference was so completely accepted that such interference was regarded as one of those unfortunate political facts of life that must be lived with and made the most of. Requesting British support did not imply the constitutionalists' approval of foreign interference any more than accepting Frank Hague's support implied Franklin Roosevelt's approval of big city bosses, or accepting Joe McCarthy's support implied Dwight Eisenhower's approval of McCarthyism. In fact, an almost exact parallel with the role of foreign support in Iran can be found in the relationship of the two American parties to the AFL-CIO and NAM pressure groups. Just as the Democrats looked to labor for support and the Republicans to business, so the constitutionalists looked to the British and the Court looked to the Russians. The moral implications for the constitutionalists were hardly more serious than for the American parties.

The opening phase of the constitutional revolution was marked by the march of the religious leaders to take bast in Qom. Soon a delegation of merchants requested permission of the British Legation for a sizeable group of merchants to encamp in the spacious summer legation grounds. It is unfortunate that the revolutionary leaders were not able to hear the discussion their request provoked in the legation. The Iranians may well have assumed that their request would stir a profound discussion as to whether Britain's devotion to her ideology or to correct diplomatic behavior should

[5] *Habl al-Matin*, May 25, 1901.

prevail; in fact, British diplomatic correspondence indicates that the request was seen as a ridiculous bore. There is little indication that the British viewed the Court or the opposition seriously enough to grant either respect.[6] To be sure, Mr. Grant Duff, acting minister, in response to a direct question said he would not expel anyone taking bast at the legation, but he made this decision with the greatest reluctance, and the actual British role throughout can best be described as passive. In Iranian eyes, however, the British had given their full support to the constitutional movement; the Russians had opposed it, as witness the attitude of the Russian-officered Cossacks.

Both views were gross exaggerations. The diplomatic correspondence makes clear that both legations favored the granting of the constitution. Since the sloth and corruption of the Court were not only repulsive but carried an inherent threat to the stability that Russia and Britain wished to see in Iran, any reform movement was to be welcomed. When Mozaffar al-Din appeared to be equivocating, both the British and the Russian ministers made representations to him urging the fulfillment of his promise to grant a constitution.[7] Whatever differences there were in the attitudes of the two governments, they were differences of degree, not of kind.

For the Iranian constitutionalists the year following the successful revolution was given over to total immersion in the victorious liberal democratic nationalist ideology. Probably both the intensity of their involvement and their tendency to see society and politics in blacks and whites can be explained by the very shallow history of political thought in Iran. Liberal democracy was good and was personified by the British government. Absolute monarchy was bad and was personified by Russia. It was as simple as that—a struggle between good and evil. British popularity, especially with the intellectuals, could not have been greater, the British being placed in the improbable role of ideological messiah. Of course this view of them was wholly unrealistic, but it had wide acceptance.[8]

[6] *State Papers 1909, Persia No. 1*, p. 4.
[7] *Ibid.*, p. 5.
[8] See in particular *Habl al-Matin, Neda Vatan*, and *Majlis* for the year 1906.

Had this fantasy faded gradually, the result could have been a more realistic liberal nationalist world view. Unfortunately, the mythical image of Britain vanished with a suddenness that was shocking, and in the deeply offended Iranian mind a new myth appeared, equally fantastic, yet one that persists to this day.

Britain and Russia: The Agreement of 1907

In 1907 Britain and Russia were preparing an alliance for meeting the threat posed by Imperial Germany. Logic seemed to call for the elimination of zones of conflict between the two allies. Since Iran was such a zone, the two governments agreed to institutionalize their respective positions in order that no disagreement should arise in that tangential area. By the terms of the Anglo-Russian Agreement of 1907, Iran was divided into British and Russian spheres of influence with a neutral buffer zone in the center. It is difficult not to conclude that this treaty was badly misguided. As their statesmen should have known, British-Russian rivalry and suspicion would not so easily be eliminated. There was a certain sophomoric logic to the sphere-of-influence idea, however, and there is no reason to question the motivation behind the treaty.

From the Iranian viewpoint the Agreement was utter disaster. Even for those few who saw the world in clear perspective, the treaty was of top importance since it meant that Anglo-Russian rivalry would henceforth be on a more dangerous plane: the next step could be the partition of Iran. For the idealistic Iranian constitutionalist the shock was immense. Suddenly, the Western power that had seemed to personify the liberal ideal had joined with the power that was the antithesis of that ideal in an alliance that threatened not only the liberal cause in Iran but even the existence of the nation.[9] It was inconceivable that such a betrayal could occur, and many liberal constitutionalists were ready to believe him when Sir Cecil Spring-Rice on behalf of the British Foreign Office signed a memorandum of reassurance. The Agreement did not threaten Iran's independence, Sir Cecil wrote; on the contrary, it was a source of security to Iranian independence

[9] See for example *Habl al-Matin,* September 10, 1907; Kasrevi, p. 458; Mirza, p. 122; Dolatabadi, II, 180; *Mosavat,* October 27, 1907.

since it would destroy the basis for Anglo-Russian rivalry in Iran.[10]

The more sophisticated Iranians understood that the reason for the treaty was to remove a source of Anglo-Russian conflict. They understood, but since the Agreement was at their expense they could hardly have been expected to approve. As *Habl al-Matin* wrote in bitter irony on September 11, 1907, "There is sweetness, kindness and love in the Agreement. The Russian government will grant the English government opportunities for commercial activity in the northern sphere of influence and the English will kindly grant permission to the Russians to do the same in the south. What right have the Russians in Iran to grant or not grant—from north to south—that which belongs to us? We aren't so youthful as to want a protector and we aren't mad or insane and hence in need of one." [11] The English argued that Germany was a threat to liberal democracy, but the Iranians were not convinced. After all, the despotism of Russia was close at hand while that of Germany was far away. The Anglo-Russian alliance was sad proof to the Iranians that the exigencies of power politics would always take precedence over the ideological conviction of the British government.

Sir Cecil's memorandum was meant to be the sugar coating of a bitter pill, but the statement in it that the Agreement would eliminate or at least drastically reduce a dangerous rivalry and hence a proclivity to interfere was certainly meant sincerely. For the British to have believed otherwise would have meant a recognition on their part that the Agreement served no useful purpose. Within the next several months, however, when the position of the constitutionalists was under increasing attack, more than a suspicion lurked in the liberal mind that foreign interference was being felt. When Anglo-Russian interference, generally against the interests of the constitutionalists, became more open, the words of Sir Cecil appeared as a bitter, contemptuous mockery. Those Iranians who had exaggerated out of all proportion British devotion to Iranian liberalism felt that in the light of later developments the memorandum compounded hypocrisy. The

[10] Browne, *The Persian Revolution,* pp. 172–96.
[11] *Habl al-Matin,* September 11, 1907.

conviction that the British never say what they mean, which endures to this day in Iran, owes much of its strength to Sir Cecil's unfortunate memorandum. As *No Bahar* wrote: "To whatever gathering we go and talk, the name of Russia is forgotten and the true meaning of the memorandum [of Sir Cecil] is breathed. We made a great mistake when our hearts embraced with love the government of England. It is good that we understand!! Today we know that the state of England of the future is the same as the state of Russia." [12]

The Agreement of 1907 was a major turning point for Iranian nationalism: the roots of the so-called anti-Western aspects of mid-twentieth century Iranian nationalism gain much of their nourishment from the memory of this treaty. Another legacy of the Agreement is the belief in the existence of a secret Anglo-Russian understanding. As will be seen later, this belief does much to confuse the ideological struggle of the Cold War.

The violent Iranian reaction could not help having its impact on British attitudes toward the Iranian constitutionalists. Up to the signing of the Agreement of 1907, Iran was better understood by individual Englishmen than by men of any other nationality. The brilliant British Iranist, Edward Browne, probably understood the emerging liberal nationalist movement more fully than any man, Iranian or foreign.[13] Within the British Legation in Tehran there had been some acute observers and reporting on Iranian politics was of high quality. This awareness was reflected in the understanding of the Iranian situation in the foreign office.[14] After 1907 an abrupt change took place. Once the constitutional movement began to complicate the British position in Iran, dispatches to London began downgrading the importance of the liberal nationalists. For example, despite a unanimous press reaction which reflected a shocked dismay when the Agreement of 1907 was made public, the British minister reported comfortably that "on the whole the Agreement has been well received." [15]

The Agreement of 1907 should not have been the turning point

[12] *No Bahar*, December 4, 1910, p. 2.

[13] This is shown particularly in his *The Persian Revolution*.

[14] On February 27, 1907, Sir Cecil Spring-Rice wrote that nationalistic sentiment was in Iran to stay. *State Papers 1909, Persia No. 1*.

[15] *Ibid.*, p. 60.

for Iranian nationalism. It just wasn't that important. Had the Iranians seen the world in better perspective, the treaty would never have been considered a betrayal. But if the lion's share of the blame for this exaggerated impact belonged to the Iranians, the British were not blameless. The blindness of Iranians to the real motivation of the British was matched by the British refusal to see that a profound social revolution was under way in the land so brilliantly satirized by Morier in his *Haji Baba of Isfahan*. One wonders if Morier's book, because of its very brilliance, did not do Britain real damage, not because it offended Iranians, which it did and does, but because too many British diplomats had trouble remembering that it was, after all, fiction.

Britain and Russia: Controlled Rivalry 1907–12

The 1906 revolution brought a fundamental change to Iran. A half-century of historical data makes this conclusion obvious, but it is not surprsing that British and Russian observers in 1907 failed to recognize it fully. The event was too near to upset a century's assessment of Iranian society and politics; it had had too many comic aspects to be taken seriously; and, after all, only a veneer of the population had been affected, while the vast majority had continued undisturbed in their familiar routine. Neither power understood that the bitter resentment generated by the Anglo-Russian Agreement of 1907 among the constitutionalists would make Anglo-Russian interference more rather than less likely in Iran. But even if the revolution had not occurred for another decade, it is likely that the Agreement would have resulted in increased rather than decreased interference. The establishment of spheres of influence implies the acceptance of a certain responsibility by each power for its sphere, and in early twentieth-century Iran, with or without the revolution, this responsibility would have necessitated taking measures to maintain internal security.

The revolution had occurred, however, and Iran had changed far more basically than Iranians or foreigners imagined. A period of ferment and political maneuvering was inevitable, because the revolution had been only the first round in a continuing struggle for power between the Court with its reactionary allies and the formless merchant-clerical-intellectual alliance. The only clearly predictable result of the revolution was that a period of extended instability would follow, and instability was what both Britain and Russia feared most in Iran.

The ideal internal situation for Anglo-Russian objectives would have been an Iranian government strong enough to maintain internal security but not so strong as to challenge the privileged Anglo-Russian position in the country. But this ideal was impossible. Mohammad Ali Shah would have liked to establish strong control over Iran and almost certainly would have accepted the special Anglo-Russian position. However, the Shah was a strangely indecisive man given to spurts of furious activity followed by days and weeks of passive brooding. Furthermore, the security force available to him, despite its Russian officers, was anything but a formidable body. The constitutional coalition may have been formless and may have been representative of only a small percentage of the total population, but numerically it was not insignificant, and in spirit and energy it stood clearly superior to its enemy. Obviously, only foreign interference could have thrown victory to one side or the other.

Increasing numbers of Iranians thought they saw foreign interference in favor of the Court. This conclusion was only to be expected, considering the Iranian view of international affairs. In this view Russia was the champion of despotism and could not tolerate the emergence of liberal democracy in Iran, and Britain had surrendered her own ideology in the interests of Anglo-Russian harmony. Therefore, no force stood to halt the inevitable effort to destroy Iranian democracy in its infancy. When Mohammad Ali openly manifested his opposition to the constitution, the liberals, believing as they did that the Court had long before sold itself to the Russians, could only conclude that the green light had been given by the Russians. After all, the real leader of the Persian Cossacks was the courageous, competent Colonel Liakhoff, whose devotion to the Russian Court was beyond question; and Colonel Liakhoff was perhaps Mohammad Ali's most trusted advisor. Could the picture have been more clear?

The answer is that as far as the British were concerned the picture was clear enough, but one quite different from that the

Iranians thought they saw; and the Russian picture was confused and muddled. Mr. Marling wrote to London that he and the Russian Minister, M. de Hartwig, were in full agreement that Mohammad Ali should remain in power, but as a constitutional monarch.[16] Each minister made at least two representations to the Shah urging him to abide by the constitution and not to overturn it.[17] They reasoned that since the Shah and his opposition stood in fairly equal balance, neither could expect victory; and since continued struggle would result in an instability that would inevitably place a strain on Anglo-Russian harmony, the best solution would be for Mohammad Ali to accept the constitution. The British diplomatic correspondence demonstrates that the British took at face value M. de Hartwig's professions of support for a constitutional monarchy. But the Iranian liberals' argument that Russian policy favored interference against them is not easily quashed since it really does approach the inconceivable that so loyal an officer as Colonel Liakhoff would act without at least the tacit agreement of his legation. Perhaps the Russian Legation was bitterly divided or possibly M. de Hartwig was engaged in clever deception. In any event, the Iranian suspicion is fully understandable.

In 1908 Mohammad Ali, utilizing Colonel Liakhoff's troops, defeated the constitutionalists in Tehran. The Shah then ordered the Russian officers and troops to Tabriz to strike what was hoped to be a death blow at the constitution. At the time of their departure Colonel Liakhoff addressed his men as follows: "You must know that should you return victorious, you will be overwhelmed with money and favors from both the Russian and the Persian sovereigns." [18] Shortly thereafter the Russians proposed that the powers jointly grant Mohammad Ali a loan.[19] With evidence such as this, the Iranians could only conclude that the new government was the property of the Russians and, to a lesser extent (since they refused to go along with the loan proposition), of the British.

[16] *Ibid.*, pp. 93–94.
[17] *Ibid.*, pp. 92–98.
[18] Browne, *The Persian Revolution*, p. 258.
[19] *State Papers 1909, Persia No. 2*, p. 43.

Again, however, the British diplomatic correspondence makes clear the error of this view. Both the new British minister, Mr. Barclay, and M. de Hartwig asked the Shah to restore the constitution in November 1908 because they realized that opposition to him was still intense.[20] Then in April 1909 the Russians proposed that they and the British insist that Mohammad Ali abide by the constitution and dismiss the reactionaries in his government.[21] The British demurred since Mohammad Ali's refusal would have necessitated his overthrow if Anglo-Russian prestige was to be maintained, and the British did not wish to become so deeply involved.

The lifting of the Tabriz seige by Russian troops was not regarded as support for Mohammad Ali. On the contrary, both the Iranians and the foreigners regarded it as a victory for the nationalists; [22] and both the Russians and the British lamented that the relief of Tabriz would aid the nationalists and damage Mohammad Ali's position.[23] In their correspondence the British indicated for the first time a predilection for one side in the Iranian conflict—for Mohammad Ali and his followers. From this point on, an emotionally based hostility toward the nationalists is clearly discernible in much of the British diplomatic correspondence, and this attitude must be ranked along with other factors in explaining the evolution of British policy.

Britain and Russia placed pressure on Mohammad Ali to reinstate the constitution, but this pressure, largely thanks to the British, was toothless. When the nationalists appeared to be determined to capture Tehran and to depose Mohammad Ali, the diplomatic activity of the two powers, and especially of the British, became much more intense. The commanders of the Isfahan and Rasht forces were contacted by the British and urged to desist from their plan. Ignoring this request, the Rasht-Isfahan army moved within striking distance of Tehran. The Russians and British extracted a promise of major concessions from Mohammad Ali and attempted to use these concessions to stop the nationalist attack

[20] *Ibid.*, p. 3.
[21] *Ibid.*, p. 90.
[22] Browne, *The Persian Revolution,* p. 274; Kasrevi, p. 888.
[23] *State Papers 1909, Persia No. 2,* p. 100.

ers.[24] That the British and Russians could have imagined the nationalists would forgive Mohammad Ali when they were on the threshold of victory is indicative of their almost absolute inability at this time to understand the Iranian nationalist viewpoint. This lack of understanding had been demonstrated a few weeks earlier when Mr. Barclay informed a delegation of nationalists that he thought two of their demands on the royal cabinet were unreasonable: that Colonel Liakhoff be dismissed and that the strong-willed but reactionary governor of Tabriz, Ala al-Doleh, be removed.[25] Barclay considered that these men were vital for the preservation of internal security, and in his eyes internal security was the ultimate goal. He did not understand that he thereby told the nationalists that Britain gave full support to the strong men of the Russian-sponsored, anticonstitutionalist regime.

Lest perspective be lost it should be noted that Mohammad Ali could have been maintained on his throne with a minimum of Russian effort. Russian troops had landed in Rasht and were in the vicinity of Qazvin, just two or three days marching distance from Tehran, when the capital fell. Anglo-Russian antagonism to the nationalists was certainly growing, but it had not yet reached the point of an open break.

In the two and one-half years that followed an open break almost occurred several times. Even before the new constitutional regime was six months old, the British consul in Shiraz wrote a dispatch in which he urged that immediate foreign intervention was necessary to restore internal security.[26] An increasing number of British merchants demanded the dispatch of troops to protect the southern caravan routes. Despite violent objections on the part of the Iranian government climaxed by an anti-British riot in Tehran in November 1910, troops were sent to police the caravan routes.[27] They proved incapable of providing security, and the British gained only ill will by their intervention. If anyone in the British Foreign Office chose this moment to dwell on the Spring-Rice memorandum of 1907, the confident prediction that the

24 *State Papers 1910, Persia No. 1,* pp. 32, 75.
25 *Ibid.,* p. 41.
26 *State Papers 1911, Persia No. 1,* p. 19.
27 *State Papers 1912, Persia No. 3,* p. 27.

Agreement of 1907 would bring an end to interference in Iranian affairs must have carried a plaintive ring.

Meanwhile the Russians moved ever closer to direct intervention. In the summer of 1911 Mohammad Ali suddenly appeared on the east Caspian shore with Turkoman tribal support and prepared to march on Tehran. Two years earlier the deposed monarch had taken up residence in a handsome villa near Odessa, Russia, apparently prepared for a life of luxurious exile. The Russians announced that they had no forewarning of his return to Iran, and the British consul in Odessa and the ambassador in Moscow reported that the attack was a complete surprise to the Russians.[28] Iranians, on the other hand, regard this point as too absurd to warrant argument. They find it incredible that the secret police would not have observed an ex-monarch stealing away from his ostentatious villa and embarking at Baku with men and materials. Moreover, an event that took place after the invasion offers support for the Iranian belief in Russian sponsorship. When the Tehran government wished to arrest a pro-Mohammad Ali leader in Azerbaijan, the Russians not only refused to permit his arrest, but permitted him to lead an antigovernment force toward Tehran.[29] Understandably, Iranians regard Mohammad Ali's defeat as the defeat of an indirect Russian invasion.

But unconcealed intervention by Russia was left for 1911, the Morgan Shuster period. After initially approving the appointment of the American financial expert, the Russians became suspicious of Shuster's role in Iran. No episode so well illustrates the reason for this Russian hostility as does the appointment of Major C. B. Stokes to head tax collection in Azerbaijan. Stokes was one of a breed of Englishmen found in Iran and other such lands who "go native." He understood Persian, was familiar with the customs of the people, and, most important of all, sympathized with them. Not unnaturally he shared their strong Russophobia. Why should such a man be sent to Azerbaijan, the heart of the Russian sphere of interest? Shuster insists that Stokes was his best man and was hence sent to Iran's most important province.[30] Possibly that

28 *Ibid.*, p. 105.
29 *Ibid.*, pp. 120, 129.
30 W. Morgan Shuster, *The Strangling of Persia* (New York, 1912), pp. 70–75.

explanation was true, but if so Shuster emerges as a less sensitive and more naive man than other aspects of his career indicate him to be. As his own book demonstrates, Shuster accepted without hesitation his position as an employee of the Iranian government, and a more loyal employee Iran had never seen. He entered energetically into the task of defeating Mohammad Ali; indeed, more than a little credit for the ex-monarch's defeat is due Shuster. It was precisely his loyalty that made the few months of Shuster's residence in Iran one of the high points in the history of Iranian nationalism. The Iranian government had refused to recognize the Anglo-Russian Agreement of 1907, but no official prior to Shuster had dared to defy the treaty. Considering Shuster's whole-hearted support for the nationalist regime, it is difficult to believe that flouting the Russians was not at least one aspect of his motivation for appointing Stokes.

The Russians reacted furiously to the Stokes appointment; they believed that through it Shuster was working with the British to upset the Anglo-Russian balance and to invade the Russian sphere of influence. This conclusion was nonsense, but Iranian twentieth-century history is a weird study in conflicting irrationalities. The Iranian authorities were advised by Russia in the strongest possible terms to withdraw the Stokes appointment. Both Iran and Shuster stood their ground, and the removal of Stokes came about finally through the personal intervention of British authorities with Stokes, who reluctantly resigned.

To the British the entire Shuster experience was ridiculous and annoying.[31] Shuster disturbed Anglo-Russian relations with an exuberance that some described as puerile. British hostility dated from his earliest weeks in Tehran and was due at first not to his irreverence toward the Agreement, but to his refusal to observe diplomatic niceties. Shuster insisted that as an Iranian government employee he had no diplomatic function. He was technically correct, but he succeeded in annoying men for whom diplomatic protocol was important. Once Shuster began his attacks on Anglo-Russian prerogatives, the British hostility intensified.

His greatest single accomplishment was in collecting taxes. He

[31] This is seen clearly in the diplomatic dispatches of the period published in *State Papers, Persia.*

organized a gendarmery and ordered them to collect back taxes from delinquent grandees. While the gendarmery carried out his orders, an incredulous population watched. In November 1911 Shuster ordered the gendarmery to take possession of the confiscated dwelling of Shoa al-Soltaneh, a Qajar prince who was in exile in Russia. When the gendarmery was refused entry by a contingent of Russian troops, Shuster ordered it to take possession, and it did so.[32]

This was the beginning of the end. Since the Russians could not submit to such a rebuff from Iran, they sent two ultimatums, the first demanding an apology and the second Shuster's dismissal. Russian troops reinforced the Enzeli garrison, and one detachment moved on to Qazvin. But even though Iranian officials realized that the end was only a matter of time, public opinion would not permit them to accede to the ultimatums. Russian goods were boycotted; fighting with Russian troops broke out in Tabriz and Rasht; huge demonstrations were staged in Tehran, where shouts of "death or independence" filled the air; a pro-Russian minister was assassinated; and the Majlis stood unanimously against giving in to the Russian demands.[33]

As the Russian troops drew nearer to Tehran, the government accepted reality and resigned. A new government was formed, extralegally, that was prepared to surrender. But the bitterness of the Iranians was deep, and the wound is even today far from healed. Grey assured the enmity of Iran for Great Britain when he announced in the House of Commons that the British government was in full accord with the Russian ultimatums: "The solution of the present crisis must be such as to secure a Government in Persia which will conform to the principles of the Anglo-Russian agreement, and not disregard the special interests which the two powers respectively have in that country." [34] Circumstances gave Grey no choice: he had to convince the Russians that the British had been true to the letter and spirit of the Agreement. To Iranians, however, the Grey statement was a gratuitous affront, and it

[32] *State Papers 1912, Persia No. 4,* p. 33.

[33] *Ibid.,* pp. 86, 119–20, 126–27, 137–40; *The Near East,* December 22, 1911, p. 196; December 29, 1911, p. 221; January 5, 1912, p. 263; January 12, 1912, p. 290; Mostofi, II, 502–04.

[34] *State Papers 1912, Persia No. 4,* p. 102.

reaffirmed their conviction that British ideology was not for export. *Tazeh Bahar* echoed the sentiments of many intellectuals when it editorialized: "The Russian ultimatum presented our government overthrew our independence but the government of England was the founder of this ultimatum. As we have said repeatedly before, whenever Iran is vulnerable, the government of England carries out the preliminaries for the Russians and then is a spectator." [35] Few Iranians doubted that Russia was dedicated to despotism. The Russian role in Iran was reprehensible, but consistent. The British role, viewed as hypocritical, was to many more despicable than the Russian.

Iranian nationalism had been defeated, but it was not the kind of defeat to shame an emerging nation. The internal battle had been won, and the forces of reaction had been routed. In a brief moment of glory Iran had even defied the Russian and British giants. The nation had stood united against the foreign enemy, and no man had dared call for surrender until Russian troops were in sight of Tehran. But this wasn't reality; this was only the gilt edge of reality. In fact, Iranian nationalism had long been hovering near defeat—a defeat to be administered by the overwhelming political, social, and economic problems a victorious nationalism had faced in 1906 and again in 1909. What the constitutionalists needed more than anything else if Iranian nationalism was to blossom into a healthy, positive force was responsibility. They needed to learn how to solve the immense problems that stood between Iran and the twentieth century. The real tragedy of foreign intervention was that responsibility was denied the constitutionalists: the maturing process that the 1906–12 period should have witnessed never occurred. On the contrary, since the nationalists could believe with some justice that foreigners in league with Mohammad Ali had administered the first defeat and then in 1911 had openly administered the final defeat, they could explain their failures as entirely due to foreigners and their domestic allies. Consequently, Iranian nationalism focused on a destructive goal, the nationalists being convinced that their main task was the negative one of destroying foreign interference and domestic reaction.

[35] *Tazeh Bahar,* December 1911.

Britain and Russia: Condominium 1912–17

A general Iranian view is that after the dismissal of Morgan Shuster Iran was under the complete control of the British and Russians.[36] There is very little exaggeration in this picture of Iran prior to 1914 and almost none after 1914. Russian troops were garrisoned in Tabriz, Enzeli, and Mashhad and therefore were in actual control of the three major northern Iranian provincial centers. Iranians were still appointed to the positions of governor general of each of the northern provinces, but these men were at least approved, if not selected, by the Russians. The extent of Russian control is illustrated by the choice of Shoja al-Doleh, one of the most hated men in Iran, as governor general of Azerbaijan. In addition to dictating the choice of Iranian officialdom, the Russian troops interfered in other ways. There are many examples of disciplining tribes and removing individuals considered to be troublemakers. A moderate liberal but strongly nationalistic mullah, the Seqat al-Islam, was executed and the rabble were permitted, probably hired, to defile the body. The Shahsevan tribe was chastised; and most outrageous of all, the most holy of Iranian mosques, the Imam Reza of Mashhad, was bombarded as a disciplinary measure.[37]

Even prior to Shuster's ejection, British troops were brought into south Iran. After 1911 these troops were reinforced, and garrisons were located in Shiraz and Isfahan, the proud provincial cities of west central and southwest Iran.[38] The British activity in these areas paralleled that of the Russians: the governor generals of the south Iranian provinces were as notorious for being British agents as was Shoja al-Doleh for being a Russian agent. The British carried out no wanton murders of provincial nationalists nor bombardments of sacred shrines, but though their occupation was less brutal than the Russian, it was hardly less offensive.

Anglo-Russian interference in Tehran, only slightly less blatant than that in the area of occupation, was consistently in opposition to the liberal nationalist element. When a contingent of Bakhtiari troops refused to fight for the central government, reportedly

[36] Dolatabadi, IV, 26.
[37] *State Papers 1912, Persia No. 5,* pp. 6, 9, 74, 97.
[38] *State Papers 1913, Persia No. 1,* p. 115.

because of its loss of independence, the British minister, Mr. Townley, wrote: "Under these circumstances my Russian colleague and I deemed it advisable to make a strong representation to the Bakhtiari Prime Minister and Minister of War to the effect that, if they cannot persuade their tribesmen at the front to do their duty and refrain from meddling in politics, we shall feel constrained to withdraw our support from the Bakhtiaris both at the capital and in the provinces." [39] At the time of the 1913 Majlis elections, the two ministers urged the cabinet to take care "to insure the return of more suitable members of Parliament than was the case in the two previous occasions." [40] "Suitable" meant that they not be liberal nationalists. An instruction from Sir Edward Grey to the British minister demonstrates that this type of interference was understood and sanctioned at the highest levels: "You should also require the Persian Government to restrain extremists in Tehran and elsewhere, and induce the Najaf and Karbala clergy to recant their recent incitations and use their influence to secure a more friendly attitude on the part of tribal chiefs." [41]

How were instructions such as these carried out in areas not under British occupation? The Iranians insist that the British made full use of local agents, private British citizens, and the leverage of a favorable or unfavorable credit rating at the British bank. Since the British and Russians admittedly had a great influence over appointments, it cannot be doubted that many ambitious Iranian politicians sought British and/or Russian sponsorship and, in the eyes of their nationalist compatriots, sold their souls. This Anglo-Russian policy of working through Iranian agents has engendered the conviction which still endures in the minds of Iranian nationalists that mullahs, tribal chiefs, the Court, and right-wing politicians count among their numbers a great many men who are traitors to their country.

The limits of Anglo-Russian interference were defined when the two powers attempted to maneuver the election of a reputed Russian agent named Sa'd al-Doleh as prime minister. As Sir

[39] *State Papers 1913, Persia No. 1*, p. 188.
[40] *State Papers 1914, Persia No. 1*, p. 134.
[41] *State Papers 1913, Persia No. 1*, p. 6.

Edward Grey said, Sa'd al-Doleh seemed an ideal candidate because the "establishment of a stable government appeared . . . more probable under him than anyone else." [42] As usual the British did not consider Iranian opinion—and Sa'd al-Doleh was notoriously disliked throughout Iran. Rioting and demonstrations by Sir Edward's "extremists" broke out in Tehran, and a major revolution appeared to be in the making. At this point the British and Russians chose to withdraw their sponsorship of Sa'd al-Doleh; to have persisted in it would have necessitated the ordering of occupation troops into the capital. Obviously, Sir Edward's assessment was totally incorrect. Far from being the man most capable of establishing a stable government, Sa'd al-Doleh was demonstrably among the least capable. He was least capable, not because he lacked determination, decisiveness, and ruthlessness—all these he had—but because he lacked the reputation for sincere devotion to Iran which would have given him the backing of public opinion. But if one denies that public opinion exists in Iran, as did Sir Edward Grey and even to this day does many a British policy maker, then backing from public opinion should matter not at all. When riots and demonstrations proved that public opinion did exist, Sir Edward dismissed it as activity of "extremists," which in some mysterious manner differs from "public opinion" and need not be taken into account.

Considering the above, Iranians can be excused for believing that the Anglo-Russian objective was to reduce Iran to the status of a colony. Nevertheless, the evidence is strong that this was not their objective. In 1913 the two powers advanced a £400,000 loan, half of which was to be used for the Swedish-officered gendarmery, and the British added another £100,000 for the use of the gendarmery in south Iran.[43] Had the British objective been to establish colonial control, this sizeable sum could have been better spent on a British-officered elite corps. That the gendarmery was anything but under Anglo-Russian control was demonstrated when its Swedish officers supported Germany in World War I. The most likely conclusion is that the British objective was precisely what they said it was countless times in their diplomatic correspondence —internal stability. The case is not so clear for the Russians. In

[42] *Ibid.*, p. 224.
[43] *The Near East,* May 9, 1913, p. 2.

June of 1914 they reorganized the Iranian Cossacks in such a way as to make them, in effect, a Russian force.[44]

When World War I broke out, the liberal nationalist element in Tehran was overwhelmingly pro-German and pro-Turk. Large numbers of these people left Tehran for Kermanshah in order to join forces with the Central Powers there. Nor was this pro-Central Power sentiment limited to the liberal nationalists. Christopher Sykes reports that even among peasants and tribesmen, for whom World War I had only the vaguest of meaning, a hatred for Russia was a strong sentiment.[45] In south Iran peasant and tribal antagonism was directed at the British, and tribal rebellion became so extensive that they were compelled to organize the South Persian Rifles, an Iranian force commanded by British officers.

Even the captive Tehran government was so openly pro-German that the Russians ordered a contingent of troops to advance on the capital. For a time it appeared that the government might move to Qom, ninety miles to the south, but as the more energetic members left for Kermanshah and open participation on the German-Turkish side, the government lost heart and resigned. With the departure of the nationalist elite, the successor governments were willing and pliant tools in the hands of the allies.

Conclusion

The 1906–17 period was a generic one for the belief system of Iranian nationalists. Myths were created in this twelve-year span that are to be found virtually unaltered today and give an unreal coloring to the Iranian perspective. At the beginning of this period men with liberal, democratic, and nationalist values pushed aside those with traditional values and assumed a tenuous direction of the Iranian political process. Somewhat naively they expected to receive the sympathetic support of the British diplomatic staff in Tehran; after all, the British held these same values. But this was not to be.

In the first place, and not at all unnaturally, the British failed to recognize the immense potential of the change simply because the changed attitudes were confined in 1906 to the very few. The traditional leaders, within whose social circle the British diplomats

[44] *The Near East,* June 5, 1914, p. 141.

[45] Christopher Sykes, *Wassmuss, the German Lawrence* (London, 1936), p. 64.

moved, and the visible mass of the people were the least affected. British diplomatic correspondence leads to the conclusion that the British were anything but ready to think of Iranian liberals as ideological brothers. Consequently, they persisted in diplomatic operations which can only be described as crude interference. The traditional elements could take a casual view of this behavior, but men who held high the values of independence and dignity for Iran could not, and an intensely hostile nationalistic reaction against the British became inevitable.

Second, the fact that nationalistic values had a place in the value systems of both Iranian modernists and the British does not imply a harmony of interests. The Iranians were devoted to the national interests of Iran, and these interests did not necessarily coincide with the national interests of Great Britain. For example, in pursuance of their perception of their national interests the British negotiated the Anglo-Russian Agreement of 1907 and thereby deeply offended the Iranian nationalist's sense of national dignity.

Third, the liberal-democratic-nationalist values of the modernist Iranian led to an assault on the traditional status quo in Iran. Since the British had a primary goal of stabilizing the Anglo-Russian balance and since the modernist assault on the status quo threatened this balance, they opposed the modernist forces. In pursuit of their own national interests, the British offended every aspect of the modernist Iranian's value system.

The consequences of this interaction were circular and reinforcing. Because the British seemed to be running counter to their own values in their Iranian policy, Iranian nationalists became convinced of British hypocrisy. As a result, the Iranian nationalist reaction led to increasing Anglophobia which in turn added to British antagonism toward what the British called the Iranian "extremists." Iranian traditional elements could bring the stability the British wished, and they were therefore the natural allies of the British. By accepting this alliance, however, the traditionalists in the eyes of the modernists moved down a path of treason. Furthermore, the point was quickly reached at which the Iranian modernist nationalist could not distinguish between his struggle against indirect colonialism and his struggle against social and political injustice at home.

12

IMPERIALISM AND NATIONALISM: CONFRONTATION

Few doubt today that the March and November revolutions in Russia in 1917 will stand among the most dramatic and vital events of world history. In many countries they had little meaning at the time, but for Iran the major role that the Tsarist regime had played in Iranian internal affairs made the revolutions of immediate importance. Suspicion of Russia was too ingrained to disappear overnight, and while Kerensky was still in power, *Bahar,* with uncanny prescience, wrote: "It is demonstrable that an even coarser tyranny will rise . . . out of the despotic soil of Russia." [1] Many Iranians shared this skepticism, but nonetheless there was a tremendous emotional release in Iran following the revolutions. Reports tell of dancing in the streets of Tabriz, Iranian with Russian, and on the anniversary of the Iranian constitution the Russians are said to have joined in the celebrating. The rejoicing approached abandon in the mass celebrations that were held in Tabriz and Tehran when, in January 1918, the new Soviet regime renounced the old treaties of the Tsars, including the infamous Agreement of 1907,[2] and ordered Russian troops to return home. As the Russian troops marched northward across the border, Iranians were ready to believe that a new era had begun.

They were soon to be disillusioned. Much of the good effect of the withdrawal was obviated by Soviet interference in Gilan. But even earlier the Iranians had been reminded of a truth that had slipped their minds: Iran owed its independence to Anglo-Russian rivalry. With Bolshevik Russia fighting for its existence, there was no longer a major Russian influence in Iran, and, as if to fill the void, British troops left their familiar haunts in south Iran and

[1] *Bahar,* June 5, 1917.

[2] Fatemi, pp. 7–8; *The Near East,* July 13, 1912, p. 210; October 5, 1917, p. 451; May 10, 1918, p. 382.

were garrisoned in the former Russian headquarters of Qazvin and Enzeli. Iranians began to wonder if, after all, the Russian Revolution had been such a blessing.

Suspicions that the British hoped to extend their colonial empire into Iran were exacerbated at the Paris Peace Conference in 1919. An Iranian delegation had demanded that it be received at the conference in order to present the case for compensation for Iranian suffering in World War I.[3] The Iranian territorial claims against Turkey, Mesopotamia, and the Caucasus were far beyond reality. Still, few nations had suffered more than had Iran during the war, and equity demanded that at least courtesy be extended to the Iranians. Instead, at British instigation the delegation was refused entry. This British move, combined with rumors of an Anglo-Iranian treaty under negotiation in Tehran, seemed to confirm Iran's worst fears.

Shortly afterwards, on August 19, the terms of the Anglo-Persian Treaty of 1919 were announced. In the preamble Iranian independence and territorial integrity were guaranteed, but the terms of the agreement clearly indicated that Iran would enter a protectorate status in all but name. Iran would be granted a £2,000,000 loan at 7 per cent interest with which to finance a massive development program. British financial, administrative, and technical advisors, who would be paid by the Iranian government, would be sent to help plan and execute this program, and British officers, also paid by the Iranians, would train and develop an Iranian army.[4]

The Anglo-Persian Treaty was fathered with loving parental care by the British Foreign Minister, Lord Curzon, who, according to Harold Nicolson, saw in the agreement the climactic achievement of his career. Curzon ". . . had always, and with full sincerity, been in favour of Persian independence and integrity. He had always and sometimes out of season been the enemy of Russian infiltration into Central Asia. It seemed incredible to him that the Persians could fail to recognize in him their constant, their lordly, their disinterested and their inspired friend." [5] With these

[3] Fatemi, p. 20.
[4] Sir Percy Sykes, *History of Persia,* pp. 520–24.
[5] Harold Nicolson, *Curzon: The Last Phase 1919–1925* (New York, 1934), p. 128.

words Nicolson captures the heart of the best of the British policy toward Iran; but, as events were to show, the best was sadly lacking in comprehension. As Nicolson admits, Curzon felt ". . . that in general we should assume towards Persia the role of a determined although liberal protector."[6] The treaty was too transparent to be a serious effort to deceive Iran and the world as to the British intention. After all, the British could argue, Iran was in a chaotic state and sorely in need of outside tutelage and assistance. With Russian influence at a low ebb, it would be to the mutual advantage of both countries that Iran should pass under the benevolent protection of Britain and thus be securely beyond Russian grasp.

The British Legation and the correspondent of the *Near East* reported that the Iranian reaction to the treaty was, as expected, favorable.[7] Despite this opinion, Iranian reaction was far from unanimous. There undoubtedly were many Iranians—particularly among the aristocratic element with whom British diplomats had long moved socially—who saw in British protection the only hope for security and stability. However, within a year even the British had to admit that their optimism was not soundly based and that when the Anglo-Persian Treaty had been announced, the Iranian press and public had been generally "indignant."[8] But the British Legation was not ready to concede that this indignation was a reflection of public opinion. On the contrary, they argued that the protests were staged by the French, who were jealous of British success, or by the ruling clique, which feared that British hegemony would end the corrupt system they had so easily dominated, or by both groups.[9]

The evidence against this British view is overwhelming. Of twenty-six periodicals being published in Tehran at the time, all but one, Sayyed Zia's *Ra'd,* denounced the treaty—and at the risk of suppression by the government of Vosuq al-Doleh, which had signed it. The argument that all twenty-five journals were in league with wicked and corrupt grandees, the very men who had

[6] *Ibid.*, p. 133.

[7] *The Near East,* November 28, 1919, p. 599; *Documents on British Foreign Policy, 1919–1939,* (London, 1952), 1st Ser., IV, 1127.

[8] *The Near East,* September 16, 1920, p. 394.

[9] *Documents on British Foreign Policy, 1919–1939,* 1st Ser., IV, 1138–39.

always opposed nationalism, is not plausible. Furthermore, the tenor of the attacks belies the British assessment. The articles denouncing the treaty were couched in strongly nationalistic and sometimes sophisticated language.[10] If, as the British contend, there was no public opinion, to whom were these articles appealing? Surely they were intended to influence the public; otherwise there would have been no point in the expenditure of time, effort, and money by twenty-five periodicals. And the type of article published must have been indicative of the publisher's assessment of the reading public to which he was appealing. If these deductions are granted, the press campaign proves that it was not the five-rials-a-head type of mob that was being stirred against the treaty, but rather men with the requisite education to respond to a sophisticated line of reasoning.

The assessment of the Iranian reaction by the American minister in Tehran, John L. Caldwell, flatly contradicted the British opinion. Caldwell claimed that although the presence of British troops in Iran and the willingness of the government to arrest those opposed to the treaty inhibited open denunciations, Tehran was seething with resentment. Yeselson, who made a complete survey of the published State Department documents on Iran for this period, writes: "Caldwell asserted that the only supporters of the agreement (these included the Shah, the Prime Minister, and the Foreign Minister) had been bribed by Britain, and said further that he had not found one single honest disinterested person who approved of this treaty." [11]

The first significant departure by the United States from a traditional noninterference doctrine in Iran was brought about by the publication in *Ra'd,* which was assumed in Tehran to be an unofficial mouthpiece for the British, of a statement that America had tacitly consented to the Anglo-Persian Treaty as part of a noninvolvement policy. Caldwell made a statement denying that America had been aware of the treaty in advance, implying that his country was unhappy with the treaty, and assuring the Iranians

10 See the following: Mostofi, III, 35–125; Dolatabadi, IV, 126; Maki, I, 1–2; M. Bahar, pp. 29–30; Fatemi, p. 28; Balfour, p. 208; Sheean, p. 24.

11 Abraham Yeselson, *United States–Persian Diplomatic Relations 1883–1921* (New Brunswick, N. J., 1956), p. 164.

that the United States delegation had tried to gain a hearing for Iran at Versailles. He and his staff publicly distributed the statement.[12] Tehran had not been so exhilarated by a foreign action since the days of Morgan Shuster.

The estimate made by Iranian historians of the period coincides with Caldwell's account. Iranians believed, furthermore, that the two of their countrymen most responsible for the agreement had received £131,000 for their trouble.[13] This sum was theoretically to have been used to purchase a favorable public reaction, but most Iranians regarded it as a payoff. In any case, the rumor of the payoff was widely believed, and the British were discredited. Convinced that the French and Americans would stand with them against the British, the Iranians gained the heart to step up their anti-treaty campaign: they formed a secret society, the Mojazaad, with the expressed policy of murdering all "lovers of England," and launched a campaign of assassination and terror.[14] Reluctantly the British admitted defeat. When Sayyed Zia, the former editor of *Ra'd*, announced the rejection of the treaty after his *coup d'état*, Iranians regarded the announcement as an open British admission of failure for their plan to establish a protectorate.

Iranian nationalism had won a great victory. Although Iranians had been prevented from utilizing Anglo-Russian rivalry to stave off the bid of the British to make of Iran a dependency, they had, on their own, stood firm and had temporarily humbled one of the world's great powers and one of Iran's traditional enemies. This episode ranks with the 1906 revolution, the deposition of Mohammad Ali, and the Shuster interlude as one of the most glorious events of Iranian nationalism.

But, from another point of view, little was gained by this victory. The belief that Britain could not tolerate the emergence of an independent Iran had been tragically confirmed by the Anglo-Persian Treaty combined with Soviet revelations that in negotiating the Treaty of Constantinople in 1915 the British had been ready to agree to the partitioning of Iran. Furthermore, even while the British were attempting to convince Iran that the agreement

[12] Fatemi, p. 36.
[13] *Ibid.*, p. 24; Sheean, pp. 24–27.
[14] Fatemi, p. 120; Dolatabadi, IV, 126.

would not impair Iranian independence, they had interfered blatantly in Iranian affairs.

The British chief of military mission, General Ironsides, believed that the Iranian Cossacks could not be reorganized until White Russian officers who remained after the Russian army's withdrawal had been removed. Ironsides argued that these Russians had little interest in Iran and would likely involve the Iranian Cossacks in their efforts to overturn the Soviet regime. The Iranians viewed the Russian officers as a vitally necessary counterbalance to increasing British inroads in the Iranian Cossacks; and the government of Moshir al-Doleh, the only postwar prime minister whose patriotism was questioned by no one, refused to remove the Russian officers. Ironsides demanded of the Shah that his recommendations be accepted and hinted that if they were not, the British would withdraw and permit the Soviet force in Gilan, which had already gained control of the Kuchek Khan movement, to do as it willed. Moshir al-Doleh resigned, and a prime minister friendlier to the British was appointed.[15]

Had the Anglo-Persian Treaty and its rejection resulted in a truer understanding on the part of the British and the Iranian nationalists, its long-term effects would have been beneficial. Instead, the opposite was true. Refusing to admit that a genuinely outraged public opinion had been the chief reason for the rejection of the treaty, the British persisted in their unwillingness to accept Iranian nationalism as a fact. The nationalists, on the other hand, assumed that the British had recognized them as a formidable enemy and that they were implacably determined to destroy nationalism, along with freedom and prosperity. This assumption seemed to confirm all of their exaggerated notions of Iranian agents of the British. And thus the negative, intensely anti-British aspect of Iranian nationalism was strengthened, and the prospects for a positive evolution dimmed.

The Bolshevik Dilemma in Iran

As part of the allied anti-Bolshevik campaign following World War I, British troops in Iran were transported to Baku, the capital

15 See Mostofi, III, 168–237; Maki, I, 31–41; Dolatabadi, pp. 157, 184; M. Bahar, p. 59; Fatemi, pp. 102–18.

of the briefly independent Azerbaijan Republic. But in 1920 a Soviet force overwhelmed the British in Baku and then pursued them across the Caspian Sea to the Iranian province of Gilan. Had the Soviet troops that disembarked at Enzeli confined their activities in Iran to a pursuit of the British, there is reason to believe that their intervention would have been accepted and even welcomed. Russia had long been the symbol of reactionary despotism and aggressive imperialism, but some Iranians had already accepted as a fact that Russia was now the chief opponent of reaction and imperialism, and many others were wondering if this assumption were not true. Since Britain was clearly the aggressor against the Soviet Union in 1920, many believed that the Russians were justified in sending troops to oust the British from Iran.

However, the dynamics of the Russian southward drive had not been destroyed by a mere revolution. On the contrary, they now combined with the messianic zeal of the new communist faith to convince the Bolsheviks that by moving into Iran they were not acting as imperialists, but as liberators. Consequently, the Russians sought to rally Kuchek Khan in Gilan and then Khiabani in Azerbaijan to join with them in their holy crusade.[16] In Iranian eyes this was another act in a century-old drama. Once again Qazvin and Tehran trembled at the approach of a Russian army. Once again Iranian sentiment turned sharply against the Russians. The revolution had not, after all, changed much; the historical view of Russia was reinforced.

Regardless of the Iranian view, Russia had drastically changed and that change was reflected in the Russian attitude toward Iranian nationalism. Many writers speak of the hostility of Karl Marx toward nationalism, but they do him an injustice. Marx, in spite of himself, may have had an emotional antagonism toward nationalism, but his intellectual treatment of that subject was logical and consistent and not tied to any value judgment. Marx saw in nationalism one of the major instruments by which the bourgeoisie was able to establish and maintain its control. Nationalism appeared with the bourgeoisie power challenge, and nationalism would disappear when the bourgeoisie finally fell before the proletariat onslaught. It was therefore an essential aspect of the

[16] See Chapter 8.

dialectical process; whether it was a progressive or reactionary force depended entirely on the stage of the dialectic. Hence in the highly industrialized West, where the proletariat was strong, nationalism was a force for reaction. Conversely, in colonial or semicolonial areas such as Iran, nationalism was a progressive force since it would help the bourgeoisie overthrow feudalism, which had to go before the proletariat could make its challenge. Lenin accepted this view wholeheartedly and added to it his own refinement—that nationalism in Asia would serve as a weapon to use against the imperialistic stage of capitalism. The doctrinal line, then, was clear, but regardless of communist doctrine, Russia was a major power and hence subject to the same power drives that characterized other great powers. Also, since the Russian economy was almost totally disrupted at this time, the very survival of Bolshevism demanded a prior concern for internal economic needs. It was inevitable that doctrine, great power drives, and the needs of the internal Russian economy had to conflict.

At the Baku Conference of 1920, however, doctrinal purity was in full ascendance. This conference consisted of delegates from all parts of Asia and was held for the purpose of propounding an Asian policy for international communism. Marx could have been proud of the results: nationalism was to be fostered as a means of speeding up the dialectical process and of combatting imperialism. Democratic elements were to be supported, and the propaganda would focus its attack on the wealthy and the imperialists. Such a line was tailor-made for maximum appeal in Iran and in much of Asia. Furthermore, makers of Soviet policy gave expression to these decisions by negotiating a series of self-denying treaties with Middle Eastern states.[17] By the Treaty of Friendship of 1921 with Iran, for example, Russia renounced the hated capitulations, turned over all Russian assets except the fishery industry to Iran, and promised to withdraw Russian troops from Gilan as soon as the British evacuated south Iran.

All Iran, not only the nationalists, greeted this treaty joyfully, but with a pleasure tempered by a deeply ingrained suspicion.[18] The events in Gilan were too fresh in mind for them to have

[17] Lenczowski, *Russia and the West in Iran,* pp. 6–9.

[18] *Ibid.,* p. 49; Mostofi, III, 250, 266; Dolatabadi, IV, 157, 184; Maki, III, 385; M. Bahar, p. 164; *Kaveh,* August 6, 1921.

reacted otherwise. However, the Soviet trade policy toward Iran which was inaugurated in 1922, even though a trade agreement had not been negotiated, did much to allay these suspicions. This policy was part of a general Soviet trade plan by which merchants from the East would be permitted to market their goods personally in the Soviet Union; Soviet industrial goods would be sold at a lower cost in the East than elsewhere; and the Soviet Union would not insist on a favorable balance of trade with the East.[19] No claim was or could be made that this trade policy was purely for the purpose of encouraging the growth of a bourgeoisie. But this purpose was one of the motivating factors. The effects of the application of this policy for Iran were economically very salutary. Since trade with the Soviet Union, particularly of the northern Iranian provinces, rapidly expanded, all sections of the Iranian population were pleased and wished only to see this trade conventionalized.

Ironically, however, the Iranian government that accepted the Treaty of 1921 was that of Sayyed Zia al-Din Tabatabai, a government that Iranians considered British-sponsored. In all likelihood, the Russians shared this Iranian assessment. Even after Sayyed Zia had fled and Reza Khan had become the real power in Iran, they may well have agreed with the Iranians that British influence was being exerted in Iran through Reza Khan. This British involvement was a real dilemma for the Bolsheviks. What should their attitude be toward a man who was attacking the powers of the wealthy and who sounded so much like a nationalist, but who probably owed his rise to power to the British? Had the Russians been the coldly rational dialecticians they thought they were, there should have been no dilemma. All but the blind could see that Reza Khan was speeding up a profound social revolution. He was doing far more to give Iran a bourgeoisie power base than the communists had any right to expect. So what if the British did sponsor him? In doing so they were merely helping construct the basis for their own inevitable fall from influence in Iran.

This should have been the communist reasoning, but it wasn't. The Bolsheviks, being the successor government of the Tsars, inherited the traditional rivalry with the British in the Middle East littoral area. It was beyond even their ideological devotion to

[19] Lenczowski, *Russia and the West in Iran*, p. 91.

reason away the British challenge. Besides, the alleged British sponsorship of Reza Khan and the 1919 treaty conformed to the concept of capitalist encirclement. Therefore, the Bolsheviks chose to follow a policy of disapproval toward Reza Khan, and not until the latter overthrew the Sheikh of Mohammarah did they give him any applause.[20]

The possibility of exploiting the sentiment of the Kurds for separatism was in stark conflict with communist doctrine but very much in harmony with Russian imperial aims. If George Agabekov can be relied upon as a source, the question of whether or not the Kurds should be supported caused a major policy crisis in the USSR. The OGPU argued pro and the foreign office con, and the foreign office won. The Armenians presented the same kind of opportunity to the Russians, and, in fact, a great many were utilized as agents by the communists.[21] But it was not until Stalin decided to sponsor the Azerbaijan Republic that the choice was made against treating Iran as an indivisible nation.

Another incident forced the Soviets to choose between doctrinal and power political goals. The Iranians were anxious to have their oil in northern Iran developed, but they did not want either a British or a Russian concern to be involved. They preferred a company from a disinterested and far away land such as America. When Sinclair Oil expressed an interest the Iranians were elated. But the difficulty lay in the transporting of the oil. By the terms of the concession of the Anglo-Iranian Oil Company, no other oil company could transport oil across the AIOC concession area without AIOC permission, a permission that could only have been purchased at a heavy price. There remained, however, the possibility of sending the oil to Baku and from there overland to the Black Sea. At first the Russians indicated they would agree to this route. From the doctrinal point of view they should have agreed, for the development of northern oil resources could have hastened the social revolution and hence, by communist theory, the dialectical process. But power political considerations won out; transit was refused, and Sinclair left Iran.[22]

[20] Maki, III, 267.
[21] See Chapter 6.
[22] Maki, II, 145–46.

Even more destructive of the doctrinal approach were the internal economic problems that the Soviet Union faced. The overly generous trade policy of 1922 was found to be placing too great a drain on the crippled Soviet economy. Within a year of the inauguration of this liberal program, the Soviets demanded that their trade representatives in Iran be given diplomatic status and that Iranian tariffs on oil imports from the Soviet Union be lowered. For three years, from 1923 until 1926, the Soviet economic attitude vacillated between the liberal and the bullying. Then in 1926 Soviet policy crystallized. A tight embargo was placed on Iranian exports, and a number of Iranian merchants in Baku were arrested. Although this policy produced severe suffering in northern Iran, the merchants inaugurated a boycott against Russian goods, rather than ask their government to capitulate. In 1927 a treaty was concluded which stabilized the situation somewhat. But even after this time, the Russians engaged in transit obstruction and dumping practices to harass the Iranian economy.[23] Such fluctuations continued throughout the thirties. Once the Five Year Plans were in operation, trade between Iran and Russia fluctuated with the needs of the Russian economy. Gone were any thoughts of using trade to develop the bourgeoisie and thereby to expedite the dialectic.

The Soviet interwar policy toward Iran followed a predictable pattern. An early concern with what should be done according to communist doctrine soon gave way to the necessities of domestic economy and big power rivalry. But, in spite of the economic annoyances, the consequences of Soviet policy in Iran in the days of Reza Shah were not of much significance: the historical anti-Russian bias of Iranian nationalism was not strengthened, although sufficient Russian provocation existed to maintain it.

Britain and the Pahlavi Dictatorship

Iranian nationalism may have won a brilliant victory in forcing the British to abandon their plans for establishing a protectorate, but by late 1921 many ardent patriots were wondering if the

[23] Violet Conolly, *Soviet Economic Policy in the East* (London, 1933), pp. 53–75; *The Near East and India,* February 17, 1927, p. 171; Conolly, "The Industrialization of Persia," pp. 70–73.

triumph had not been Pyrrhic. The domestic situation could hardly have been worse. Ahmad Shah, still an immature youth, showed every sign of being an indecisive monarch; internal security was virtually nonexistent; the Iranian Cossacks were under British influence; and the landowner majority in the Majlis had no interest in seeing a strong regime take over the reins of government. Much of the paralysis was due to a widespread conviction that the British would not permit any improvement. The fact that this conviction was based on false premises detracted not at all from its force and effectiveness.

Most Iranians knew that their country was in dire need of a strong government. Furthermore, it was widely accepted that this government must bypass the Majlis and come into power through a *coup d'état*. In his volume on the *coup d'état* Maki lists the names of six men who were thought to be candidates for leading the *coup*.[24] Tehran debated the merits of the various contenders as if they were to be elected to the office of the "Overthrower of the Government." The Iranians accepted it as axiomatic that the British would be deeply involved in any *coup d'état*. The British had been humbled, true enough, but no one imagined that this would end their interference. On the contrary, all the victory meant was that British interference would be carried out more by Iranians than by Englishmen. Maki even quotes one of the unsuccessful candidates, Nosrat al-Doleh, to the effect that Lord Curzon had asked him to lead a *coup* and that he had refused, not because of principle but because in the bargaining the British had insisted on retaining too many controls over him.[25]

This was the picture as the Iranians saw it. The reader should not be surprised to learn that the next scene thrown on the Iranian screen is of a brilliantly planned and executed British-sponsored *coup d'état*. No "t's" are left uncrossed and no "i's" undotted. Acting through Messrs. Howard, Smart, and Norman, the British selected as the first strong man Sayyed Zia al-Din Tabatabai, and to provide him with military backing they chose an obscure colonel whom British officers believed to be decisive, courageous, and shrewd—Reza Khan. With the actors carefully selected, the play

24 Maki, I, 77–88.
25 *Ibid.*, I, 83.

was produced flawlessly. Now the Anglo-Persian Treaty could be forgotten. Britain had gained control of Iran and at very slight expense—or so goes Iranian reasoning.[26] Just how much of this story is truth and how much is fiction, future historians may possibly tell us. What is pertinent from the point of view of this study is that Iranians from left to right, from lower class to upper class, from democrat to communist accept it as true.

There may be truth in the Iranian account of the *coup d'état,* but the conclusion often drawn from it that Reza Khan was a British agent contains very little truth. Even some of Reza Khan's strongest detractors admit that he had to take into account the viewpoint of the British Legation; British power in Iran was too great for him to do otherwise. But the term "agent" and the concept "treason" carry an absolute flavor that obscures actuality. Assuming that Reza Khan knowingly worked with the British to overthrow the constitutional Iranian regime, was he thereby committing an act of treason? Since they are convinced that the British objective is one of reducing Iran to a colonial status, many Iranians answer in the affirmative. Having thus concluded that Reza Khan was a "traitor," those using the word are forced by its absolute tenor to attempt to prove that throughout his career he remained one. The same individuals who thus describe Reza Khan see no inconsistency in their own willingness to cooperate with a foreign power that would help place in office a regime they regard as patriotic. It was not his working with a foreign power that caused many to view Reza Khan as a traitor, but rather the particular foreign power with which he chose to work and the type of regime he sought to install.

Anyone reading Maki's "History of Twenty Years," for example, will find the unquestioned assumption that the British picked Reza Khan as the potential strong man and then guided him toward the goal of absolute control. This assumption is extraordinarily unlikely. The British may have wanted a strong man in Iran, but their choice was almost certainly the suave, sophisticated Sayyed Zia, who was well schooled in political intrigue, rather than the obscure, barely literate colonel of the Cossacks, Reza Khan. To

26 For this interpretation see the following: Maki, I, 88–98, 100–04; M. Bahar, pp. 62–66, 109–10; Dolatabadi, IV, 219–29; Khajenuri, pp. 83–84; Mostofi, III, 70–72.

believe that even before the *coup* the British foresaw the tortuous path Reza Khan would follow to supreme power is a profound demonstration of the willingness of many nationalists to grant the British a prescience that is truly god-like.

Shortly after he came to power Reza Khan eliminated British influence from the Iranian Cossacks. According to his detractors, this is no argument against the widely accepted view that he only carried out British orders. Those condemning Reza Khan merely counter that the British understood that his popularity had suffered from his reputation of being their agent, and they ordered him to kick them publicly—a logical view, but again one that grants too much cunning to the British. A major argument against the policy of interfering in the affairs of another nation is that interference carries a dynamic quality of its own. The action must be carried out through men who are suddenly raised to power and these "figureheads" come to enjoy their new influence too much to willingly surrender it. General Ironsides had already discovered this truth when he compelled Moshir al-Doleh to resign. A far more likely guess concerning British reaction to Reza Khan's action was that they surrendered their position in the Cossacks reluctantly, rather than accept the alternative of an open break with the strong man. Maki spends many pages developing his thesis that the overthrow of the Sheikh of Mohammarah was engineered by that hapless Sheikh's past protectors in order to boost Reza Khan's popularity.[27] Evidence to the contrary, such as the stong British protests against Reza Khan's advance into Khuzistan, is dismissed as maneuvering to disguise the true British intention.

Although the conclusion that the British guided Reza Khan to power is in error, there is every reason to believe that they were gratified by his forceful control of Iranian affairs. Throughout this study the conclusion has been that the real British objective for Iran was the kind of stability that would not upset the international power balance and would permit British commercial activities to proceed unimpaired. If this conclusion has validity, then the British could only regard the Pahlavi dictatorship as approaching their ideal.

[27] Maki, III, 153–221.

Most of the men in Iran who bear the reputation of being agents of the British have been of the upper class, which under Reza Shah's reign suffered both financially and politically. Yet, there is no evidence that this setback disturbed the British. As the diplomatic correspondence quoted in the previous chapter makes clear, the British supported upper-class politicians in the previous decade only because these were the men thought most capable of maintaining order. The British had no special devotion to this class, as was demonstrated by their willingness to blame its members for leading the agitation against the Anglo-Persian Treaty. Still, the very fact that the British were pleased with the rule of Reza Shah, until the later pro-German part of his reign, gave substance to the widespread conviction that he was their man.

Even the most imaginative of those claiming that Reza Shah was an agent of the British could not explain the increasingly open pro-German stance of the government in the late 1930's. But, they insist, when Reza Shah broke his British leash his doom was sealed; the Anglo-Russian invasion of 1941 was the most natural of consequences.

Impact of Stalin's post-Stalingrad Policy

As the Iranian press and Majlis debates demonstrate, the Anglo-Russian invasion of 1941 and the pathetic dissolution of the much heralded Iranian army produced an intense shock.[28] Today in Iran, with the memory of his tyranny over two decades old, Reza Shah is gaining in popularity. But in 1941 he was seen as an almost sadistically cruel tyrant whose early purposefulness had increasingly given way to a cynical concern for power for its own sake. Thus his deposition was greeted with relief. But it was a relief heavily intermixed with chagrin. Despite the mythology of his having been a British agent, by 1941 most Iranians understood that Reza Shah, however oppressive he might have been, was their own leader and not the lackey of any foreign government.

Reza Shah's overthrow by Iran's two traditional enemies acting in concert brought back bitter memories that had begun to fade. Thirty-four years after the Anglo-Russian Agreement of 1907,

[28] Hossein Kermani, *Az Sharivar 1320 ta Fejeah Azerbaijan Zenjan* (Tehran, n.d.), pp. 250–80.

Iranians again found cause to believe that Great Britain and Russia always operate with secret agreements that only occasionally come to light. Nothing seemed to have changed since the Anglo-Russian condominium of 1914–17. Iranians once again were somewhat pro-German, not because they admired fascism, except in rare cases, but because Germany was fighting their enemies. However, the presence of the United States on the Anglo-Russian side and the understanding many educated Iranians had of Hitler's antiliberal political philosophy reduced the German appeal; the enthusiasm for the German side among liberal nationalists during World War I did not find its parallel in World War II.

The Soviet occupation policy in Iran prior to the Battle of Stalingrad was frightening enough.[29] North Iran was, in effect, sealed off from the rest of the country; foreign correspondents were not permitted to enter the area; economic intercourse from north to south was disrupted. Anglo-American relief measures were needed to keep Iran from starving, because much of the Azerbaijan grain surplus was sent to Russia. These were the days during which Soviet survival stood in precarious balance, and the exclusive concern of Soviet policy in the Middle East was to utilize the resources and transit facilities of that area to defeat the Germans. But very shortly after the critical battle for Stalingrad had been won, Soviet policy makers turned their attention to postwar plans for the Middle East.

With regard to Iran, specifically, the Soviets in 1944 disclosed their two major immediate objectives. During this year Pishevari converted the Azerbaijan branch of the Tudeh Party into the Democrat Party of Azerbaijan, while announcing that Azerbaijan wished and was entitled to political autonomy; he thereby telegraphed the Soviet intention of separating Azerbaijan from Iran. In the late summer of 1944 a Soviet delegation arrived in Tehran to discuss the granting of a major oil concession in northern Iran. Iranian reaction to both lines of attack must have been disappointing to the Soviets. No appreciable separatist sentiment burst forth in Azerbaijan. Instead, the press in Tehran was filled with forebodings of a Soviet plot to seize the province. The Soviet request for an oil concession was met with a bill, sponsored by Dr.

[29] For an excellent description see Lenczowski, *Russia and the West in Iran.*

Mohammad Mossadeq and rushed into law, that prohibited the granting of any concession to any foreign power so long as foreign troops were in Iran.

But these setbacks were minor. Although Iranians like to believe that they had a great deal to do with thwarting the Soviet plans, their role was a minor, though essential, one. Even without the appearance of widespread enthusiasm for a separate Azerbaijan and in spite of an increasingly violent nationalist hostility, the Soviets proceeded with their plan to set up a puppet Azerbaijan regime. Robert Rossow, Jr. has perceptively indicated that the intense Soviet military activity in Azerbaijan coincided with similar military activity on the Bulgarian-Turkish border and with an intensive propaganda campaign for the return to the Soviet Union of Kars and Ardahan and for Soviet control over the Dardanelles. Rossow concludes that the real target of the Soviet maneuvering was Turkey.[30] A broader study may reveal that Rossow's conclusions were too narrow.

The vital ingredients in the Soviet southward move were all to be found in Western weakness. British power had been much reduced; by 1946 many had concluded that henceforth Britain would be a second-class power in international society. The United States, the only nation strong enough to oppose the USSR, was demobilizing as rapidly as possible. Soviet policy makers may have concluded that Western resistance to a major southward drive would be weak or nonexistent and may have decided to go as far as they could without seriously risking a major war.

In all probability the Soviets grossly miscalculated Middle Eastern reaction. The Turks stood firm, as might have been expected, but so did the Iranians to a surprising degree. Had they not done so, the Soviets possibly could have succeeded in their plan. Nevertheless, the government of Ahmad Qavam began to retreat in 1946: Qavam went to Moscow; communists were included in his cabinet; the rightist press was suppressed; Sayyed Zia was arrested and imprisoned. The Qashqai revolt, which many believed was a British-inspired effort, had little lasting effect. Although Qavam dropped the communists from his government, his drift toward acquiescence to the Soviet demands continued.

[30] Rossow, p. 21.

The significant battle raged elsewhere. The United Nations Security Council considered the Iranian protest against the continued presence of Soviet troops in Iran long after the date of their promised withdrawal. In the debate Secretary of State Byrnes strongly asserted the United States' intention to do everything possible to compel the USSR to evacuate Iran. This statement of American intentions, together with the obvious Western determination to assist Turkey in its resistance, must have demonstrated to the Soviets that their plan to move into the Middle East would not be unchallenged.

On April 4, 1946, the break came. The Soviets agreed to withdraw their troops within a month, and the Iranians agreed to establish a joint-stock oil company with the Soviets in which the Soviets would have 51 per cent ownership. Many observers saw this agreement as a great Soviet victory,[31] but in fact it was the beginning of a major retreat. Ahmad Qavam agreed to the oil agreement, but, as he and the Russians well knew, the Majlis had to give its approval. The Fourteenth Majlis had expired. By its own decision, a new election could not be held until foreign troops had left Iran. Thus, the Fifteenth Majlis would be elected and would consider the joint-stock oil company proposal when there were no Soviet troops to compel approval. The United States Ambassador, George V. Allen, gave energetic support to the Iranian determination to resist the Soviets,[32] and with his backing and with pressure from the Shah, the Qavam government moved troops into Azerbaijan. Once again all Iran was under Tehran's control. The Fifteenth Majlis not only refused to accept the oil proposal, but in short order dropped Ahmad Qavam.

The costs of this fiasco from the Soviet point of view were immense. Whatever progress had been made since the Bolshevik Revolution in convincing the Iranian people that Soviet Russia bore no resemblance to the old imperialistic Tsarist Russia was lost. Iranian nationalists came to view the Tudeh Party as analogous to the early twentieth-century pro-Russian aristocrats. Both had demonstrated a willingness to work against their own government and in cooperation with the Russians. Within the Tudeh

[31] *The New York Times,* April 16, 1946, 12:2.
[32] Lenczowski, *Russia and the West in Iran,* p. 310.

Party deep chasms developed. Many Tudehites understood for the first time that the objectives of Iranian nationalism and international communism were inherently contradictory. A considerable number of them, including the brilliant theoretician, Khalil Maleki, left the Tudeh Party at this time. For once, the atavistic attitude of the Iranian nationalists was working in favor of the West. By permitting the nationalists to draw a close parallel between the Soviet policy and that of the Russian imperialists, the Soviet Union engendered a hostility to communism in Iran that many years of Western propaganda could not have produced.[33] Unfortunately, the postwar Western policy did not seize upon this advantage, but persisted in muddying the ideological waters until the Iranian nationalist could see little difference between Western and communist imperialism.

Oil and Nationalism

More frequently than not the politics of Iran are described as orbiting around the question of oil. The reader is entitled to wonder, then, why the oil question has been so lightly considered? In answer, one conclusion of this study, whose primary purpose is to attempt to place Iranian nationalism in perspective, is that nothing has done more to distort the Western image of nationalism in Iran than the overwhelming preoccupation with the subject of oil. Obviously in a country as poor as Iran, the impact of this tremendous resource is economically and politically massive. But Iranians are not mere appendages of their oil supply. They are a proud people with a great history and culture, and they had won an important position in world history long before oil was even thought of. The impact of oil on Iran is so recent that the dominant aspects of the character of Iranian nationalism predate its importance. When the political impact from oil did strike Iran with great force, much of the Iranian nationalist belief system had already been constructed. Consequently, its impact was felt mainly in the strengthening or weakening of already existing beliefs.

[33] *Shahed,* pamphlet on the Tudeh Party, 1952, pp. 57–68. See also Ann K. S. Lambton, "Some of the Problems Facing Persia," *International Affairs,* April 1946, p. 265; Laurence Elwell-Sutton, "Political Parties of Iran: 1941–1948," *Middle East Journal,* January 1949, pp. 54–55.

Failure to understand this point is one of the reasons for the difficulty of resolving the oil dispute. Western negotiators far too frequently have failed to comprehend that their difficulties lie in deeper historical recesses.

In 1901, ten years after the tobacco concessions, an Australian, William Knox D'Arcy, was granted an oil concession by Mozaffar al-Din Shah. By the terms of this concession D'Arcy agreed to pay the Iranian government £20,000 cash, another £20,000 in shares, and 16 per cent of the annual net profits of the company.[34] This compares with the £15,000 the tobacco concessionaires had agreed to grant annually. Not until 1908, a year after the Anglo-Russian Agreement and at the time of the climactic struggle between Mohammad Ali Shah and the liberal nationalists, was the first geyser tapped. Furthermore, not until 1912, after Shuster had left and the first great period of Iranian nationalism had been replaced by Anglo-Russian control, did the oil begin to flow abroad in appreciable amounts. But 1913 was the most important year in the history of oil in Iran. At this time the British Admiralty decided to convert from coal to oil and Iranian oil achieved a profound importance for the British. In 1914 the Admiralty purchased a majority of the shares of the oil company,[35] and from then on oil was destined to become deeply involved in Iranian affairs. But there is little to suggest that prior to 1914 the oil interests in the south were out of proportion to other British commercial interests in Iran as determinants of British policy.

Iranian realization of the importance of the oil resource was delayed a little longer. Nationalist leaders and the rank and file were preoccupied with the war until 1918, and the oil resources were in distant Khuzistan, which had long been virtually autonomous. Confronted with this lack of concern from Tehran, the British, as usual, dealt with the tribal chiefs and local potentates who could establish internal security in the oil producing area. These included, notably, Sheikh Khazal and certain clans of the Bakhtiari tribe, which were paid a handsome subsidy. But the Bakhtiari, hoping to see an improvement in their own position, took advantage of British preoccupation with the war to harass the

[34] Lenczowski, *Russia and the West in Iran*, p. 77.
[35] *Ibid.*, p. 78.

oil producers, particularly by cutting the pipelines. Few acts better illustrate the British attitude in Khuzistan than their response to this harassment. They must have reasoned: "We are suffering considerable financial loss as a result of marauding tribal action. Isn't it absurd to pay Tehran 16 per cent of the profits when the Iranian armed forces make no attempt to control the tribesmen?" They announced to the Tehran government that the costs of repairs due to Bakhtiari raids would be subtracted from Tehran's royalty.[36]

Had the British mobilized their best brain power to draw up the plan most likely to offend the Iranians and least likely to make their own position in Iranian oil secure, they could have done no better. Although Iranians were awakening to the value of their oil resources and would sooner or later have insisted on a renegotiation of the oil concession, it is ironic that the British themselves so rudely hastened the awakening. The Iranians believed that the 16 per cent payment was a ridiculously small figure and placed them under no obligation to protect British equipment. The oil the British were removing was a part of Iran, and the royalty was a payment for the purchase of a vital resource, not a subsidy paid in return for services rendered. Also, in Iranian eyes the British were responsible for the weakness of the Tehran government: in fact, that government was more British than Iranian. When an Iranian government in 1911 had begun to move toward real internal security, the British had helped the Russians destroy it. Furthermore, the British, by paying the Bakhtiaris a subsidy, had made that tribe's independence from central control even greater than before. The British failure to foresee this Iranian attitude was due not so much to obtuseness as to a British inability to empathize. The result was that in the agitation against the Anglo-Persian Treaty, oil for the first time played a significant part. Great Britain's oil policy had added an exclamation mark to a well-established view of British arrogance.

A much misunderstood doctrine attributed to the Mossadeq government was the so-called "oilless economy." Here, as so often in political affairs, terminology can be sufficiently misleading to

[36] Alan W. Ford, *The Anglo-Iranian Oil Dispute of 1951–1952* (Berkeley, 1954), p. 17.

help produce major errors of judgment. An "oilless economy" sounds like the doctrine of an irrational fanatic, and since this was the image of Dr. Mossadeq in many Western minds the phrase was interpreted literally. In fact, however, responsible Iranians have never held such an idea. Their view can be summarized as follows: "Iran has a magnificent, God-given resource which if properly utilized can raise the standard of living of the people, establish a healthy industrial-agricultural economy, and restore much of the prestige and dignity Iran has lost. However, this resource is not an unlimited one and possibly will be exhausted in a half-century. Consequently, it is this generation's duty to posterity to achieve the maximum returns from this great resource. Not only must the monetary returns be at the maximum, but the Iranian government in power must be totally devoted to the holy purpose of utilizing the oil revenues justly. Such a government cannot be the lackey of foreigners, nor, which is saying the same thing, can it be based on the power of the effete ruling families who have no interest other than their own immediate profit. If no such monetary returns can be attained and if no such government can secure and retain office, then it is best that Iran's oil stay underground until these conditions are achieved, despite the suffering that cutting off the oil revenue would produce."

This view, held by many Iranian nationalists, predates Mossadeq. In fact, there is reason to believe that it had the sympathy of Reza Shah. As early as 1922 the Iranians decided on an oil development policy that seemed very sound. They wished to exploit their oil resource in the north and to gain freedom from the British oil monopoly. Consequently, the Majlis agreed that a company of a disinterested power should be invited to explore and develop any northern oil fields that could be located. Standard Oil, an American company, was interested, and negotiations were begun. However, the Anglo-Iranian Oil Company (then called the Anglo-Persian Oil Company) refused to permit the transporting of oil over its area of concession, and since this route was the only economically feasible one, Standard was compelled to negotiate with AIOC. The agreement reached by the two companies would have given AIOC 40 per cent of the profits. Standard officials were surprised that the Iranians refused to accept this arrangement.[37] Given their premises, the Iranians could not have done otherwise; for instead of creating a force which could be used to counterbalance the political weapon that was the AIOC, they would have strengthened the AIOC political leverage by accepting these terms.

A year later, when the Sinclair Oil Company responded to the Iranian invitation, the AIOC again refused to grant permission to transport the oil over their concessional territory. But this time it appeared possible that Sinclair could solve the dilemma by transporting the oil across Russia. As was described earlier, the Russians decided against this possibility, and Sinclair's hopes were dashed. But the Iranians attribute Sinclair's departure to the British.

In 1924 the American consul general, Major Robert W. Imbrie, wandered with an American who was his prisoner to the scene of a religious ceremony at a holy fountain. Imbrie appears to have been a zealous amateur photographer, for he rashly took out his camera. Moments later the crowd, spurred on by a fanatical mullah, fell upon the hapless American and his prisoner with shouts of the "evil eye." Imbrie was beaten to death and his prisoner wounded. A camera was an object of great suspicion among religious elements and the violence of the crowd's response was not abnormal. Feeling ran high in Tehran, and the government only with great difficulty was able to punish those responsible. The interpretation placed on the incident by Iranian nationalists was that the British, who were known to subsidize mullah rabble rousers, had paid to have Imbrie killed in order to frighten off Sinclair.[38] Undoubtedly, the threat to American lives thus manifested had a bearing on the Sinclair decision, but the accidental nature of the encounter makes the Iranian interpretation highly improbable. Its importance lies in the demonstration it gives that as early as 1924 the AIOC had become in Iranian minds part of the British apparatus for daily political interference on every level of activity.

[37] *The Near East,* August 10, 1922, p. 174; August 24, 1922, p. 240; M. Bahar, p. 214; Maki, II, 67–68.

[38] *The Near East,* August 14, 1924, p. 166; August 28, 1924, pp. 214–15.

The first great clash over oil between the British and the Iranians occurred in the depression year 1932. AIOC's royalties and consequently the Iranian government's returns were falling off. Many Iranians, for whom the facts of economics have always been obscure, saw the decline in AIOC's payment as a plot. The press of this period, by now tightly controlled, was filled with such assertions.[39] On December 27, 1932, at the climax of a violent press campaign, Reza Shah cancelled the AIOC concession. For a time it appeared that the British would resort to direct action, but on May 28, 1933, they signed a new contract valid for sixty years and far more favorable to Iran. Henceforth Iran was to receive 20 per cent of the dividends on ordinary shares and four shillings for each ton sold or exported, with a minimum annual guarantee of £1,050,000. The area of the concession was reduced, and AIOC agreed to an accelerated program of training Iranians to assume important positions in the company.[40] In 1944 AIOC voluntarily raised the minimum annual guarantee to four million pounds sterling.[41]

When the Iranians rejected the Russian oil agreement in November 1947, they felt the time was propitious for entering new negotiations with the British. Viewed from the economics of the dispute, there should have been no insoluble problem. Iran wished to engage in an ambitious developmental program that necessitated a marked increase in oil revenue. Britain hated to make any concessions. Oil sales were the chief source of badly needed dollars, and better terms for the Iranians would reduce the dollar inflow. Furthermore a revised agreement with Iran would provide a model for similar revisions elsewhere in the Middle East.

The problem was difficult and major compromises were in order, but it should not have produced an impasse that resulted in a break in Anglo-Iranian diplomatic relations. The precedent for a fifty-fifty solution had been set in Venezuela, and most of the other Iranian demands, which focused on the training of more Iranians and equal treatment by the AIOC of the Iranian and Royal Navy markets, were neither impossible nor unreasonable. Indeed, after

[39] The *Messager d' Tehran* summarizes all of the press for this period. Countless articles following this line are reprinted in that newspaper in the 1932 period.

[40] Lenczowski, *Russia and the West in Iran*, pp. 79–80.

[41] H. H. Hamzavi, *Persia and the Powers* (London, 1947), p. 19.

long and bitter negotiations, the AIOC reportedly agreed to the fifty-fifty formula, an increased minimum guarantee, and a more extensive employment of Iranians in managment.[42] But AIOC, obtuse to the end, had delayed too long. On the seventh of March 1951, before he could present the new, more generous terms to the Majlis, Premier Ali Razmara was assassinated. A few days later, while the conservative royalist Hossein Ala was prime minister, a bill calling for nationalization of the oil industry was rushed through the Majlis. Three weeks after Razmara's death Dr. Mohammad Mossadeq was prime minister, and with overwhelming popular support prepared to implement the nationalization act.

Demands for nationalization had not been noticeable in the early days of negotiations, but by January 1951 they had achieved such force and volume that Ali Razmara was compelled to denounce nationalization as impractical. Iran did not have the technicians to produce and refine the oil nor the tanker fleet and marketing facilities to dispose of it. The British, who persisted in denying the existence of public opinion in Iran, apparently believed that the demands for nationalization were staged by the Iranian negotiators in a clever move to strengthen their hand. They continued to treat the dispute as a bargaining problem in which British technicians and marketing facilities were ranged against Iranian physical possession. But the oil dispute was not this simple for the Iranians. Their goal was to destroy the British ability to interfere in Iranian political affairs through the oil company. If the Mossadeq government and its successors were to put the oil revenue to good use, they had to be responsible only to Iranian public opinion, not to the wishes of the British. The Iranians insisted and deeply believed that they had documentary evidence to prove AIOC political interference.[43] Any settlement they agreed to must end, once and for all, the possibility of such interference.

[42] *Tolu',* September 20, 1951.

[43] This situation was reported fully in the Tehran press in 1951–1952, based on documents allegedly seized when AIOC official offices were raided. It is clearly implied in Mossadeq's first letter to Eisenhower of January 9, 1953, "US Position on Iranian Oil," *Department of State Bulletin,* July 20, 1953, p. 76.

13

MODERN IMPERIALISM: THE REVIVAL OF NATIONALIST MYTHOLOGY

Enter America

Much has been heard of the Yankee-Go-Home campaign in the latter days of the Mossadeq regime, but very little has been written of the strong pro-Americanism of the early Mossadeq days. In 1951 pro-Americanism was one of the most striking features of Iranian nationalism; yet Iran's attitude toward America changed with a dramatic suddenness that is equalled only by its reversal toward Britain after the 1907 Agreement with Russia.

The intensity of the pro-Americanism of early 1951 did not appear overnight. The United States had inherited a legacy of good will from the good works of a number of private American citizens. Morgan Shuster was one of the greatest assets of American diplomacy in Iran. The memory of his wholehearted contribution to Iranian nationalism is very much alive today, and if Shuster made mistakes they were the kind of mistakes that endeared him all the more. The American Presbyterian missionaries were also an asset. Within any large group of individuals such as the missionaries, there were inevitably some who made bad impressions. But these are hardly remembered today, while such men as Dr. Samuel N. Jordan, the head of Alborz College, made a lasting and favorable impression. By their work in the medical and educational fields and by their genuine sympathy for the people, they gained the respect and friendship of many Iranians, including a large number of leaders who were educated in the missionary schools.

Pre-World War II United States foreign policy was scrupulously, sometimes exasperatingly, noninterventionist. But the only time in which the United States ever departed from this policy, over the issue of the Anglo-Persian Treaty of 1919, it did so spectacularly and in favor of the nationalists.[1] This intervention added a great deal to American popularity.

Nor did American participation in the World War II occupation of Iran do any lasting damage to American popularity. The G.I. was a different kind of American from the missionary; but the inevitable unpleasant incidents were offset to a large extent by the good-natured generosity of the troops. Furthermore, there were many excellent American technical missions in Iran during the war.

From 1922 to 1927 Reza Shah made good use of a talented American financial advisor, Arthur Millspaugh. Though the Iranians had wished to have Shuster again, Millspaugh's record was a good one and confirmed their high opinion of the United States.[2] In 1942 Millspaugh was recalled to Iran as a virtual economic tsar. He brought the same competence and energy he had exhibited in his earlier mission; but both Millspaugh and Iran had changed vastly in this twenty-year period. Millspaugh had lost most of his flexibility and Iran had gained a technical bureaucracy that, not unnaturally, regarded itself at least as competent as Millspaugh and his assistants. The combination was an unhappy one, and Millspaugh soon found himself at odds with almost the entire Iranian press and officialdom. As Millspaugh himself laments, the American Embassy in Tehran gave him little support.[3] From the point of view of maintaining rapport with the Iranians, this lack of support was a very wise American decision. Ironically, the British were blamed more for Millspaugh than were the Americans. Millspaugh's most spirited defender in the Tehran press was *Ra'd Emruz,* the organ of Sayyed Zia al-Din Tabatabai, and an open British Embassy endorsement would have produced no more negative an impact on the Iranian nationalists. Perhaps the greatest proof of Millspaugh's personal failure is his book *Americans in Persia,* which reeks of bitterness toward Iran and the

[1] See Chapter 12, pp. 184–85.

[2] Sheean, pp. 135–40. Sheean points out that the Iranian aristocracy did not share this good opinion.

[3] Arthur Millspaugh, *Americans in Persia* (Washington, D. C., 1946), pp. 218–19. This lack of support characterized the second period of the Millspaugh mission.

Iranians and concludes with the startling suggestion of an Anglo-American-Soviet postwar tutelage of Iran.[4]

In 1946 American nonintervention in Iran ended dramatically with the forceful support by Ambassador George Allen of the anti-Soviet policy of Ahmad Qavam and his successors. Allen's vigorous policy did much to repair whatever wartime damage there had been to American popularity among the nationalists. At the same time the United States replaced Great Britain as Soviet enemy number one in Iran, and henceforth became the top priority target of communist propaganda. The chief Soviet tactic was to tar the United States with the British brush by trying to identify American objectives with those of British imperialism. Azerbaijan had done too much to discredit the Tudeh Party for this line to be effective immediately; but memories are short, and by 1953 it had achieved extraordinary success.

In the fall of 1949 Mohammad Reza Pahlavi made a trip to the United States, apparently in the expectation of receiving a handsome and generous gift. America was spending billions of dollars on world economic recovery in order to forestall the communist advance, and Iran stood on the communist threshold. Furthermore, Iran had amply demonstrated its seriousness of purpose. The Iranian government had had the Morrison-Knudsen Company prepare the preliminaries for an economic plan, and in 1948 the government brought Max Thornburg and a group of specialists, organized as the Overseas Consultants Incorporated, to draw up a detailed and philosophically integrated plan for economic and social development. Surely the stage was set for a major loan. But, apparently much to his chagrin, the Shah received from the Truman administration little more than lectures on the necessity of carrying out reforms and ending corruption.[5]

The United States failure to permit the Shah to return home bearing gifts is often denounced by those commenting on this period, but there is a great deal to be said for this type of diplomacy. Without question, the Shah's prestige did suffer, but that of the United States did not. This period was one in which the so-called thousand families were in firm control of the Majlis and the top

[4] *Ibid.*, pp. 244–65.

[5] *The New York Times*, February 14, 1950, 22:1.

bureaucracy. To give the Shah what he asked for would have been to confirm a belief that the United States need only be approached correctly, i.e. in terms of an anticommunist struggle, in order to gain lavish loans which could then be parcelled out among the deserving.

Six months later General Ali Razmara was appointed prime minister, and it was widely believed in Iran that Razmara was the American as well as the British choice.[6] Much of this belief was due to a misimpression created by the activities of a member of the American Embassy staff. If the Iranian press is to be believed, this man entered into Iranian political intrigue in behalf of Razmara with such energy and in a manner so contrary to traditional American diplomacy that it is difficult to believe his activities were authorized.[7] However, since this type of working-level interference was expected in Tehran, Iranians cannot be blamed for assuming that his actions represented official policy. Besides, enthusiasm for Razmara was widespread among Americans, as *The New York Times* dispatches of this period demonstrate.[8] Furthermore, since Razmara was believed to be a strong-minded reformist, his appointment seemed to be a natural follow-up to the Shah's disappointing American tour. Americans and other Westerners writing of this period are almost unanimous in condemning the failure of the United States to give greater support to Razmara. He was identified as the United States choice for prime minister; he was described as being pro-Western; he was a tough leader; and he was willing to inaugurate reforms.

Modern Iranian history has more than its share of mythology; and Iran, the Soviet Union, and the Western powers seem to have been in wild competition for top honors in self-delusion. Since interpretations of the Razmara regime reflect this massive confusion, the objective historian of the period has great difficulty sifting the fact from the fiction of the various interpretations. Razmara was called reformist-minded, but the men whose elections to the Sixteenth Majlis were engineered by the Army, of

6 *The New York Times,* March 8, 1951, 1:6.

7 Throughout the 1951–52 period the name of Gerald Dooher and descriptions of his activities at the time of the premiership of General Ali Razmara made an almost daily appearance in the Tehran press.

8 See for example *The New York Times,* January 26, 1951, 7:1.

which Razmara was chief-of-staff, were among the most reactionary in the Majlis. Razmara was called pro-West, but he did far more to accommodate Iranian policy to the USSR than did Dr. Mossadeq. Happily, the meaning of the Razmara regime and of its alleged American support is clear with respect to Iranian nationalism. Nationalism reigned supreme after Razmara's assassination, and the overwhelming sentiment among the victorious Nationalists was that Razmara's removal, even by assassination, was fully justified. In fact, the Mossadeq government was condemned for jailing Razmara's assassin, who a year later was released under popular pressure.[9]

The widespread belief that Razmara had been the choice of the United States did not do the damage to American prestige that might have been expected, because of a strange, largely fictional, but not unnatural Iranian conclusion. Iranian politicians had long regarded the major foreign embassies or legations as prime sources of domestic political power, and as good politicians they had made careful investigations of the views of the embassy personnel. They discovered that these views varied greatly within embassies. For the Iranian political mentality the internal embassy conflicts presented challenges bursting with potential for exploitation. In post-World War II Iran the American Embassy became a political target, and Iranians thought they saw there a major difference in attitude toward Razmara and the Nationalists. Consequently the American Embassy as a whole was not blamed for the United States support given Razmara; a faction within the embassy was blamed. And when Mossadeq came to power, the Nationalists were ready to believe that the pro-Mossadeq faction in the embassy could work with them.[10]

A word must be said at this point of the usage in this study of the capitalized "Nationalist." There were and are many men in Iran who stood in solid opposition to Dr. Mossadeq and yet who must be described as "nationalists." Razmara was surely such a man, as were a number of his followers. However, at the time of

[9] Denunciations of the Nationalists for this imprisonment were not limited to *Zelzeleh*, the organ of the Fedayan Islam, but in nationalistic journals generally his imprisonment was regarded as an injustice.

[10] The Iranian newspapers described the head of the United States Information Agency in Iran, Edward Wells, as the leader of this faction.

the Sixteenth Majlis election, a group of Iranians with Dr. Mossadeq as their accepted leader adopted the title "Melliyun," which comes very close to the meaning of "nationalist." The title stuck, and even today when the term "nationalist" is used in Iran the meaning it connotes for most is that of a follower of Dr. Mossadeq. A "Nationalist," then, as used in this study, is one who sought to destroy British influence and thousand-family control and who supported Dr. Mossadeq. It is a belief of this study that from March 1951 to July 1952 the coincidence of Nationalist and nationalist was almost one to one. After midsummer 1952, however, many nationalists began drifting away from the Nationalists.

The policy of the United States in the first year and one-half period of Dr. Mossadeq's government seemed to confirm the view that many American officials looked upon the Nationalists with favor. The United States was widely credited with having used pressure on the British to abstain from outright military intervention and to engage in active negotiations with Mossadeq.[11] Other signs of favorable United States policy were the continuation of the American military mission to Iran and the inauguration of a Point IV program at the rate of twenty-three million dollars per year.

But the Nationalists viewed the struggle with the British as an absolute one which could only be settled by the total destruction of the British ability to interfere. Thus, whereas the United States gained popularity by placing pressure on the British, it offset this popularity by placing pressure also on the Iranians,[12] which, of course, it had to do, considering the Anglo-American partnership in the Cold War. The Iranians could only have been satisfied by a 100 per cent espousal of their position by the United States. Since such a policy would probably have been unwise even if only Iran had been taken into account, the propaganda opening for the communists was a large one. The use they made of it was brilliant.

11 Although assertions to this effect were made repeatedly in private conversations, it is a significant indication of the sensitivity of the Nationalist press to the charge that they served the Americans that no article to this effect was published in the Nationalist newspapers.

12 See Mossadeq's letter to Eisenhower for an example of this attitude. *Department of State Bulletin,* July 20, 1953, pp. 74–77.

The Iranian belief that the Mossadeq government had the support of the American Embassy was both the greatest asset and the greatest liability for the American government. This paradox was true because of a historical contradiction which was not recognized until Mossadeq's time. Iranians simultaneously believed that (a) all of Iran's ills could be ascribed to foreign interference and hence foreign interference per se was an evil, and that (b) foreign interference was inevitable and Iran needed a disinterested foreign power which would support Iranian independence against the avarice of the British and the Russians. Thus Iranian Nationalists wanted all-out help from the United States, but such help would clearly be interference and they opposed interference. Since the articulate element of the population believed in the inevitability of foreign interference, they could be much more enthusiastic about Mossadeq because he was thought to have the added strength of foreign support; their enthusiasm would have been less if he were viewed as a heroic but futile figure bashing his head against the foreign power wall. But these same individuals resented foreign intervention, even on their side, and responded to denunciations of that intervention.

The ambivalence being only too obvious, the Tudeh press made the most of it. *Besu Ayandeh,* for example, stated, "Dr. Mossadeq, by following the policy of obeying the instructions of the Americans, is wasting the fruits of victory this nation has obtained in its movement to free Iran from the clutches of the imperialistic oil magnates." [13] The long-standing Tudeh propaganda theme that American policy was similar to British policy was constantly pushed, together with the assumption, either implicit or explicit, that Mossadeq was the tool of the Americans. Thus pictured, the two primary American-Mossadeq objectives were to betray the Iranian desire for independence by selling oil to the Americans or to an American-British partnership and by converting Iran into a gigantic military base. According to *Razm,* "Dr. Mossadeq and his friends in the so-called National Front are dancing to the tune of imperialistic America. They have no other intention but to arrange a quick victory for the American oil-eaters in

[13] *Besu Ayandeh,* September 26, 1951.

their campaign against imperialistic Britain."[14] *Besu Ayandeh* wrote, "Loy Henderson, the American Ambassador, interferes in all our foreign and internal affairs. The Iranian Army and Gendarmerie are under the complete control of the American advisors. American secret agents are constantly among the Iranian tribes in the interests of American imperialism."[15] The best summary of Tudeh propaganda appeared in the small paper, *Moadda*. "An old man of eighty [Mossadeq] who was called 'Man of the Year' by the American [magazine] *Time* together with another man [Kashani] who calls himself a spiritual leader have conspired to change their old masters with American masters. The British are not as prosperous as before. The Americans are richer."[16]

Of course, the Tudeh was vulnerable on the count of having a foreign master, and the meaning of Azerbaijan had not yet faded. Furthermore, the Nationalist press, in particular the newspaper *Shahed,* hammered at the theme of the Tudeh treachery. But the National Front, not the Tudeh, was in power, and even those readers who condemned the Tudeh as a Soviet tool were impressed with its propaganda line. *Besu Ayandeh,* the largest of the Tudeh papers, had a circulation of several thousand and ranked among the most popular papers in Iran. Many noncommunists read it, for politically aware Iranians follow several newspapers, including those with which they agree and a selection of those with which they disagree.

The Tudeh propaganda succeeded in placing the National Front on the defensive—a very great achievement. The Mossadeq government believed that it had American support and wished to retain and strengthen that support; but the suspicion of Anglo-American collaboration was strong, and when former Ambassador Henry Grady hinted in 1951 that the State Department was following British advice, Iranian Nationalists nodded knowingly.[17]

[14] *Razm,* October 1, 1951.

[15] *Besu Ayandeh,* February 1, 1952.

[16] *Moadda,* January 22, 1952.

[17] See the interview of Grady in *US News and World Report,* October 19, 1951, pp. 13–17, and an even more explicit statement in *The New York Times,* October 18, 1952, 5:5. For the Iranian view see *Bakhtar Emruz,* March 30, 1951.

Every time the United States put pressure on the Iranians to negotiate, the Iranian fear and suspicion grew.

If ever American policy makers had an excuse for failing to comprehend a situation, this was the time. The Iranian atavistic attitude was incomprehensible to men who tried to see the oil dispute in modern perspective. When Averell Harriman was sent to Iran in July 1951, he suggested the only logical and practical compromise: that the British accept Iranian ownership and the Iranians agree to utilize British technicians and marketing facilities. Both parties were willing to negotiate on these terms, and the Labor government's negotiator, Richard Stokes, was realistic and sympathetic. A solution to the dispute seemed possible. But negotiations failed on an issue that appeared to be absurdly picayune. The British proposed that the industry would be operated by an organization composed primarily of Britons, although Iranian supreme authority would be recognized. The Iranians insisted that the British technicians could only be employed on an individual contract basis, an arrangement to which the technicians had announced they would never agree.[18] The Iranians stood firm on this point, and the negotiations failed.

The Iranians believed that the proposed British oil organization would have continued the past policy of political interference and that nationalization would have been to no avail if the Stokes terms had been accepted. What must have appeared to Stokes as exasperating fanaticism was actually a deeply held conviction that had been in genesis for almost fifty years. Had this fact been recognized, it is conceivable that the British either could have given such guarantees to their technicians as to have persuaded them to accept the Iranian terms or could have taken other steps to prove to the Iranians that their oil officials would not again engage in internal political interference. But this most crucial fact was never recognized, and by the time a proposal of the International Bank was under consideration the Iranian view had hardened to the point where no British technicians would be accepted.[19]

Throughout the period of futile oil negotiations, American-

[18] Ford, p. 96.
[19] *Bakhtar Emruz,* January 6, 1952.

Iranian relations became more and more strained. Ambassador Henderson continued in his efforts to mediate the oil dispute, but no progress could be made. Furthermore, the Mossadeq government was weakening perceptibly. Kashani, Hossein Maki, and Dr. Mozaffar Baqai, who had been among Mossadeq's most powerful supporters, broke with the government; the aristocratic right was gaining heart, and its leader, General Fazlollah Zahedi, was engaged in open intrigue. Also, an increasing number of clerical leaders were moving into the open opposition. As his coalition narrowed Mossadeq was driven in the direction of dictatorship, and as he became more dictatorial his moderate, middle-class support began falling off.

In this period Mossadeq desperately needed United States support, and he swallowed his pride to ask for it directly. Even before Dwight Eisenhower had assumed office, Mossadeq sent him a letter in which he appealed for the support of the new administration. In this letter Mossadeq placed his cards squarely on the table:

> Unfortunately the government of the United States, while on occasions displaying friendship for Iran, has pursued what appears to the Iranian people to be a policy of supporting the British Government and the former company. In this struggle it has taken the side of the British Government against that of Iran in international assemblies. It has given financial aid to the British Government while withholding it from Iran and it seems to us it has given at least some degree of support to the endeavors of the British to strangle Iran with a financial and economic blockade.[20]

Having received a neutral, noncommittal reply, Mossadeq tried again. On May 28, 1953, he wrote:

> The Iranian nation hopes that with the help and assistance of the American Government the obstacles placed in the way of the sale of Iranian oil can be removed, and that if the American Government is not able to effect a removal of such obstacles, it can render effective economic assistance to enable Iran to utilize her other resources. This country has natural resources other than oil. The exploitation of these resources would solve the present difficulties of the country. This, however, is impossible without economic aid.
>
> In conclusion, I invite your Excellency's sympathetic and responsive

[20] *Department of State Bulletin,* July 20, 1953, pp. 76–77.

attention to the present dangerous situation of Iran, and I trust that you will ascribe to all the points contained in this message the importance due them.[21]

This was an audacious message, approaching effrontery. The United States was known to believe that a settlement of the oil dispute was the only solution for Iran. But Mossadeq ignored even the possibility of such a settlement and demanded United States support anyway. Implicit throughout his letter was the threat that the alternative to American assistance was communism. Much of modern diplomacy has a tinge of blackmail, but this letter reeked of it. Nor was the communist threat an idle one. Theoretically the Tudeh Party had been outlawed in 1949, but its operations through front organizations were increasingly arrogant. Its vigorous press included papers that appealed to every major interest group except the landowners. The Yankee-Go-Home campaign, obviously the Tudeh's, was just as obviously conducted with Mossadeq's permission. Still, it was not true that the Tudeh and the National Front were in alliance. Prior to July 21, 1952 (known as 30 Tir), they had been in bitter opposition. After the collaboration of 30 Tir, although the Nationalists firmly refused Tudeh proposals for a popular front,[22] anti-Tudeh activities of the government slackened and the party was permitted considerable freedom. This change was a far cry from coalition, but it was enough to frighten many Americans.

Why did Mossadeq pursue this policy? There are two major reasons, one ideological and the other tactical. Ideologically the National Front has never subscribed to the view that communism can be destroyed by physical suppression. It has argued that the roots of communism must be located and their nourishment eliminated. This view is a respectable one to which many in the West would subscribe. But the question can legitimately be asked if the occasion might not arise when the danger of a communist victory would be great enough that suppression would be justified in order to gain time to deal with the root cause.

The tactical side of the Mossadeq policy had little justification. He refused to suppress either the Tudeh or the feudalistic right,

[21] *Ibid.*, p. 76.

[22] *The New York Times*, July 23, 1952, 1:1; July 24, 1952, 1:2; July 28, 1952, 5:5.

even though many of his followers demanded that he suppress both. In Mossadeq's mind the Tudeh was the Soviet party and the feudal right the British party. The role of Iranian statesmen during the preceding fifty years had been to maintain a balance between these powers, and Mossadeq was attempting to govern in this tradition. American people were known to be frightened of communism almost to the point of hysteria. Surely, then, the best policy would be to permit the Tudeh to play the bogeyman role. This view pretended to be realistic. But it underestimated the strength both of the right and of the Tudeh; it overestimated the tie-in of the right with the British; and it demonstrated a gross misunderstanding of American psychology. By toying with American fear of communism, Mossadeq unleashed a force that was to destroy him.

Exit Britannia

Even in the final days of Mossadeq's rule, when the tide of nationalism was ebbing and the old man was becoming increasingly dictatorial, the press was, in spite of a severe but sporadically invoked press law, surprisingly free. In the earlier Mossadeq days Iran had known real freedom for the first time since the early period of the constitution, and freedom of the press approached license. It was then that Iranians gave vent to their wrath toward the British, an unhealthy fury composed of hatred and veneration. Nowhere in the world is British cleverness so wildly exaggerated as in Iran, and nowhere are the British more hated for it. The picture that emerges from a study of the Iranian press and its rantings about the British in those days is a weird fantasia. Nor were the attacks limited to the communist and Nationalist press. On the contrary, many of the wildest charges were recorded by men of the far right, men, many believed, who protested too much. That Britain should be blamed for Iraqi hostility to Iranian claims to oil-rich Bahrein Island should surprise no student of the Middle East; [23] but the revelations that the British authored Turkey's hostile Iranian policy and originated the mediation efforts of Pakistan's ambassador to Iran [24] must have shocked both coun-

[23] ***Ettelaat,*** May 4, 1952; ***Keyhan,*** May 8, 1952; ***Bakhtar Emruz,*** April 23, 1952; May 5, 1952; ***Nabard Bayar,*** May 6, 1952.

[24] ***Farman,*** May 3, 1952; ***Pan-Iranism,*** April 24, 1952; ***Siassi,*** March 6, 1952.

tries. Likewise, British sponsorship of the ousting of Nahas Pasha in Egypt through the instrumentality of King Farouk [25] bears a familiar ring for those who follow Middle Eastern nationalism; but the description of the International Bank as an agent of British imperialism [26] is an Iranian addition to Anglophobic mythology.

The old belief that the landowning "ruling class" and the clergy were frequent recipients of British subsidies found expression in the communist and Nationalist press and even in the supposed organs of the landowners.[27] Similarly, the conviction that the British have done much of their intriguing in Iran through the medium of the tribes was demonstrated in the spring of 1952 when the British chargé took a trip to Shiraz and the press literally followed him every step of the way, speculating as to his dishonorable plans. When the British consulates were closed in provincial centers, the press assumed that the Iranian government had so acted because the consulates were primarily engaged in tribal intrigue.[28]

The belief that the British were seeking among rightist strong men the ideal Iranian ruler had deep roots, and it had been reinforced within recent years by the conviction that Reza Shah was British sponsored. The leading National Front evening paper, *Bakhtar Emruz,* carried a series of articles describing British efforts to discover another puppet ruler to replace their favorite for the job, Ali Razmara, who had been assassinated.[29] The rightist *Tolu'* agreed fully that the British had sponsored Razmara, but *Tolu'* claimed Razmara had held out for too favorable terms for Iran in the negotiations with AIOC, and "therefore the British shot him." [30]

25 *Shahed,* January 31, 1952; *Bakhtar Emruz,* May 28, 1952; *Asia Javan,* January 30, 1952; *Besu Ayendeh,* February 19, 1952.

26 *Bakhtar Emruz,* January 6, 1952; January 8, 1952; *Keyhan,* March 10, 1952; *Iran,* March 17, 1952; *Asnaf,* January 5, 1952; *Ettelaat,* February 3, 1952.

27 For typical examples see *Shahed,* January 30, 1952; *Pan-Iranism,* April 12, 1952; *Bakhtar Emruz,* April 14, 1952; *Dad,* January 5, 1952; *Nabard Bayar,* May 26, 1952; *Atesh,* February 25, 1952.

28 *Bakhtar Emruz,* January 10, 1952; January 13, 1952; March 5, 1952; April 7, 1952; April 13, 1952; *Ettelaat,* January 20, 1952; *Farman,* May 31, 1952; *Nabard Bayar,* April 12, 1952; *Atesh,* September 19, 1951; October 10, 1951.

29 *Bakhtar Emruz,* February 25, 1952; March 6, 1952; March 12, 1952.

30 *Tolu',* September 20, 1951.

A foreign visitor viewing Iran for the first time and attempting to understand its politics would have been astonished to learn in the press of 1951–52 that all Iran's politicians, without exception, were British agents. If he read the rightist or communist press of the time, he would see that the Nationalists were American agents with secret British sponsorship; in the Nationalist and communist press he would learn that the rightists were long-term British agents; and in the Nationalist and rightist press he would discover that the Tudeh Party was the joint property of the British and the Russians.[31] As *Shahed* wrote: "Political circles in Iran say that the Tudeh Party has now been divided into the British and Soviet groups. The British control the propaganda and financial sections of the party." [32] This statement reflected the belief that a secret Anglo-Russian understanding always existed, a belief which found expression at many other points. For example, a stiff Russian protest at the receipt of American armed assistance was regarded as proof of an Anglo-Russian alliance, since the effect of the note weakened the Iranian government at the moment it needed all of its strength to fight the British.[33]

Those who know Iran will recognize that there is no exaggeration in this picture. The really lunatic allegations against the British, and they are legion, have been ignored here, but the reader should understand that locust plagues, drouths, and crop failures have been ascribed by the more primitive to the evil design of the British. No greater mistake could be made by those attempting to understand Iran than to dismiss or minimize the significance of this disturbed thinking. Many of the saner allegations have factual, historical precedents, and their atavistic force remains strong.

In 1952 the Iranians enjoyed the ultimate satisfaction of

[31] See the following examples: Communist press—*Besu Ayendeh,* January 10, 1952; February 12, 1952; March 19, 1952; March 27, 1952; April 1, 1952. National Front—*Keyhan,* October 29, 1951; *Bakhtar Emruz,* January 30, 1952; June 3, 1952; *Pan-Iranism,* March 13, 1952; April 12, 1952; May 20, 1952; *Shahed,* December 8, 1951; April 12, 1952. Rightist—*Farman,* February 2, 1952; *Tolu',* September 19, 1951; September 20, 1951; December 13, 1951; January 11, 1952; *Atesh,* October 1, 1951; October 7, 1951; *Nabard Bayar,* April 7, 1952; *Nabard Mellat* (Fedayan Islam) February 28, 1952; *Dad,* January 14, 1952; May 21, 1952.

[32] *Shahed,* January 29, 1952.

[33] *Shahed,* May 27, 1952.

breaking diplomatic relations with Great Britain and watching the English leave the soil of Iran. Very few were sorry to see them go. The historically conscious Iranians understood the balancing role the British had played in the past, but the British were no longer needed for this purpose. America was now the strongest power of the West, and the American government had expressed its determination to help secure the Middle East from Soviet aggression. Why maintain relations with the British? No progress was being made toward settling the oil dispute, and the belief that the British had no intention of ever settling it with Dr. Mossadeq had become a firm conviction. This belief led to one assumption: that the British in time-honored fashion would try to overturn Mossadeq. They had many weapons at their command: oil revenues had been cut off; a tight economic blockade had been imposed; and the pro-British "ruling class" was waiting like a great vulture to devour the emaciated National Front frame. Thus nothing was to be gained as long as the British remained in Iran, and much was to be lost since they would be free to contact their allies among the rightist opposition.

Ambassador Grady, who had close dealings with the British diplomats, has indicated that he was in fairly close agreement with the Iranian assessment.[34] Although confronted with a massive demonstration of Iranian public opinion, the British persisted in their refusal to recognize this opinion as fact. The great majority of the moneyed interests were opposed to Mossadeq, but the British continued to believe that the popular eruption was purchased and staged. Where the National Front could have found the financial means to do so was never made clear. Since the British may have underestimated the internal communist threat and, in any case, knew that the communists were pouring vast sums into fighting Mossadeq, it is unlikely they saw the source of the funds in the USSR. Some British oil men were said to believe that the Americans might be taking advantage of the Mossadeq movement to break the British oil monopoly in Iran. But it is the conclusion of this study that on the whole the British did not engage in this line of reasoning. They seemed to accept as a mat-

[34] *The Saturday Evening Post,* January 5, 1952, p. 30.

ter of faith the cliché, "There is no such thing as public opinion in Iran."

Nationalism need not be "extremist," negative, and a source of disruption; on the contrary, it can be a vital positive force. The British did a great deal to mold the character of the emerging nationalism in Iran, and by refusing to accept nationalism as a fact and by opposing its every manifestation, they bear a major responsibility for its extremism and negativism.

USSR: Years of Recuperation

In the immediate postwar years, both British and Soviet policy in Iran attracted the enmity of Iranian nationalists. But whereas the supposedly realistic British refused even to admit the existence of this enmity, the Soviets, who are popularly viewed as rigidly doctrinaire, were perfectly capable of making a fundamental reassessment of their situational assumptions. The nationalist line in the Tudeh press recognized all of the subtleties of nationalist folklore and made the most of them. Having failed spectacularly in 1946, the Russian bear quietly licked its wounds for the next few years, and the Tudeh propaganda organs worked to repair the damage of the Azerbaijan fiasco. For the unemployed intelligentsia, who were willing to believe that only a reactionary social order stood between them and social prestige and economic prosperity, the Tudeh had a made-to-order appeal. Most of this group were nationalistic, however, and the appeal was blunted by the suspicion that the Tudeh was a tool of historic Russian imperialism. The Tudeh met this suspicion squarely. Instead of denying any Tudeh-Soviet alliance, the Tudeh propagandists developed the theme that the old Russian imperialism had no connection with present Soviet objectives. The Soviet Union was depicted as the one great power that fully sympathized with Iranian nationalist aspirations.[35] Even the Azerbaijan question was met head-on. The Tudeh insisted that Western propagandists had grossly misinterpreted the Soviet role there and that actually the Pishevari regime was a patriotic Iranian regime which wished to overturn the British-feudal class alliance

[35] *Asr No*, June 9, 1952; *Jarras*, November 20, 1951.

that governed in Tehran.[36] This approach was probably the best possible under the circumstances, and it provided a rationalization for those seeking an answer to their own social and economic insecurity.

However, the sudden appearance of the victorious Nationalist regime of Dr. Mossadeq upset the Tudeh plans and confronted the Soviets with a major dilemma. Had the old doctrinaire dialectical approach of 1920–23 been relied on, the obvious line would have been to support the National Front. But the Iranian policy of the USSR has little comfort to offer those who see Soviet policy as doctrinairely based. The National Front was initially anticommunist, partly because it wished to attract sympathetic United States support. Since the Soviet Union was fighting any and all American inroads in the area, it could hardly look with tolerance on the new regime—a regime which was that much more dangerous for having such overwhelming popularity.

The policy the Soviets chose to follow was violently anti-Mossadeq. The Tudeh press attempted to smear Mossadeq and the United States with the imperialist brush and to depict themselves as the only true nationalists.[37] But this propaganda line fell flat as American-Mossadeq relations became increasingly strained and as Mossadeq became a symbolic force rather than an ordinary leader. Unquestionably the line did have an effect, but one chiefly manifested in compelling the National Front to maintain its nationalist purity and to refuse any political compromise that would have lent credence to the Tudeh argument. Consequently the Tudeh propaganda damaged its own base of credulity.

After 30 Tir (July 21, 1952) the criticism of Mossadeq in the Tudeh press eased, but members of the National Front, particularly those such as Khalil Maleki who had once been in the Tudeh, were attacked. There is not much doubt today, with the benefit of hindsight, that the Soviet line was a major error. In an effort to maintain their hold on the Tudeh faithful, the Soviets permitted the isolation of the Tudeh and the Soviet Union from the extremely popular Nationalists. Therefore when the United States began moving further away from Mossadeq, the National-

[36] See *Rahnema Mellat,* October 28, 1951.
[37] See pp. 212–13.

ists were not able to believe, as were Arab nationalists later, that the USSR offered alternate support. Suspicion of the Soviet Union increased among the Nationalists as a result of the Tudeh attacks on Mossadeq; and when Mossadeq did attempt to frighten the United States with the Tudeh, he frightened many of his erstwhile supporters as well. The West can be very thankful for these Soviet tactics. Had the Khrushchev foreign policy been in effect from 1951 to 1953, the history of the last decade in Iran might have been very different.

Normally the Soviets were content to work through the Tudeh press, but in 1952 they took an open stab at the Mossadeq government. The question at issue was the continuation of American military aid. Many Nationalists had favored its discontinuation, but Mossadeq, after persuading the State Department to interpret away most of the strings Congress had specified for such aid, agreed to its continuation. The Soviets responded with a strong, implicitly threatening note. This note unified Iran as few things have done—and the Tudeh received its most stinging setback since 1946. *Tolu'* charged, "The Soviet note is a stab in the back and reminds one of Mussolini's attack on France in 1941." [38]

Twenty-Eight Mordad

When Mossadeq wrote his final letter to President Eisenhower in May 1953, the stage was being set for a major development. The internal opposition to Mossadeq had crystallized, and both his strength and weakness had been fully revealed. The opposition, a large section of which had recently come out into the open, included most of the Court, the landowners, the big merchants, the general officers of the armed forces, and the right wing clerical leaders. Splits had occurred within the National Front, and even the loyal element lost much of its past enthusiasm.

The National Front had believed that it possessed a tremendous lever to apply against Britain and the West because the West needed Iran's oil. But within a matter of months the disruption to the world's oil supply resulting from the closing of Abadan was overcome, and many oil producers feared that the reopening of the Iranian oil supply would upset the new equilibrium. The

[38] *Tolu'*, May 25, 1952.

Iranian lever proved to be a weak reed. Mossadeq's supporters could anticipate little but economic stagnation and growing unrest, and the enthusiasm of 1951 was transformed into despair. Something had to be done to reverse the trend, or the Mossadeq regime would fall of its own weight. Deprived of the lever of oil, Mossadeq boldly seized another lever: the threat to go communist which was implicit in his letter of May 28 to President Eisenhower. This time Mossadeq succeeded in prodding the American government into action. But the American policy response was the reverse of his expectations.

On June 29, 1953, Eisenhower replied to Mossadeq. He concluded:

> I fully understand that the Government of Iran must determine for itself which foreign and domestic policies are likely to be most advantageous to Iran and to the Iranian people. In what I have written, I am not trying to advise the Iranian Government on its best interests. I am merely trying to explain why, in the circumstances, the Government of the United States is not presently in a position to extend more aid to Iran or to purchase Iranian oil.
>
> In case Iran should so desire, the United States Government hopes to be able to continue to extend technical assistance and military aid on a basis comparable to that given during the past year.
>
> I note the concern reflected in your letter at the present dangerous situation in Iran and sincerely hope that before it is too late the Government of Iran will take such steps as are in its power to prevent a further deterioration of that situation.[39]

Eisenhower's letter was made public and was broadcast to Iran over the Voice of America. All Iran knew that Mossadeq had gambled and lost in his attempt to force the United States into active support. Here was the cue for the fence sitters to leap as far from Mossadeq as possible. The rightist opposition was elated; the Nationalists were deeply depressed. For Mossadeq the Eisenhower letter opened a new and inglorious phase of a career of public service that had known moments of real glory. The man who had been devoted to liberal democracy now accepted dictatorial leadership and even staged a typically totalitarian plebiscite in which over 99 per cent of the people voted as he wished. His instinct to be suspicious, always highly developed, became almost

[39] *Department of State Bulletin,* July 20, 1953, pp. 75–76.

paranoid, and his colleagues found him increasingly difficult to work with. Still he persisted with the gamble he had already lost. On the afternoon of 30 Tir the Tudeh was permitted to hold a public meeting in Parliamentary Square following a parallel meeting of the National Front in the morning. The Tudeh crowd was said to have outnumbered the Nationalists by five or even ten to one and to have attracted between 50,000 and 100,000 demonstrators.[40] Still Mossadeq refused to recognize his great danger. The United States had publicly announced its total lack of confidence in him; his followers were drifting into apathy; and the Tudeh was emerging as the strongest organized political force in the nation.

On August 16, 1953, the right wing of the Army struck. Armed with a royal order appointing General Fazlollah Zahedi prime minister, a coalition of retired and active officers, mostly of the rank of colonel or above, attempted a *coup d'état.* They failed miserably. The Shah fled the country in inglorious haste, and the right wing beat an undignified retreat. *Ettelaat,* the nation's largest newspaper and one whose publisher, Abbas Masudi, was a known sympathizer with the *coup,* published attacks on the Shah.[41] All but a fraction of the press followed suit. Mossadeq and his more responsible advisors floundered in indecision while the Tudeh and the more extremist elements of the National Front, led by Foreign Minister Hossein Fatemi, demanded the Shah's abdication.

In the following two days the Tudeh turned victory into defeat for Mossadeq, and it is difficult not to conclude that herein lay poetic justice. Mossadeq had tolerated Tudeh lawlessness to counter the right and to frighten the United States. Now suddenly the right had been defeated and had taken cover, and every knowledgeable Iranian assumed that the United States and Britain had been defeated with them. Mossadeq was now confronted with Tudeh lawlessness as the chief threat to his regime. Tudeh mobs roamed Tehran raising red flags and pulling down statues of Reza Shah.[42] Richard Frye writes that in Gilan the Tudeh had

40 *The New York Times,* July 23, 1953, 1:5.
41 *Ibid.,* August 28, 1953, 4:2.
42 *Ibid.,* August 18, 1953, 5:1.

taken over the government.[43] Many of Mossadeq's moderate and anticommunist supporters and many nonpolitical religious leaders saw in these Tudeh mobs confirmation of all that had been written in the rightist press of the imminence of the communist danger. Pressure must have been mounting on Mossadeq. On the evening of August 18 he struck. Tudeh mobs were ordered to disperse, and those refusing were clubbed into acquiescence.[44] The Tudeh had grossly overplayed its hand, and by midnight August 18 it was in bewildered retreat.

On the morning of August 19 little groups began to form in south Tehran. The groups merged into a seething, shouting pro-Shah mob which marched into the northern part of the city. The mob was led, as was described in Chapter 3, by a conglomeration of religious leaders and chaqu keshan leaders. The evidence available indicates that the rightist perpetrators of the August 16 *coup* were astonished at the sudden appearance of the mob, but by afternoon of August 19 they had returned to the attack and by evening Tehran was in their hands. The remainder of the country accepted the new government with scarcely a murmur—an indication of the disillusionment with Mossadeq. Iranian politics are almost monopolized in Tehran, but the provincial centers have a small middle class which two years earlier would have responded differently.

The *coup* of August 19, 1953, or as the Iranians call it, 28 Mordad, will long stand as the most important date in the history of Iranian nationalism. Today the visitor to Iran finds that politically articulate Iranians from right to left believe the *coup* was Anglo-American sponsored. Some approve of the foreign role, but many more do not. Both the Tudeh and Nationalist undergrounds have published pamphlets describing in detail the events of those days and spelling out the role allegedly played by Americans, American "agents," and British "agents." The phrase "Behbehani dollars" is in common usage as a description of the payment made to the mullahs and chaqu keshan leaders of the 28 Mordad mob. The conclusion of this study that Zahedi and his

[43] Richard N. Frye, "Iran Under Zahedi," *Foreign Policy Bulletin,* February 1, 1954, p. 8.

[44] *The New York Times,* August 19, 1951, 1:4, 5.

supporters were surprised by the appearance of the mob is denied by most Iranians, who point to the fact that chaqu keshan leaders do not act unless they are paid. This fact, of course, is true, and the Zahedi people undoubtedly did pour a good deal of money into the hands of mullahs and chaqu keshan leaders. Buying support is standard operating procedure for any Iranian politician. But the evidence still indicates that Zahedi was surprised both by the timing of the demonstration and by its size. If the truth is ever fully known, the answer may well be that those leaders who were paid by Zahedi three days earlier were joined by a great many others who were not paid but who were terrified at the prospects of a Tudeh government.

With regard to United States involvement, Iranians claim to have proof from an American source. The source is a *Saturday Evening Post* article of November 6, 1954, which was part of a series entitled "The Mysterious Doings of CIA" by Richard and Gladys Harkness. This article has been widely read in Tehran and has had a great impact there. The fact that in the United States it passed almost unnoticed is an interesting commentary in itself on the post-World War II American attitude regarding interference in the affairs of other nations. The relevant portions of this article are as follows:

Another CIA-influenced triumph was the successful overthrow in Iran in the summer of 1953, of old, dictatorial Premier Mohammad Mossadegh and the return to power of this country's friend Shah Mohammad Riza Pahlevi.

On May 28, 1953, President Eisenhower received a letter from Mossadegh amounting to a bare faced attempt at international blackmail. . . .

The White House stalled Mossadegh for one month; then turned down the crafty premier with a blunt no. This was a calculated risk at best. It was a daring gamble, in fact, that Mossadegh would not remain in power to carry out his threat. It was, as well, a situation which required a little doing. The doing began in short order through a chain of stranger-than-fiction circumstances involving [Allen] Dulles, a diplomat, a princess and a policeman.

On August tenth Dulles packed his bags and flew to Europe to join his wife for a vacation in the Swiss Alps. The political situation in Tehran was becoming more conspiratorial by the hour. Mossadegh was consorting with a Russian diplomatic-economic mission. Loy Henderson, United States Ambassador to Iran, felt he could leave his post for a short "holiday" in Switzerland. Princess Ashraf, the attractive and strong-willed brunette twin sister of the Shah, chose the same week to fly to a Swiss alpine resort. It was reported that she had had a stormy session with her brother in his pink marble palace, because of his vacillating in facing up to Mossadegh.

The fourth of the assorted characters in this drama, Brig. Gen. H. Norman Schwartzkopf, at this time took a flying vacation across the Middle East. His itinerary included apparently aimless and leisurely stops in Pakistan, Syria, Lebanon—and Iran. Schwartzkopf is best known to the public as the man who conducted the Lindberg kidnapping investigation in 1932, when he was head of the New Jersey state police. But from 1942 through 1948 he was detailed to Iran to reorganize the Shah's national police force. Schwartzkopf's job in Iran was more than the tracking down of routine criminals. He protected the government against its enemies—an assignment requiring intelligence on the political cliques plotting against the Shah, knowledge of which army elements could be counted on to remain loyal and familiarity with Middle East psychology. Schwartzkopf became friend and advisor to such individuals as Maj. Gen. Fazlollah Zahedi, his colleague on the police force, and the Shah himself.

Schwartzkopf returned to Iran in August of 1953, he said, "just to see old friends again." Certainly the general will deny any connection with the events that followed his renewal of acquaintanceships with the Shah and Zahedi. But as Mossadegh and the Russian propaganda press railed nervously at Schwartzkopf's presence in Iran, developments started to unfold in one-two-three order.

On Thursday, August thirteenth, the Shah suddenly issued a double-edged ukase: Mossadegh was ousted by royal decree and his successor as premier was to be General Zahedi. The Shah ordered the colonel of the Imperial Guards to serve the notice on Mossadegh. Two days later, at midnight of Saturday, August fifteenth, the colonel went to Mossadegh's residence to find himself and his platoon surrounded by tanks and jeeps. The colonel was clapped in jail, and Mossadegh proclaimed that the revolt had been crushed. The Shah and his queen, taking events at face value fled to Rome by way of Iraq.

On Wednesday, August nineteenth, with the army standing close guard around the uneasy capital, a grotesque procession made its way along the street leading to the heart of Tehran. There were tumblers turning handsprings, weight lifters twirling iron bars and wrestlers flexing their biceps. As spectators grew in number, the bizarre assortment of performers began shouting pro-Shah slogans in unison. The crowd took up the chant and then, after one precarious moment, the balance of public psychology swung against Mossadegh.

Upon signal, it seemed, army forces on the Shah's side began an attack. The fighting lasted a bitter nine hours. By nightfall, following American-style military strategy and logistics, loyalist troops drove Mossadegh's elements into a tight cordon around the premier's palace. They surrendered, and Mossadegh was captured as he lay weeping in his bed, clad in striped silk pajamas. In Rome a bewildered young Shah prepared to fly home and install Zahedi as premier and to give Iran a pro-Western regime.

Thus it was that the strategic little nation of Iran was rescued from the closing clutch of Moscow. Equally important, the physical overthrow of Mossadegh was accomplished by the Iranians themselves. It is the guiding premise of CIA's third force that one must develop and nurture indigenous freedom legions among captive or threatened people who stand ready to take personal risks for their own liberty.[45]

Whatever the truth behind this account, with its puerile innuendoes and glossy distortions (for example, Mossadeq was not found lying weeping in bed—he escaped and turned himself in to the new governmental authorities twenty-four hours later), it was a mischievous article that has done the United States a great disservice. In particular its description of the August 19 mob, which every Iranian would recognize as a typical mercenary chaqu keshan group, and its allusion to the precision timing by which Zahedi and his men joined forces with the mob constitute a denial of the spontaneity of the August 19 developments. And it was the spontaneity of August 19 that Iranian Nationalists need to recognize if they are ever to understand the significance of 28 Mordad. Regardless of foreign participation, Mossadeq could not have been overthrown if significant elements of the population had not lost faith in his leadership.

Another very damaging aspect of the Harkness article is the implication that Zahedi's and the Shah's religious and rightist supporters were examples of "indigenous freedom legions" which CIA had sought to "develop and nurture." Iranians read "indigenous freedom legions" as a euphemism for agent groups and the reference to the CIA's role as a confirmation of the widespread belief among the Nationalists (not necessarily among all nationalists) that the Shah and Zahedi were virtual American agents. And so the vicious circle is completed.

[45] Richard and Gladys Harkness, "The Mysterious Doings of CIA," *The Saturday Evening Post,* November 6, 1954, pp. 66–68. Reprinted by special permission of *The Saturday Evening Post.* © 1954 The Curtis Publishing Company.

Two facts emerge from this speculation, both of which are vitally important. The first is that Iranians credit or blame, depending on their loyalties, the United States and Britian for Mossadeq's overthrow. The second is that, as the Harknesses wrote, the United States from the time of Eisenhower's letter gambled on the fall of Mossadeq, and Eisenhower abandoned any further effort to influence the Mossadeq government from within. With regard to this second fact, those who are interested in United States foreign policy must ask themselves if such an all-or-nothing gamble is (a) good diplomacy and (b) a permissible function of the American executive without congressional approval or, at least, knowledge. This is not the place for a consideration of these points. However, it is well to remark that following the failure of the August 16 *coup*, the United States gamble was to succeed mainly thanks to the stupidity of the communist leadership. Had the Tudeh not overplayed its hand, the inevitable popular revulsion at the real and imagined Western role might well have resulted in the very development the United States most feared—the passing of Iran behind the Iron Curtain.

There was a very real danger from communism in Iran, and Mossadeq was exasperatingly stubborn, not only in his refusal to recognize this threat, but in his willingness to toy with such a dangerous weapon. Clearly, energetic American diplomatic action was called for. But gambling on Mossadeq's overthrow was not the only alternative. There were within Mossadeq's coalition many, such as Khalil Maleki, who fully understood the great danger in Mossadeq's tactics and who made every effort to dissuade him from pursuing them. Had the United States thrown its very significant influence and diplomatic support to these men, the gamble would have been far smaller and the resulting political situation could have been much healthier.

Anglo-American Condominium?

Needless to say, the primary psychological consequence of 28 Mordad for the Nationalists was the revitalization of the mythology that had led to the negativism and unwillingness to compromise of the Mossadeq movement. Once again, in Nationalist eyes, Iran had a government that was virtually the property of foreigners, but this time the condominium was Anglo-American rather than Anglo-Russian. A mysterious family of brothers, the Rashidians, announced openly that they were top British agents, and they had the agencies of a number of British commercial firms to hold up as proof for their contention. Whether their claim was true is less important than the fact that it was believed and that rightist and opportunist politicians beat a path to their door seeking political favors. The pattern was a familiar one for Iranians, and no great adjustment was necessary. It was the Mossadeq period that was unreal. For a brief euphoric moment Iranians had deluded themselves into believing that they could assert their independence. Now they could see that this had been a dream and that the British once again, this time working through the Americans, had demonstrated their ability to turn back even the strongest Iranian challenge. So these are the facts of politics, and life must go on. Surely it would be futile and senseless to fight more.

Since this reaction was typical, the result for the majority has been inertia, a refusal to think about or become involved in politics. Inevitably, though, the elite of the Nationalist element could not suddenly cast aside the habit of many years and sink into an apolitical apathy. For them the struggle of a half-century must continue; but here a crushing blow had been administered. Ever since the early days of the nationalist movement, the theoreticians had looked to the entrance of a third, disinterested power as the only hope for salvation in the Anglo-Russian squeeze play on Iran. Before and during World War I and again before World War II, the power looked to had been Germany. But during and after World War II, until 28 Mordad, the third power was the United States. Must this hope be dropped as an unrealistic dream? The majority of the Nationalist elite apparently felt not.

In spite of their conviction that the United States had been the most active of the two powers in executing the *coup d'état* against Mossadeq, many Nationalists believed there was still hope. The communists had worked with more than a little success to convince the Iranian people that the chief drive of the United States was to break into the British oil monopoly in Iran. A great many of the Nationalist leaders were and are socialists to one degree or another and hence were ideologically prepared to respond to this propaganda line. The image of America for the Nationalists, as for all Iranians, was not a distinct one and necessarily was filled with many contradictions. Without doubt most Iranians viewed America as a capitalist nation driven by its hunger for profits to struggle for control of Iran's great resource. But, by itself, this image did not ring true. Whereas British, German, and Japanese attempts to expand their commercial activities in Iran were intense and were supported by their respective embassies, the Americans seemed to be lackadaisical in comparison. When the oil consortium was inaugurated, many Iranians believed the United States, with its 40 per cent interest, would seek to dictate policy; but after a few months of experience Iranians had to admit that the American interests, divided as they were among many oil concerns, willingly acquiesced in Dutch and British leadership. Then, finally, the extremely generous financial assistance of the United States was increasingly accepted as genuinely motivated by a desire to bring prosperity and stability to Iran.

Further confirmation for the growing belief that the United States was sincerely interested in helping Iran came on the political plane. The mythology of the ubiquitous British agent did not appear solely from the Iranian imagination, fertile though that may be. The mythology could not have achieved its force and longevity were not much of it based on fact. As this study has shown, the British did interfere and interfered openly in favor of the right wing, landowning element. Any Iranian politician can list the names of men believed to be British agents at any time. Sometimes the men so classified attempt to advertise their British connections. But they must constantly prove their credentials, and this can only be done by the demonstration of a considerable and mysterious influence, usually today the procurement of lush government contracts or the placement of a man in the Majlis or in a high bureaucratic post.

Following 28 Mordad, Iranians expected to see the same pattern emerge with American agents. They thought they saw one such man in the Zahedi cabinet, but he was unceremoniously dropped when Zahedi was replaced by Hossein Ala. Gradually the suspicion began to grow that the United States, incredibly, had no agents in top positions. Tying together their political and economic experience with the Americans, the Iranians began to see a new image of America, and for the Nationalists it was an image with some hope. The American was a naively simple, cultureless character, totally ignorant of Iran and easily deluded by his infinitely clever British cousin. But the American was warm-hearted and sincerely wished to help Iran and thereby save it for the free world. The password to the American heart and money supply was anticommunism. Standing side by side with this caricature and often accepted by the same men was the Marxist creation of the American as the crude and grossly materialistic capitalist. The end result was an image of America that was at once a source of optimism and of pessimism for the Nationalists. If the American was really interested in the social, economic, and political welfare of Iran, then perhaps he could be shown that anticommunism would best be served by supporting the only group that commanded popular noncommunist support.

American prestige among Nationalists and among most Iranians fell sharply as the corrupt and tyrannical character of the Zahedi government began to emerge. But in November 1956, when the United States did so much to compel the British and French to give up their plan to topple President Nasser of Egypt, American prestige with the Nationalists returned to a zenith it had not seen since 1951. Finally, Iranian Nationalists permitted themselves to believe, the United States had decided to support the Middle Eastern people instead of their colonial oppressors. Every word uttered by Secretary Dulles or President Eisenhower was scanned for a hint of a new policy for Iran—one that would compel the Shah, now firmly established as an absolute dictator, to give up his new prerogatives and return to the position of constitutional monarch with a Nationalist government. The Eisenhower Doctrine, announced with such fanfare, was as meaningless for Iranians as for the rest of the world, but when James Richards, the former chairman of the House Foreign Affairs Committee, was commissioned to go to the Middle East, the Nationalists hoped to convince him that a complete reappraisal of American policy in Iran was necessary.

The Iran Party, a semiunderground, pro-Mossadeq party of which more will be said later, issued a manifesto on the eve of Richards' arrival in Iran which expressed its acceptance of the Eisenhower Doctrine with all of its anticommunist implications. The manifesto implicitly accepted the Zahedi-negotiated Oil Agreement and, even more startling, the Baghdad Pact.[46] It would be difficult to exaggerate either the risk involved for the Iran Party in having made this bold bid for American support or the compromise of doctrinal Nationalist purity involved. Whereas it may well be that the Nationalist leadership had become convinced that the oil agreement with modifications should be allowed to stand, very few leaders had shown any inclination to compromise on the Baghdad Pact. This unwillingness to compromise on the Baghdad Pact did not mean that the Nationalists were all neutralists. Probably a majority were neutralists, but many were not. A regional defense pact negotiated by a future Nationalist regime is still a distinct possibility. However, the Baghdad Pact was not regarded as a defense pact but rather as a means for maintaining in power reactionary and slavishly pro-British governments. By making these concessions, therefore, the Iran Party was risking the loss of much of its support within the Nationalist community.

The Shah's response was violent. His hand-picked deputies in the Majlis prepared to pass a bill which, in addition to outlawing the Iran Party, forbade any member of the party, past or present, from holding a position in the government.[47] Since the Iran Party's chief source of support was from young professional men, many of them bureaucrats, the consequences could have been disastrous. The bill was permitted to reach a final stage and then was held in Damoclean fashion to paralyze the Iran Party. A vigorous press campaign was waged to demonstrate that the party was insincere in its manifesto and that it was actually procommunist.[48] An incident that occurred in 1946 was resurrected and heavily publicized. In that year the Iran Party, Ahmad

[46] The Iran Party Manifesto was published in the Tehran press April 1957.

[47] See *Ettelaat* for April 1957.

[48] *Ibid.* For the nearest thing to a coverage in the United States press see *The New York Times*, December 29, 1957, 6:1; January 2, 1958, 5:3.

Qavam's Democrat Party, the Tudeh Party, and Pishevari's Democrat Party had negotiated on the possibility of an alliance for the Fifteenth Majlis election. Although the negotiations had failed, the fact remained that the Iran Party and its leader, Allahyar Saleh, had seriously considered the proposition. Many of those leading the campaign to smear the Iran Party had themselves been involved in the negotiations, but the Iran Party was vulnerable on this issue.

From Tripoli James Richards sent a message to the Shah praising him in the fulsome manner of a South Carolinian politician, and probably with no more seriousness of purpose in mind. For the Iran Party, however, this message seemed to be their answer. In a way it was. Top American policy makers, including John Foster Dulles and Loy Henderson, had obviously participated in the decision to oppose the Mossadeq government. Consequently they had a vested interest in the correctness of that decision, and both were still in power in 1956. To expect them to reverse the decision, especially in the face of trouble caused by nationalists in the Arab world, was to hope for too much. Only the gravest kind of crisis could have brought the sudden, dramatic reversal that the Iran Party sought. The American image of Mossadeq—that of a weepy, old fanatic who played footsie with the communists—was still firmly implanted, and the manifesto could not dissipate strongly felt grievances and suspicions. But the Iran Party manifesto served a useful function, for it demonstrated that one of the most important segments of the Iranian Nationalists was capable of responsibility and statesmanship. Americans needed to learn this lesson if their own perspective was to be clear.

Just as the Iran Party incident illustrates the mutual impact of the United States and the Nationalists, the relationship between Great Britain and the Nationalists can be viewed in one event. Iranians are almost unanimous in the belief that Freemasonry is an instrument of British imperialism and that the Freemason organizations include many Iranians who have accepted British support to advance their political careers. The attitude of the average politically aware Iranian toward Freemasonry resembles the average American's attitude toward a communist front group. Therefore one could expect that a budding Iranian politician's attitude toward Freemasonry would also resemble his American counterpart's attitude toward a communist front, i.e. not only would he stay clear of the organization, he would do his best to avoid anyone who did not do the same. In fact, however, post-Mossadeq politicians have sought energetically membership in Freemason organizations.

In March of 1957 Dr. Manuchehr Eqbal became prime minister of Iran. Eqbal was the president of a Freemason organization, and ten of the men he chose for his cabinet were also Freemasons.[49] Eqbal and his ten colleagues may have been the most patriotic of Iranians, and the British Embassy may have had nothing to do with their appointment. But since the Shah and Eqbal were both aware of the Freemasons' reputation, the selection of so many Masons for cabinet posts demonstrates either a profound disregard for public opinion or deliberate flaunting of it. Iranian Nationalists were neither surprised nor annoyed at these appointments; they scarcely felt that the Freemason complexion of the cabinet was worthy of comment. For them it was merely one more proof of a British control that was approaching the absolute. The bad effect was on those nationalists who had broken with Mossadeq because of his intransigent refusal to compromise. These people believed that Mossadeq made major and inexcusable mistakes, but to them this obvious British domination made Mossadeq's judgment seem, in retrospect, to be increasingly wise.

The Shah and the Soviets

After 28 Mordad the Tudeh, and no doubt their Soviet sponsors, went through a period of highly critical introspection—an introspection that would surprise many Western writers who mistakenly refer to the Mossadeq-Tudeh relationship as a "collaboration" rather than what it actually was, mutual toleration. The chief conclusion of this reevaluation was that the Tudeh should have supported Mossadeq. Had it done so, the members reasoned, Mossadeq's attack on them on the evening of August 18 would not have occurred, and on the morning of August 19 the Tudeh and the National Front could have easily defeated the mercenary south Tehran mob. Instead the Tudeh was disorgan-

[49] List of Freemason members, *Farman*, December 1956.

ized and in hiding, and the dispirited National Front could not deal with the challenge.[50]

Zahedi and the Shah had no intention of repeating Mossadeq's error of permitting the Tudeh to act openly, even lawlessly. The new government moved with energy and imagination against the Tudeh. In the fall of 1954, by a stroke of good luck and bad communist management, the government obtained a list of Army officers in a secret Tudeh organization. The membership totaled more than 400 officers, including many of Iran's most competent men. This figure was proof of the danger of Mossadeq's game, but, unfortunately, many Nationalists, probably most, refused to accept the full meaning of the revelation. They preferred believing that the big majority of these men were Nationalists who had been framed.

The government campaign against the underground Tudeh continued until there was virtually no effective organization left. Many top Tudeh officials escaped, however, and prudence dictates the conclusion that alternate Tudeh organizations exist abroad—probably behind the Iron Curtain and in France. Iranian Nationalists, while conceding that the Tudeh organization has been largely crushed, insist that popular receptivity for communism has not been affected and that the communist danger in Iran is as great as ever. There is much truth to this Nationalist assertion, which will be discussed further in the conclusion.

Stalin died in early 1953, well before 28 Mordad; and under the premierships of Malenkov and Khrushchev a period of thaw characterized Soviet foreign policy. But could this thaw include Iran when the Soviets had suffered a major setback? Not only had they failed to make allies of the Nationalists, but now the far right government of Zahedi and the Shah was destroying their chief instrument of policy. Whether or not to include Iran in the thaw must have been a major dilemma for the Soviets. Since the Nationalists were bitterly disillusioned with the West, the time was ideal for the Soviets to court the Nationalists. And since the Nationalists continued to represent the majority of articulate opinion, there was a good possibility of a Nationalist govern-

50 See the Tudeh pamphlet, *28 Mordad,* published for underground distribution in 1954.

ment in the near future; were that government to be pro-Soviet, the USSR would have won a great victory. Furthermore, a strongly pro-Nationalist Soviet line could help bring a *rapprochement* between underground Tudeh and Mossadeqist elements.

Yet the Soviet policy makers chose to include Iran in the thaw. There were mutterings in the Soviet press when some of the Tudeh officers were executed, but the Soviets had written off the Tudeh and the Nationalists, at least for the time being. The Harknesses in their article refer to Mossadeq's "consorting with a Russian diplomatic-economic mission," but throughout 1956–58 the supposedly pro-Western government of the Shah received countless Soviet missions, economic, political, cultural, and athletic. Soviet trade missions were enjoying particular success.[51] The Soviet ambassador, Nikolai Pegov, who arrived in 1956, was of the smiling, hail-fellow variety, and scores of Iranians were being received at Soviet diplomatic functions. Soviet propaganda in early 1958 reached a peak in adulation of Mohammad Reza Pahlavi and his father, referred to by the Soviets as "Reza Shah the Great." [52]

At first glance the Soviet policy appears to have been based on a decision to attract the favor of the government of Iran by friendship, increased trade, and noninterference with the Shah's government, even though this meant antagonizing the high percentage of articulate Iranians who disliked the government. However, a closer investigation indicates that the Soviets had little to lose and the possibility of achieving major long-term gains by pursuing a progovernment policy. Only a veneer of Iranians, including the Shah and his lieutenants and the Nationalist elite, were aware of the pro-Shah Soviet propaganda line. The former would be attracted by the Soviet line; the latter suffered few illusions about the Soviets anyway, and had demonstrated their attitude by an unwillingness to make any kind of agreement with the Tudeh even when they were in no position to reject help from any quarter. Of far greater importance, the trend in Iran was in the Soviet favor. Since apathy increasingly characterized

[51] For example see *The New York Times,* January 13, 1957, 25:5.
[52] *The New York Times,* January 5, 1958, 21:1.

the Nationalist rank and file, it was highly questionable that the Nationalist elite could reassert its leadership if the Shah's dictatorship were suddenly lifted. The Tudeh, on the other hand, could quickly move back to Iran and probably could recoup its popular following. Continued deterioration and disillusionment were in the long-term communist interests, and Soviets could afford to wait.

This Soviet friendship offered the Shah a new opportunity for exerting diplomatic leverage on the West, particularly the United States, and he used his advantage with far more success than had Mossadeq. However, on July 14, 1958, the Nuri al-Said government in Iraq was overturned, and the Western mythology about the Middle East should have been disclosed for the romantic fiction it was. The revolution in Iraq dramatized the truth that a government without any significant popular backing is no bulwark against communism regardless of how anticommunist that government is or claims to be. Most British and many American policy makers failed to learn this lesson—another demonstration that mythology, Iranian or Western, is long-lived. But the Shah understood. He is reported to have said that such a *coup d'état* could easily occur in Iran,[53] and for several days following the assassination of Nuri al-Said, the Shah waited in Turkey, where he had been visiting, before returning home to his tank-surrounded palace. Iraq had demonstrated that even the strongest-willed regime with all-out foreign backing could be toppled. Here was proof of the Shah's vulnerability for all who thought that his regime was indestructable because of American-British support.

In the months that followed, the Shah asked that the United States equip two more divisions, guarantee to come to Iran's support in case of attack, and grant more military and economic aid.[54] In each case the United States either refused or said more time was necessary for a decision. Secretary Dulles sought to reassure the Shah and other Middle Eastern allies by a series of bilateral agreements, which he hoped would be signed at the Karachi meeting of the Baghdad Pact beginning January 26,

[53] *Ibid.*, February 12, 1959, 1:7.
[54] *Ibid.*, January 13, 1959, 11:1.

1959.[55] However, the Soviet Union in an official note on January 16, 1959, warned Iran against signing and suggested that the two countries discuss the matter.

What happened between this date and January 29 remains a mystery. On January 29, while the Cento delegates at Karachi marked time, a high-ranking Soviet delegation consisting of Vladimir S. Semeyonov, Deputy Foreign Minister, Alexesei P. Pavolov, Chief of the Near East Division of the Foreign Ministry, and Ambassador Pegov arrived to negotiate a nonaggression treaty. By this treaty Iran would agree not to sign the bilateral pact with the United States and the Soviet would renounce Article Six of the 1921 treaty. Article Six, the Soviets had insisted, permitted the movement of their troops into Iran if Iran is used as a base for foreign troops who in the Soviet view are likely to attack the Soviet Union.[56] The Soviets claim that the Iranians had initiated the talks and that before the Russian delegation arrived in Tehran the Shah had ordered the drafting of a treaty which was generally satisfactory to the Soviets.[57] The Iranians claim that the negotiations were Soviet initiated.[58] In any case, the Soviets had been led to believe that a treaty would be signed; otherwise they would not have risked their prestige by sending a top-level negotiating team. Premier Eqbal and the West seemed to share the Soviet view. Eqbal is said to have threatened to resign if the Shah did not break off negotiations; and Eisenhower, Macmillan, Turkish President Bayar, and Pakistani President Ayub all sent messages urging the Shah to stand firmly with his Western allies.[59] The Shah agreed and the talks were discontinued in an undiplomatic fashion—the Shah announced that he was ill and Eqbal left town. *Ettelaat* reported: "Informed quarters said today that Iran would press for more United States military and economic assistance during coming talks with George McGhee and Admiral Arthur W. Radford, who arrived here yesterday as President Eisenhower's committee to study the aid program." [60]

[55] *Ibid.*, January 17, 1959, 5:7.
[56] *Ibid.*, February 12, 1959, 1:7; February 13, 1959, 4:4; February 17, 1959, 5:7.
[57] *Ibid.*, February 13, 1959, 4:4.
[58] *Ibid.*, February 17, 1959, 5:7.
[59] *Ibid.*, February 12, 1959, 1:7.
[60] *Ibid.*, February 9, 1959, 4:4.

Though the picture remains hazy, some aspects are clear: the Shah was frightened of his own domestic situation and of the Soviet threat; the Soviets felt strongly about the possibility of the establishment of American bases in Iran and were willing to push Iran to the limit to prevent the signing of the bilateral agreement with the United States; and the Shah came far closer to coming to terms with the Soviets than the West or his own government had believed he would and a great deal closer than Mossadeq had ever considered going. Khrushchev commented in a speech that the Shah had engaged in a very dangerous game of brinkmanship,[61] implying that he had used the Soviet mission to force the United States to grant more aid to Iran. But the clumsiness of the maneuver belies this interpretation as the whole answer and indicates that the Shah was vacillating, as he often does, in the face of a serious Soviet threat.

However, the end result was that the Soviet Union received a rebuff and consonant loss of prestige and that henceforth, as the Soviets themselves announced, Iran had "joined the ranks of the enemies of the Soviet Union." [62] From January 29 until midsummer 1959, when there was a dramatic though temporary change, the Soviet radio and press attacked the Shah. According to *The New York Times,* more broadcast time was being devoted to programs in Persian than in any foreign language except English.[63] What has been the effect of these attacks? Some say that even Iranians who are not supporters of the Shah are angry at what they regard as crude interference. This belief is probably overly optimistic with regard to Nationalists. The Russian propaganda is very clever in repeating what Nationalists believe to be facts: the Shah is little more than an Anglo-American agent; [64] he has invested large sums of money safely abroad; [65] little good use is being made of the huge oil income because of the Court and its sycophants.[66] For example, after describing many unhappy circumstances in Iran today, the Soviet Radio concluded that "the

[61] *Ibid.,* February 27, 1959, 7:5.
[62] *Ibid.,* February 13, 1959, 1:5.
[63] *Ibid.,* February 24, 1959, 9:3.
[64] *Tass,* May 25, 1959.
[65] *The New York Times,* February 27, 1959, 7:5.
[66] Soviet Near Eastern Service, broadcast in Persian, March 17, 1959.

crime implicit in this state of affairs can be directly blamed on the Shah and his clique, who have handed over these resources to the imperialists who have stretched forth their hand of oppression against the great achievement of the Iranian people, that is to say, against the law nationalizing Iran's oil."[67] Such propaganda couched in phrases that the Iranians themselves often use could not fail to hit its mark.

[67] *Ibid.*, July 23, 1959.

14

LIBERAL NATIONALISM: BIRTH AND ECLIPSE

There is much conceit and even more ambiguity in the phrase "impact of the West." There is conceit because the phrase seems to appropriate for the West that which generically is due to centuries of cultural interaction. There is ambiguity because the term "West" is beyond precise definition. For each Western reader "West" will have a different meaning, a meaning that is intertwined with his own value system. For many, liberal democracy is dominant in "West," and without question it deserves an important place in any definition. But it does not merit the predominance it has often been given.

In discussing the impact of the West on Iran, nothing is easier than to exaggerate the role of liberal democracy in Iran. One of the few good sources of late nineteenth- and early twentieth-century Iranian thought is the newspapers of the period, and the prerevolutionary exile press is soul-satisfying to a Western adherent of liberal democracy. Although papers such as *Adab* and *Shahanshahi,* published in Iran, were drab organs of the Court, *Qanun,* published in London, *Sabah,* published in Istanbul, *Habl al-Matin,* of Calcutta, and *Parvaresh* and *Soraya* of Cairo demonstrate that liberal democracy had passionate adherents among Iranians.

But these papers show much more than that liberal democracy had adherents in Iran. With the exception of the simply-styled *Qanun,* the prerevolutionary exile press was esoteric and pretentiously literary. Considering this style, the probability that no more than 1 per cent of the population was literate, and the extraordinary difficulty of getting the papers into Iran, it is obvious that the impact of the liberal press was not widespread. Its influence was confined to a veneer of the elite of society.

Most of the schools in pre-twentieth-century Iran were religious institutions conducted by men who refused to admit the validity of any addition to human knowledge in several centuries. From these schools came the better-educated mullahs as well as doctors and lawyers. But it is unlikely that these men would have had much interest in Voltaire, Montesquieu, or Locke, the favorites of the exile press. There were two important secular schools established prior to the 1906 revolution: Nasr al-din Shah founded the Madrasah Shah, a college with a European curriculum and European instructors, and in 1901 Abdollah Mostofi organized the School of Politics. In these two schools the young Iranian made contact with the ideas of the West and the philosophers who had helped develop the liberal democratic concepts. Also, after the mid-nineteenth century, Iranians in small but increasing numbers traveled abroad. In particular, royal visits to Europe offered large numbers of young men of the retinue the opportunity to see European society for themselves.

These men had the training and experience to understand the exile press, but they were the sons of the Court, of the aristocracy, or of the most prosperous merchants. Paradoxically, the class that benefited most from the status quo was the only class that could comprehend the liberal democratic concepts that, if put into effect, would destroy the status quo. Some members of this class became passionate followers of liberal democracy and worked actively to create the educated base they thought necessary for democracy. In 1897, for example, a group primarily composed of young courtiers established a society for furthering a national grammar, secondary, and college educational program.[1] But no revolutionary leadership came from this group, whose members found the role of theoretical liberal comfortable and intellectually satisfying.

However, the impact of the West had been felt by two other groups—the mercantile and the clerical elite—for whom the status quo was far less comfortable and who, as we have already seen, were the activists of the revolution. Among the mercantile and clerical groups, liberal democracy was rarely understood and endorsed. For them the impact of the West was non-ideological

[1] Kasrevi, p. 33.

and was manifested in the form of a basic challenge to their self-interest. Since the Court had willingly acquiesced in the commercial and cultural inroads of the West, the merchants and clergy needed governmental institutions that would curb the powers of the Court and would be more responsive to their interests. Also needed was a program. The intellectuals, who had been passive in the first stages of the revolution, could and did provide both the blueprints for the institutions and the program. Once the revolution was successful, the intellectuals did become active and gave the constitutional movement its ideological base of liberal democratic nationalism, an import from Western Europe.

By the turn of the century the compound of liberalism-democracy-nationalism had given France, England, and the United States an eminently satisfactory ideological base for their socio-political systems. But transplanted suddenly to Iran, the same compound could have thrived only with good luck and careful, understanding nurturing. Liberalism-democracy-nationalism is not always stable even in the West. Liberalism, with its overriding concern for the dignity of the individual, is fully understood only by a small sector of the population. In normal times this group is well represented at top governmental levels, but many demagogues have demonstrated that the ideologically convinced liberal democrat can be bypassed and that, sometimes in the name of democracy and nationalism, liberalism can be attacked and defeated.

Of all the aspects of the Western impact on Iran, none is more important than its having set into motion a trend of steady growth in the popular base of political awareness. By opening new vistas for commercial activity, Western merchants and their representatives broke the chains of economic stagnation. Slowly at first, but with steadily gathering momentum, Iranians turned to new economic pursuits. The dynamics of the new trend demanded both a steady growth in the size of the middle class and, eventually, an educated and skilled working class. Then as the newly awakened middle-class elements began to appear, they made more demands of the socio-political system; and just around the corner were similar demands from an aroused working class. Any political value system that could have attracted the support of these people had to rationalize their drive for power, prestige, and security. Democracy and nationalism were admirably suited to this task. Democracy could provide the means for acquiring power; and nationalism, with its egalitarian implications and its predilection for a more centralized society, could replace the old quasi-feudalism with a social order that would be far more beneficial to the middle and working classes and could, at the same time, provide the security of an ultimate political loyalty. Few could be expected to see much value in liberalism, and yet without liberalism the newly emerging classes could easily fall victim to a tyranny far more oppressive than the one they sought to escape.

As the impact of the West began to be felt in Iran, political awareness began to move rapidly downward into the mass of the population; but education and an understanding of politics could proceed downward only at a much slower rate. The result was that the elite had placed upon it a great responsibility. Nationalism was not at stake, but liberalism was. The critical question was whether or not the elite would be able to establish a firm tradition of liberal-nationalism before the mass base of political participation became so large that a demagogue appealing to the mass in nonliberal but nationalistic terms could bypass the liberal democratic elite.

The 1906–11 Period of Liberal Nationalism

If the intellectuals were more or less passive observers during the 1906 revolution, they soon compensated for their inertia. As if driven by a compulsion to fulfill a historical mission, they launched in that year a massive educational program. They recognized that although many Iranians understood the need for placing curbs on the power of the Court, very few had any idea of an alternate political system. The constitution, presented as a solution to this problem, was generally accepted as such, but very few understood what the constitution really was. Clearly, if the constitutional experiment were to survive, the interested population must be educated to the point of understanding the workings of the constitution and the political ideology behind it. To do the educating the intellectuals had two instruments: the anjumans and the press.

As has been suggested in the story of the Tabriz anjuman, the development of these discussion-activist groups was remarkable.[2] In Tehran 180 anjumans were formed,[3] and others appeared throughout the provinces. These anjumans were societies which developed out of private discussion groups, most of which had met clandestinely prior to the revolution. Following the acceptance of the constitution, they came into the open and expanded in number and size. They were not, of course, all of the same political complexion, but the large majority were nationalist and, to one degree or another, liberal. Many of the anjumans sponsored regular lectures and discussion groups to acquaint their members with the essentials of the parliamentary system and with the liberal, democratic, nationalist ideology. Many of the teachers were ill-informed, often ludicrously so, but the people were exposed to new ideas. Professor Browne agrees with many Iranian historians that large numbers of Iranians gained an understanding of liberal democracy and nationalism through the anjumans.[4]

The anjumans were more than debating societies or centers for adult education. Much of the policy of the constitutional movement was formulated in the anjumans, for most of the liberal deputies in the Majlis were members of one or more of the groups. The great period of the anjumans was 1906–08. Although many anjumans were reactivated after Mohammad Ali was deposed in 1909, they never regained their former preeminence. It is often said that the hour produces the man, but no towering figure appeared to lead the liberal cause in 1906, and no man had achieved prominence by 1908. Then when the nationalists returned to power, they did so under the command of Sardar Asad, the Bakhtiari chieftain, and of the Sepahdar, the leader of the Rashti force, an extremely wealthy opportunist who never understood the movement he helped lead. Neither man was the kind of leader

[2] See Chapter 9.

[3] Mostofi, II, 350.

[4] Edward G. Browne, *A Brief Narrative of Recent Events in Persia* (London, 1909), p. 21; Kasrevi, pp. 262, 265, 267; Dolatabadi, II, 151; Mostofi, II, 245.

the liberals could rally behind, and yet both could rightfully claim leadership of the national movement. The anjumans had failed to produce a great leader, and by 1909 they were confronted with strong leaders who did not share their philosophical orientation. Consequently their influence suffered a major decline.

The anjuman movement was a spectacular example of the concept of "spillover." Prior to 1906, awareness of the liberal-democratic-nationalist value system was confined to a mere handful of individuals. Societal receptivity existed for a significant broadening of the base of ideological awareness, however, and the anjuman movement amounted to a spillover of the liberal-democratic-nationalist values from a small group into a much larger group. But the failure of the anjuman movement to produce a great leader reflects accurately the stage of development of Iranian society in the first constitutional period. Even after the spillover, only a small fraction of the Iranian population had been educated politically. For a man to become a great popular leader, there must exist a means by which he can communicate to a large sector of the population his answer to their frustrations and problems. In Iran in 1906–08 only religious leaders had the ability to reach below the educated veneer.

Intellectual enthusiasm in 1906 also burst forth in the press. By early 1907 thirty newspapers were published in Tehran.[5] The dull, semiofficial organs that Tehran had previously known gave way to stimulating, provocative, and astonishingly educational newspapers. Of the thirty papers, twenty-seven were liberal nationalist, and the largest of these, *Majlis,* reached a circulation figure, according to Browne, of 10,000. The circulation of several others was approximately 3,000.[6] Prior to this time no journal had sold more than a few hundred copies, and nothing better illustrates the intense enthusiasm of the period than the burgeoning press. Even the most popular of the papers carried long articles by learned men on such subjects as parliamentary government, liberal democracy, the essentials of patriotism, freedom, and the rule of law. The names of some of the newspapers indicated the temper of the times: "Hope," "Freedom," "Unity of the Nation,"

[5] *State Papers 1909, Persia No. 1,* p. 28.
[6] Browne, *The Press and Poetry of Modern Persia,* pp. 24–25.

"Justice," "Roar," "Fatherland," "Voice of the Fatherland," "New Year," "Civilization," "Dawn of Truth," "Progress," "Humanity," and the "Language of the Nation."[7]

Indeed the press was a barometer of nationalist success or failure. After the July 1909 *coup* by Mohammad Ali, the liberal press disappeared or fled abroad. Although it reappeared a year later, after the restoration, it reflected the discouragement of the 1909–12 period. Gone were the enthusiasm, the verve, the crusading spirit. Very few educational articles were published, and the papers indulged more and more in bitter attacks and innuendo. In circulation, too, the decline in nationalist fervor was faithfully registered; the readership of *Iran No,* the largest paper, rarely reached 3,000.[8]

On the practical political plane, liberal nationalist idealism was on the decline. The dilemma posed by adherence to the concept of democracy was serious. As followers of Locke and Voltaire, the theoreticians of the constitutional movement could scarcely oppose democracy, and yet the inevitable result of democracy in a country in which the landowners exercised political control over the peasants was upper-class domination. But even for the doctrinaire liberal, suffrage need not be universal. The West offered many precedents for property qualifications and other limitations.

Nor were the liberal nationalists in Iran doctrinaire on the point of suffrage. Women were excluded, and in 1906 Tehran was purposely given a heavy overrepresentation in the Majlis. But what was necessary if the liberals were to predominate was a literacy requirement for voting. Only by excluding the illiterates could the ignorant peasants and urban lower class be kept from voting as their landowner, mullah, or chaqu keshan leaders directed. But the liberals were not strong enough to impose such a restriction. The clerical leaders had been extremely influential in bringing about the success of the revolution, and they would not favor a plan for disenfranchising the bulk of their supporters. The result was that the liberals, for all their enthusiasm, were relegated to a minority position in the Majlis throughout the 1906–12 period.

[7] For these and others see Kasrevi, pp. 268–75, 528, 540.

[8] Browne, *The Press and Poetry of Modern Persia,* p. 25.

The liberals in the Majlis grouped themselves into a faction known as the Democrat Party. There were ideological differences within this faction, chiefly on the issue of incorporating the Shariat into the law of the land, but by and large the group was the nucleus of the liberal, democratic, nationalist movement. However, of 136 deputies, only fourteen were consistently in this camp.[9]

The chief competing faction was the 'Etedal Party, which was the conservative faction. Herein were grouped the clerical deputies as well as many wealthy conservatives. The 'Etedal faction numbered about thirty.[10] The remaining ninety-two deputies were independents. Since most of the independents bent with the prevailing winds, they did not constitute the obstacle indicated by their numbers. The demonstrations of a large mob of proconstitution Tehranis, which could be gathered in front of the Majlis at any moment, counted for far more than the numerical strength of the nationalists there. Whenever a test of strength was at hand, the anjumans could be counted on to rally heavy popular support.

Thus the situation stood as follows: although the press and the anjumans were vociferously liberal, the liberal element in the Majlis was never more than a small minority. The liberal forces together had a solid veto and were able to stand firmly against any infringements from the reactionary majority on the power of the Majlis and against any easing of the restrictions on the Court. But, at the same time, the liberals were stopped by parliamentary maneuvering from furnishing positive, constructive leadership.

After the deposition of Mohammad Ali, the Court no longer served as a rallying point for the reactionaries. Furthermore, the nationalists now had genuine leadership. But this leadership proved to be more of a liability than an asset for the liberal nationalists. Both the Sepahdar and Sardar Asad associated themselves with the conservative 'Etedal faction, and neither was willing to launch a genuinely reformist program. The two men were bitter rivals, each with his personal following within the 'Etedal. The result was utter paralysis. The Democrats, disillusioned and dispirited, did very little. For the heroes of Tabriz, Sattar Khan and Baqer Khan, the situation was intolerable. They saw that the

9 *State Papers 1911, Persia No. 1*, p. 45.
10 *Ibid.*

will of the large majority of the literate, articulate element could be thwarted by men whose power rested on the votes of the ignorant and apolitical. Consequently, they organized groups, referred to as fedai, outside the Majlis for the purpose of goading the Majlis and the government into action.[11] Since their efforts became increasingly terroristic, these groups weakened rather than strengthened the liberal cause.

The strange Shuster interlude demonstrates what leadership could have done. When genuine progress was being made, largely thanks to Shuster, enthusiasm returned to the Majlis, to the press, and to the anjumans. But when this enthusiasm was met by a British-supported Russian ultimatum, despair took its place. Although the constitutional experiment had been an exhilarating experience for some, it had brought with it an insecurity that added to the misery of the lives of most Iranians. Little wonder then that personal security began to acquire a place in the value system of the average man far above that of any ideological conviction.

Nationalism in Eclipse

Visitors from democratic countries who for the first time see a city under the control of an authoritarian regime are often surprised at how normal everything seems. The dour, frightened looks and the lines of heavily armed security police that they had expected are not to be seen. On an average day the neighborhood policeman jokes with his friends, and laughter is to be heard with normal frequency. Normalcy is all the more evident in a city such as Tehran which shows the impress of an ancient heritage. In the steady, rhythmical pounding of the coppersmith, the cries of the vegetable vendor, and the ceaseless flow of people moving through the routine of daily life, there is a timeless quality that even the noise of automobiles cannot change. Wild political demonstrations may drown out the din of the city for brief moments, but as the demonstrators disperse they are enveloped again in timelessness. In 1908 after Mohammad Ali's successful *coup,* Tehran was changed only by the disappearance of the cacophony that had been added to the music of the city by the constitutional mobs. And in

[11] Dolatabadi, II, 133–37.

1953 after the 28 Mordad mob had returned to its south Tehran haunts, the din and the routine of the city reached out to erase the evidence of the entire Mossadeq era. Today the foreign visitor has difficulty believing that in this tranquil setting the Mossadeq upheaval could have occurred. But it did occur, and before it many other eruptions.

In 1911 the Democrats of Tabriz, staging a "huge" demonstration, made this announcement: "Our country and our religion have passed out of our hands. The foreigners have taken them. We are going to fight to get them back." [12] Then when a few Russian soldiers appeared on the scene the crowd quietly dissolved. That incident is symbolic of Iranian nationalism at that point. Heroic efforts had been made to popularize the new ideology of the constitutional regime, and the results had been impressive. In a few years the number of people who could comprehend the new ideology had multiplied many times. But in percentage they were still only a small fraction of the total population, and their opponents were many and powerful. Apathy of the masses, antagonism from the upper class, hostility and open enmity from Britain and Russia, and the immensity of the task before them were enough to extinguish the fire of the early nationalists.

But the coals of the old enthusiasm continued to smolder, and with each fresh breeze the flames leapt up again. In 1915, when the Germans and the Turks seemed to have a good chance for victory in World War I, an epidemic of new newspapers suddenly appeared and called for joining the holy war against Britain and Russia.[13] A few of the more doctrinairely liberal papers worried about the illiberality of the Central Powers but rationalized such worries away with the observation that Russia was even less liberal than Germany and that the behavior of Britain and France in Asia was not of the variety to attract any liberal adulation.[14] But by and large the press ignored this ideological contradiction and treated the war as a battle of good vs. evil. Then when the British and

[12] *The Near East,* January 12, 1912, p. 298.

[13] For example see *Shuzi,* December 1914 to June 1915; *Aftab,* May to November 1915; *Asr Enqellab,* November 1915; *Parvardin,* November 1915; *Bamdad Roshan,* May to June 1915.

[14] See for example *No Bahar,* published in Tehran, December 20, 1914; January 1, 1915; February 3, 1915; November 11, 1915.

Russians tightened their control in Iran and the tides of battle began to flow more in their direction, the press quietly disappeared.

In 1917 the press appeared again as suddenly as it had disappeared.[15] After the Russian February Revolution new hope of independence swept Iran. The enthusiasm reached a climax after the terms of the Anglo-Persian Treaty of 1919 had been announced, when a huge crowd gathered to greet Ahmad Shah on his return from Europe with shouts of "Death to Vosuq al-Doleh." Iranian nationalism at this point was on its way toward winning its most important victory since 1909: the British were forced to give up their effort to institutionalize a tutelary role in Iran. But disillusionment followed victory, and again the press reflected the retreat of nationalism from euphoric heights to depressive depths.

The key to the explanation of these spurts of intense activity and then long periods of quiescence is to be found in the numerical weakness of the national movement. During the years 1912–21 there had been no substantial growth in the popular base of nationalism. Though adherents were to be found in influential families, among merchant elements, and throughout the intelligentsia, they were not yet powerful enough to take over the affairs of government. They were powerful enough, however, to create a considerable stir among the articulate element of Tehran and of some of the provincial centers. Thus they were able to agitate so successfully in favor of the Central Powers that the British and Russians were compelled to control the Tehran governments openly; and later they were able to prevent the acceptance of the 1919 treaty. But they did not have the strength to form a government which could have provided the progress and security so badly needed.

A survey of the press in the 1910–21 period reveals a subtle but highly significant change from the earlier nationalist era. Exhortations in favor of patriotism and bitter attacks on Western imperialism made their appearance, but less space was devoted to the virtues of liberal democracy and more space was given to the necessity of establishing law and order and building a modern Iran. No writer was ready to admit that liberal democracy had

[15] By 1919 there were twenty-five journals in Tehran. See Fatemi, p. 79.

failed. Possibly few had admitted this failure to themselves. But there was a tacit admission of failure in 1921 when Tehran was debating the merits of the contenders for the position of strong man.

Nationalism sans Liberalism

In 1921 the strong man Iran sensed it needed did appear and he began a long process of consolidating absolute power in his hands—a process that culminated with his coronation as Reza Shah Pahlavi. Few Iranians recognized at the time and many Nationalists even today refuse to admit that with the triumph of Reza Shah came total victory for Iranian nationalism. The liberal nationalists who had been struggling for victory since 1906 cannot be blamed for failing to see in Reza Khan their messiah, for a more improbable leader for Iran could hardly be imagined. In Iran, the soldier was scorned. Yet Reza Khan was a soldier. In Iran with its great cultural tradition, evidence of breeding and culture were regarded as necessary in any great leader. Yet Reza Khan was unlettered, crude, and uncouth. In Iran the national movement, having been based on an awareness of the teachings of Locke and the French Encyclopedists, was deeply concerned with the dignity of man and with humanism. Yet Reza Khan was a ruthless egocentric who lacked a shred of sympathy for liberalism and humanism.

Could such a man inherit the leadership of the Iranian struggle for independence and national respect? The answer is that he could and did; but the early leaders of the struggle were never to recognize this fact. The national movement had been essentially a power struggle in which the middle class with intellectual leadership sought to upset the monopoly position of the landowning aristocracy. Reza Khan replaced intellectual leadership with his own and brought to the middle class power, prestige, and prosperity. Since the old status quo, predominated by landowners, tribal chiefs, and conservative clerical leaders, was as much anathema to Reza Khan as to the middle class, the two were natural allies.

For the rank and file nationalists the ideological goals of liberal democracy had never been vital. Far more important for them were the halting of tribal and robber depredations, the breakdown of feudal restrictions on commerce, and westernization. If the liberal intellectuals had been capable of providing these essentials, the rank and file would probably have remained loyal to them. But the liberal intellectuals had failed where Reza Khan succeeded. Under him tribal chiefs were disciplined and lawlessness was ended, feudal barriers to trade were torn down, a trans-Iranian railroad and a highway network were constructed, and Iranian industry and commerce were given every encouragement and assistance. The newly respectable officer corps and the bureaucracy offered many job opportunities for sons of the middle class. Elementary and secondary education were expanded sixfold, and a system of universities and technical schools was inaugurated which gave Iran a larger educated and technically trained population. Even the Majlis and the diplomatic corps became realistic goals for talented members of the middle class.

Reza Khan attracted middle-class support. It was a section of the middle class that backed his scheme for establishing a republic, and it was the essentially middle-class officer corps that kept him from falling before the massive clerical-led attack in 1924. Nevertheless, the middle class at no time regarded Reza Khan as their savior. Whereas the majority of the middle class could not respond to the esoteric values of liberal democracy, they fully understood anti-imperialism, and on this score Reza Khan was vulnerable. The suspicion that he was sponsored by British imperialism was too strong to permit even the relatively unsophisticated to take him to their hearts. Then as time passed and the personality of Reza Shah evolved, the increasing tyranny, the gross corruption, and the cruelty of the Pahlavi dictatorship were easily comprehensible. Iran had gone far on the road to westernization, and law and order had been established, but much of the middle class felt personally insecure. The military, the Shah's coddled favorite, became steadily more arrogant and oppressive; personal fear of Reza Shah extended far down into the ranks of the public servants. This atmosphere was not the type to engender enthusiastic loyalty.[16]

[16] This can be seen by the public relief with which Reza Shah's abdication was greeted. See for example *Baba Shemal,* an excellent, satirical nationalist paper, for the year 1323 (1944). See also *Great Britain and the East,* Sept. 25, 1941, p. 107; "Iran and the Anglo-Russian Occupation," *Asiatic Review,* October 1941, p. 856.

But if the middle class could not accept Reza Shah as their ideal leader, neither were they any longer willing to follow the liberal intellectuals who had given them much excitement but little comfort. Deserted by most of their rank and file following, the liberal intellectuals slid deeper into a tragic dilemma. For many of these men nationalism without liberalism was a fraud, and, at any rate, how could anyone who knew of Reza Shah's British sponsorship take seriously his claim to be a great nationalist? Like so many liberal nationalists of the West, the Iranian intellectual had not considered the possibility that nationalism could be shorn of liberalism. Integral nationalism, that grotesque malaise of modern society, had appeared only in the writings of the theoreticians by the early 1920's; the Iranian can be excused for failing to recognize the qualities of integral nationalism that were appearing in Iran at this time. Today, with the history of Hitler and Mussolini still fresh in their minds, the Iranians understand much better that Reza Shah, regardless of any British sponsorship, was a nationalist.

Most of the liberal nationalists in the early 1920's moved naturally into the opposition to Reza Khan. Forced to choose between liberalism and nationalism, they unhesitatingly if not quite consciously chose the former. And having made this choice, they fell naturally into an alliance with the very elements of society that had always been their bitterest opponents: feudal, royalist, tribal, and reactionary clerical elements. In their overriding objective of combatting the Pahlavi antiliberalism, the liberals, who had called for a modern, centralized society, supported the anachronism that was Sheikh Khazal of Mohammarah; the liberals, who had worked unceasingly for more of a secular flavor in government, supported the clergy in their struggle against secularization; the liberals, many of whom had long looked with favor on the republican form of government, fought bitterly Reza Khan's efforts in this direction; and the liberals, who had hoped to inaugurate social and economic reforms that would have broadened the base of the politically aware, fought such reforms when they were inaugurated by Reza Khan.

The press was no longer the barometer it had been, registering the rising and falling of nationalist fortunes. As the Pahlavi dictatorship was consolidated, the newspapers took on the characteristics of the controlled press to be found in any authoritarian system. Even before Reza Khan finally became prime minister, the press had begun to bow to his will. Liberal editors were arrested and harassed by military authorities, and one particularly intransigent liberal editor, Mirzadeh Asheqi, was murdered by Reza Khan's men.[17] Liberalism disappeared from the press, and nationalism was enthroned. Nationalist propaganda dominated almost every issue of every paper, the reader being exhorted to love his country and to appreciate its great history and culture. Text books were rewritten to stress nationalism, and the entire education system was rallied to propagandize in favor of love of nation. Military training, in particular, reached the saturation point in stressing patriotic devotion. Boy scouts and girl scouts were organized and their leaders were instructed to inculcate nationalism in their youthful charges' minds.

Outside Iran two newspapers appeared that reflected widely varying views of Iranian intellectuals. *Habl al-Matin,* of Calcutta, did not join the Iranian liberal intellectuals in absolute condemnation of Reza Shah. Instead it praised his accomplishments and his dynamic leadership but pleaded with him to be more humane, more liberal, and to grant greater freedom.[18] The really interesting response was from *Farangistan,* which was published in Germany. Those contributing to this journal fully understood the social reasons for the failure of the liberal, democratic, nationalist experiment. They recognized that the social base for liberalism in Iran was too small and that the triumph of liberalism could never occur until that base had been widened. In order to achieve that goal *Farangistan* was willing to discard, temporarily, all liberalism and all humanitarianism. Its formula for success was a strong dictatorship and a blood bath that would totally destroy the effete aristocracy. Reza Shah was not, naturally enough, the ideal leader. What was called for was a tough-minded intellectual who could be as ruthless as Reza Shah but who would combine with this ruthlessness an intellectual comprehension of the liberal democratic goal.[19]

[17] Maki, III, 34.

[18] See for example *Habl al-Matin,* December 21, 1926.

[19] See *Farangistan* for the year 1924.

However, the specific programs *Farangistan* spelled out—extension of education, commerce, communications, etc.—were identical with the programs of the Pahlavi dictatorship. Reza Shah may have lacked the comprehension *Farangistan* wanted, and he certainly lacked the fundamental devotion to liberalism, but he succeeded in going a long way toward accomplishing just what *Farangistan* called for, i.e. the creation of a social base broad enough to support a liberal and democratic as well as nationalistic regime. The Mossadeq era could never have been possible without him.

But just as he built the social base of support for the Mossadeq era, Reza Shah deprived that era of the quality of leadership that was so desperately needed. During his rule Iranians learned to read literature, learned the facts of history, and gained an understanding of mathematics and the sciences, but they were denied the kind of free inquiry that could have prepared them for democratic political leadership. Some remarkable men served under Dr. Mossadeq, it is true, but a great many more were needed.

Reza Shah was more than an Iranian nationalist. His ambitions for Iran were intensely personal; like Charles de Gaulle, Reza Shah saw himself and his country virtually synonymous. But unlike de Gaulle in France, Reza Shah was never able to sell this personal image to the Iranian people. This accomplishment was reserved for Dr. Mohammad Mossadeq.

15

LIBERAL NATIONALISM: BRIEF TRIUMPH

It is one of the ironies of recent Iranian history that Reza Shah, a man who held liberalism and liberals in contempt, gave the Iranian liberal nationalists another, and possibly last, chance. The Iranian liberal is unlikely to admit his debt to the Pahlavi dictatorship, and, of course, Reza Shah's assistance to liberalism was totally inadvertent. But as a result of the Pahlavi economic and social program, the liberals were given a mass base which could furnish political support, the lack of which had been their chief deficiency. Likewise Reza Shah's unwillingness to permit the development of independent leadership within the greatly expanded middle class played into the hands of the liberal-intellectual element still led by the upper class. The middle class had nowhere else to turn for leadership.

The dynamics of growth of a mass society made this post-Reza Shah period the crucial moment for liberal nationalist leadership. Although the politically articulate element of the population had been expanded several times by Reza Shah's policies, probably no more than 10 per cent of the population belonged to this category. They were small enough in relative numbers and weak enough in leadership to respond to an offer of leadership from the liberal nationalist intelligentsia. Yet they were large enough in absolute numbers to be able to furnish their liberal nationalist leaders with the popular strength necessary to join battle with the Court and its landowner allies.

At this moment it seemed that if the liberal intellectuals rose to their historical opportunity and seized power, the chances would be good for a stable union of liberalism and nationalism. If the liberals consolidated this power, there was a possibility that they could control political and social developments in the difficult period ahead when the huge laboring and peasant mass began with an accelerating tempo to move into the ranks of the articulate. But should the liberal intelligentsia fail to secure leadership, there might well be no other opportunity. As the articulate base widened, the average of political sophistication was certain to fall and the opportunities for the demagogue or military dictator were certain to expand proportionately. The point would soon be reached at which the intellectual elite would have the greatest difficulty in gaining and maintaining leadership. The tragedy of the Mossadeq era is all the greater because the liberal intellectuals did rise to the occasion and assert their leadership, but they lacked the wisdom and good fortune to retain it.

In the fall of 1949 Iran yawned and prepared for another farcically staged election—this time for the Sixteenth Majlis. The Minister of Court, Abdol Hossein Hazhir, was believed to be an important power behind the throne and the man charged with rigging the election. At this moment Mohammad Reza Shah was preparing to leave for the United States to seek what he regarded as badly needed financial assistance. There was some concern in Tehran that Washington would be reluctant to grant aid to a government as corruption-ridden as that of Iran was rumored to be.[1] But there is no evidence that either Tehran or Washington was concerned because the coming election was rigged. However, on October 14, 1949, Dr. Mohammad Mossadeq and a group of followers, including many of Iran's outstanding intellectual leaders, took sanctuary in the palace grounds in order to protest the election. Immediately the issue of the rigged election became significant, since it highlighted the charge that Iran was led by a corrupt oligarchy.

Five days later a deeply embarrassed Shah promised Mossadeq that if an investigation showed that the election had not been free, a new one would be held.[2] Mossadeq and his followers dispersed, and an investigation was held. Most Iranians expected the inquiry to be a skilful whitewash; possibly a whitewash was planned. But on November 4, 1949, Hazhir was shot and on November 5 he died. Reminiscent of earlier assassinations in Iran, the death of Hazhir forced the Iranian oligarchy to realize that the gulf

[1] *The New York Times*, February 14, 1950, 22:1.
[2] *Ibid.*, October 19, 1949, 24:6.

separating them from the predominantly middle-class opposition was dangerously wide. The oligarchy might have reacted by suppressing the opposition leadership, but instead they followed their usual pattern of retreating in the face of violence. On November 11, 1949, the Tehran elections were declared invalid and new elections were ordered.[3] Between this date and the holding of elections, the Shah journeyed to Washington and was given to understand that significant financial aid would be forthcoming only after the Iranian house had been placed in order.[4] Returning to Iran, he called for a program of reforms. When the new Tehran elections were held in February the Shah permitted them to be relatively free.

In looking back over his career, Mohammad Reza Shah may well regard his decision to permit free elections in Tehran as his greatest mistake. Yet it is easy to see why he fell into this trap. He undoubtedly understood that Mossadeq and his colleagues would win in Tehran. But after all, his father had sometimes agreed to the victory of opposition candidates in order to give to the election a veneer of authenticity, and he had suffered no ill effects from this gesture. The Tehran delegation would, in any event, constitute only a small minority of the total, and the overwhelming majority of the provincial deputies met with the Shah's approval.

But times had changed. The parallel between Reza Shah's and Mohammad Reza Shah's parliaments was far from exact. The most fundamental difference was to be found in the attitude of the middle class. Reza Shah's base of support had been middle class, but that of his son was upper class; and in 1950 the middle class, now significantly large, was ripe for the emergence of new leadership. Thus while an opposition deputy in Reza Shah's day had been limited in his appeal to the thoroughly cowed upper class and to a handful of intellectuals and clerical leaders, the opposition deputy in 1950 could appeal to a significantly large body of politically articulate and dissatisfied voters.

The Shah did not see the danger signals until after the February elections. Indeed, very few people in Tehran took seriously the claim that the election would be free. *The New York Times*

[3] *Ibid.*, November 11, 1949, 7:6.
[4] *Ibid.*, February 14, 1950, 22:1.

correspondent reported that there was almost no indication of voter interest or activity.[5] But Dr. Mossadeq and seven ardent Nationalists, including Ayatollah Kashani, were elected, and the Sixteenth Majlis gave promise of being the most interesting since the First and the Second. Dr. Mossadeq and his allies had been granted a forum from which they could seek leadership of the nationalistic middle class. Barely fourteen months after the apathetic election in Tehran, Iran had a government which was able to attract enthusiastic mass support. In these fourteen months, Iranian nationalism, amorphous and leaderless, had crystallized into Iranian Nationalism guided by a great leader and possessed of a feeling of an almost mystical national mission.

Descriptions of postwar Iranian leadership in Western journals and books commonly describe the leaders of Iran's oligarchy as "pro-West," whereas Dr. Mossadeq and his followers are commonly dismissed with the "anti-West" label. This is a melancholy commentary on mid-twentieth-century America. Quite conceivably the dictates of *realpolitik* may call for a working arrangement or even alignment between the feudalistically-oriented Iranian oligarchy and the democratic West. But such cooperation, if it is necessary, should be undertaken only after a careful and honest analysis of both the internal political situation and the consequences, within and beyond Iran's borders, resulting from an alliance with elements that by no stretch of the imagination can be described as sharing the ideological convictions of the West.

For reasons that seem to inhere deeply in Americana, however, the American public and the American leaders appear to be driven by a necessity for rationalizing such alliances ideologically. Thus the term "pro-West" with reference to Iranian leaders may have meant at first simply a willingness to associate openly with the West in the Cold War and the term "anti-West" may have meant no more than an unwillingness to engage in such an open alliance with the West; but the meanings of both terms soon broadened until the feudalistically-oriented upper class and the increasingly totalitarian-minded Shah were thought of as ideological allies, and such men as Mossadeq, whose attachment to liberal democracy in 1952 may well have led to his overthrow in 1953, were regarded as

[5] *Ibid.*, February 10, 1950, 11:1.

ideological enemies. With the infinitely complex Iranian political situation reduced to the ideological simplicity of a television melodrama, decision-making in Washington became easy.

Some Iranians sincerely question the honesty and the patriotism of Dr. Mossadeq, but there are probably fewer adverse opinions of Mossadeq than of any Iranian statesman who was prominent in the past 150 years. Born with the security of wealth and a firm position within the Iranian oligarchy, including blood ties with the Qajar dynasty, Mossadeq was nevertheless a logical candidate for leadership of an essentially middle-class movement. The date of his birth is unknown, although the year 1880 is not a bad guess. In any case, he was a convinced liberal democrat by the time of the 1906 revolution. He had spent his formative years in French and Swiss educational institutions, and upon returning to Iran became one of a number of upper-class liberals who until the days of Reza Shah were to provide the intellectual direction of Iranian nationalism. Following his political eclipse during the Pahlavi dictatorship, when Mohammad Reza Shah, breaking tradition with his father, chose to associate his own political fortunes with those of the old oligarchy, Mossadeq became the rallying point for the leaderless middle class. He had a masterful but extravagant sense of drama, and even within the Iranian culture, where a public display of emotions is the norm, his histrionics skirted the narrow line between the effective and the overdone. Many Western observers could not take him seriously because of his public weeping and fainting. But partly because of his histrionics, Mossadeq was able to bring to Iranian nationalism a personal leadership that soon became symbolic.

A widely prevalent view in Western circles is that liberal democracy cannot establish itself in the developing Afro-Asian states until after the appearance of a politically mature public. Although the case of India and Nehru argues strongly that this pessimistic view is not always valid, the history of liberal democracy in most of Asia demonstrates that there is much to be said for it. A comprehension of liberal democracy is difficult enough to achieve for educated Westerners. For the workers and peasants who are emerging into political awareness in the developing societies, such a comprehension is impossible. It is doubtful that liberal democracy could survive in the newly independent states without the appearance of a remarkable individual who is able to capture the support of the newly awakened and yet who is, and remains, a firm advocate of liberal democracy.

Nehru is such a man and Mossadeq could have been. From the time of his election to the Sixteenth Majlis until his triumphant return from the United Nations in early 1952, Mossadeq was accepted by an ever-expanding public as an absolutely trustworthy leader who deserved their wholehearted and uncritical support. A large majority of the middle class came to this view in early 1951, and by January 1952 a significantly large and expanding percentage of the urban lower class and peasantry was beginning to share this opinion. Mossadeq was rapidly becoming the personification of the Iranian striving both for international independence and dignity and for the replacement of oligarchic control. That he was also a liberal democrat was no more than incidental for most of his following; but for the complexion of Iranian nationalism his devotion to liberal democracy was a primary determinant.

The appearance of this symbolic leadership was essential for the vitality of the Nationalist movement. By itself, however, the appeal of the Mossadeq personality could not have given life to the movement. Of equal importance was the formation of a coalition of leaders supported by the middle class who were able to unite behind Mossadeq in a struggle against the political predominance of the oligarchy. The history of the Mossadeq era demonstrates that the pro-Mossadeq leaders and Mossadeq himself had to remain within a recognized ideological framework if they were to retain middle-class elite support or run the risk of ostracism and a loss of influence. At the same time, most of the elements in the Nationalist coalition had not evolved into the type of formal organization that would warrant the appellation of "party."

The political groupings that came closest to meeting the requirements for a definition of "political party" were to be found on the left wing of the National Front. Furthest to the left was the Toilers Party, headed by the strong-minded, dynamic Dr. Mozaffar Baqai. But the Toilers Party was in several respects a transitional party which contained within its membership and leadership elements of the old and the new in Iranian group politics. Dr. Baqai was one of the outstanding Nationalist leaders, and, in fact, could reasonably regard himself as Mossadeq's heir apparent. However, it was this very prominence of its leader that militated against the Toilers' becoming a modern political party. A sizeable percentage of the leadership was completely loyal to Baqai and was prepared to follow him through the many ideological twists and turns he was to make in the next few years. The Toilers Party was a coalition itself of Marxist but anti-Stalinist intellectuals and of socialistic but undoctrinaire labor organizers. It was the latter group that remained loyal to Baqai. The former group, however, led by Khalil Maleki, was much less flexible ideologically and was destined eventually to split away from the Toilers Party and to form a Titoist party, the Third Force (Niru Sevvom) . Maleki had been a leading Tudeh Party theoretician but had been disillusioned primarily by the Soviet attempt to set up a puppet government in Azerbaijan.

A far stronger case for being a genuine political party can be made for the Iran Party. Until the creation of the Third Force, only the Iran Party of the noncommunist groupings could be described as clearly independent of the leadership of one man. Allahyar Saleh, who was generally recognized as the Iran Party leader, was popular and highly respected but in no sense an indispensable leader. Had he given up the leadership of the party, there is no reason to believe that the party would have lost much vitality. Although the Iran Party lacked the ideological rigidity of the yet to be born Third Force, it had a consistently Fabian socialist shading along with its intense nationalism. The membership was drawn primarily from professional people, including a surprisingly high percentage of the best qualified of the young bureaucrats. Doctors, lawyers, engineers, journalists, professors, and teachers were more frequently found in this party than were businessmen.

Saleh may have been dispensable, but his successor would undoubtedly have come from one of a clearly-identifiable group of Nationalist elder statesmen. Younger Nationalists who shared the general goals of the Iran Party leadership but differed strongly in their view of strategy and tactics wanted a larger voice in policy determination. The nucleus of this opposition was to be found in a group of young intellectuals and professional men who formed a group called Mardom Iran and who had merged with the Iran Party in 1950. In the inner party councils this group had one-third representation. The issue came to a head in February 1952, when Mohammad Nakhshab, one of the founders of the Mardom Iran, was expelled, taking with him up to 50 per cent of the party. The Mardom Iran, whose leaders included Nakhshab, Hossein Razi, and Dr. Mohammad Ali Shariatmadari advocated what they called "spiritual socialism" along with intense nationalism. But the ideological differences were less important than the challenge to party leadership. The Iran Party-Mardom Iran conflict parallels closely similar conflicts in the highly bureaucratized French Socialist party and indicates that upper-class Nationalist politicians had so institutionalized their control of the Iran Party that they in fact constituted a structured party bureaucracy.

Comparable political organizers were not to be found either in the center or in the conservative right of the National Front. In the center, however, were to be found most of the closest associates of Dr. Mossadeq. Each of these men had his own supporters, but few were thinking in organizational terms. The National Front itself was centrist-dominated for the simple reason that its leader, Dr. Mossadeq, belonged there. Post-Mossadeq developments indicate that the nucleus for centrist political parties existed in organizations of medium to prosperous merchants, usually with strong religious overtones and with allies among both the faculty and the student body of the University of Tehran.

On the conservative right of Mossadeq's followers were to be found most of the large merchants, landowners, and senior military officers. At first their number was substantial, and though the earliest defections from the coalition came from this group, many remained true to the end. There is nothing to indicate that this group was approaching an organizational stage.

Outside of the left-right classification were to be found the nationalist-extremist and the predominantly religious organizations. The nationalist-extremist groups were clearly influenced by European Fascism. The pan-Iranist press of the Mossadeq period demonstrates conclusively that the anti-Semitism, anticapitalism, anticommunism, and the wildly imperialistic claims of this political group bore an uncomfortable resemblance to Hitlerian dogma. The so-called Pan-Iran Party attracted adherents chiefly from middle- and lower-middle-class secondary school students, but it also had an appeal for athletic society toughs. Pan-Iran suffered a series of bewildering splits, each splinter group claiming to be the authentic Pan-Iran party. The most loyal and largest of these groups was headed by Dariush Foruhar, but at its height this group could not have numbered more than a few thousand and was largely confined to Tehran.

Defying classification on any right-left scale stand the religio-political organizations that either were allied to or were integral parts of the National Front. The Fedayan Islam almost by definition could not have been associated intimately with the National Front. Composed of the most bitter opponents of the secular trend, the Fedayan was the natural enemy of the Nationalist movement. The accusation has been made that Dr. Baqai, Ayatollah Kashani, and several other leading members of the National Front had given their blessing to the planned assassination of Premier Razmara. Kashani, for his part, almost too readily admitted the charge. He understood that Razmara's assassination was more widely applauded than condemned. But the Fedayan-National Front alliance did not survive the formation of the Mossadeq government.[6] Since Kashani's organization, the Mojahadin Islam, has been described in Chapter 10,[7] little needs to be added here other than the reaffirmation that both its strength and its weakness lay with the leadership of Kashani. His personality and attitudes dictated organizational policy, and since his leadership was vital and dynamic Kashani was a source of great strength to the Mojahadin Islam. But, as will be seen later, when Kashani broke with the National Movement he carried his organization to destruction.

There were a great many politically minded religious leaders who, although deeply devoted to the National Movement, did not identify themselves with the Mojahadin Islam because of an inability to work with Kashani or because of disapproval of his rabble rousing. These leaders made little effort to organize rival

[6] See Chapter 10, pp. 151–52.
[7] See Chapter 10, pp. 152–55.

organizations, since opposition was not needed at this time. Nevertheless, included among these men were some of Iran's most able and popular religious figures; Kashani's monopoly of religio-political power was nowhere nearly as complete as he and many Western observers imagined.

The National Front coalition, then, embraced elements from all sections of the body politic—religious and secular, upper class and peasant, right and left. To be sure, the center of political gravity lay with the middle class and with those on the center left economically; nevertheless the coalition was of so disparate a nature that only the broadest kind of program could have held it together. In all probability unity could have been maintained only by the type of program that the National Front endorsed, i.e. one that in its immediate and specific objectives was overwhelmingly negative and in its general objectives was all encompassing in its vagueness. The specific objectives concerned destroying all aspects of the oligarchical-imperial alliance, especially that most important of political weapons, the Anglo-Iranian Oil Company. The general objective was to build an economically healthy, independent Iran. This program was essentially revolutionary, and, as has been the case with most revolutionary movements, the negative objectives were far more concrete than the positive.

For most of the intervening fourteen months following the February 1950 elections in Tehran and prior to the total Nationalist victory, the Iranian premier was General Ali Razmara. When Razmara was assassinated in March of 1951 much of the Nationalist element rejoiced. Yet Razmara's record indicates that he was a nationalist, and he had the potential in personality, temperament, and talent of becoming a great leader of Iran. His failure was the failure of most Iranian leaders and of most Western statesmen concerned with Iran: the inability to understand that the political attitudes of the interested public must now be considered in Iran. A significant element of the population had become politically articulate, had acquired opinions and aspirations, and was seeking political leadership. There was nothing inevitable about Mossadeq's emergence as the symbol of Iranian aspirations. Razmara might just as well have become the popular idol had he recognized that social and social-psychological evolution had proceeded to the point where public idolatry mattered. There was political consensus in Iran on the necessity for waging a struggle against oligarchical and Western imperial control. Razmara could easily have satisfied the public on this issue, but instead he gave the appearance of allying himself with both the oligarchy and the Western imperialists. By March 1951 it was too late, even had he lived. Already nationalist sentiment had focused on Mossadeq, a man who intuitively understood the popular wish and, even more important, shared it.

Today, references to the early Mossadeq period are rare. Especially in the West, where there is an almost pathetic effort to paint the Shah as an ideological good-guy, this period is treated as a demagogic flash in the pan. The breadth and intensity of the public support for Mossadeq is difficult to recreate. That *Time* magazine, for example, should have chosen Mossadeq as its man of the year in 1952 seems now to have been almost aberrant. *Time's* cover story of Mossadeq could hardly have pleased Mossadeq's supporters; but they ignored the story and revelled in the implications of Mossadeq's selection. The choice of Mossadeq was made because he symbolized the emergence in the Middle East of a popular force capable of establishing itself in power. Mossadeq ultimately failed, and world attention has focused on another Middle Eastern leader who gives personification to a popular force. But Mossadeq's premiership remains extremely significant; both the triumphs and the eventual defeat of Iranian Nationalism need to be surveyed if Iranian nationalism is to be understood.

The facts show the tremendous popularity of the National Front as the leadership of Iranian Nationalism, and the two most telling indicators were the Majlis and the press. No more than twelve of more than 130 deputies in the Sixteenth Majlis could have been described as Iranian Nationalists, and the majority of the deputies were known to have been very happy with the status quo ante; but this same Majlis voted unanimously for nationalization of the oil industry and overwhelmingly for the premiership of Mossadeq. Their lack of sincerity was demonstrated many times when at the slightest glimmer of hope for the removal of Mossadeq the deputies were ready to withdraw their support. In private conversation they showed that they were never really on his side. The deputies, most of whom represented the old oligarchy, were merely following their established pattern of bowing before overwhelming force. The point is that they recognized this force existed in the form of an aroused public opinion.

For the first year and a half of the Mossadeq government the press gives an equally clear picture. The Tudeh press and the rightist opposition attacked Mossadeq and the National Front bitterly, even violently,[8] but their frame of reference was nationalistic. Both groups of opposition papers accused Mossadeq of being an agent of imperialism, this time American imperialism. Both affirmed again and again that the British and the oligarchy were Iran's great enemies, insisting that their backers could far better wage the holy battle against these enemies than could the National Front. In so doing both indicated a full awareness of the pervasiveness of the sentiment for the Nationalist program.

The great tragedy of the Mossadeq period was that the immense energy that had been unleashed was not harnessed to a constructive program; the tragedy is all the greater since this energy could have been so harnessed. In the foregoing pages the disparity of forces aligned in the National Front has been noted and the comment made that this coalition could exist only as long as the common goal was negative. But very soon after he took office public faith was invested in Mossadeq to a spectacular extent, and at this point the fringe elements of the Mossadeq alliance could have been dropped without perceptibly weakening the government. Not until the closing days of his regime did Mossadeq seem to understand that the immensity of his popular support gave him a freedom of action that no Iranian statesman had ever enjoyed. It was not that Mossadeq failed to recognize that he had this support. On the contrary, he always understood that fact. What Mossadeq failed to understand was that this domestic support gave him great independence in dealing with the British. It was his overestimation of the peril from the British that compelled him to maintain his cumbersome alliance far past the point of marginal utility.

The Mossadeq government did have a positive program. Since the young professional class gave Mossadeq overwhelming support, a reservoir of dedication and talent was always available, and there

[8] See Chapter 13, pp. 212–13.

was much energetic planning. Some programs materialized, the most important of these being agricultural reform. Much has been made in the Western press of Mossadeq's unwillingness to cooperate with the widely advertised program of land distribution inaugurated by Mohammad Reza Shah. Invariably the comment appears that Mossadeq as a great landowner sought to preserve the old estates. This supposition is but one example of the gross misinterpretation of Mossadeq's case in the Western press. In fact, had Mossadeq's program of agricultural reform been extended and carried out after his overthrow, Iranian agriculture and Iranian villages could by now have shown much progress.[9]

Experience has demonstrated time and again that turning over land to a peasant who is largely ignorant of modern agricultural methods rarely benefits him. Generally the peasant soon falls into the hands of the loan shark, who replaces the old landowner as a new and far less benevolent master. In Iran, where entire communities depend on a very costly and difficult-to-maintain irrigation system, this sequence of events is especially true. For land distribution to be really meaningful in Iran, the peasant must be sufficiently educated to understand seed selection, marketing, how to obtain low interest loans, and, most important, the necessity for a cooperative enterprise with his fellow villagers for the maintenance of the irrigation system. Very few peasants approach this understanding.

The National Front agricultural program was less spectacular than that of Mohammad Reza Shah, but far more fundamental. By this program the percentage of profits a landowner could legitimately claim was limited by law. The landowner was required to pay 20 per cent of his profits back to the village, half for the peasants and half for community improvements. These improvements would be directed towards the long-range goal of educating the peasants to the best methods of agricultural practice. The village council, which the law attempted to place under village rather than landowner control, would plan a community-wide approach to the problem of health, sanitation, and irrigation. For its part Tehran would provide highly trained advisors to help the

[9] Albion Ross, "Mossadegh: Prophet or Buffoon," *The New York Times*, September 28, 1952, Sec. 6, 16:1. This article is the best journalistic study on Mossadeq.

council plan improvements. Point IV can claim a major share of credit for the inauguration of this program and for the training of a group of young, educated Iranians who became a nucleus of community experts.[10] Of course, such a program could only begin slowly, hampered as it was by the lack of a sufficient number of trained technicians and by the difficulties of enforcement.

There were other positive programs in the fields of education, health, and industry. Iran's Plan Organization, which was responsible for economic and social planning, had a devoted and high-caliber staff under the direction of Ahmad Zanganeh. But the Plan Organization lacked the financial means for executing any program it might have devised, a deficiency which could only have been removed by the concluding of an oil agreement; and, of even greater importance, it did not have the full support and interest of Mossadeq and his chief lieutenants that was necessary for success. The Plan Organization failed to receive the attention due it for the same reason that all other aspects of the positive program were neglected. Mossadeq and his advisors were overwhelmingly preoccupied in the negative battle against Britain and its real or imagined domestic allies.

The focal point of this negative struggle was the oil issue. As has been described above, the dispute was for the Iranians primarily a political dispute. The comments of the Nationalist leaders regarding the economics of this dispute indicate that their conception of the financial complexities of oil was simple to the point of being childlike. Such economic primitivism reflected their belief that economic aspects were not of prime importance. Their overriding objective was to make sure that Iran's oil industry could never be used as a weapon to maintain political control in the hands of the British-backed oligarchy. There may be more than an element of truth to the Nationalists' claim that they found much evidence of political interference by AIOC, but the conclusion is nonetheless justified that the Nationalists grossly exaggerated the quantity of such interference and the malevolence of motivation behind it.

The late Ambassador Henry Grady, writing after he retired from the Foreign Service, demonstrated a lucid comprehension of

[10] *The New York Times,* September 28, 1952, Sec. 6, 16:1.

the fact that Iranian fear of future British political manipulations was the chief stumbling block to an oil settlement. Grady deplored the lack of reality in this Iranian belief and expressed strong concern that the exaggerated fear could itself lead to disaster.[11] But, as Grady pointed out, the situation could still have been salvaged by the British. Had they accepted Grady's premises there is reason to believe that the British could have removed the major obstacle preventing the Nationalist movement from moving in a constructive direction. These premises were (a) that the Nationalist movement was a genuine expression of Iranian public opinion, (b) that the Nationalist leaders were the least corrupt and most dedicated group in modern Iranian history and were sincerely concerned with achieving independence for their nation and modernizing it, and (c) that the Nationalists, leaders and public alike, believed that the British were engaged in minute, day-by-day interference in the internal affairs of Iran for the purpose of maintaining oligarchic control over a weak, raw-material-producing, semi-independent Iran. But the Iranians were not alone in their unreality. The British, who for practical and psychological reasons could not accept any of the above premises however strong the supporting evidence, persisted in their antiquarian conviction that the Iran of 1951 differed little from the Iran of 1901.

If the British had accepted Grady's evaluation, the oil negotiations could have been conducted on a realistic plane. They could have been based on plans for removal of historical and largely invalid Iranian suspicions rather than on the less relevant economic points. However, the policy pursued by the British was hopelessly out of touch with reality. They were faced with the need of convincing Iranians that they would not again interfere in Iranian affairs to block political and economic progress. But their actions had exactly the opposite effect. They first considered sending a naval force to the Persian Gulf. Having been dissuaded by the American government, they inaugurated an economic blockade. This policy was doubly unfortunate because it resurrected and reinforced the historical Iranian belief that Britain did

[11] *US News and World Report,* October 19, 1951, pp. 13–17.

not wish to see a prosperous Iran.[12] This policy provided Iranian Nationalism with a much needed scapegoat for their failure to reconstruct Iran more rapidly. Here was moral justification for a continued negative orientation; the Iranian Nationalist could tell himself that no progress was possible until the enemy of that progress had been defeated. Thus the British response strengthened the negativism of the Iranian challenge.

A strong case can be made for the hypothesis that, paradoxically, Mossadeq's strong belief in liberal democracy helped set in motion the forces that were to lead him and the National Movement to defeat. Mossadeq was determined that the Seventeenth Majlis election should be free. Convinced that the people supported him, he saw little reason to fear a popular verdict. In this thinking Mossadeq was incredibly naive. Although it was true that articulate opinion in January 1952, when the elections began, was overwhelmingly pro-Mossadeq, the majority of Iranians were not articulate. Tehran and Tabriz would support Mossadeq, but what of the thousands of villages in which no more than a handful of peasants were politically aware? Traditionally these peasants had allowed themselves to be herded like cattle to vote for the candidate of the landowner. What of provincial centers such as Yazd, where only a thin veneer of the population could understand and endorse the National Movement and where the lower classes voted for the candidates of the leading citizens with the same docility as did their peasant counterparts? And finally, although the National Front could be described as being pro-Mossadeq, it was a diverse coalition in which the Iran Party and the centrists were much closer to Mossadeq than were the religio-nationalists or the extremes on the right and left. Would it be wise to sit back passively while the demagogic Kashani and Baqai thoroughly routed the moderates?

The early returns from the Seventeenth Majlis elections provided the answers to these questions. Elections were traditionally staggered in Iran, and among the first districts to vote in 1952 was that of Zanjan, a border Azerbaijan district. The city of Zanjan is a middle-sized Iranian provincial center. Due largely to its location

[12] This was an almost daily topic for discussion in the Tehran press in the Mossadeq period. See for example *Keyhan*, September 18, 1951.

at the center of a rich agricultural area and on the Tabriz-Tehran road, Zanjan was perhaps above average in the percentage of its population that was politically aware. But a powerful family, the Zolfaqari clan, traditionally dominated the politics of the area. Although there were Mossadeq supporters in Zanjan, active interference would have been necessary from the Ministry of Interior to secure a Mossadeq victory. Mossadeq refused to interfere in the election, even to the extent of preventing the landowners from herding their peasants to the polls, and when the returns were in the Zolfaqaris had won.

The victory was no tragedy for Mossadeq. Although the Zolfaqaris could not be described as Nationalists, they had demonstrated that they were nationalists by their courageous opposition to Soviet designs on Azerbaijan at a time when many landowners were collaborating with the communists. Nevertheless, the middle-class Mossadeqists in Zanjan were bitterly disappointed at the election of the Zolfaqaris, and Mossadeq suffered a loss of prestige.

The worst was yet to come. If the Zolfaqaris were politically moderate and unquestionably patriotic, other newly elected deputies were of the unreconstructed oligarchy. Most notorious of all the election results were those in the city of Yazd, one of Iran's major provincial centers. Three men regarded by the public as servants of the British were elected. Since in a city the size of Yazd only a minimum of official interference would have been sufficient to tip the scales in Mossadeq's favor, middle-class Nationalists began to wonder if Mossadeq's membership in the upper class was not the real reason for the middle-class defeat.

Tehran, of course, voted overwhelmingly in favor of the National Front candidates.[13] The communists ran a poor second and the right opposition an almost negligible third. Tabriz was not so encouraging, however. The nine men elected from that district were totally committed to the support of Mossadeq, and neither the Tudeh nor the right opposition made a substantial showing; but, unlike in Tehran, where the diverse elements of the National Front had been represented in the victorious official slate, in Tabriz the National Front was split. An active campaign was

[13] *Ettelaat,* February 17, 1952.

waged between the religio-nationalist element and the more moderate intellectual leaders. The result was a stunning victory for the candidates Kashani had endorsed and vigorously supported. The two top posts went by a huge vote to two prominent clerics, Angaji and Milani. Three others among the victors were religious candidates, and of the remaining four victors the centrist National Front had not wanted two of them.

By now thoroughly alarmed, the Iran Party and the center seriously proposed abrogating the Tabriz election and holding new elections. But Mossadeq's support could not be enlisted, and the proposals died. However, the National Front center understood at this point that a major retreat from idealism would have to be made if the right and Kashani were not to gain complete control of the Seventeenth Majlis. Kermanshah, Kerman, Rasht, and Kashan had elected staunch supporters of Mossadeq, but indications from Shiraz, Isfahan, and especially from Mashhad were that Kashani forces and possibly Kashani-right candidates might win if the government did not interfere. Only in those rural constituencies in which leading families happened to be pro-Mossadeq was there hope for a Nationalist victory.

The final blow to the doctrinaire idealism of the Mossadeqist election was delivered by the Shah himself. There were a number of districts in Iran which were in military zones and under the control of the Army; and the Army in Iran reported directly to the Shah. In one of these districts, Meshgin Shahr, the Army engineered the election of Mehdi Mir-Ashrafi, the thoroughly corrupt, opportunistic editor of *Atesh,* a sometime Mossadeqist, sometime rightist opposition paper. Mir-Ashrafi had no claim to represent the Azerbaijani district in which his election was engineered, and his selection was greeted with dismay throughout the National Front. Mossadeq's response to a now desperate situation was still not to rig the remaining elections, but rather to halt any further elections after a bare quorum of sixty-nine deputies had been elected. Traditionally in Iran elections in various districts are put off indefinitely, but never before had the election for almost half of the deputies been postponed.

By putting off the remainder of the elections Mossadeq had not extricated himself. Only twenty-five of the sixty-nine elected deputies were to prove totally reliable for the National Front, and close to a majority were from the beginning privately opposed to Mossadeq.[14] These deputies gave Mossadeq overt support as long as he was the overwhelming choice of the articulate elements. But in July 1952, when it was generally believed that Britain and the United States were in favor of Mossadeq's replacement by Ahmad Qavam, they voted against Mossadeq. Then after the ouster of Qavam by an immense popular upsurge, these privately oppositionist deputies returned to their policy of public support of Mossadeq. This pattern held true as long as the opposition was confined to the landowning right. Not until a major split occurred within the National Front did energetic leadership for the opposition materialize.

The National Front split became complete in the winter and spring of 1953. The results of this split were to be (a) a demonstration that Mossadeq's personal standing among the Nationalists had become unassailable, (b) proof that the unwillingness of Mossadeq to rig the election was, paradoxically, a fatal error if liberalism were to triumph in Iran, (c) the forcing of Mossadeq to move in the direction of the very dictatorial control he had so long fought, and (d) a great advantage to those working for Mossadeq's overthrow.

In the Seventeenth Majlis elections in Tehran the recipient of the highest vote was Hossein Maki, a strong Nationalist, but a man of only mediocre abilities. Maki regarded himself as the Mossadeq government's expert on the oil question and, after the Tehran election, as Mossadeq's heir apparent. Maki, who was no match intellectually, socially, or politically for many of his rivals, found himself being relegated more and more to the background. Eventually his disaffection came into the open, and in early 1953 the public became aware of his split with their idol.[15] The result was a total popular eclipse of Maki. Virtually none of those who had voted for Maki were willing to follow him out of the National Front. On the contrary, the suspicion, so carefully nurtured

[14] The hard core of Mossadeq's strength, thirty deputies, was demonstrated by the vote on July 18, 1952, for the premiership of Ahmad Qavam. *The New York Times*, July 18, 1952, 1:2. Following the defections of Maki, Baqai, and Kashani the number of regular supporters fell to twenty-five.

[15] *The New York Times*, January 9, 1953, 1:2.

previously by the right opposition, that Maki had been in secret collaboration with the British was thereafter given much wider credence.

The next to break openly with Mossadeq was Dr. Baqai. His break was far more serious for the National Front than that of Maki had been. In contrast to Maki, Baqai was a forceful, highly intelligent man with loyal organizational support. Baqai claimed as his reason for the break Mossadeq's soft policy towards communism, but this statement need not be taken too seriously. As the leader of a strong political organization, as publisher of the influential Nationalist newspaper *Shahed,* and as a longtime close ally of Ayatollah Kashani, from whom he could expect strong support, Baqai could lay serious claim to the leadership of the National Front. But Baqai, like Maki, had failed to comprehend the charismatic quality of Mossadeq's personal appeal. As Baqai began to split with Mossadeq, the largely Titoist intellectual element of his Toilers Party left him and formed a new and loyal Mossadeqist party, the Third Force; and when Khalil Maleki, the leader of Third Force, and others ceased writing for *Shahed,* that paper lost its intellectual excellence and its strong popularity. After the split Baqai was left with only a few intellectual followers, and henceforth his organization was dominated by men who differed only in degree from the chaqu keshan leaders. Because his strength had been greater than Maki's, Baqai's sudden political destruction was even more spectacular, and the indication of Mossadeq's popular strength was greater.

By far the most critical of the splits, however, occurred when Kashani broke openly and angrily with Mossadeq in January 1953.[16] Maki and Baqai had both looked for much of their support from the secular-minded middle-middle and upper-middle classes, but Kashani's strength had always been with the lower-middle class, which traditionally responded to religious leadership. Although Mossadeq's victory over Maki and Baqai proved his supreme strength with the middle-middle and upper-middle classes, his appeal to the lower-middle class was yet to be demonstrated. There were grounds for believing that a Mossadeq-Kashani split would result in each leader's taking with him a large block of

[16] *Ibid.,* January 19, 1953, 1:2.

the public. Actually, the split destroyed all of Kashani's broad support. Inside the Majlis only two of the religious deputies remained with him; the remainder, including the popular and powerful Tabriz delegation, chose to remain loyal to Dr. Mossadeq.[17] Even more of a blow to Kashani, the majority of the religious-oriented guild leaders in the covered bazaar chose to follow Mossadeq's leadership.[18]

The mistake of each of the three men who split was the failure to understand that his opponent was not just an Iranian politician by the name of Mohammad Mossadeq, but a man around whom a vital, intense popular movement had crystallized. Since his followers were convinced that Mossadeq's crusade was mainly directed against foreign imperialism, the logical conclusion was that anyone who turned against him was in league with the imperialists. Thus Maki, Baqai, and Kashani were not only shorn of support, but were regarded by many of their former supporters as having sold out to the foreign enemy.

Mossadeq's personal victory over his rivals was almost total. Nevertheless, the three were to have their revenge. A strong case can be made for the assertion that their defection tipped the balance against the National Front. First, even though only a minority of deputies joined in the defection, Baqai and Kashani and their allies were able to give the timorous landowner opposition the type of affirmative leadership that was needed to mobilize the anti-Mossadeq forces. Second, Maki, Baqai, and especially Kashani had been the three men most capable of bringing out the mob support the National Front had enjoyed in the streets. Following the split, Kashani demonstrated his continuing ability to produce a mob, but it was the typical chaqu keshan mob rather than the earlier Kashani-organized mob that had had an element of genuine nationalist fervor. Other National Front leaders remained who had influence among the lower-middle class from which the mob arises. But none of these men compared with Kashani or Baqai in their ability to create and control such mobs. Consequently, the National Front could not be expected to rally the amount of street support of former years.

17 *Ibid.*, January 20, 1953, 1:4.
18 *Ibid.*, April 16, 1953, 6:3.

The full impact of this development was soon felt. Mossadeq was probably still congratulating himself on his victory when, on February 27, 1953, a howling mob attacked his house and sent him scurrying, pajama clad, over the wall of his compound into the neighboring Point IV office and from there to the Majlis. The "spontaneity" of the mob was clear to any seasoned observer of Tehran. The leader of the mob was the most notorious of all the chaqu keshan chiefs, Shaban Ja'fari, nicknamed the "Brainless." It was obvious that the mob had been purchased by Kashani's group. Mossadeq did not leave these conclusions to the imagination. He stated flatly that Kashani had organized the mobs in collaboration with the Court and, inferentially, with the British.[19] Several days earlier Mossadeq had stated that an oil agreement could be quickly negotiated were the British not hopeful that his enemies would topple him, leaving the way clear for a more favorable settlement of the oil issue.[20]

By March of 1953 the situation had crystallized for Mossadeq. Lines by now were clearly drawn. The National Front, with the withdrawal of Maki, Baqai, and Kashani, was a tighter, more homogeneous and potentially stronger organization; but for the time being because of their representation in the Majlis the three defectors were a thorn in Mossadeq's side. The rightist, landowner element in the Majlis could be counted on to remain docile unless there was a clear show of strength on the part of other anti-Mossadeq forces. The Court was obviously in collaboration with the opposition, but the Court proper was little threat, and it was possible that the Shah might yet become a constitutional monarch who would support a moderate political, social, and economic reform program. The Tudeh was making a strong bid for collaboration with the Mossadeqists, but the latter had severely rebuffed the Tudeh,[21] and did not regard as serious the subversive potential of the communists. There was one major danger spot as seen by Mossadeq. The general officers in the Army were less than enthusiastic about the regime, and an energetic group of retired officers led by General Fazlollah Zahedi was openly antagonistic.

19 *Ibid.*, March 1, 1953, 24:3–6.
20 *Ibid.*, February 24, 1953, 10:5.
21 *Ibid.*, March 4, 1953, 8:1.

Since the Shah retained primary control over the Army, this was Mossadeq's Achilles' heel. General Zahedi openly proclaimed his intention of ousting the regime, and, as an additional complication, it was believed that the British were in close liason with Zahedi and his men.

Clearly, then, the Army was the key to the situation. Therefore, Mossadeq set about the task of bringing the Army under the control of the prime minister and his cabinet. He had appointed a "Committee of Eight" deputies who could make proposals as to the proper constitutional role of the Court. This committee, several members of which were moderate nationalists, recommended that the Shah accept a limited constitutional role and that the control of all the armed forces be vested in the cabinet.[22] Mossadeq's seriousness of purpose is reflected in the fact that he was willing to give up his hard-fought-for plenary powers in economic affairs as a bargaining point if the opposition would accede to his demand for control over the armed forces.[23] The opposition knew that with control of the military, Mossadeq could consolidate his power. Were the "Committee of Eight" report ever to be voted on, however, the docile landowner deputies would certainly support Mossadeq. Consequently, the opposition's tactic was to prevent the gathering of a quorum of deputies. At each crucial moment a group of opposition deputies would suddenly leave town to see their sick grandmothers, and the vote would not be held.[24]

Mossadeq was securely caught in his own trap. As the days passed it became obvious that the impasse could only be broken by extralegal means. For a time it appeared that the answer lay in completing the elections, and this time the election officials would make certain that only National Front supporters could be elected. However, since the approval of a quorum of Majlis deputies was necessary before the credentials of a newly elected deputy could be accepted a handful of deputies was able to block the seating of the new deputies just as they had blocked the approval of the "Committee of Eight" recommendations.[25]

[22] *Ibid.*, April 7, 1953, 1:7.
[23] *Ibid.*, March 17, 1953, 10:5.
[24] *Ibid.*, April 17, 1953, 6:3.
[25] *Ibid.*, April 21, 1953, 18:2.

On April 21, 1953, Mossadeq's loyal and energetic police chief, Mohammad Afshartus, disappeared after telling Mossadeq of a mysterious rendezvous he was making. A few days later his body was discovered. An investigation soon implicated Baqai (Afshartus was murdered in the house of Hossein Khatibi, a Baqai henchman, and now Court favorite), General Zahedi and his associates, a leading merchant, and a son of Ayatollah Kashani.[26] Mossadeq could no longer doubt the desperate nature of his situation, and the appeal of extraconstitutional measures became stronger. The only alternative that remained, the Mossadeqists seemed to believe, was to compel the United States to come to Mossadeq's aid. When this attempt was rebuffed in Eisenhower's letter of June 29, 1953, Mossadeq felt he had exhausted all legal alternatives and proposed that a referendum should be held in which the people could endorse his policy and permit him to call for new elections without the Shah's concurrence. First, however, he asked his supporters in the Majlis to resign in order to destroy forever the present quorum. Twenty-seven deputies resigned on July 14, and by July 17 fifty-two had resigned.[27]

For a man who had carried his idealism to the ultimate degree in refusing to interfere in the early Seventeenth Majlis elections, Mossadeq had gone a long way toward accepting dictatorial control. His reluctance to take this step is apparent. Still the referendum, held August 3–15, 1953, was a travesty. The final vote was 2,043,389 to 1,207 in Mossadeq's favor.[28] Voting was not secret. If a citizen were brave enough to vote negatively he was compelled to go before a jeering pro-Mossadeq mob to do so. The pro-Mossadeq and anti-Mossadeq election boxes were placed in different parts of the city or town so that there would be no doubt as to the identity of the anti-Mossadeqist.

But the elections had a certain significance. The opposition boycotted the vote; and Mossadeq's move toward dictatorship had not progressed to the point where he could herd voters to the polls (he did not control the Army to that extent). What compulsion

26 *Ibid.*, April 22, 1953, 11:1; April 27, 1953, 1:5; April 28, 1953, 5:1; April 29, 1953, 7:7.

27 *Ibid.*, July 15, 1953, 11:1; July 17, 1953, 4:5.

28 *Ibid.*, August 14, 1953, 1:8.

there was came largely from Tudeh toughs who were mobilized by their party to bring out a big vote. The Tehran vote was 101,396 to 67.[29] This was 29,000 votes fewer than the number of votes cast in the relatively free January 1952 election.[30] Considering the fact that the National Front had lost its main chaqu keshan leaders in the defection of Kashani and Baqai, this vote was significantly high. There is no way of determining what percentage of the vote was due to Tudeh support. In the districts outside of Tehran the meaning of the big vote was even more clear. The large turnout demonstrated Mossadeq's ability to outdo the landowners in getting the inarticulate peasants to the polls.

As described in Chapter 13, the opposition to Mossadeq had by this time crystallized. It included the Court, most general officers, landowners, and large businessmen, and a growing number of clerical leaders. When joined by the three National Front defectors and their followers, this was a significant force. In addition, the rebuff by President Eisenhower brought many fence sitters into the opposition. The Tudeh Party did its important bit to solidify the opposition by its Yankee-Go-Home campaign and its remarkable showing in the 30 Tir (July 21, 1952) demonstration.[31] Nationalists insisted that British agents worked to swell the size of the Tudeh mob in order to frighten the United States. But accepting this logic calls for an acceptance of the Nationalist assumption that the Tudeh Party was an Anglo-Russian enterprise, an assumption that few Western observers can make. Furthermore, if reports that the 30 Tir Tudeh mob was "disciplined" [32] are correct, this in itself is strong evidence that the participants were not hired. Chaqu keshan-led mobs are never disciplined.

Coincident with the crystallizing of the opposition, there was a significant decline in the *esprit* of the middle-class Mossadeq support. The pro-Mossadeq demonstrations decreased in size and came to include more of the fascistic Pan-Iranists. The hitherto loyal speaker of the Majlis, Dr. Abdollah Moazemi,[33] opposed Mossadeq's order to the National Front Majlis deputies to resign;

29 *Ibid.*, August 4, 1953: 1:2, 3.
30 *Ibid.*
31 See Chapter 13, p. 216.
32 *The New York Times,* July 22, 1953, 1:5.
33 *Ibid.*, July 16, 1953, 5:1.

his distaste for the increasingly dictatorial trend in the Mossadeq government was probably reflected throughout much of the liberal intellectual community. This group was shocked by the referendum. Although there is little evidence that the referendum resulted in any large-scale defections, it may explain much of the reason why the liberal-intellectual population remained indoors on August 19 and permitted Mossadeq to be overthrown. The invigoration of the opposition was met by the Mossadeq camp with disillusionment and despair.

By January 1953 Mohammad Mossadeq had been caught in a dilemma from which he could extricate himself only by compromising drastically with the liberal democratic ideology he had so warmly embraced. He accepted this necessity, but only with such great reluctance and hesitation that by the time he had moved decisively into the extralegal realm, the situation was beyond salvation. By January 1953 liberal, democratic nationalism was already on the road to defeat and could have been saved only by skillful leadership. That leadership was not forthcoming.

In essence, Iranian Nationalism foundered on the shoals of its own irrationality. It had won a victory of immense proportions in March 1951, but failing to understand how near victory it was, Nationalism consumed itself in a negative struggle with forces which it had virtually defeated. Although a mass movement of the size and intensity of the National Movement will inevitably be to a large degree based on an irrational appeal, rationality can prevail if the leadership rises above the emotionalism of the mass and gives sensible direction. The conclusion is inescapable in this case that Mossadeq was as much a prisoner of the irrationality as were many of his least literate supporters.

Mossadeq's atavistic view of British influence in Iran and the Middle East prevented him from understanding that the battle had been won when the British accepted the principle of nationalization of oil. Under either the Stokes or the World Bank proposals, there is every reason to believe that a popular and powerful Iranian government could have neutralized any effort that might have been made by the British government to use British oil personnel as instruments for interference. The behavior of the thousand families and the Court in 1951 and1952 demonstrated that they would have docilely accepted the transfer of political power to a middle-class-based regime. Had Mossadeq fully understood the great power which his own popularity gave him and had he concluded an oil agreement, he could have moved in the direction of progress; and the free world, with the minor exception of the colonial wing of the British Tories, would have applauded. The oil revenue Mossadeq received would probably have been honestly invested in Iran's future, although certainly not always wisely, and the possibility of real economic and social progress would have been great. Politically, the National Front could easily have evolved into an organization resembling that of the Congress Party of India.

Saddest of all, history is unlikely to grant a liberal democratic Iranian leader another opportunity so favorable as that given Mossadeq. As the concluding chapter will indicate, the day of liberal intellectual leadership of Iranian nationalism may already have passed.

16

"POSITIVE" NATIONALISM AND ROYAL DICTATORSHIP

As supporters of the Shah's government often state, Dr. Mossadeq and his followers had no monopoly of Iranian nationalism. At its zenith, Iranian noncommunist nationalist support of Mossadeq approached the point of unanimity, but by August 1953 there had been significant defections and a general disillusionment with Mossadeq. Conceivably the successor government of General Zahedi could have attracted the support of some and the acquiescence of other former Mossadeqists. To have done so, however, Zahedi would have had to demonstrate that he was devoted to the Iranian nation and was in no sense a tool of foreign imperialism. Considering the means by which he came to power, this task would have been at best extremely difficult. But enough was known of Iranian nationalism to draw up a blueprint for appealing to one-time Nationalists.

After two and one-half years of relative freedom of expression, the attitudes of Iranian nationalism could have been fully aired. Therefore, the Zahedi government could have deduced which courses of action were proscriptive and which were permissible if Nationalists were to be attracted to the support of the regime. Since Iranian political attitudes are personalized to a large degree, policy can most easily be explained to the public through the type of appointments made. For example, if Nationalists were to be attracted to support the regime, those selected for cabinet positions should have been men who were not suspected of dealings with foreign powers. If the support of disillusioned Nationalists was to have been wooed, the governmental appointments should have included such highly respected men as Dr. Abdollah Moazemi, who had struggled against Mossadeq's dictatorial trend, or Khalil Maleki, who was the most bitter of the anticommunists in the

Mossadeq coalition. Such a policy would have asked a great deal, possibly too much, from both Zahedi and the Nationalist leaders. For Zahedi, it would have meant disappointing the oligarchical clique to which he belonged and from which he had received so much support in overturning Mossadeq. For the Nationalists it would have meant risking political death as had Maki, Baqai, and Kashani a few months earlier.

A less attractive but still conceivable alternative for Zahedi would have been to attempt to rebuild the popularity among nationalists of Zahedi's August 19 allies, Baqai and Kashani. But Zahedi apparently looked on Baqai and Kashani as rivals, and he exiled Baqai to Baluchistan and sharply curtailed Kashani's activities.

This discussion is academic, however, because there is no evidence to indicate that either Zahedi or the Shah ever proposed to follow the kind of policy needed to attract Mossadeqist support. Nor is there much evidence to indicate that the sensibilities of nationalists were ever taken into consideration. The high priority given to a restoration of diplomatic relations with Britain and the renewal of serious negotiations for an oil settlement confirmed the Nationalist assumption that this was an imperialist-imposed regime. The pulling of the teeth of Mossadeq's agricultural reform and the placing of conservative members of the oligarchy in most policy-making positions underscored the Nationalist assumption that the imperialists would once again work through the least progressive elements of society.

Most ridiculous of all was the treatment given Dr. Mossadeq. Mossadeq was regarded as an honest and sincerely patriotic man, even by those who welcomed his overthrow, and he should have been permitted a dignified departure from Iranian politics. Nothing was to be gained by mistreating him. Instead, he was brought to public trial. As if motivated by a desire to furnish the grand old man a final and spectacular exit from Iranian politics, the Zahedi government granted Mossadeq a rostrum from which he could outline his charges against those who had overthrown him. He rose to the occasion and gave one of the most impressive performances of his career. Since Zahedi's government was far more restrictive than Mossadeq's had been even in its darkest days, any conclusion as to the attitude of the Iranian public at the time of the trial can only be impressionistic. It is the opinion of this study, however, that by the end of his trial Mossadeq had regained most of the popular support he had earlier lost.

When the judge sentenced Mossadeq to three years of imprisonment, officially described as solitary confinement, he gave the old Nationalist the political advantage of martyrdom. The sentence did much to deny to Zahedi and the Shah the likelihood of ever attracting much Nationalist support.

From the year of Mossadeq's overthrow until 1960, Iran moved steadily from a loose authoritarianism in the direction of totalitarianism. Much to the surprise of many observers, dictatorial control passed to the Shah, whose image was one of weakness and vacillation, rather than to the strong-willed General Zahedi. The latter dealt with the middle-class opposition harshly enough but did not challenge the prerogatives of the oligarchy. He very quickly found himself limited in support to members of the oligarchy and even here the widely-believed rumors of spectacular corruption in the Zahedi government reduced that support. The Shah had no difficulty removing him from office and establishing a personal dictatorship. The oligarchy acquiesced in this dictatorship because the Shah did not, except for a brief period in 1954, seriously challenge the social and economic position of the thousand families. He steadily reduced their political power, however, despite the fact that the Majlis, the cabinet, and the top bureaucracy were filled with obedient aristocrats. Increasingly the Majlis and the cabinet were compelled to hew to the Shah's line, and few men in the post-Zahedi governments had any independent power. The Shah exercised control through the government's security organs—the army, the gendarmery, the police, and the steadily growing Iranian equivalent of the Gestapo which bears the ominous-sounding initials of SAVAK.

The Shah unquestionably wished to expand his base of political support. Despite his reliance on the oligarchy for primary support during much of his career, the evidence is strong that he recognized the inherent weakness of that support. In order to provide long-term stability for his regime he needed the support of a much larger sector of the population. But he was denied the support of the nationalistic middle class, at least temporarily, because he had helped overthrow the symbol of Iranian nationalism, Dr. Mossadeq, and hence was regarded by much of the middle class as little more than a foreign tool. He was not yet strong enough vis-à-vis the oligarchy to attract the support of the peasantry by inaugurating a serious land reform program. In fact he had to retreat on this front. The Mossadeq law requiring the payment of 20 per cent of the landowner's profits from his land back into the village was amended to 5 per cent, but the percentage is of little consequence since the enforcement provisions were weakened to the point that very few landowners were paying even 1 per cent.[1] His hands were also tied with labor. The Ministry of Labor prepared some fairly advanced legislation, but any possibility of improvement in labor was destroyed by government control of the labor leadership. Labor was compelled to submit to chaqu keshan leaders whose chief talent lay in an ability to herd their flocks to demonstrations and elections. But a turning to genuine labor leaders would have meant turning to Mossadeqists or communists.

The one bright exception to a bleak picture was the important Plan Organization. This organization had, by law, control over the planning and execution of short- and long-range economic projects. Under the energetic, if dictatorial, direction of Abol Hassan Ebtehaj, this organization became the one hope for long-term stability in Iran. Ebtehaj and his organization were subject to abuse from both the oligarchy and the Nationalists. The latter were convinced that Ebtehaj was a servant of the British in spite of the fact that he had left a top position in the British Bank after a violent disagreement with British officials. The former were annoyed with him for not approving projects that would bring them personal profit. Ebtehaj insisted on a free hand and received it. He understood that success of the Plan Organization demanded the appointment of honest and competent employees, and his record in personnel selection is an excellent one. Many bright young Nationalists were among those employed in his organization. Corruption, which is believed to have been of immense proportions, occurred in the contracting and sub-contracting stages of the projects, which were beyond the control of Ebtehaj. In the spring of

1 Series of articles by Kazem Zarnegar appearing in *Keyhan*, May and June 1958.

1959 the Shah submitted to right-wing pressures and removed Ebtehaj. The Plan Organization was placed temporarily under the control of the prime minister, Manuchehr Eqbal, whose willingness to compromise with the influence seekers was known well.

The Shah's determination in standing by Ebtehaj as long as he did was the most impressive argument in favor of His Majesty's claim that he was determined to bring progress and stability to Iran. There were other indications. In 1954 the Shah inaugurated an attack on the economic and social position of the oligarchy. This campaign evoked a strong reaction which, although focused on the Shah's front man in the Majlis, Jahangir Taffazoli, was a potential challenge to the Shah personally. The Shah could not rely on his security forces to the extent that he could after 1958, and he could not turn to the hostile middle class for alternate support; thus he gave way completely and permitted Taffozoli to become the Majlis whipping boy.[2]

Another indication of the Shah's desire for progress is his sponsorship of two political parties instead of the traditional single party of the totalitarian system. In 1957 the Shah called for the formation of a liberal and of a conservative party, both of which would give loyal support to the Court. The Shah regarded these parties as bringing to Iran the beginnings of a two-party system which would in the future provide a stable base for the Pahlavi dynasty. Yet in operation they were artificial to the point of being grotesque. The "liberal" party was led by Amir Assadolah Alam, one of Iran's great landowners and a member of one of the most notorious of pro-British families. A less likely leader for the rallying of liberal support could not have been found. As an alternative, Iranians could look to the "conservative" party of Dr. Eqbal and his Freemason friends.[3] Iranians universally regarded

[2] The Shah gave several speeches in 1954 promising fundamental social reforms and demanding that the landowners distribute their lands among the peasantry. The Majlis debates as recorded in *Ettelaat* in this period demonstrate that Jahangir Taffazoli was the spokesman for this program. Landowner deputies attacked Taffazoli strongly but never the Shah. When it became clear that the Shah would not follow through with his program, the attacks on Taffazoli became even more vicious. He was sent shortly thereafter to France as director of Iranian student affairs.

[3] This party has been given the name "Melliyun" in an obvious move to try to confuse the electorate since the Mossadeqists have traditionally been referred to by that name.

these parties as farcical, many arguing that the Shah would have had more to gain from admitting his dictatorial control than from attempting to camouflage it so crudely. Although there is little reason to question the Shah's sincerity in this venture, he was unwilling to grant the two parties the independence of choice both in leadership and policy that would have permitted their growth into genuine parties.

The Shah was aware of his failure to attract popular support, and he made two independent efforts to attract nationalist (not necessarily Nationalist) support. One of these was on the propaganda front. Through his speeches and the controlled press he insisted that he, not Mossadeq, was the true nationalist. He described his nationalism as "positive," which means that it was directed toward a real program of improving the welfare of the people, whereas Mossadeq's nationalism was negative and self-destructive. This propaganda carried a hollow ring when viewed in the context of a regime under which corruption had flourished, luxury imports and luxury real estate had consumed much of the oil revenue, the wealthy were virtually untaxed, agricultural reform had suffered a stinging reverse, labor had become the prisoner of criminal elements, and men regarded as servants of foreigners were in high position.

The other approach was the Shah's sponsorship of a "tame" nationalist opposition under the leadership of one Ahmad Aramesh. Aramesh, who is regarded by many leading Nationalists as a close friend of Britain, established a party called "Devotees of Progress." The relationship between the Shah and Aramesh was one of the most bizarre in Iranian history; nothing better illustrates the failure of the Shah to comprehend the thought processes of Iranian nationalists. It was naive to believe that a man whose own patriotism was in question could attract the support of people long conditioned to view an alliance between foreign imperialists and members of the local oligarchy as their chief target. The Shah was not dealing with an amorphous mass, but with an element of the population that had focused its full support on certain leaders and policies. The Shah could succeed in attracting these people only by compromising with their leaders, sincerely adopting some of their policies, and paying close attention to their symbols. Conceivably the leaders could be replaced, but to replace them would require a long campaign; and in any case the substitute leaders must of necessity have unsullied records.

If propaganda could have made Aramesh into a new Mossadeq, the Shah-Aramesh venture would have succeeded. Aramesh moved about Tehran, at least with tacit royal approval, speaking the language of the extremist wing of the Mossadeq coalition with impunity. In an astonishing series of articles, which all Tehran believed was ghost written by Aramesh, the policies of the United States were roundly denounced.[4] The series was widely read and discussed, but even in Iran, familiar with intrigue, this maneuver of the Shah was baffling. Since even the least literate Iranian understood that such a series could appear in Tehran's tightly controlled press only with official sanction, its violent attacks on the United States were not without significance. A possible explanation is that the Shah and Aramesh continued to entertain the hope that such attacks would persuade nationalists to rally to the government. If so the campaign was a total failure. In order to maintain his control the Shah had to continue to rely on the repressive instruments of a twentieth-century police state.

The years after Mossadeq's overthrow until 1960 were increasingly disastrous for the Nationalists in Iran. As the foregoing pages have indicated, Zahedi and the Shah were unwilling to appeal for nationalist support in any meaningful manner. Instead the royal dictatorship steadily narrowed the area of freedom of action for any opposition group. Confronted with a hostile, repressive dictatorship, the Nationalist leadership moved reluctantly into a semi-underground position. The liberal intellectuals who had surrounded Mossadeq had little taste for clandestine activity, and they took the view that any activity directed against the government would fail because of American and British support of the regime. Consequently what leadership they asserted was primarily directed toward appealing to the United States for a change of attitude. Chapter 13 has described their lack of success.

Considering this situation, two opposite developments were

[4] These articles were published in several journals but most noteworthy were those in *Tehran Mosavar* in the spring of 1958 entitled "Chahar Rah Khavar Mianeh" ("Crossroads of the Middle East").

inevitable. The rank and file Nationalists and nationalists moved toward apathy. The University of Tehran, for example, formerly the center of nationalism, rarely witnessed a political discussion and almost never a demonstration. The prevailing attitude was one of hopelessness combined with fear of the consequences of any expression of opinion. Simultaneously, however, there had to appear a group of potential leaders who would rebel at the passive acquiescence of their old leaders and seek to replace them. Such men exist, but since they operate in underground fashion this study can make no pretense of identifying them or estimating their strength.

It is known that in the semiunderground the pro-Mossadeq forces were divided broadly into two competing camps. On the one side was the intellectual-dominated Iran Party and its allies. On the other side was the merchant-religious-university coalition called the National Resistance Movement (later the National Freedom Movement). Both groups claimed to be the rightful inheritors of Mossadeq's favor, and both were intransigently opposed to participation or even acquiescence in any of the Shah-dominated governments. Younger members of both groups could be found in high level bureaucratic positions, but not in the policy-making positions. Since these organizations believed the Shah and many of his lieutenants to be little better than foreign agents, compromise was extremely difficult, if not impossible. Had the issues separating the Nationalists from the Shah been simply ideological, compromise would have been a possibility; but the Nationalists' belief that their antagonist was guilty of treason made any type of mutual dealings difficult. Since treason is an absolute term, those who use it to describe the Shah could hardly cooperate with him without incurring some of the opprobrium.

Some erstwhile Mossadeq supporters accepted positions in post-Mossadeq governments, but their history is not conducive to emulation. A few men, such as Khalil Taleqani, profited financially from these activities, but they have been condemned by their ex-colleagues with greater bitterness than have consistent royalists. In addition, there was one significant dissent by a loyal Mossadeqist from the policy of total opposition. After his release from prison, Khalil Maleki, the leader of the Titoist Third Force, argued publicly for a policy of accepting political realities. Maleki said that Mossadeq's overthrow, whatever the immediate causes, would not have been possible had the base of social support for nationalism been larger. Therefore, the Nationalists should drop their intransigent opposition and instead seek to cooperate with the liberal wing of the "ruling class" until social evolution had progressed further. Maleki stressed that this "ruling class" should not be viewed as a monolith—all of one color and traitorous—but rather as a group of men whose views range from the reactionary to the liberal. Were the Nationalists to throw their strength to the liberal wing, an evolutionary trend could be set into motion which might bring the Nationalists back into positions of influence.

Maleki's arguments were published in his magazine *Elm o Zendegi* and were read widely. But instead of convincing his colleagues, Maleki was charged with having sold out to the Court and the imperialist powers. For a man who had lost most of his worldly possessions after the *coup* and had spent many months in prison because of his unwavering devotion to the Nationalist cause, the realization that many of his supporters now questioned his loyalty was surely a heavy blow. Yet in a day when censorship was increasingly strict, *Elm o Zendegi* had appeared without repercussions; and Maleki had called for collaboration with the men who had overthrown the greatest of Iranian leaders, Dr. Mossadeq. To many Nationalists the case against Maleki was a clear one. The Third Force split into pro- and anti-Maleki factions. The pro-Maleki wing atrophied; *Elm o Zendegi* ceased regular publication, and Maleki joined Maki and Baqai in obscurity.

Ironically, a significant part of the explantion for the weakness of the Nationalist semiunderground was that Dr. Mossadeq was still alive. A little less than three years after his overthrow, Mossadeq was released from prison, theoretically a free man. But the Shah could not permit this man, idolized as he was, to move freely in the country. Nor did he feel that he could permit Mossadeq to go into exile; from Switzerland Mossadeq could have served as a rallying point for the opposition and could have altered the Shah's international image through his access to the world press. The problem was solved in a crude manner that further alienated the articulate element of the population. Mossadeq left Tehran for a village he owned fifty miles to the west. Shortly after his arrival there, an anti-Mossadeq demonstration was held near the village; the demonstrators called Mossadeq a traitor and demanded his death. Mossadeq telephoned for police protection, which the government willingly provided.[5] The "protection" was never withdrawn. The leader of the "spontaneous" demonstration was none other than Shaban the Brainless. No one was fooled by this maneuver except for some foreign newspapermen, but it was a uniquely Iranian way of dealing extralegally with a man who for political reasons had to be confined.

But even had Mossadeq not been a virtual prisoner, there is reason to believe he would neither have left his village nor have received visitors. Rumor said that he was convinced of a plot to murder him and trusted virtually no one. Yet as long as Mossadeq lived the question of succession could not be resolved. There was no obvious heir apparent, although the leader of the Iran Party, Allahyar Saleh, was probably the next most popular of the Nationalists. Saleh, however, was not noted for decisiveness.[6] Besides, the merchant-clerical section of the National Front would not have liked the Mossadeq mantle to fall to the Fabian-minded Iran Party. At the same time, the NRM lacked a leader who was as well known to the public as were four or five Iran Party and several independent leaders. Were Mossadeq to have relinquished his leadership, a disruptive power struggle would have inevitably followed, complicated, of course, by its being fought underground; but from such a struggle a leader of real stature and ability might have emerged. Mossadeq has repeatedly stated to the Nationalist leaders that he has retired from politics. But as long as Mossadeq remains in confinement, no Nationalist leader could take this statement at face value.

The distinction made between the concepts of totalitarianism and authoritarianism is useful as long as it is understood that the two concepts differ only in degree not in kind. Nineteenth-

[5] *Ettelaat,* August 9, 1956.

[6] Saleh was Minister of Interior at the time of the seventeenth Majlis elections and was largely responsible for Mossadeq's failure to rig the elections.

century authoritarianism blends into twentieth-century totalitarianism imperceptibly, and no purpose is served by attempting to determine any dividing line between the two. Such an attempt risks losing sight of the simple truth that the essential difference lies in the degree of control of the individual. The twentieth century has witnessed an intensification of totalitarianism largely because of extraordinarily rapid technological developments and because of the equally extraordinary growth of mass political awareness and participation in every part of the world. Both developments have made possible a demagogic manipulation of mass irrationality that can lead to increasingly totalitarian control.

Mossadeq in 1953 and the Shah in 1960 were caught in trends that appeared to be moving Iran in the direction of totalitarian control. But the control systems that the two men utilized were very different and reflected each of the twentieth-century developments just mentioned. Mossadeq, lacking firm control over the security forces, was compelled to rely on his great popular appeal as a control mechanism. The Shah, lacking the ability to attract any significant popular support, was compelled to rely on the instruments of terror under his control. It is problematical whether Mossadeq could have been capable of reversing the trend toward totalitarianism had he been successful in wresting control of the security forces from the Shah. But by 1960 the Shah seemed to be a prisoner of his totalitarian trend. Every effort made to attract broader support having failed, the Shah turned to the security forces to remain in power. His regime became increasingly dictatorial, and with the growth in dictatorship came a steady deterioration in the Shah's relations with the foci of power that had been allied with him, especially the landowners, large merchants, and religious leaders. These groups naturally resented the reduction of their own powers, and as they moved toward passive opposition the Shah's dependence on the security forces increased still more.

The difficulty with depending on the instruments of terror for control is that the instruments may devour the master. The Shah's ability to control the Iranian security forces proved to be considerable; he appointed several tough, competent, and ambitious men to the various top security posts and relied on their conflicting ambitions to neutralize each other. Although the game almost failed in 1958, when a military-civilian *coup* was thwarted only at the last minute, the longevity of the Shah's rule is due largely to his success in balancing his security chiefs against each other.

As suggested earlier, however, the Shah's attitude toward his position of control appears to have been characterized by a major ambivalence. Although he was clearly willing to utilize instruments of terror to remain in power, he nevertheless was probably sincere about wishing to bring economic, social, and political reform to his country. The establishment of two competing parties can hardly be explained otherwise. By the summer of 1960 the totalitarian trend was well advanced, but at this point the Shah's ambivalence came close to costing him his throne.

Elections were scheduled for late summer 1960, and the Shah seemed determined to play seriously with his two parties. Since neither party had been permitted the independence to develop a distinctive personality, however, the fascination of this game was limited to the Shah and the candidates. Rumor in Tehran had it that Melliyun ("conservative") had been allotted two seats for each seat given Mardom ("liberal"), and as the returns began coming in this appeared indeed to be the pattern. The Shah was so confident of his ability to control the election and still maintain a democratic motif that he permitted an influx of correspondents from the world's press.

Despite the trend in that direction, however, Iran was not yet totalitarian, indeed was far from it. The Mardom Party may have been regarded by the Shah as His Majesty's Loyal Opposition, but articulate Iranians were aware that a genuine opposition existed semiovertly. In July 1960 some of the best known leaders of this opposition came out in the open and called for free elections. Since the Shah was very obviously concerned with the "progressive democratic" image so painstakingly created abroad, he could ill afford to deal harshly with the new National Front. One member of the National Front, Abdolrahman Barumand of Isfahan, went so far as to test the willingness of the government to permit National Front candidacies. The answer came swiftly. Mr. Barumand was jailed. The Shah and Prime Minister Eqbal argued that although the elections were free, "traitors" could not be permitted to run, and their jailing of Barumand made clear that the National Front leaders were "traitors."

But the fact was that Iran had not yet progressed far enough along the road to totalitarianism to enable the Shah to carry out an elaborate election drama in which the rigging was concealed by means of skillful play-acting on the part of the two legal parties. The National Front could be immobilized by the charge of treason, but other opposition elements could not. Several men, possibly disappointed by their failure to be selected by the government, took the promise of electoral freedom seriously and announced their candidacies. The Shah had only two choices: to permit the election to continue, with the serious risk of losing control of the situation; or to utilize SAVAK and the other security forces to suppress all opposition, even though this would involve the loss of a benign international image. The Shah chose the former course, and the trend in the direction of totalitarianism was abruptly reversed. Several minor and two major personalities seized control of the election campaign and were able to demonstrate so clearly the actual rigging of the election that even the Mardom Party had to join in the attack. The major figures were Dr. Ali Amini and Dr. Mozaffar Baqai.

Amini was the head of one of Iran's great landowning families with ties to the Qajar dynasty and also to Vosuq al-Doleh and Ahmad Qavam. He was personally brilliant, capable, and possessed of a remarkably clear perspective. But in many ways he was ill-equipped for his opposition role. An early Mossadeq supporter, he had broken away and moved into the opposition well before 28 Mordad. After Mossadeq's overthrow he appeared in the Zahedi cabinet as finance minister; it was he who directed the Iranian team in the oil negotiations. With this history, Amini inevitably was charged with treason by the Nationalists, and even the most sophisticated regarded him as an opportunist for whom patriotism was of little consequence. And he was little more popular in the Court. The Shah viewed Amini as a man likely to challenge his authority. He therefore sought to remove him from the political scene by appointing him ambassador to the United States. But Amini continued his political activities from Washington. A widely-held belief in Iran was that Amini was deeply involved in the plans for the *coup d'état* of 1958. He was recalled at that time, ostensibly because of an ill-considered speech.

Amini therefore fell into that category of Iranians whom the Nationalists have at one time accused of treason, but who by subsequent acts have blurred the charge. Although there is no evidence to indicate that the treason charge, once made and widely accepted, can be neatly withdrawn, it can be blunted to the point that a temporary alliance becomes possible. When the practical grounds for this alliance disappear, however, there is every reason to believe that the treason charge would return with considerable force. In the election campaign of late summer 1960 Amini was helping to set into motion a liberalizing trend, and the Nationalists were grateful. Later, in the spring of 1961, when Amini was appointed prime minister they could assume a fairly benevolent attitude toward him because of his service the year before.

With regard to Baqai much has been said. No one doubted his courage or his cleverness, but even a temporary Nationalist-Baqai rapprochement was unthinkable. His crimes had been too serious for the Nationalist elite, and as long as this elite remains in control of the movement it seems clear that he cannot regain significant power among the Nationalists. But Baqai understood the receptivity for a nationalist propaganda line and utilized it as far as he dared. He was careful to underscore the point that violence should be avoided, but, having said that, he resurrected many of the Nationalist clichés and propaganda themes. His attack was focused on Prime Minister Eqbal, whom he described as a "traitor." Since anyone of sophistication in Iran understood that Eqbal was the servant of the Shah, this came close to being an assault on the throne. The attack was so successful that the other opposition leaders adopted it, and the Shah was compelled to drop Eqbal and to annul the election returns.

The Shah suffered a severe defeat in September 1960. Having permitted the elections to get out of control, the Shah's control over the security forces also was reduced. The security chiefs were not restrained in their ambitions so much by loyalty to him as by rivalries with each other, and the weakening of his position might increase the willingness of one or more of these men to accept the risks involved in planning a *coup*. Once the foreign correspondents had left Iran after the election, the Shah had the option of tightening his control over his people and over the security forces with very little international publicity. For reasons that are by no means clear, however, he chose to permit the liberalizing trend to continue. As his prime minister he selected a one-time Mossadeqist, Engineer Jafar Sharif-Imami, and as head of the Plan Organization Sharif-Imami's brother-in-law Ahmad Aramesh.

Sharif-Imami undoubtedly regarded himself as a liberal nationalist if not a Nationalist. He had little in common with the conservative landowners, and his appointment seemed to be an appeal by the Shah to the middle sector of the Iranian public. The inclusion of Aramesh and several longtime Aramesh associates in the government strengthens the hypothesis that the Shah had decided to meet head-on the problem of his unpopularity with most of the middle sector. But in making this appointment the Shah once again demonstrated his unwillingness to accept the fact that he was not dealing with an amorphous political mass but rather with a well-structured political movement whose leadership and attitudes were easily identifiable.

Sharif-Imami and Aramesh demonstrated by the propaganda line they followed a clear understanding of middle sector attitudes. Their policy statements in many cases would have differed very little had they been prepared by the National Front. But their appeals to the Nationalists fell on deaf ears. Included in the belief system of the Nationalists was a rigid categorization of Iranian leaders into the patriotically pure and the patriotically suspect. The Shah clearly belonged in the latter category, and since Sharif-Imami and Aramesh were his selectees, they too were suspect. Their loudly proclaimed liberal nationalist views were regarded as sheer pretense. For those Nationalist leaders who regarded Aramesh as a British tool, his maneuvers had the more ominous overtones of a typically subtle British plot.

The Shah may have expected that this appointment would create a "tame" nationalist movement, but the results were the opposite. The new government could hardly hope to achieve any support if the hated security forces remained in evidence. Consequently security control was further relaxed, and the liberalizing trend picked up momentum. But instead of resulting in increased popularity for the regime, this relaxation permitted long quiescent forces to stir. Life returned to the politically-minded university students, and the National Front became increasingly bold, even going as far as scheduling a press conference to demand the holding of new and free elections. This was too much for the government. The press conference was forcibly cancelled. But this was a minor setback rather than the reversal of a trend. Elections were held, and although they could still be classified as rigged, a genuine effort was made to select more popular candidates. The new men were largely representatives of the middle sector who were willing to make their peace with the government. Many political unknowns were elected, and they were probably inferior in quality to their predecessors. Included among those elected were undoubtedly a few who thought of themselves as Nationalist "sleepers," who at the first opportunity would emerge as open followers of the National Front. But the National Front could not make a direct electoral challenge. When Mr. Barumand tried again to be elected in Isfahan the government swiftly removed him.

This latter action makes all the more inexplicable the one great surprise of that election. An open and avowed National Front candidate was elected. He was Allahyar Saleh, a man second only to Mohammad Mossadeq in Nationalist affections. Saleh's election was a great risk for both the government and Saleh. As leader of the Iran Party, Saleh had strong rivals in the National Freedom Movement who would advance the idea that Saleh did not differ from other opportunists who had agreed to the government terms. In order to combat this view, Saleh would have no alternative but to take an intransigently strong stand inside the Majlis. Possibly the government understood this and hoped (a) to widen the split within the National Front and (b) to demonstrate again to the Americans that the Nationalists were hopeless extremists. But should the split not develop and should Saleh be capable of assuming a statesmanlike attitude in the Majlis, the government would be in serious trouble. Many of the new deputies might swing over to Saleh's leadership.

When the new Majlis convened, the government's failure was

apparent. The collapse of a financial boom had caused general dissatisfaction and Saleh showed signs of exerting considerable leadership. Student demonstrations continued, and a futile effort was made by the National Front to close the bazaar as in earlier, more relaxed days. The government had once again to decide to return to control by terror or to make further concessions, concessions which could only reinforce an already rapidly moving trend.

The Shah's response was astonishing. In one stroke he removed all of the security chiefs including the extremely powerful Timur Bakhtiar. He launched a campaign to make scapegoats of the removed military chiefs. Had such relaxations of control been accompanied by a major *rapprochement* effort with the Nationalist leaders, there would have been a significant possibility of success. But the Shah's fear and hatred of the Nationalists permitted no such move. The results were inevitable. Public expressions of dissatisfaction multiplied and culminated in an incident in which two teachers among a large group demonstrating for higher wages were shot and killed. This was the end of the political road for Sharif-Imami and Aramesh.

The Shah had failed in a major effort to attract support, and he had weakened his security forces; he now had no alternative but to search for a prime minister who could bring independent strength to the government and who could deal with the financial crisis. The logical choice, indeed almost the only choice if a military leader or a Nationalist were ruled out, was Dr. Ali Amini. But to appoint Amini would be to admit that royal power was now far from absolute. The Shah's suspicions of and dislike for Amini were widely recognized. Furthermore, Amini was no Eqbal who would do the Shah's bidding. The new prime minister would insist on considerable independence and when he first assumed office could do so. But for the first time in months, good fortune smiled on the Shah. A power struggle followed Amini's appointment, and to all appearances the Shah outmaneuvered and outwitted his rival. Amini's task was an extraordinarily difficult one. Since the Shah controlled the security forces, weakened though they had been, Amini had to find offsetting strength. He had a small group of lieutenants and allies, including the brilliant but erratic Hassan

Arsenjani. But he had no popular following. The alternative available to Amini was to construct a working alliance with the Nationalists. Amini understood this and moved immediately to gain Nationalist support. But a Nationalist *quid pro quo* would involve a promise of eventual power, and Amini was unwilling to accept such an eventuality. Furthermore, the austerity program Amini had to launch would not be popular. The result was the isolation of Amini and a continued rigid polarization of the government and the Nationalists. The Majlis was dissolved, and elections, in open violation of the constitution, were not scheduled. Saleh was thus relieved of his opportunity and of his embarrassment. The National Front, seeing no prospect of compromise, began to howl loudly for free elections.

Had Amini been successful in bringing about a temporary alliance with the Nationalists, there would have been the possibility of harnessing the immense vitality of the National movement to a constructive program. Furthermore, there would have been a good chance that the more moderate Nationalist leaders would have gained preeminence in the National Movement.

But Amini's failure to bring about this alliance is easily explained when viewed in the perspective of nationalism. The point was developed in Chapter 11 that the appearance of nationalism in an Iran in which both Britain and Russia utilized Iranian political leaders in their power rivalry raised the issue of treason. This reaction was a confused and contradictory one, because the omnipresence of foreign influence meant that no politician, modernizer or traditionalist, could avoid dealing with foreign powers. What developed eventually was an unspoken but clearly implicit acceptance by the modernizers of this rule of thumb: Where foreign influence exerted through Iranian leaders is directed toward maintaining the domestic political power status quo, those cooperating Iranians are traitors. Where foreign influence assists Iranian leaders in basically altering the elite power structure, those cooperating Iranians are not guilty of improprieties.

The logical inconsistency of this attitude left the National Front somewhat vulnerable. As seen in Chapter 13, the Tudeh was able to embarrass the National Front by arguing that his acceptance of so much American support made Dr. Mossadeq an American agent. Nevertheless, the Nationalists continued to seek American support to alter the situation because of the lingering hope that America may eventually understand that a Nationalist government is the best defense against communism in Iran. The Nationalists held this view in spite of their conviction that the United States was responsible for Mossadeq's overthrow. Likewise, the hope persisted that the Shah was not totally committed to the Iranian right wing-British position. It was generally believed that the Shah joined in the plot against Mossadeq reluctantly and only after great pressure was applied. But as the Shah increased his personal control of government, this hope dimmed until the Shah became the focal point of hostility and suspicion of treason.

Sophisticated National Front leaders may be attracted by the prospect of an alliance with the government. The relaxation of restrictive measures against them would permit the setting into motion of a dynamic force that could bring them into total control. But their rank and file followers would have great difficulty in understanding their actions. Isn't Dr. Mossadeq still a virtual prisoner? And isn't the Shah's government guilty of treasonous actions? If so, how is it possible to compromise with such a government?

Were the National Front capable of a united decision to enter into a working relationship with the government, possibly the rank and file could be persuaded by some rationalization that this policy in fact helps Dr. Mossadeq. But the National Front is not capable of such unity of policy, and inevitably a less moderate element, probably the National Freedom Movement, would accuse the other leaders of compromise with treason. The demagogic appeal of such a line could not be countered by those willing to compromise. An accommodation of the government and the National Front is therefore unlikely unless the government meets the National Front demands for a free election and the end of press control. Since these measures would probably result in a National Front victory, the Shah is unlikely to accept them.

Dr. Amini remained in office until July 1962, when, on the heels of a worsening financial situation, he resigned. His performance was a highly creditable one considering the environment he operated in. Iran needs a government with a sufficient base of support to carry out an austerity program. Whether a National Front government could generate sufficient enthusiasm to accomplish this is problematical. Although such a government could control foreign exchange very tightly, there is reason to question its ability to resist demands for higher wages from government employees and teachers. Its success would depend on its ability to appeal to the patriotism of the people with a magnetism that would equal Mossadeq's.

Dr. Amini's tenure was probably prolonged because of the widely held belief that Washington had a high regard for him. His fall from power followed an unsuccessful effort to persuade the United States to meet a major share of the budgetary deficit. His failure on this score indicated to many in Iran that Washington had withdrawn its support. Amini's parting statement, in fact, seemed to confirm this view, since he petulantly commented on Washington's refusal. In any event, the Shah was more than willing to see this independent first minister returned to private life.

Dr. Amini's successor, Amir Assadolah Alam, also a member of the thousand families, was Amini's opposite in many other respects. He was known for the totality of his subservience to the Shah, and he was a member of a family with a very strong Anglophilic reputation. One of Alam's first statements, which suggested that Iran would look to others in the West besides the United States for aid, was interpreted widely as an admission of his special relationship with the British.

Surprisingly, however, Alam pursued a far more vigorous policy of approaching the Nationalists than had Amini. He met with Allahyar Saleh and two other leading Nationalists and reportedly offered as many as three cabinet positions. The Nationalists countered with a demand for free elections. Alam announced his intention of calling for new elections, but he balked at the National Front demands for measures which would insure that the elections were free. Negotiations were broken off.

The National Front response to these overtures followed a familiar pattern. Nationalist activity intensified. A reorganization of the National Front central council in December 1962 resulted in a closer relationship of the Iran Party wing and the National Freedom Movement wing. The National Front as a whole then turned to an open attack on the Shah. In so doing the National Front responded to relaxed governmental pressure, just as it had done with Sharif-Imami's government, by increasing rather than decreasing antigovernment agitation.

Whereas in 1961 Nationalist agitation against the Sharif-Imami government had compelled the Shah to turn to Ali Amini to help reestablish order, Nationalist agitation in January 1963 produced a different response. Since 1961 the security forces had been reorganized and revitalized. Under the direction of Hassan Pakravan, SAVAK had become increasingly effective. Security units of the Army stationed in or near Tehran, particularly the paratroopers, were well-equipped and officered by men carefully screened for their loyalty to the Shah. The reliability of both organizations was to be tested when severe rioting broke out in June 1963, and both withstood the test remarkably well. Furthermore, under the premiership of Ali Amini the beginnings of a major effort to attract peasant support through land reforms had produced favorable results. Therefore in 1963 the Shah was in a position to counter the Nationalist agitation forcefully.

Shortly after the formation of the new National Front central council, the Shah ordered virtually the entire council and most second-level leaders of the National Front arrested. All Nationalist political activity was suppressed. Simultaneously the Shah embarked upon a reform program designed to broaden support for the regime by attracting elements of the population that had been politically inarticulate. Apparently both the landowning and middle-class sectors were to be written off.

The Shah dramatized this new program by calling for a national plebiscite to demonstrate public approval. The points to be approved were: (a) a land reform program; (b) sale of government-owned factories to finance the land program; (c) a new election law aimed at preventing rigged elections; (d) the nationalization of forests; (e) the formation of a 50,000-man teacher corps for rural education; (f) a plan to give workers 20 per cent of the net profits from government-owned factories.

These tactics placed the Nationalists in a difficult position. They favored each of the reform measures but their opposition to the Shah's dictatorship was much too strong, especially considering the arrest of their leaders, to permit their taking a passive stand. They were compelled to call for a boycott of the plebiscite. Their main argument, that this program should be referred to a freely elected Majlis, fell flat. The controlled press had a field day describing them as opponents of progress and reform.

The reception of the Shah's approach in the United States was an additional source of frustration for the Nationalists. Except for the *Christian Science Monitor* the massive political arrests were not mentioned in the American press. But the plebiscite received extensive and favorable coverage. Then when the results of the plebiscite were known and over 99 per cent of the people had voted approval, there was hardly a suggestion that the vote had been staged.[7]

By February 1963 the Shah had once again begun moving rapidly along the road toward totalitarianism. But this was a dangerous period for him. He had failed in his effort to project the "positive nationalist" image to the middle sector, and there was certain to be a considerable time lag before his reform program could produce sustained support from the peasantry. Therefore, he had to rely on the security forces and chaqu keshan leaders as his chief instruments of control.

Resistance quickly developed. The Nationalists inside Iran were effectively controlled, but the Iranian student organization representing 25,000 students in the United States and Europe, always hostile to the Shah, moved into vigorous opposition.[8] In

[7] Compare for example the remarks of *The New York Times* editorial after the Mossadeq plebiscite with one referring to the Shah's plebiscite. In August 15, 1953, the *Times* wrote: "We thought of [Dr. Mossadeq] as a sincere, well-meaning, patriotic Iranian who had a different point of view. We now know that he is a power-hungry, personally ambitious, ruthless demagogue who is trampling upon the liberties of his own people." On June 10, 1963, the *Times* wrote: "The great mass of the Iranian people are doubtless behind the Shah in his bold new reform efforts. The national plebiscite he called early this year gave emphatic evidence of this. . . . " The vote in 1953 was 2,043,389 to 1,207. The vote in 1963 was 5,598,711 to 4,115.

[8] *The New York Times,* June 9, 1963, 18:1. See the issues for 1963 of the Iranian student newspaper *Daneshjo.*

Fars a rebellion of unknown size and duration broke out in the Qashqai and Boir Ahmadi tribal areas.[9] The primary opposition, however, came from religious leaders. Mutterings against the government were heard throughout the spring of 1963 in Tehran and in religious centers of the country. Then on June 5, 1963, severe rioting broke out in Tehran, Shiraz, Qom, and other Iranian centers. Thousands of people were involved; the bazaar became a virtual battle ground; the luxurious sports palace built for Shaban the Brainless by a grateful government was gutted; and there were many casualties.[10] The two-day rioting was led by Ayatollah Ruhollah Khomeini, an unknown figure in Nationalist circles. Although the National Freedom Front participated in the second day of rioting, the Nationalists had clearly not expected the rioting.

The government, considerably embarrassed by such a serious riot only a few months after the staged plebiscite, blamed reactionary mullahs, landlords, and a foreign power (by which they meant the United Arab Republic).[11] But the rioting in 1963 can be better explained on other grounds. That year was the third year of an economic depression in Iran which had hurt particularly the lower-middle and lower classes[12]—the elements most responsive to religious leadership. Therefore, the mullahs, reacting to governmental restrictions on their freedom of activity, were able to strike back with considerable support from their dissatisfied followers. The argument that the rioting was due to opposition to land reform and the emancipation of women is only partly true. Without question most of the religious leaders did oppose giving women the vote, but many favored extensive land reform.[13]

9 *The New York Times,* March 20, 1963, 2:8; May 12, 1963, 31:2.

10 The government, after first giving higher figures, settled on a total of 86 killed and 100 to 200 injured. *The New York Times,* June 9, 1963, 18:1. Dr. Ali Shayegan, the elder statesman of the Iranian exile group in the United States, wrote in a letter to the editors ". . . several hundred persons were killed and over 1,500 injured under the Shah's 'shoot to kill' order." *Christian Science Monitor,* June 24, 1963.

11 *The New York Times,* June 10, 1963, 3:2.

12 *The Economist,* August 24, 1963, p. 659.

13 For example, Ayatollah Sayyed Kazem Shariatmadari, one of three ayatollahs arrested in connection with the rioting, had earlier issued a statement favoring the giving of land to the peasants. *Christian Science Monitor,* June 24, 1963. See also the statement of Ayatollah Rohani, *Bulletin Jebhe Melli Iran,* October 15, 1963.

The failure of the rioting to topple the regime produced one effect that may have long-term consequences for Iranian nationalism. Both the religious and Nationalist leaders recognized the possibility that the June rioting might have been successful had there been prior collaboration of the two groups. The result has been a religio-Nationalist alliance that bears a close resemblance to that of Mossadeq and Kashani in 1951. Along with this has come an increasingly open dissatisfaction of the younger Nationalist leaders with the strategy and general leadership of the elder statesmen. In particular disrepute is the longtime supposition that the Nationalists must focus on the task of altering American foreign policy toward Iran. Younger leaders argue that a direct challenge to the Shah, regardless of American support, is long overdue.

The Shah's tactical response to the rioting demonstrated his mastery of the art of politics in Iran. Allahyar Saleh and most of the Iran Party wing of the Nationalist leaders were released from jail. But the more activist leaders, including the head of the Freedom Front, Mehdi Bazergan, and the brilliant theologian Ayatollah Taleqani were placed on trial. The public prosecutor demanded the death sentence.[14] Final sentencing was deferred for a time and these Nationalist leaders became in effect hostages. By these two acts the Shah made certain that a violent factional struggle would occur inside the National Front and at the same time placed restraints on the activists.

In September 1963 new elections were held. No effort was made to produce a turnout equal to that for the plebiscite. But no genuine opposition candidates were permitted. In place of the defunct parties, an officially sponsored organization called the "Congress of Free Men and Free Women" was formed under the leadership of Hassan Ali Mansur, who, despite the Shah's frequent public denunciations of the landlords, is a member of the thousand families. This organization prepared a bizarre election list which included peasants, workers, wrestlers, and members of various guilds. All but a handful of these candidates were elected.[15] The Shah dropped all pretense that this was a free election. When re-

[14] *Daneshjo*, October 1963.
[15] *The New York Times*, September 20, 1963, 5:1.

minded in a *New York Times* interview of charges that the members of the Majlis ". . . had been 'hand-picked' by the Government-supported Congress of Free Men and Women," the Shah replied sharply: "So what. Was it not better that this organization do it than that it be done by politicians for their own purposes?" [16]

The year 1963 was an important one for the evolution of Iranian nationalism. The Shah virtually abandoned his "positive nationalism" appeal and the National Front moved sharply away from moderation and from any hope of eventual sympathy from the United States. But it is far too early to conclude that the old guard Nationalists are about to be replaced.

Some writers, such as Walter Z. Laqueur, seem to believe that Middle Eastern nationalisms are remiss in not having social ideologies beyond nationalistic objectives of achieving national independence and dignity.[17] Such a view reveals a failure to comprehend the limitation of nationalism per se. Every nationalist has other loyalties than the nation and other objectives than national independence, and these objectives vary with the individual. Iranian nationalists include men of widely divergent economic, political, and social views who are united only by their limited common objectives. When a particular viewpoint is found to prevail throughout the nationalistic element, it is safe to assume that it has a direct bearing on national independence. For example, all Nationalists and most nationalists are opposed to the Central Treaty Organization, the old Baghdad Pact. But the conclusion should not be drawn that Iranian nationalists are likely to be neutralists. Their opposition to CENTO is due to their conviction that the Baghdad Pact was not devised to provide a defense against a Soviet attack; few Iranians believe that Iran can gain the ability to ward off a Soviet invasion. They see the motivation behind the Baghdad Pact as a desire to maintain in power an Anglo-American-controlled government in Iran. Since the present government is not believed by the Nationalists to be genuinely independent, it must be altered or replaced if Nationalist objectives are to be achieved. CENTO, by strengthening that government, is thus a

[16] *Ibid.*, September 25, 1963, 6:1.

[17] Walter Z. Laqueur, *The Soviet Union and the Middle East* (New York, 1959), p. 317.

hostile target for nationalism. Many Nationalists insist that if the government was in their own hands they would favor a regional defensive alliance and would continue to welcome American military assistance.

A hopeful sign with regard to Nationalist thinking is the present attitude toward the Oil Consortium. It was suggested earlier that Mossadeq's greatest failure was that of misunderstanding both the extent of his victory in 1951 and his enhanced ability to control any efforts at political interference from British oil technicians. Now, after several years of the Consortium arrangement, a significant number of Nationalist leaders are convinced that were a Nationalist government to come into power, the Oil Agreement should only be amended, not discarded. This change is less a reversal in attitude toward oil economies than it is a realization that the oil company's British technicians are not engaged in widespread political interference. Under the spell of future demagogues a Nationalist government might be compelled to cancel the Oil Agreement, but for the old guard Nationalists the oil company is no longer a symbol of imperial control.

17

LIBERAL NATIONALISM: THE FUTURE

In the minds of far too many Nationalists, Iran has existed in a state of suspended animation since August 19, 1953. They live on the hope that some magic means, such as American intervention to restore to power a Nationalist regime, will be found by which Iran can pick up where Mossadeq left off in 1953. But the truth is, of course, that the dynamics of social and political change are never in suspended animation. Fundamental changes have occurred in Iran in the past ten years, and they have made a return to the Mossadeq era impossible.

Foremost among these changes is the growth in the number of people who are politically articulate. Iran has received huge oil revenues in the past five years, and the expenditure of these funds has resulted in a remarkable expansion of Iran's commercial and industrial base. The impact of this expansion on society has accelerated change. Increasing numbers of peasants have moved into the urban labor force, and, responding to the demand for technicians, increasing numbers of the offspring of the urban laboring class have joined the ranks of the expanding middle class. At the same time, education opportunities have been multiplied, illiteracy has declined rapidly, and an impressive percentage of the student population has gone on to secondary schools and even college.

Reflecting those changes, the social base of political articulateness is rapidly expanding. But this rate of expansion is far slower than the growth in the numbers of men and women with a developed potential for becoming politically articulate. As long as the organs of social communication remain in the hands of those who conspire to maintain political apathy, the potential for political activity of this large group will remain unexpressed; but should a fundamental change occur in the political situation which would grant to the citizenry a meaningful political choice, the percentage of the population that would become politically active would soar far beyond the 1953 level. And it is this receptivity to political activity of large numbers of the formerly politically unaware that would radically alter the characteristics of a future Nationalist regime.

Developments in Egypt, Iraq, and Cuba furnish a parallel for the Iranian case today. In all three of these countries political receptivity had extended far deeper into society than observers had imagined. Although the middle-class intellectuals in Faruq's Egypt, Nuri al-Said's Iraq, and Batista's Cuba were openly dissatisfied with their authoritarian regimes, the mass of the population remained passive; and observers failed to recognize the emergence of a political receptivity among them. In the nonauthoritarian developing society, channels exist by which an individual who begins to become politically aware can move unobtrusively into the political stream. He can attach himself to one of the competing political elites and can be tutored in the essentials of a particular political belief system. It was in fact precisely by this means that the newly awakened in Mossadeq's Iran were being absorbed into an institutional system that incorporated many of the features of liberal democracy. Since Mossadeq's overthrow, however, the newly awakened have gravitated neither to a political ideology nor to a political elite. Instead they stand as ideal raw material for the future demagogue.

For Fidel Castro the temptation offered by the demagogic opportunities in Cuba was overpowering. Apparently in the interest of gratifying his own desire for power, Castro bypassed the middle-class and the intellectual liberals, who had been his chief source of support prior to victory, and has based his regime on his ability to captivate the newly awakened. Gamal Abdul Nasser, on the other hand, has retained to a remarkable degree the support of both elements. Whether Iran is likely to follow either of these patterns depends on the personality and ideological attachment of the future Iranian leader or leaders. Almost certainly any successor regime to that dominated by the Shah would make nationalism a central rallying point. But the coloring of this nationalism could vary from the liberal democratic to the fascistic, or from the conservative authoritarian to the communistic.

The likelihood has diminished that ideology of a successor regime will combine liberal democratic with nationalistic values. As described in the preceding chapter, the percentage of Iran's population in the postwar period up to 1951 that was politically aware was still small. In such an environment the liberal intellectual element was sufficiently influential to capture the leadership of the popular movement. There were demagogic competitors even then, but the intellectual leaders were able, with the effective histrionic assistance of Dr. Mossadeq, to stave off their challenge. But after ten years of persecution the National Front, semiunderground, has not provided an aggressively effective leadership. Even with the overwhelming majority of the politically aware basically hostile to the Shah's governments, these leaders have done little to give expression to this opposition. Should the Nationalists be confronted with a collapse of royal authority, a fierce power struggle among them would be inevitable, and it is uncertain that the old National Front leaders could survive against ruthless and demagogic competitors. The hope for another marriage of liberal democracy and nationalism seems to rest in the appearance of a new personality from among the liberal intellectuals who would have a charismatic appeal.

Charismatic appeal is an increasingly necessary ingredient for any democratically selected leader in Iran because the recently awakened now form a very large percentage of the politically aware population. Since they are exceedingly unsophisticated in their thinking, they are more likely to form an attachment to a personality who symbolizes their aspirations than to any ideology. If the leader is capable of attracting the support of the politically primitive, few ideological road blocks in his path would be insurmountable. If this leader were a liberal democrat, so would his uncomprehending mass following. Thus a future liberal democratic regime is a possibility, but the probability of such a development is in daily decline.

In January 1958 General Valiollah Qarani was arrested and jailed on the charge that he sought to overthrow the regime. There is no reason to doubt that the charge was correct and, indeed, that

Qarani regarded himself as an Iranian Nasser. The challenge to the Shah from the army was not accidental. In fact, the security forces are a more likely source of future leadership in Iran than is the intellectual elite. The use of modern technology by SAVAK makes a popular uprising steadily more difficult, and dissatisfied civilians are convinced that a revolution would have not only Iranian security forces to combat but also the active opposition of the United States and Great Britain.

Lacking any appreciable support from the politically aware middle class and being unable to count on more than the passive acquiescence of the peasant and laboring masses, the Shah is compelled to rely on the security forces as the bulwark of his regime. Since the middle and lower grades of the officer corps are filled with products of the generally hostile middle class, this "bulwark" is something less than substantial. Some of these officers are professional-minded to the extent that they would support their constitutional leaders regardless of complexion; but many others would welcome a change of regime. Although many junior officers are devoted Nationalists, the majority of the senior officers are hostile to the Nationalists and determined to keep them out of power. It does not follow, however, that these senior officers are necessarily loyal to the Shah or are unaware of the demagogic potential of nationalism. The Shah, who obviously recognizes this lack of personal loyalty, has shown great skill in placing in the top command posts men who are deeply suspicious of each other and are unlikely to be able to unite in conspiracy. But, as the General Qarani case demonstrates, even these top officers include leadership which will make the effort to overturn the regime.

Whether the leaders of a new regime hail from the Army, the intelligentsia, or elsewhere, they are certain to be dependent on the urban lower and lower-middle classes for mass support. Since these are the elements that would respond strongly to the appeal of demagoguery, they provide the most critical of the problems of popular control. Traditionally the leadership of this element of the population has been furnished by a blend of religious, bazaari, and chaqu keshan categories, and any future regime must take into account each of these categories. Of the three the chaqu keshan leader group is most likely to be adversely affected by the growth in political awareness. For maximum effectiveness these leaders need a following which will willingly follow any course of action. As political awareness becomes increasingly pervasive, the freedom of action of the chaqu keshan will be restricted in proportion to the crystallizing of political attitudes among their paid followers. But the power of the religious and bazaar leaders is likely to be enhanced in any regime responsive to public opinion. A national leader who wishes widespread support will be compelled to take into account the thinking and attitudes of both of these groups. It is inconceivable that the religious leaders, for example, could be ignored and humiliated in this era as they were by Reza Shah. In all likelihood a regime seeking mass support would be compelled to accommodate itself ideologically to that blend of religio-nationalism described in Chapter 11.

If the long-term trend in Iran is such that the appearance of an intellectual-dominated regime such as that of Dr. Mossadeq is less and less likely, the trend is even more adverse for the traditional claimants of power. The inexorable progress of political articulation is such that if the traditional elements recognize its force and seek to accommodate themselves to its power demand, they can do nothing less than surrender the traditional power structure. The passing of power from the hands of the traditional elements is inevitable. The only question is whether the process will be evolutionary or revolutionary.

One leading Iranian politician, Hassan Arsenjani, has accepted the above conclusions and has moved to offset them. If the old traditional elite structure is doomed and if the middle-class elements have focused their loyalties on identifiable leaders who stand in opposition to the Shah, then an alternative base of support must be found. The alternatives would appear to be two: the urban lower class and the peasantry. Since the former is fairly well-controlled through the chaqu keshan and since authentic labor leaders might move into an alliance with middle-class leaders, any effort to enlist a positive support from labor would seem unwise. Arsenjani, who served as Minister of Agriculture under Amini and for a time under Alam, believes that the peasantry can be transformed from an acquiescent element into a source of positive support for the Court. With full backing from the Shah, he moved energetically to distribute land to the peasants with long-term repayment provisions. Reports of newsmen covering turn-over ceremonies invariably agree, as would be expected, that this move is popular among the peasants and that the Shah is given full credit. The suspicion that the patriotism of the Shah is questionable is no problem here. As discussed above, the horizons of the peasantry generally are too limited even for a comprehension of the concept of nation.

However, there is reason to conclude that Arsenjani's expectations are overly optimistic. The Shah is gaining popularity because he has satisfied an extraordinarily important value of the peasants, that of land ownership. But the peasants are not prepared for their good fortune. They lack capital and an understanding of where and how capital is available. They lack an understanding of marketing, seed selection, and animal husbandry; and there is nothing approaching an adequate staff of technicians to advise them. As the peasants fall into financial difficulties, the regime will, almost inevitably, cease appearing to be the granter of land ownership and instead will seem to be aiding those who threaten that ownership. The opportunities granted demagogues at this point are incalculable.

For the communists the long-term trends are favorable. True, the communist organizational apparatus within Iran has been crippled to the point of ineffectiveness. But nothing has been done in the past few years to reduce the respectability of communism. For a regime whose own patriotism is in question to describe the communists as traitors is less a liability than an asset for the communists. The bases for the attractiveness of communism that existed in 1951 exist today. Intellectual unemployment, the desire to progress more rapidly than the democratic process can permit, the conviction that a fundamental social revolution is an essential prerequisite for progress, and the belief that the primary external enemy is Western imperialism—all are as important today as they were a decade ago. But added to this is a new and even greater asset for the communists: disenchantment of the noncommunist elites among the modernizing elements. The communists probably have in working order abroad a complete leadership structure which could return to Iran in a matter of days; but the noncommunist, antigovernment elites exist primarily within Iran and there in a badly crippled state. If freedom to organize were granted to each, the process of recovery for the noncommunists would be more arduous and prolonged than for the communists. It is difficult not to conclude, therefore, that the situation in Iran is fundamentally more favorable to Soviet than to Western objectives.

Those who formulate United States foreign policy toward Iran face the problem of reversing this unfavorable long-term trend. The overthrow of the government of Dr. Mossadeq was an audacious, romantic, and hopelessly unsophisticated approach to the Iranian problem. The extent of United States involvement in that event is unlikely to be known for many years, but enough evidence is available to indicate that the United States encouraged the royal *coup d'état*. In essence this was a short-term approach to a problem that is as fundamental as the social revolution occurring in Iran. For the United States to have thrown its total support to the traditional elements at a time when the dynamics of social change clearly demonstrated that the replacement of the traditional leadership group was inevitable indicates a failure to take the most basic step in the foreign policy decision-making process: the preparation of a careful and objective estimate of the situation.

Confronted with a long-term trend that was obviously more advantageous to the Soviet Union than to the West, the United States policy makers moved dramatically but attacked only the symptomatic manifestations of the trend. An argument for the anti-Mossadeq policy could be made if United States policy immediately following Mossadeq's overthrow had directed itself to meeting the fundamentals of the problem; there is something to be said for a short-term policy designed to gain time with which to maneuver a reversal in an unfavorable long-term trend. But there is no indication that the Department of State made any serious effort to persuade the Shah and General Zahedi to accept the necessity of attracting the support of the middle classes. On the contrary, the haste with which the Zahedi government restored diplomatic relations with Great Britain and negotiated an oil agreement and the enthusiasm of the Shah for the Baghdad Pact all serve to show that the Shah, Zahedi, and the Americans regarded as irrelevant the support of the middle classes. Each of these actions was intensely unpopular with the Nationalists, and they served to reinforce a conviction within the middle classes that the Shah was a tool of Western imperialism.

The pose of United States policy in the Dulles period was that of hard-headed realism, but the conclusion from this study is that, instead, United States policy toward Iran in the Dulles years was romantic and intuitive. Political analysis may lack tools of scientific precision, but the tools available are sufficient to isolate long-term political trends and to enumerate the political probabilities and variables of a given situation. The indications are that these tools were not used with regard to the Iranian situation. Consequently, the phenomenon of Iranian nationalism and, more explicitly, of the Mossadeqist movement was never understood. In the place of analysis there were intuitive value judgments. Once the decision was made to turn against Mossadeq, an elaborate mythology was constructed to justify this action—and the unraveling of this mythology now stands as the most difficult problem.

United States policy toward Iran in the Kennedy years cannot be accused of favoring a foredoomed status quo or of ignoring long-term trends. On the contrary, the Kennedy policy seems to have been dedicated to the objective of pushing the Iranian economy to the "take off point" after which, presumably, the goal of a stable, noncommunist government will be achieved. The conclusions of this study do not support these expectations. The political and social consequences of an extraordinarily rapid economic growth will unquestionably be profound, and one of these consequences will be a much wider acceptance of nationalist values. The steady movement to the cities from the villages which is accompanying the economic growth will cause a growing awareness of Iran as a nation. But a central proposition of this study is that these newly awakened Iranians are unlikely to look to the liberal intellectual nationalists for leadership. They will prefer the demagogues, who will appeal to their aspirations, frustrations, and hatreds. The paradox is that in the interest of combatting communism the United States has been pursuing a policy of economic determinism that might well produce not a Nasser- but a Castro-type leadership.

18

FIFTEEN YEARS LATER

The last paragraphs of the previous chapter were written a few months after the Shah had emerged victorious from the 1960–63 crisis. For fifteen years following that crisis the Shah's control appeared to be so solid that Iran was regarded externally as having one of the world's most stable regimes. But as this chapter is being written in late 1978 the Shah's control has passed through a period of rapid disintegration. My expectations of fifteen years ago, easily inferred from the previous chapter, did not include a decade and a half of surface political tranquility. Far less surprising to me is the overwhelming evidence being manifest in Iran in the final weeks of 1978 of the fragile base of support the Shah actually enjoyed. But both periods tell much about the impact of nationalism on Iran. The fifteen years of political tranquility were possible in spite of nationalistic forces and therefore suggest some limitations to nationalism as a political determinant. But the turmoil of Iran in late1978 can only underscore the ultimate importance of nationalism in giving direction to Iranian politics.

Iran fifteen years ago was beginning to move toward the economic takeoff point. Since then, the easily identifiable trends associated with rapid economic growth have indeed occurred. Iranians have moved to the cities in large numbers, and public awareness of Iran as a nation has increased faster than expected. Furthermore, evidence is strong in support of my most important assumption: that the regime would not be able to convince important sections of the Iranian public of its nationalist purity. Twenty-five years after the overthrow of Mossadeq there is no longer any doubt of the primacy of the role of the Central Intelligence Agency in that operation.[1] And

[1]Although the CIA role is referred to frequently and without official denial, there is

a new generation of Iranian oppositionists continues to see the regime as American-imposed and American-controlled. Yet the fact is that, in spite of this liability and contrary to my expectations of fifteen years ago, the regime of Mohammad Reza Pahlavi, Aryamehr, Shah-in-Shah of Iran, has been remarkably stable. This stability has been achieved in large part because, until recently, the regime successfully attracted the enthusiastic support of some middle-class Iranians, and the acquiescence of more. To be sure, the core of the opposition to the regime includes middle-class youth and intellectuals, and behavioral evidence suggests that even those who support the regime respond sluggishly to its efforts to manipulate nationalist symbols. Indeed, the regime appears to have made surprisingly little recovery from the onus of having achieved power through a *coup* directed by foreigners. The failure to anticipate the growth in the regime's stability, therefore, was not a consequence of underestimating its ability to achieve nationalist legitimacy but of overestimating the difficulties posed by the lack of such legitimacy. The demogogic potential for exploiting the regime's nationalist vulnerability persists, as can be seen from the opposition's success with Iranian students living abroad. But the fifteen-year failure of the opposition inside Iran cannot be explained simply by the inhibitions imposed by the Iranian security organization, SAVAK, and other instruments of coercion. The stability of the regime depended to a substantial degree on satisfying the demands of broad sections of the political and economic elite for influence and material goods.

The governing style of Mohammad Reza Shah bears little resemblance to that of his father, Reza Shah. Whereas the father was simple, direct, and often crudely brutal, the son is complex, sophisticated, and subtle in approach. Yet with regard to nationalism their attitudes are strikingly parallel. Both appear to have seen Iran, dynastic interests, and their ego

no carefully documented and serious analysis of the event. The account of the Harknesses in *Saturday Evening Post* in 1954, obviously biased and distorted, remains the basis for all succeeding descriptions. Richard and Gladys Harkness, "The Mysterious Doings of CIA," *Saturday Evening Post,* November 6, 1954, pp. 66–68.

interest as inseparably blended, and hence can be considered profoundly nationalistic; but neither was able to project to the Iranian people a credible image as a nationalist. This inability to win clear public acceptance on nationalist grounds in turn compelled both father and son to resort to strongly repressive policies to control the Iranian people.

In explaining the current regime's longevity and stability, much of the credit must be given to the qualities of leadership of the Shah. Few would have predicted that Mohammad Reza Pahlavi, who appeared to be so vacillating and timid at the time of Mossadeq's overthrow, would become by 1978 a primary example of an absolute ruler. In terms of decisional control, few leaders in modern history can compare. In possibly the most astonishing of a series of brilliant interview portraits, the Italian journalist Orianna Fallaci has captured some of the essence of Mohammad Reza Shah's self-image and demeanor.[2] Confessing to an abiding mysticism, the Shah strongly asserted his contention of divine ordination. "I believe in God, and that I have been chosen by God to perform a task. My visions were miracles that saved the country. My reign has saved the country, and it has done so because God was on my side."[3] By 1973, at the time of this interview, he was aggressively and publicly contemptuous of Western liberal democracy,[4] boastfully proud of having the strength to order the shooting of dissidents,[5] confident in claiming omniscience concerning matters of importance to Iran, and willing to flaunt his and Iran's power before the entire world. "I know everything there is to know about oil, everything. I'm a real specialist and it's as a specialist that I tell you: the price of oil must rise—it's only fair that, from now on, you should pay more for oil. Let's say—10 times more."[6] Any man who achieves the kind of decisional control that the Shah exercised in Iran must be considered, because of his mortality, the prime source of regime vulnerability. His very

[2]Oriana Fallaci, "The Shah of Iran," *New Republic*, September 1, 1973, 217:16–21.
[3]*Ibid.*, p. 7.
[4]*Ibid.*, p. 18.
[5]*Ibid.*
[6]*Ibid.*, p. 21.

dominance precluded the growth of institutions that could work for easy succession. This lack of institutional base was painfully apparent as the regime disintegrated in the fall of 1978. But the most important accelerating force behind that disintegration was the Shah's loss of personal control. Once again he was the vacillating, timid, and uncertain man that the Americans and British saw in 1953 when they looked to General Zahedi, not to the Shah, to be Iran's dictator.

Of course the regime owed a great deal to the generosity of nature in granting Iran vast oil reserves. Already in the decade from 1963 to 1973 Iran's oil income had approached and then exceeded $1 billion annually; and in the same period, when inflation was a minor factor, the annual increase in gross national product varied from 4.5 per cent to 15.3 per cent.[7] Thus Iran was experiencing growth at a rate approaching Japan's; the impact was observable in the form of real standard-of-living improvements for most of the population. Following the escalation of oil prices in 1973 the growth rate in Iran skyrocketed—34 per cent in 1974, 42 per cent in 1975, and 17 per cent in 1976.[8] But inflation became a serious factor, especially in real estate, and often stood at 30 to 35 per cent.[9] There is little question that both the stability of the years from 1963 to 1973 and the serious public disturbances of 1977 and 1978 reflect the growth in real income for most Iranians in the first period and the grave economic distress for all but the enormously wealthy few in the second period.

Paralleling Iran's economic transformation is the transformation of its position in international society. From 1953 to 1963 Iran could be described not only as an American client state but as an American dependency. The regime required full American diplomatic and security support not so much for protection against an external aggressor as for its internal survival. Had American support been withdrawn, the regime would in all likelihood have been overthrown.

In the decade from 1963 to 1973, thanks in large part to

[7]*Economist,* October 31, 1970, 237:48 (survey, p. xxv).
[8]*New York Times,* February 4, 1976, 1:5.
[9]*Economist,* June 21, 1975, 255:66.

economic conditions, this dependency began to fade. A survey of the Shah's interviews[10] in that period reflects a steady growth in confidence, assertiveness, and, by the end of the period, unconcealed arrogance. As outlined below, the Shah's diplomacy began to have a major, even dominant, impact on developing alliance patterns in South Asia. He intervened in intra-Arab politics and occupied a critical bargaining position in the Arab-Israeli conflict. Since 1973 the Shah manifested his oil leverage with consummate skill while explicitly denying any intention to use oil as a political weapon. Oil granted him a world role, and his own statements leave no doubt as to his determination to exercise influence at the level of West Germany.[11]

This overview suggests an enviable internal and external power position for the Shah and his regime. But it points as well to the vital importance of nationalist legitimacy for a regime. The regime's stability rests basically on the utilization of an enormous oil income in such a way that the material demands of essential elements of society are satisfied. But in spite of Iran's transformation from an American dependency to a major regional power with global aspirations, there is surprisingly little manifestation of nationalistic pride. Indeed, it is a common opposition interpretation that in foreign policy, Iran is a tactical executor of American strategic decisions. In that view Iran lacks even the dignity of a surrogate. Among the passive regime supporters, and most Iranians are in this category, the predominant attitude appears to be one of disinterest. Only among those whose vested interests are tied to the regime—the security force, technocrats, and elements of the newly rich—is there genuine enthusiasm. The nationalistic exuberance of the early fifties has no parallel in the late seventies. The experience of the fifteen years, from 1963 to 1978, has much to tell about nationalism as a determinant of the rhythm and direction of political developments.

[10]The Shah's interviews are easily available in the issues of *Kayhan International* (published in English).

[11]For the clearest expression of the Shah's aspirations see his *Towards the Great Civilization* (Tehran, 1978).

The Role of Coercion

Iranian dissidents contend that there were one hundred thousand political prisoners in Iran in 1977.[12] The government agreed to a figure of between three thousand and thirty-five hundred.[13] In all probability, and even though the government figure was surely a self-serving one, the dissident figure was seriously inflated. No opposition group has yet been willing to compile a list of names and biographies which could give credence to its claims. Similarly in contention is the question of torture of political prisoners. The government claimed all torturing ceased in 1977. Oppositionists admit that well-known prisoners in 1977 were not being tortured but insisted that less well-known prisoners in provincial jails were subject to a regimen of daily torture.[14] Since Iran was incontestably a closed society, there was no way the outside observer could evaluate the relative claims. But from the point of view of effectiveness of control, the inability to substantiate figures is of little relevance. What appears to be a fact is that Iranians inclined to oppose the regime accepted as valid the figure of fifty thousand to one hundred thousand prisoners and the contention that torture is standard procedure. This belief may have embarrassed Iranian authorities concerned with Iran's international image, but it was a highly effective deterrent to the opposition.

SAVAK achieved the ultimate objective of a security organization charged with deterring antiregime activity. It was assumed to be ubiquitous, efficient, and ruthless. Each element of the highly factionalized opposition abroad was inclined to see infiltration and control by SAVAK of many if not most of its competitors. Nor can any oppositionist have doubted that his own group was infiltrated. This was a climate in which conspiracy theories flourished, and regardless of an opponent's tactics, his behavior was likely to confirm suspicions. Was he

[12] *Zendan,* November–December 1977, 1 (no. 3):1.

[13] The Shah stated this figure in a Columbia Broadcasting System interview with Mike Wallace in 1976. In an interview with *Aftenposten,* Oslo, June 17, 1978, he used the figure of 3,300 for 1977 but stated that in mid-1978 the number was less than 2,000.

[14] See the June 1978 issue of *Payam e Mujahid,* p. 1, for a detailing of torturing long after the Shah claims tortures had ceased.

advocating a tough, uncompromising position? SAVAK was trying to splinter and thereby destroy. Was he advocating a course of compromise and reconciliation? SAVAK was trying to use him to gain control of additional elements of the opposition. Similarly, inside Iran an individual inclined to be open in his advocacy of direct action was suspected of provocation. If he was arrested and quickly released, this proved his arrest was for purposes of establishing his credibility. If he was arrested and sentenced to a long prison term, SAVAK was taking more pains to establish his credentials.

How efficient was SAVAK? There is really no way of knowing. Some Iranians in opposition, especially those involved in urban guerrilla activities, made explicit efforts to demonstrate the incompetence of SAVAK in order to muddy its image. But without a free press to describe their encounters, the true story could be known to very few.[15] The reputation of SAVAK was such that dissident Iranians were unlikely to reveal their thinking to anyone with whom they had not established a high trust relationship. Such individuals would have been even more cautious in considering direct action. A major objective of any organization such as SAVAK is to destroy the potential opposition activist's sense of efficacy. If this is achieved, the affected individual is likely to adopt an attitude of pessimism and cynicism about his fellow nationals and about himself and will accommodate to the regime. To a very large extent SAVAK in 1977 had achieved this goal.

Still, whatever the correct figures, a significant number of Iranians tested the coercive control system and became political prisoners. Inside Iran students demonstrated and engaged in strikes despite the certainty of brutal repression. Outside Iran approximately 10 per cent of Iranian students participate to some degree in opposition activities.[16] They had little real hope that the masks they wore could conceal their identity since they

[15]Opposition newspapers published abroad detail such successes in virtually every issue. See, for example, *Khabar Nameh* and *Payam e Mujahid,* published in the United States.

[16]This conservative estimate is based on actual participation at demonstrations or in the Iranian Student Association.

assumed some of their fellow demonstrators were agents of SAVAK. Why then did they take these risks? Among the reasons for their dissatisfaction, and taking their own statements as evidence, an offended sense of nationalism ranks high. From 1963 to 1973 real standard-of-living improvements were apparent to most politically attentive Iranians. From 1973 to1978 inflation resulted in distress for all but the very wealthy. But the percentage of Iranian students abroad involved in opposition activities remained relatively constant. Thus the conclusion is defensible that, although mass receptivity for agitation varies directly with economic satisfaction and dissatisfaction, the opposition of the politically most interested in Iran rests far more on the persisting belief that the royal regime lacks nationalist credentials.

Presumably the regime would have preferred to rely less on coercion as a form of control. Not only were SAVAK and the secret police terribly expensive, they were potentially dangerous. Controlling the instruments of terror is always difficult when those instruments are a primary source of regime stability. The presumption must be made that members of the domestic security forces, aware of their special position of influence, will harbor ambitions to seize control of government. That the Shah, a man with a particularly cynical view of his fellow countrymen,[17] should see an exaggerated danger in his security forces is virtually certain. Surely then the Shah would, if he could, seek to attract the positive and enthusiastic support of broad sections of his public. Such support would relieve him of a heavy reliance on his security agencies. His inability to attract that kind of positive support, especially from the most politically interested youth, is directly related to his difficulty in projecting an image of a great national actor.

The Role of Symbol Manipulation

Opposition newspapers frequently characterized the Shah's rule as "fascist." Implicit in this charge is a definition of fascism

[17]See the discussion of Hassan Arsenjani in this chapter, under "The Shah and Nationalism."

that is an authoritarian rule that rests on commercial middle-class elements and serves the economic interests of that class. But the twentieth-century regimes that were described as "fascist" all were characterized by an ability to excite the nationalistic sentiments of major segments of the public. Without exception, fascist leaders were masters at the manipulation of symbols, foremost of which were national symbols. And their ability to utilize symbol manipulation as a means of control reduced their dependence on instruments of terror. If a definition of fascism were to incorporate the use of symbol manipulation as a primary control device, the regime of the Shah was not fascist.

Certainly the Shah made every effort to meet this expanded definition of fascism. A glance at any newspaper legally published in Iran or at the text of any official speech is sufficient to discover the favored symbol of the day. In 1978 the most frequently used expression was the "Shah-people revolution." And that symbol is of the genre that has been most effectively used by the regime: modernization symbols. "White Revolution" and the "Pahlavi era" conjure up the image of rapid economic and technical change. Such symbols relate directly to the primary basis of regime stability, that is, its ability to satisfy the material needs of important sections of society. But, unlike symbols that relate directly to individual identity, these cannot be used to stir a people into a frenzy of excitement. In Iran the symbols that could relate more directly to identity are dynasty, nation, and religion. The Shah made a major effort to present himself as the latest and one of the greatest of a line of Iranian kings that extends for twenty-five hundred years, a monarch who rules by divine ordination and with divine guidance, and a monarch totally devoted to the Aryan people and the Iranian nation. But his efforts had only meager results.

Evidence of the Shah's awareness of the importance of the dynastic symbols is not difficult to find. His various titles were cue enough. One might think the traditional title, Shah-in-Shah, or King of Kings, would suffice—especially since his father took the historically glorious family name of Pahlavi. But the Shah incorporated another historic title, Aryamehr, the Light of the Aryans, into the daily image. In addition he was often referred to, especially in a military context, as "Khodegan," a word translated as "outstanding leader" but which gives the flavor of being a leader approaching the divine.

On two major occasions the Shah spent lavishly to produce ceremonial spectaculars designed to focus on his role as monarch, on the antiquity of the institution, and on his claim to be in the glorious tradition of his favorite predecessor, Cyrus the Great, the conqueror of Egypt. In 1967, on his birthday, Mohammad Reza Pahlavi was granted an official and long delayed coronation. In October 1971 the twenty-five-hundredth anniversary of the Iranian kings was celebrated. The *New York Times* reported that $100 million was spent for the latter,[18] including funds to beautify roads to the airports, city squares and minarets, and to build new monuments. It culminated in a great banquet at Persepolis, where French chefs prepared breast of peacock for royalty and dignitaries from around the world. A magnificent relief in Persepolis depicts a procession of vassal kings bearing homage to the Achemenid King of Kings. The celebration was to symbolize the restoration of Iran to imperial greatness.

The coronation generated little enthusiasm but also little overt resentment. But the anniversary celebration was a major fiasco. Months before the festivities, university students struck in protest. Within intellectual circles the celebration was a central topic of conversation and for many an object of chagrin and humiliation. Even within the entrepreneurial class there was much grumbling at what amounted to forced levies, large monetary contributions to the celebration. For an outside observer, the intensity of the hostility of the opposition was both surprising and instructive. In terms of wasting precious oil income, the amount spent on the celebration was insignificant when compared with expenditures for new weaponry to deal with currently nonexisting foes. But the deep resentment at the effort to legitimize the brief Pahlavi dynasty by placing it on a par with the Achemenid and the Sassanid dynasties is indicative of the major difficulty the Shah had in gaining acceptance as a

[18] *New York Times,* October 12, 1971, 39:2.

great Iranian king. Then, added to a disappointing domestic response, the celebration was treated in the international press as a supreme example of high camp.[19]

The assumption that because the Iranian people have an ancient monarchial tradition they are attached to the institution of the monarchy is widely held by Western commentators[20] and is frequently explicated by the Shah.[21] If that assumption is valid, the monarchy as a symbol should lend itself to manipulation by a royal regime seeking to attract positive popular support and to legitimize its own position. But behavioral evidence in the modern era, the only era in which there has been mass political activity, is far from conclusive. The only leader who came to personify in a symbolic sense the Iranian nation for most of Iran's politically aware was Dr. Mossadeq, and in Mossadeq's rhetoric[22] the monarchy is given scant attention. The element of the public that appeared to be genuinely alarmed in 1953 when the future of the monarchy was in question was the same element that in 1925 resisted the efforts of Reza Khan to abolish the monarchy and to establish a republic: the religious and traditional-minded urban mass. Since these people are closely akin to the peasantry, it is reasonable to infer that the peasantry too would respond positively to a manipulation of the symbol of the monarchy. But the pervasiveness of its appeal among the highly attentive and opinion-formulating elements is in serious doubt. Indeed leading Shiite intellectuals in the 1970's have been asserting that the institution of the monarchy is contrary to the tenets of Islam. In any event, the efforts of Mohammad Reza Pahlavi, Shah-in-Shah of Iran, Aryamehr, Khodegan, to make use of the symbol of the Pahlavi dynasty have achieved only modest success.

As his interview with Orianna Fallaci demonstrates, the Shah not only is religious, but is a self-proclaimed mystic who feels

[19]See, for example, *Time,* October 25, 1971, 98:32–33.

[20]See in particular Edward Bayne, *Persian Kingship in Transition* (New York, 1968).

[21]The Shah gives a clear picture of his own conception in three books, *Mission for My Country* (Tehran, 1958), *The White Revolution* (Tehran, 1967), and *Towards the Great Civilization* (Tehran, 1978).

[22]Mossadeq's speeches have been compiled and published in eight volumes, *Nutqhai Dr. Mossadeq,* (n.p., n.d).

the personal presence of God at his side. His espousal of the divine right of monarchy therefore should carry the force of deeply and sincerely felt conviction. And for the second member of a new dynasty seeking to establish the legitimacy of that dynasty, the sanction of clerical authorities would be an invaluable asset. Yet not only has the Shah failed to attract such sanction, he has made little serious effort to do so. Indeed he has attempted to make a virtue of the failure by constructing an image of a progressive leader achieving spectacular gains in the face of opposition from the black reaction of traditional Islam. More recently he has attempted to couple opposition clerics symbolically with communism. The major demonstrations of 1977 and 1978 are attributed to "Islamic Marxists," and the Shah enjoys elaborating on that theme.[23]

There is little mystery in the Shah's tactic. The last major challenge to his regime in 1963 came from urban rioting inspired by religious leaders. And the 1977–78 challenge to the regime came from exactly the same source. The symbolic importance of having one of the most highly respected leaders of Shiite Islam, Ayatollah Ruhollah Khomeini, issuing periodic fatwas that sharply deny the regime's legitimacy was too little noticed and too often minimized in analyses of the regime.[24] The extent to which the Shah had in effect written off any real ability to alter this picture is indicated by his willingness, in the middle of the year of human rights, 1977, to sentence one of Iran's most respected theologians, Ayatollah Taleqani, to ten years in prison. To be sure, there were a great many Shiite religious leaders who were not only willing but anxious to sanctify the regime. This included, of course, all those with official appointments. And religious oppositionists were splintered into at least three camps, thus diluting for a time the effectiveness of this opposition. But the prominence of those in opposition was so substantial that the Shah was effectively

[23]See *Kayhan International,* May 7, 1977, p. 1.

[24]Press reports of Iran's 1978 riots usually accept the Iranian government's assessment of the religious opposition as seeking a return to traditional Islam and being opposed to all reforms, particularly those concerning women. Actual statements by Khomeini and other prominent leaders are easily available in the publication *Payam e Mujahid.*

denied the ability to use, in his own and his dynasty's behalf, the sanction of Shiite Islam.

Far more puzzling were the Shah's persisting difficulties in gaining acceptance as a man who had modernized Iran and transformed it from a minor American dependency to a major regional power and an aspiring world power. Without minimizing the difficulties implicit in his having come to power as a result of a CIA-backed and in large part CIA-directed *coup,* there were several reasons for believing that over time the onus of that event would fade. As this study has illustrated, foreign interventions in Iran were more the rule than the exception, and, indeed, the Nationalists were quite willing to solicit American support openly. The Shah's own acknowledgment to Edward Bayne that he needed time and a stronger domestic base to make possible the casting off of inordinate foreign influence[25] is persuasive given this historical context. Besides, the Shah was not a central figure in the 1953 *coup.* Quite clearly the American, British, and Iranian participants saw General Fazlollah Zahedi emerging as Iran's dictator, not the Shah. Firsthand accounts of the *coup* agree that a major obstacle that had to be overcome by its perpetrators was the Shah's reluctance to participate.[26] Then, finally, the image of the Shah as an American agent should have been vulnerable to clear evidence that the Shah was willing to pursue a course of action that the American government disapproved of. As the following pages indicate, the Shah on many occasions followed a sharply independent policy line—one that produced some nervousness in Washington.

There are in any society individuals, given to conspiracy theories, who find no difficulty in dismissing or in interpreting away evidence contradictory to a favored thesis. Thus it is no surprise that there are Iranians who can interpret any evidence in such a way as to reinforce the image of a Shah who faithfully executed American orders. But this view in Iran is held, at least to a significant degree, by a broad section of the best-informed

[25]Bayne, *Persian Kingship,* Chapter 2.

[26]David Wise and Thomas B. Ross, *Invisible Government* (New York, 1964), pp. 110–14.

people and is not limited to those who are temperamentally predisposed to see conspiracies. The term "agent" implies absolute control, and even healthy-minded Iranians find inconceivable the notion that the American government would allow the Shah, a man who owed his position to American action, any significant independence in the area of foreign policy. The unwillingness of successive American administrations to voice serious criticisms of the Shah's behavior reinforced Iranian oppositionist reluctance to alter a long and intensely held view. Yet, in important respects, the Shah's policy did not coincide with American interests.

Most important of these was the Shah's oil-pricing policy. As the quote from the Fallaci interview illustrates, the Shah on occasion was brutal in his insistence that Iran would charge a price for oil that the market could bear.[27] At other times, especially when the demand-supply equation was not in his favor, the Shah adopted a pose of self-sacrifice and responsibility in pricing policy.[28] Yet the fact is that in the critical days of 1973 when oil prices escalated, the Iranian government was a primary advocate of the price rise. Given the severity of the crisis this produced and the near hysteria of some American public responses, one might assume that this Iranian policy alone would damage or destroy the Shah-as-American-agent image. But offsetting this evidence for Iranians, especially those in opposition, was the fact that the multinational oil companies were profiting enormously from the situation, and Iranians have long assumed a close connection between the American government and American financial enterprises. Furthermore, the multibillion-dollar arms purchases from the United States were seen as a sophisticated device for laundering petro dollars. Thus, although average Americans may suffer from Iran's oil-pricing policy, those Americans closest to the decisional center profited. This reasoning denied the Shah the political capital he might otherwise have gained as a nationalist assaulting his onetime mentor.

The Shah's policy toward the Soviet Union, presumably the

[27]"The Shah of Iran," p. 21.
[28]*Kayhan International,* November 26, 1977, p. 5.

epicenter of American interest in Iran, has been somewhat alarming for Americans of the cold war persuasion. Iranian purchases of Soviet military equipment, including personnel carriers, trucks, and artillery, has been substantial,[29] and such purchases are not to be expected of America's Middle Eastern surrogate. Furthermore, economic relations with the Soviet Union have been good. The Soviet Union provides a good deal of technical assistance, an impressive manifestation of which was the construction of the Isfahan steel mill.[30] The Soviet Union has been the largest consumer of Iranian exports other than oil.[31] Yet this evidence of independence too was lost on the Shah's suspicious countrymen. Seeing the Soviet-American conflict more and more as a charade, Iranian oppositionists were not inclined to take this behavior as serious evidence of the Shah's independence.

For the most part, however, the Shah's security policy in the Middle East was pleasing to American policy makers. Indeed, Iran was almost a model for application of the Nixon doctrine. Here was an Asian country willing to invest heavily in military preparedness and for the most part willing to make the appropriate foreign policy utterances. Particularly favored was the "trip wire" hypothesis as a rationale for Iranian security policy. By this thesis Iran, though surely no match for an all-out Soviet assault, was a respectable military power and not one that could be dismissed casually. Iran therefore could deter any Soviet or Soviet-inspired move other than one that heralded a major military assault on South Asia. Even in the event of an all-out assault, Iran could delay the Soviet advance and furnish precious time for an appropriate American response.[32]

Scenarios advanced by Iranian and Western writers on strategy[33] describe an Iranian fleet in the Persian Gulf protect-

[29] *New York Times,* March 19, 1975, 47:2.

[30] Ali Banuazizi, "Iran: The Making of a Regional Power," in A. L. Udovitch, ed., *The Middle East: Oil, Conflict and Hope* (Lexington, Mass., 1976), p. 491.

[31] *Ibid.*

[32] For an explication of the "trip wire" thesis see Shahram Chubin, "National Security in a More Plural World: The Case of Iran," unpublished paper..

[33] See especially Robert Burrell and Alvin J. Cottrell, *Iran, the Arabian Peninsula and the Indian Ocean* (New York, 1972) and the same authors, *Iran, Afghanistan and Pakistan:*

ing oil lines from a Soviet or Soviet-inspired attack. They see an Iranian paramilitary force able to extinguish Soviet-installed regimes in the Arabian peninsula and possibly beyond, and they see an Iranian fleet in the Indian Ocean helping neutralize the naval power of the Soviet Union and its clients. But Iranians opposed to the regime have difficulty taking these scenarios seriously or even in believing that they are meant seriously. Why a superpower with a twelve-hundred-mile land border with Iran should carry out an act of war against Iran through the Persian Gulf where supply lines are several thousand miles long is not altogether clear. They see as far more likely a scenario in which the United States, acting through Iran, is seeking to control the area for exploitation by multinational corporations. Iranian opponents of the regime see a Soviet Union which long ago ceased to encourage any opposition movement and which has been hardly less a supporter of the Shah than is the United States.

Despite the problems of logic in the American position and the lack of supporting evidence of Soviet aggressive intent in the area, both American policy and the statements of American leaders suggest that American policy makers see the role of Iran in South Asia in late cold war perspective. But a gradual atrophy of that view may be occurring. There was one brief but frightening moment in 1971 when, during the Bangladesh independence struggle, a late cold war alliance system in South Asia appeared to be crystallizing. Supporting Pakistan were Iran, the United States, and the People's Republic of China. Supporting Bangladesh were India, the Soviet Union, and Iraq. The Shah's diplomacy in this era was vigorous and revealing. Anticipating a possible dismemberment of West as well as East Pakistan, he clearly telegraphed an intention to help preserve the territorial integrity of West Pakistan or, failing that, to absorb several of the pieces.

This broader crisis coincided with an ongoing dispute with Iraq. The two governments were locked in controversy over

Tensions and Dilemmas (Beverly Hills, 1974). See also Shahram Chubin, "Naval Competition and Security in South West Asia," unpublished paper presented at the Annual Conference on Sea Power, Ronneby, Sweden, September 1975.

their border on the Shatt-al-Arab River, the confluence of the Tigris and Euphrates. By the Erzerum Treaty, the border of Iraq (then the Ottoman Empire) was defined as the east bank of the river. Iranians almost universally considered this foreign-imposed, archaic, and obviously inequitable. In 1971 the Shah proclaimed that the border would be the channel of the Shatt-al-Arab. Iraq did not challenge this Iranian act directly, but the difficult relations between the two governments had already degenerated into a mini-cold war. Iraq further extended its hospitality to Iranian dissidents, particularly those in alliance with Ayatollah Khomeini, who lived in exile in Iraq. In addition, Iraq supported by propaganda and some direct assistance Arab separatists in southwest Iran and Baluchi separatists in southeast Iran. At moments of severe tension the Iraqis would summarily and brutally expel Iranian citizens who lived in the Shiite shrine centers of Iraq. Iran gave parallel assistance to Iraqi dissidents and, according to Baghdad,[34] was directly involved in several attempted *coups* in Iraq. Border incidents were common, and with the battle lines being drawn in South Asia, the Iranian-Iraqi conflict had the potential for accidentally setting off a major war.

The Bangladesh crisis had a strange anticlimax. After it was clear that Bangladesh, with active Indian support, would be able to establish its independence, the Nixon administration sent an impressive naval task force into the Bay of Bengal. This array of gunboats, presumably meant as a show of American force in the face of the defeat of an ally, had all the appearance of impotent rage. Certainly the Shah interpreted American policy in the Bangladesh crisis in that light. Iranian analysts saw American behavior as an indication of the limits of its resolve in South Asia.[35] The lessons of Indochina and Bangladesh were the same. Iran must follow its own policy in the region and prepare itself militarily for the role of a major regional power.

Striking evidence that there is an atrophy of cold war behavior, if not of cold war rhetoric, in South Asia is to be found

[34]*New York Times*, January 22, 1970, 2:3 and January 23, 1974, 4:4.

[35]See Shahram Chubin and Sepehr Zabih, *The Foreign Relations of Iran* (Berkeley, 1974), p. 245.

in the disintegration, since the Bangladesh crisis, of developing alliance patterns. India, Pakistan, and Bangladesh each moved away from its respective mentor. On the highest conflict level, an apparent pattern—of Sino-American cooperation opposed to the Soviet Union and manifesting itself in terms of regional conflict—did not survive the crisis. Presumably, had the great powers perceived either urgent threat or great opportunity in the area, this or some other clear pattern manifesting the conflict would have developed. For the Shah this situation presented an opportunity not to be resisted. Once satisfied that Pakistan would not disintegrate further, he moved to improve relations with India, Bangladesh, and even Afghanistan. Particularly after the rise in oil prices in 1973, the various South Asian regimes responded gratefully to any and all Iranian suggestions for improved economic relations. The Shah's still nascent Indian Common Market proposal[36] was particularly welcome.

In fact, the thesis is a strong one that the Bangladesh crisis and its aftermath marked the emergence of an Iranian foreign policy for which the primary motivation was grandeur, both national and dynastic. Indeed, the surprising feature is that this policy has generated so little nationalistic excitement within Iran. In the years 1951–53, when Iran under Dr. Mossadeq was asserting its right to independence in world affairs, there was great excitement. But in the 1970's when the Shah was proclaiming credibly that Iran would play a role in world affairs comparable to that of West Germany, the reaction was more one of ennui. Why was this so? There is no mystery in the lack of response of the nationalistic opposition. As explained above, they simply rejected the thesis and saw instead a Shah dutifully executing American orders. The lack of response on the part of a clear majority of Iranians, described as acquiescent, was in tune with their general demeanor. Theirs was an attitude of detachment. The policy and the grandeur was the Shah's, not Iran's. Yet even among the Shah's active supporters, there were few signs of spontaneous excitement. The media and the

[36] Ralph Joseph, "The Selling of an Indian Ocean Common Market," *Kayhan International*, March 18, 1978, pp. 4–5.

politicians were effusive in their praise for the policy. But all of the enthusiasm appeared to be artificial. Indeed, the lack of any real excitement in the face of spectacular growth in Iran's exercise of influence in regional and world affairs gave strong evidence of the enduring price paid by the Shah for his mode of achieving power. A lack of nationalist legitimacy had not proved important enough to bring down the regime, but it had denied it depth of support. The claim is made that the Shah was virtually the sole author of Iran's foreign policy,[37] and that case is a strong one. However, when viewed in terms of decisional latitude, the lack of any real popular enthusiasm for his foreign policy was sharply limiting. It denied the Shah the kind of adventurousness in world affairs that he might otherwise have indulged in. The Iranian people acquiesced in the expenditure of a third of Iran's vast oil income for a weapons system that seemed far in excess of Iranian needs. But would they have acquiesced in an adventure that produced large casualty figures? This analysis argues that they would not, and there is some subtle but real evidence for that conclusion.

In 1973 Iran became involved in a limited war. A rebellion developed in Dhofar, the westernmost province of Oman. The rebellion was in part a spillover from the revolutionary change occurring in the People's Democratic Republic of Yemen and in part a manifestation of indigenous grievances. It was viewed by the United States government in cold war terms: a manifestation of Soviet expansion through subversion. In fact, the rebellion did receive military, economic, and technical assistance from both the Soviet Union and China.[38] When the Sultan of Oman asked for Iranian assistance, the Shah happily agreed, with the blessing of the United States and the United Kingdom. But whereas the American interest was spelled out in cold war terms, the Shah gave C. L. Sulzberger of the *New York Times* a different picture. "Imagine if these savages took over the other side of the Hormuz Straits at the entrance to the Persian Gulf. Our life depends on this. And these people fighting against the

[37] This is the central thesis of Chubin and Zabih, *Foreign Relations*.
[38] *Ibid.*, pp. 310–12.

Sultan are savages. They could be even worse than Communists."[39]

The episode is significant for a number of reasons. As the Shah's statement indicates, he did not see his moves as a battle against international communism. But he did understand that the United States saw it as a battle against Soviet expansion and that China feared the outcome of the rebellion might result in an expansion of Soviet influence. The Shah asked Peking to withdraw its assistance, and, rather than offend a regional ally, Peking agreed.[40] Furthermore, the Shah showed no fear that Soviet retaliation might take the form of a deterioration of Soviet-Iranian relations, and no such deterioration developed.

The Shah's description of the rebels is an example of a classic imperial view in which the target people are judged with cultural contempt. Such a view generally accompanies a perceived opportunity for the expansion of influence.[41] For their own good the "savages" should be suppressed and civilized. The setting was ideal. The Iranian force was there by invitation. Sultan Qabus of Oman thus became as much dependent on Iran as the Shah ever was on the United States. Furthermore, here was a locale in which Iranian armed forces could gain combat experience and could achieve a cheap victory. Accounts of the conflict vary,[42] but the outcome was predictable, given the overwhelming superiority of Iranian arms. Yet the entire episode was given minimal attention in the tightly controlled Tehran press. Neither casualties nor victories were stressed. Apparently the regime assumed that enthusiasm could not be generated for the adventure in Dhofar.

Another episode that reveals much of the Shah's policies and his decisional freedom was his campaign against Iraq. Significantly, the details of this episode do not come from the Iranian media but from documents that were made available to the so-called Pike Committee of the House of Representatives

[39]*New York Times,* March 19, 1975, 47:2.

[40]Chubin and Zabih, *Foreign Relations,* pp. 310–12.

[41]For a development of this point see Richard Cottam, *Foreign Policy Motivation: A General Theory and a Case Study* (Pittsburgh, 1977).

[42]Compare that of Chubin and Zabih, *Foreign Relations,* with that of Fred Halliday, *Arabia Without Sultans* (New York, 1974), pp. 316–73.

appointed to investigate the role of the CIA in American foreign policy.[43] In 1972 the Shah suggested to Richard Nixon that Iran and the United States foment another rebellion of the Kurds against the Iraqi government. The government of Iraq had gone a good distance toward meeting the demands of its Kurdish minority, and there is a real possibility that without external stimulation a modus vivendi of Kurd and Arab in Iraq would have developed.[44] But the Shah correctly understood that Mullah Mustafa Barzani, the Kurdish traditional leader in Iraq, could not resist the promise of external support. Both Nixon and Secretary of State Henry Kissinger liked the idea, and a joint strategy was developed. Soviet arms captured from the Arabs by Israel would be smuggled into Iraqi Kurdistan by American and Iranian agents. This would serve the dual purpose of giving the Kurds the means to rebel and of generating suspicions in Iraq of Soviet intentions. At the same time the Shah and the Americans agreed explicitly not to allow the Kurds victory. The goal was to weaken Iraq without stimulating the interest of Iranian Kurds in independence. In 1974 the rebellion was triggered, but it went badly. By the winter of 1974–75 Iraq was close to military victory, and Iranian forces were compelled to give military support to the Kurds, advancing as much as nine miles into Iraq.[45] Then in March 1975 mediation by President Houari Boumédienne of Algeria was successful, and an Iraqi-Iranian agreement resulted by which Iraq accepted the Shatt-al-Arab channel boundary and ceased assisting Iranian dissidents and Arab and Baluchi minorities in Iran. Iran ceased assisting the Kurds, and the collapse of the Kurdish resistance followed immediately.

This episode, like that of Dhofar, illustrates several points. The Soviet Union could not be unaware that a major provocation against Iraq involving Soviet arms was occurring right in the Soviet backyard and furthermore that it concerned an ethnic group that is found in the Soviet Union. This is hardly

[43]Published in the *Village Voice*, February 16, 1976, p. 85.

[44]See Richard Cottam, "The Case of the Kurds," unpublished paper presented at the annual meeting of the APSA, Washington, D.C., 1977.

[45]*New York Times*, March 13, 1975, 6:1.

the kind of behavior that demonstrates fear of a nearby superpower. Rather it reflects an essentially status quo view of the Soviets, and the lack of Soviet response was confirming of that view. It is, indeed, difficult to argue that Iranian policy is primarily a response to a perceived Soviet threat. Second, the policy toward the Kurds was again a manifestation of cultural contempt. The Kurdish population of Iran numbers over a million, yet the Shah was willing to toy with and ultimately betray the desire of Kurds for national dignity. Third, pressure from the press for a military confrontation that might easily have resulted in an Iran-Iraqi war was minimal. Obviously the Shah felt few limitations on his decisional freedom to accept defeat but doubted the decisional freedom to carry his people into a major war.

Iran's role in the intra-Arab conflict is apparently far greater than press coverage in Iran would suggest. Reports that Iran was a major supplier of arms to the right-wing militia in Lebanon are not reflected in any effort by the press to generate Iranian enthusiasm for the Lebanese right. Yet detailed accounts are given of Iranian interference, mainly working through traditional and ultraconservative elements of the Shiite community of Lebanon.[46]

The one major example of extraordinary press attention given a foreign adventure came in 1972 with the seizure of three small islands in the Strait of Hormuz at the entrance to the Persian Gulf. When the British announced their intention to withdraw their military forces from the Persian Gulf in 1971, the Iranian government renewed its claim to the island state of Bahrein and to the three islands, Abu Musa and the two Tumbs. In 1970 the Shah with studied magnanimity agreed to abide by a United Nations test of Bahreini sentiment, knowing that the decision would be against Iran. But after the British did withdraw, the Tumbs were invaded and Abu Musa was occupied with the permission of the sheikdom of Sharja (which had been given suzerainty over the island by the British). This

[46]Descriptions of this important aspect of the Lebanese civil war are limited to the Iranian opposition press. See, for example, the lead article of *Payam e Mujahid,* no. 57, May 1978.

act was given banner headlines in Iran. The occupation was clumsy and there were a few casualties, but the operation was brief and the price in terms of loss of life low. The act appears to have been popular.

Iran's influence in the Persian Gulf was at the hegemonic level. The Arab leaders in the Union of Arab Emirates were very friendly with Iran in spite of the seizure of the islands, and militarily Iran was overwhelmingly predominant. Iran exercised a solitary "Concert of Europe" role, guarding the region against any revolutionary change. With the construction of a naval base at Shah Bahar, Iran would become a major naval power in the Indian Ocean as well. In South Asia and the Arab world Iran was already a major influence both economically and politically. And as a major power in the Organization of Petroleum Exporting Countries, Iran played an important world role. In fifteen years this was nothing less than a revolutionary change in power position. Yet there was no parallel growth in pride of the Iranian people.

Utilitarian Strategy: The Bedrock of Control

Following the overthrow of Dr. Mossadeq in 1953, the successor regime, first under General Zahedi and then under the Shah, had no choice but to turn to the Iranian landowning class as its primary base of societal support. The middle class had been much too enamored of Dr. Mossadeq, and despite efforts to please the most conservative religious leaders, such as the persecution of Bahais, by and large the most prominent religious leaders remained hostile to the regime. Some years would be required to purge unreliable elements from the security forces, and not until 1960 was the Shah willing to risk his survival on the premise that the security forces would maintain control even if there were a shift away from the upper-class base of support.

From the fall of 1960 until January 1963 the Shah made a major effort to liberalize his administration. He permitted some degree of electoral freedom and equal amounts of freedom for the press, speech, and assembly. But the consequences were not encouraging for the longevity of his regime, and at the end of that two-and-a-half-year period his political survival was in serious question. What he had more or less wittingly tested was the willingness of the most politically attentive, largely middle-class sector of the Iranian public to be reconciled to a post-Mossadeq regime in which the Shah's personal role was a significant one. The results suggested irreconcilability, and in January and July of 1963 the Shah survived the forcible suppression of the Mossadeqist opposition and then the religious opposition.

Following the advice of Prime Minister Ali Amini's protégé and minister of agriculture, Hassan Arsenjani, the Shah moved in the direction of mooring his regime in the peasantry and labor. Land reform and progressive labor legislation were the vehicles, and without question this strategy did produce a broad base of support for the Shah. But there was a serious flaw in this strategic reasoning. The peasantry and, to a lesser extent, labor were not easily mobilizable in support of the regime. Indeed, prior to land reform, the landowners' support for the Shah had brought with it the largely uncomprehending support of the Iranian peasantry. Now there was some positive enthusiasm from the peasantry, but probably the most important effect of land reform on stability was the removal of the peasantry from the ranks of potential opposition. Peasant riots against the regime could be dangerous, but peasant support offered little strength in case of a political crisis.

For positive support, the security forces were essential. Here the regime was clearly successful. Members of the security forces, many of them of lower- and lower-middle-class backgrounds, were able to improve their social status and that of their extended families. Furthermore, the material and other rewards granted the military were impressive. Not only were salaries large and housing and automobiles frequently available, but many of the military were given the heady experience of a training course in the United States. As time passed, gratitude for a rise in status was frequently offset by annoyance over a failure to be promoted or some such careerist grievance. But still the security forces by and large were attracted to the regime and gave it their support. Satisfaction on the basis of influence and material rewards was such that the security forces could be counted as a positive base of regime support.

Less expected but probably even more significant was the positive support the regime attracted from the governmental bureaucracy. Abdol Hassan Ebtehaj's advice[47] that the most competent of Iran's educated and trained youth be recruited for positions within the Plan Organization, regardless of past participation in oppositionist activities, was of great importance for regime longevity. By the late 1970's trained technocrats occupied most high positions in the government bureaucracy. A large percentage of them had been involved in opposition activities, usually abroad, but had been attracted by an appeal to patriotism (their skills were needed by Iran), the belief that they could play an early role of decisional importance, and generous wage and other material incentives. Enthusiasm for the regime was rather muted, but accommodation to it gradually developed as the young recruit moved up the bureaucratic ladder. There was, however, among the technocratic element a strong sense of a lack of efficacy. Planning was if anything overly elaborate, but execution of plans was a slow and enervating process. The end result, always far behind schedule, often bore little resemblance to the planning conception. A sense of powerlessness accompanied an assumption that any serious change in the regime was unlikely.

Contrary to Arsenjani's assumption that the middle class was hopelessly wedded to the memory of Dr. Mossadeq and his movement, the strongest public support for the Shah emanated from a section of what must be called the middle class. Following the economic crisis of the early 1960's, entrepreneurial activity began to accelerate. Fed by a rapidly growing oil income, government expenditures increased, and the spillover into the private sector was soon reflected in an extraordinarily rapid rate of growth. Indeed, viewed from a growth-rate perspective, Iranian development has resembled that of Brazil, Taiwan, and South Korea. The private sector, far more than government planning, gave a definition to the direction of

[47]See Chapter 16, pp. 289–90.

Iranian economic development. Critics pointed out that much of the economic activity was in the form of land speculation, service, and light industry. Agriculture was badly neglected, and the government's efforts to construct a strong heavy industry infrastructure were hampered by the Shah's fascination with the most advanced and most expensive technology.[48] Training programs were neglected, and power was in short supply. In addition, the sense of corruption pervaded virtually all commercial and governmental activity. The reality of corruption was impossible for the outsider to probe, but the belief in its pervasiveness was both universal and demoralizing.

In terms of regime stability, however, there is no question that Iran's economic development had produced a large number of people, many of whom were enormously wealthy, who had a strong vested interest in the regime's survival. They can be classified as the newly rich segment of the middle class, but this is the analyst's classification. There was among this element of the population no real sense of class identity and little real concern with politics. Their prosperity rested on their ability to understand and manipulate bureaucratic regulations, and this required an acute understanding of, and access to, influence channels. To this extent they were deeply involved in the governmental politico-administrative process. But they manifested little interest in the official Resurgence Party, in parliamentary activity, and in elections. Still, they gave definition to social justice in Iran just as they gave definition to development. Income distribution, the priority granted education, and welfare programs all reflected the primacy of this element of the population. So, in fact, did labor policy. Employment was high, and, especially before the years of high inflation beginning in 1974, real wages did rise for the Iranian worker. But the single labor union was tightly controlled, and strikes were forbidden. Per capita income was statistically above $2,000 a year, but this meant little. Iran was a working example of the "trickle down" theory.

[48]For a discussion of informed American opinion on this point see *New York Times*, May 30, 1977, 24:2.

The institutional base of support for the regime paralleled the societal base of support. Most important by far were the coercive institutional base and the security force. SAVAK, the secret police, and the gendarmerie appeared to be, before the Tabriz riots of 1978, sufficient to control any overt political opposition to the regime.

After those riots the effectiveness of the military for internal security purposes was open to question. The use of tanks and helicopters in Tabriz indicated that training in riot control was deficient. Presumably that problem could be quickly remedied; the important issues would be the loyalty of officers and men and their willingness to fire on religious demonstrators.

The institution of the bureaucracy presented a mixed picture. Without question the government was successful in attracting highly qualified people into the bureaucracy. But it had great difficulty in persuading them to remain, owing in part to the Shah's decisional style. Exceedingly proud of his knowledge of domestic and foreign affairs, including complex economic questions, the Shah saw himself as *the* Iranian decision maker. Given the limited number of hours in the day, this image is of necessity illusory. But it did affect adversely the willingness of the second echelon in the decisional hierarchy to innovate and even to interpret freely the general policy instructions from the Shah. The consequence was that much of the bureaucracy busied itself in the routine of administration but lacked a sense of direction and decisional importance. Since the private sector did offer opportunities for innovation, many of the best bureaucrats were enticed by offers from that sector.

The Shah had on many occasions lamented the fact that his father failed to provide the political institutional base that is essential for regime stability and for orderly succession.[49] In his early experimenting with the Mardom and Melliyun Parties in the mid-1950's, the Shah was seeking to provide that political institutional base.[50] Seeing Mardom as a progressive but loyal

[49] Probably the most insightful set of interviews of the Shah are to be found in Bayne, *Persian Kingship*.

[50] *Ibid*.

opposition party and Melliyun as the conservative and loyal government party, the Shah quite consciously sought to emulate the British system of political parties. But his efforts foundered on the most elementary prerequisite: a willingness to grant sufficient decisional freedom to the parliamentary system for the party competition to become, and to appear to be, authentic. The formula was obvious enough. Allow the parties freedom to question any policy that does not relate directly to the Shah or the security forces. But given the Shah's decisional style and decisional image, virtually any criticism of important government policies amounted to criticism of the Shah and hence was not allowed. As a consequence, party competition had the appearance of a charade and generated more cynicism than support.

When Melliyun was dropped and replaced by the Iran Novin Party, the Shah seemed to be moving toward the traditional, authoritarian, single-party formula in which the party serves as a channel for the highly ambitious to reach positions of influence within the government. But the Shah retained Mardom and even allowed other parties to be formed. The British model was still there. However, the dangers in the model were made clear by the activities of the executive secretary of Mardom, Nasser Ameri. Ameri actively explored the limits of real criticism and was at times criticizing policies closely identified with the Shah. The Shah's response was predictable. Ameri was expelled from the party and shortly later killed in an automobile accident. The assumption that it was not an accident is widely held in Iran.

Following this experience with Ameri, the Shah abolished all the parties and substituted a single party, Rastakhiz, or Resurgence. He suggested that all Iranians join the new party, and millions quickly complied.[51] But even with this move he did not abandon completely the old model. Instead, he has attempted to construct under the Rastakhiz umbrella different ideological factions. He appointed the highly talented and progressive-minded Abdul Majid Majidi as the coordinator of

[51]*Kayhan International,* January 7, 1978, p. 1.

the progressive wing and the equally talented and progressive Hushang Ansary as coordinator of the constructive wing. Given the by now prolonged pattern and the fact that Majidi and Ansary were among the most outstanding of the Shah's officials, there is no reason to doubt the Shah's seriousness of purpose. Still, there did not emerge from the artificially created factions policy differences that would appear to the politically interested Iranian as real. In the following party congress the speeches of Majidi and Ansary were easily interchangeable. As a result, Iranian dissidents willing to consider an evolutionary approach for producing change in Iran formed their own organization, the Radical Movement of Iran, and called for the dissolution of Rastakhiz as an early basic reform.

The Majlis mirrored this picture.[52] The latitude of real debate was much too narrow to be of public interest. No real policy initiatives appeared from the Majlis, nor was there any resistance to a program known to be favored by the Shah. Interest in becoming a member of parliament was high mainly because of the access that position granted. And access in this era in Iran was easily translated into money.

Control of the press was by 1978 both positive and negative. Censorship was supplemented by inspired articles and themes. Press coverage of the Shah promoted a cult of personality. Gone were the days in which innuendo and nuance, particularly in the form of satire, gave voice to real criticism. By far the most colorful and interesting articles that appeared in the 1970's were the Shah's own interviews. As he gained self-confidence, he indulged less and less in the niceties, and his interviews sometimes made for fascinating reading.

Iranian opposition activity surprisingly lost little of its vitality in the past fifteen years, and 1977 and 1978 have witnessed a sharp increase in that activity both inside and outside Iran. The persistence of strong opposition is surprising in view of the

[52] In June 1978 Majlis deputy Mohsen Pezeshkpur and several other members of the Majlis began making both sharp and unwelcome criticisms of government programs. Pezeshkpur's suggestion that an all Iranian party be formed replacing Rastakhiz was angrily rebuffed by the prime minister. On the surface this appears to be a tentative exploring of the possibility of playing a real opposition role and a reflection of the manifestation of open popular dissatisfaction.

success the regime had in purchasing the acquiescence or accommodation of so high a percentage of Nationalist and even Marxist oppositionists in their post-college years. The rhythm was one of a small opposition core which remains almost constant in size and was in effect a professional opposition. This core was sustained and supported by a significant proportion of the most politically attentive and activist youth, particularly university students. Upon graduation those ex-students who returned to Iran were likely to gain high paying jobs and to tell themselves they would work within the system to change it. Then, gradually, accommodation begins. Some few doubtless remained as active revolutionaries, and more watched for the day in which they might work actively for change. In the summer of 1977, for example, a surprisingly large number of employees of the Ministry of Justice took the risk of publicly disagreeing with government policy procedures that were closely associated with the Shah.[53]

The aging process decimated the ranks of the old National Front. Little was heard of the Iran Party or the Mardom e Iran Party. But the Third National Front was active abroad. When some of the members of the Radical Movement of Iran took the risk of public identification in December 1977, several proved to be onetime members of the Mossadeqist Niruye Sevvom. Dariush Foruhar of the old Pan-Iran group, when he was not in jail, maintained an organization. But the one element of the old National Front that has retained and even expanded its dynamic quality is the Freedom Front. Acting in close collaboration with Ayatollah Khomeini and other leading Shiite political mullahs, the Freedom Front remains a grouping of religious, intellectual, and bazaari leaders. Religiously oriented students associated with the Islamic Youth organization provide a steady inflow of new recruits. Mehdi Bazergan, whose apartment was bombed in April 1978, was the most prominent of the lay leaders of the organization.

[53]The case involved major procedural reforms which have been interpreted as a positive response to President Carter's human rights campaign. The complaint was that the reforms were imposed on the ministry without any consultation or any possibility of ministry input.

Most oppositionist students in the United States and Europe are associated with the Confederation of Iranian Students. That organization is in fact an umbrella that shelters a multifaceted Iranian student movement. Most of the students are Marxists of one shade or another—including Maoists and Trotskyites. Since the People's Republic of China is an active if de facto ally of the Shah and since the Soviet Union is usually on good terms with the Iranian government, there is little temptation on the part of the student factions to look to the great powers for support. Close relationships do exist for some with the Palestine Liberation Organization, with Libya, and with other Arab groups, but the student factions are basically self-reliant. Connections of these student factions inside Iran have been impossible to document.

Guerrilla activity in Iran began in 1971 with a raid on the police station at Siah Kel in northern Iran. The group was decimated, but its parent organization, the Guerrilla Organization of the Devotees of the People, continued to operate. Another organization, the Strugglers of the People, also operated as a guerrilla force; there have been frequent clashes with the security forces, many bank robberies, and a number of assassinations of Iranian security officials and of some Americans associated with Iranian security.[54] Government reports always referred to the guerrillas as Islamic Marxists or "red and black reactionaries."[55]

Opposition activity inside Iran developed rapidly in 1977 and 1978. The stimulation for this activity was in part internal and in part external. Inflation by 1977 was causing genuine distress not only for everyone who lived on a fixed salary but for anyone not deeply involved in speculative ventures. Housing in particular was unattainable for anyone other than the exceptionally well off. Peasants and workers both suffered.

[54]On the guerrilla movement in Iran see A. T. Pouyan and M. Mani, *Iran: Three Essays on Imperialism* (Florence, 1972).

[55]*Kayhan International,* January 7, 1978. References to "red and black reactionaries" were a constant feature of the Rastakhiz Party congress reported in this issue of *Kayhan International,* pp. 4–5.

This internal distress coincided with President Jimmy Carter's human rights program. Given the intimate American involvement in Iranian affairs, detailed in this book, Iranians can hardly be blamed for taking seriously an American policy that proclaimed interference in the affairs of others. What was unexpected was the suggestion that the interference be conducted to broaden, not narrow, the range of human and political rights in Iran. This amounts to a return to the American policy Iranians thought they saw during the first quarter of this century, especially in the Morgan Shuster days. At least Carter's stand was worth exploring.

The Radical Movement of Iran, referred to above, was formed by a group of progressive Iranians, some of them well known. As mentioned, several had been associates of Khalil Maleki in the Niruye Sevvom. Others had been involved in the 1961 teachers' strike and with the leader of the teachers' movement, Mohammad Derakhshesh. Some were employed in the Ministry of Justice and the Ministry of Education. Their public spokesman was Rahmatollah Moghadam, a former deputy of parliament whose political career was shortened because he had the temerity to make a highly critical speech in the Majlis. The Radical Movement issued several manifestos which called for a return to the rule of law in Iran, release of political prisoners, and an end to brutality and torture by the security force.

The Iranian government, seemingly also uncertain as to Carter's seriousness of purpose, made several gestures in the direction of liberalization. A Human Rights Commission was activated; legal procedures were altered to make arrest and detention less arbitrary; torturing of prominent prisoners was halted and prison conditions improved; an organization of composers and artists independent of government control was permitted; and the increasingly bold dissent from a number of individuals and organizations was not suppressed. Responding to this, a number of prominent individuals wrote public letters highly critical of the regime and demanding extensive reform. Particularly noteworthy were the letters of Ali Asghar Haj

Sayyad Javadi. The government did not permit media coverage of these activities, and even highly attentive Iranians were unaware of them. But neither were they at first harassed.

By mid-year, however, the government's attitude began to change. Signals received from the Carter administration could only encourage the government in its conclusion that, at least as far as Iran was concerned, Carter's human rights campaign could safely be ignored. Carter's choice of ambassador for Iran, William Sullivan, was a man with, from the Shah's point of view, a safe reputation—a Vietnam hard-liner while ambassador to Laos and the man chosen to deal with Marcos in the Philippines. The administration worked hard to overcome congressional opposition to the sale of planes to Iran equipped with the highly sophisticated electronic warning system known as AWACS. This decision was particularly important because the AWACS system is precisely the kind of security instrument that Iranians can see as being of no use to them in any conceivable conflict but could be of great importance to the United States. Then the president included Iran on his itinerary for a friendly visit in December 1977. But, most important, the administration took no note of dissidents' activity in Iran even though their risky decision to surface was in direct response to President Carter's proclaimed interest in advancing the cause of human rights abroad. In late summer 1977, the Iranian government abruptly sentenced one of Iran's most prestigious thelogians, Ayatollah Taleqani, to ten years in prison. Since Taleqani was associated with the Freedom Front and with Ayatollah Khomeini, the meaning of this action was clear. By virtue of its connections with religious leaders in Iran, the Freedom Front has an ability to reach a wide range of the Iranian public. Its opposition therefore was very dangerous especially since economic distress was producing increasing public receptivity for anti-regime activity on the part of the religiously inclined lower middle class. In the fall of 1977 several sermons from mosques were clear attacks on the regime, and a number of incidents involving police violence against religious and student demonstrators occurred.

On December 22, 1977, a statement signed by twenty-nine

prominent Iranian dissidents was distributed inside Iran.[56] The list included the name of Bazergan of the Freedom Front, Karim Sanjabi of the old National Front, Moghadam of the Radical Movement, and two or three members of the Marxist opposition. Although this list had been sent to Carter prior to his departure for Iran, he took no note in his public statements in Iran of what amounted to a broad coalition of Iranian dissidents who were calling for exactly the kind of program Carter advocated. On the contrary, he pointedly referred to the trust of the Iranian people in their Shah.[57]

Spurned by Carter, the religio-political opposition accelerated its activities. In early January 1978 a large demonstration in the shrine at Qom protested the sentencing of Taleqani and demanded the return of Khomeini from exile in Iraq. Violence flared and a number of people were killed. But it was the February 18, 1978, riots in Tabriz that raised the first really serious question of the institutional capability of the internal security force since July 1963. The riots began as a religio-political demonstration commemorating the fortieth day of mourning for victims of the bloody demonstration in Qom. Demonstrations occurred throughout Iran on February 18, and in a number of cities they led to rioting. But in Tabriz the demonstrations were massive, and the security force response was clumsy and provocative. By the time order was restored, seventy-three banks, four hotels, twenty-two shops, eight theaters, and a number of government offices were badly damaged or destroyed. There were nine deaths and over a hundred injuries by the government count.[58] Opposition sources described far greater damage and a death toll of 432 with fifteen hundred injured.[59] Reports indicated that the Tabriz police refused to fire on the crowd, and military forces had to be brought in to restore order.

[56]For the text see Committee for Human Rights in Iran, *Letters from the Great Prison: An Eyewitness Account of Human and Social Conditions in Iran* (Washington, D.C., 1978). Three additional signatories are included along with the original twenty-nine.

[57]See the Iranian treatment of Carter's statements in *Kayhan International*, January 7, 1978, p. 3.

[58]*Kayhan International*, February 25, 1978, p. 1.

[59]*Iran Free Press*, March 1978, p. 1.

Since the demonstrations across Iran followed Moslem mourning tradition and had been called for by a leading cleric, Ayatollah Sayyed Qasem Shariatmadari, the event was easily anticipated. The Shah publicly criticized SAVAK for its failures, and removed the responsible police, secret police, and SAVAK officials in East Azerbaijan.[60] A few weeks later he replaced the director of SAVAK. The performance of the internal security forces and the Shah's public criticism of them was of major significance because, as described earlier in this chapter, an image of ubiquitousness and omniscience is vital for mission performance. The Tabriz episode damaged this image and seriously reduced the deterrence capability of these forces. Furthermore, reports of police unwillingness to fire on the crowd were widely believed and placed the ability of these security forces to maintain order in serious question.

In March and April 1978 the government began resorting to paramilitary terrorist attacks on Iranian dissidents. Apartments and automobiles were blown up, and in one case the victim was kidnapped, beaten, and released. This marked a move to open and crude terror similar to the reliance on strong-arm tactics in a previous and less sophisticated era.[61]

The reliance on the transparent device of supposedly outraged citizens forming vigilante groups to punish the Shah's tormentors typified the strange, almost bizarre, nature of the Shah's response to his crisis. Mass receptivity for protest, even violent protest, against the regime was a consequence of the deep economic distress most Iranians were experiencing because of the uncontrolled inflation. Indeed, it is probably fair to say that only those Iranians heavily involved in corrupt practices were able to stay ahead of inflation.

Coincidental with this mass receptivity, the momentum of oppositionist activity was by the spring of 1978 developing to the point that fairly drastic repressive action would be necessary to reverse it. Whereas it is certainly true that initial Iranian interpretations of Jimmy Carter's human rights foreign policy

[60]*Kayhan International,* March 4, p. 1, and March 11, 1978, p. 1.

[61]These attacks are detailed in the publication *Nehzat,* the organ of the Radical Movement of Iran, published in Iran.

stance gave early momentum to opposition activities, these activities were timid and tentative. Within a few weeks signals from Washington should have made clear to the Shah that he need fear little pressure from Washington to "liberalize" and to the opposition that they could not expect even rhetorical support from Washington, at least at a public level.

The developing momentum in fact was entirely attributable to the inability of the Shah's regime to deal adequately with either the problem of inflation or the problem of maintaining the credibility of the security forces. To be sure, dealing with inflation required drastic remedies that would involve sacrificing some of the Shah's most dearly held priorities—the extravagant arms purchases that fed his need for personal grandeur, and equally extravagant economic projects such as urban development spectaculars in Tehran. Furthermore, any serious effort to deal with the problem would be at the expense of the newly rich who comprised one of the Shah's few bases of societal support. But his approach was to impose arbitrary and selectively administred price controls on merchants, many of whom were already victims of inflation. Individuals of great wealth and influence easily avoided most controls.

With regard to the problem of reinforcing his ability to exercise coercive control, the Shah was even less effective. Arbitrary dismissals of security force officials adversely affected both morale and efficiency in the security forces. Indeed, a key predictor of probable disfavor seemed to be past loyalty to the regime. Then acts of repression were inconsistently administered. Extreme brutality alternated with permissiveness and leniency. Paramilitary raids on opposition leaders were followed by the release of political prisoners. The result was both an increasing willingness by the opposition to escalate its demands and activities in response to evidence of the inefficiency of the security force and a growing paralysis and intensifying anger at apparent mindless brutality. In addition, the broadly based opposition coalition that included the Radical Movement, the National Front, the Freedom Front, representatives of religious leaders and a few socialists, was able to maintain a degree of unity that is remarkable considering its diversity, competing ambitions, and the suspicion generated by years in underground competition. The artless quality of the government response, far from exploiting inevitable suspicions, served to unify.

The climactic event occurred in August 1978 when the Rex Theater in Abadan caught on fire, apparently the result of arson. Over four hundred persons were burned. The doors of the theater had been locked, presumably as a precaution against terrorist attacks, and were not opened quickly; the supposedly ultramodern fire-fighting equipment in the city arrived late and dealt ineffectually with the catastrophe. The government charges that those responsible were fanatical Moslems opposed to the Shah's modernization efforts were accepted without question only by the American press. In Iran the government's description of the Rex tragedy was accepted by very few. This was not surprising since the initial government account was incompatible with the physical location of the theater, and the early arrests were of young high-school teachers rather than of fanatical Moslems opposed to the showing of films. A revised and very different story gained little credibility. The victims' friends and relatives indicated who they thought responsible by rioting against the government. An account that gained wide acceptance was that several Islamic activists being pursued by SAVAK took refuge in the theater; when SAVAK reported this to the Shah, he personally ordered the burning of the theater. That this account would be accepted by so many, especially given the factual uncertainty of the case, is indicative of the extent of deterioration in the Shah's popular position.

Karim Sanjabi, leader of the National Front, compared the Rex to the Reichstag fire. But the results were opposite. Instead of being able to use the episode to consolidate power, the Shah moved dramatically to appease the opposition. He removed as premier Jamshid Amuzegar, a talented technocrat who had served the Shah well for many years as oil minister. Amuzegar's replacement was in many ways his opposite. Jafar Sherif-Emami, a senator and politician with a long survival record that testified to his ability to sense change in the political climate, was given the task of reconciling the opposition. The Shah had turned to Sherif-Emami in the 1960–63 crisis with the same purpose in mind. Without question Sherif-Emami had the desired contacts. But he had no independent base of support and could not hope to attract men of any real independence into his government or into his confidence. He therefore was no threat to the Shah but neither was he of much use. In 1978 as in 1961 he could not establish serious negotiations with either the Islamic or secular opposition.

Sherif-Emami's two months as premier was the freest period in Iran since 1962. At times the press was almost free; debates in the Majlis came to life as deputies took advantage of the media exposure their position granted them and engaged in real criticism (a minority moved into apparently genuine opposition); old political parties were revived, including the National Front parties, and many new parties were born; and orderly, disciplined demonstrations took place, one of which on September 5, 1978, attracted as many as three million participants across the country. Strikes swept the country, and the government promised to offset inflation with salary increases which if fulfilled would consume much of the government's budget. At the same time, serious preparations were underway to place on trial for corruption several leading business and governmental officials. Heading the list was Amir Abbas Hoveida, the Shah's faithful premier for twelve years and his minister of court for one year. Not incidentally, part of Hoveida's family was Bahai and several of those under investigation, later to be tried, were Bahais. General Nematollah Nassiri, the Shah's loyal officer, participant in the overthrow of Mossadeq and for many years head of SAVAK, was also prominent on the list. Quite clearly the Shah was willing to take economic measures that could only appall his supporters among the newly rich in order to appeal to the opposition. Also he was willing to risk his support in the government by placing on trial men who had served him faithfully if not terribly well. He was even willing to offer as sacrifices to what he obviously saw as Islamic bigotry members of the Bahai community who had been among his stronger supporters. The act left the religious opposition bemused, angry, and possibly a little embarrassed. Ayatollah Khomeini in a statement made explicit his promises that in the Islamic republic he advocated there would be religious tolerance.

Yet the Shah coupled his efforts to appease the opposition with harsh acts of repression. Most serious of these occurred on September 8, 1978, a few hours after martial law was declared. A large crowd was fired on and many people were killed. The government issued the figure of seventy-eight but opposition spokesmen in Iran claim they can prove that at least forty-five hundred were killed and reports of seventeen thousand deaths were being circulated. Only three days earlier, a million demonstrators in Tehran had given troops, police, and SAVAK officers flowers and had expressed feelings of brotherhood.

After two months, in November 1978, the Shah gave up his efforts to reach and accommodate the opposition. He appointed General Gholam Reza Azhari premier of a new military government. Schools and universities were closed, the press was suspended (and then refused to publish), gatherings of more than three people in Tehran were prohibited, efforts to break strikes of oil workers and government employees were made, opposition leaders were arrested, and parliament was recessed. The Shah promised that these measures would be temporary, but confrontations with the opposition were, as these lines were written, easy to forecast.

By far the most interesting development of 1977 and 1978 in Iran was the growth in popularity of Ayatollah Ruhollah Khomeini. When the riots of June 1963 occurred in Tehran the name of Khomeini had little currency among Iran's Nationalists. But the breadth of Khomeini's appeal among lower-middle-class and working-class Iranians quickly became apparent. The ease with which the Shah had suppressed the secular National Front stood in sharp contrast to the nearly fatal rioting by Khomeini's followers. In the years that followed, there was a close working relationship between the Freedom Front, led by Mehdi Bazergan, and Ayatollah Khomeini and his supporters. As such the Khomeini movement was fully within the tradition of Islamic reform and revitalization in alliance with secular liberalism and nationalism that has been a characteristic feature of Iran for the past century. The Freedom Front certainly regarded itself as the most legitimate manifestation of the Mossadeq movement. Yet this secular-Islamic alliance has always been an uneasy one. Secularist distrust of Islamic leaders was apparent in the 1906–12 period particularly among the Azerbaijani anjumans. And that attitude is widely pervasive today. But the National Front easily accommodated a number of powerful religious leaders. Mossadeq's political sensitivities were nowhere better demonstrated than by his skillful accommodation of sectarian and secular forces.

Nevertheless, the suddenly apparent Khomeini popularity necessitated a shift in balance. In the years since Mossadeq's ouster, political awareness and readiness to participate in politics has become far more pervasive in Iran. It may well be that the proportion of secularist Iranians in the population is higher than it was in 1953. But among the large majority of new participants there is obviously a predisposition to look to religious leaders. The massive demonstrations crying for Khomeini's return in 1977 and 1978 were very different in their societal core from the smaller Mossadeqist demonstrations of the early 1950's. University students joined the demonstrations of 1978 and shouted for Khomeini, but they were not the heartbeat of the crowd as they were so often in the 1950's.

In short, Iran in 1978 had its second leader of the twentieth century who can be described as charismatic. Like Mossadeq, he personifies the dignity of the nation but he personifies as well the dignity of Shiite Islam. The blend of the two communities is less classically nationalistic and the ties to the enlightenment are less explicit than was true in the Mossadeq case. Khomeini is in no way Mossadeq's successor. (Khomeini's statements and those of his followers refer only occasionally to Mossadeq albeit usually very favorably.) But the phenomenon of Khomeini is unique in Iran's history. The National Front in 1978 clearly recognized the popular force of the Khomeini movement and has apparently made its adjustments. Khomeini's preeminence has been recognized. But programmatically this adjustment may not be as dramatic as is the shift in leadership. The Freedom Front is philosophically in tune with the National Front, and the social, economic, and foreign policy preferences seem to be generally close.

Nevertheless, the balance of nation, Islam, humanism, and liberalism that is emerging in Iran is a significantly different balance than that of the Mossadeq era. The Iranian whose writings reflected most sensitively the new mix was Dr. Ali Shariati, whose untimely death in his London exile is viewed with deep suspicion by many Iranians. The migration in Shariati's thinking toward Islam and humanism expressed both the direction in which the new balance was tending and the tension and excitement of the new intellectual environment.

Unlike Mossadeq, Ayatollah Khomeini gave every indication of understanding very well the power his enormous popularity granted him. At or near the age of eighty, he brushed aside suggestions that he assume political office in Iran. Rather he chose a role that may be described as boundary setting. By declaring the institution of the monarchy as contrary to the tenets of Islam, he closed the door to compromise with the Shah and the Pahlavi dynasty. In so doing he made extremely difficult any transitional regime designed to accommodate the Pahlavis in the role of constitutional monarch with a broad coalition of oppositionists. Due to Khomeini's influence, Karim Sanjabi, speaking for the National Front, had to refuse to participate in such a regime. He did this even though a widely held view within the secular opposition was that a transitional regime would be the best means of maintaining a momentum that would lead inevitably first to the abdication of the Shah and then the termination of the dynasty. Rejecting that alternative, they felt, played into the hands of the American- and Israeli-backed security force leaders who believed that much of the status quo ante could be restored.

But the force of Khomeini's influence is such that, regardless of the outcome of the political confrontation, governmental policy must remain within the necessarily imprecise boundaries of Khomeini's dicta. Furthermore, the movement is strong enough to play a major boundary-setting role even with the passing of Khomeini. Corruption, gross inequities in income distribution, favoritism for large enterprises in commerce and even more certainly in agriculture, luxury imports, and brutality by the internal security forces—all as defined by the Khomeini people—cannot return to their pre-1978 level if Iran is to enjoy internal tranquility.

In foreign policy too the boundaries are imprecise but clear in direction. Future policy must manifest clear independence in dealings with the United States, the Soviet Union, and the People's Republic of China, all of which have been more or less supportive of the Shah' regime and must be alert to subversive efforts from any quarter. But Iran must continue to sell its oil, to enter fully into commercial dealings with other countries, and to seek technical assistance where it is truly necessary. Iranian policy must be far more sensitive to the needs of the world Islamic community. Clearly that requires an end to a de facto alliance with Israel and a shift away from Sadat, but since Khomeini and his followers see no truly Islamic regimes anywhere this general dictum is otherwise open to wide interpretation.

The Shah and Nationalism

The problem for any study of nationalism as a determinant of political behavior is that nationalism is only one of many major behavioral determinants and the behavioral outcome is a result of the mix. Isolating the particular impact of a factor such as nationalism is an impossibility. Yet patterns do suggest themselves, and with enough case studies some defensible propositions may emerge. How important, for example, is the tarnished nationalism of the Shah in the strong and persisting opposition to him year after year among university students? Evidence of its importance is easy to come by. The epithets "traitor," "American agent," and "puppet" are used by every opposition group regardless of ideological complexion. But so are "corrupt," "tyrannical," "murderer."

A comparison of the leadership of the Shah and Mossadeq suggests that an image of national purity is helpful in inducing a willingness to accept major material sacrifices for the good of Iran. Signs of sacrifice are not very evident in the Iran of 1978. Mossadeq's followers responded with great enthusiasm to the image of an Iran finally able to assert its independence in a hostile environment. But the Shah has had difficulty generating any excitement for a credible image of an Iran exercising world influence at the level of the highest of the second-rank states. Iranians at the time of Mossadeq extolled the virtues of the Iranian culture and the Iranian national character. But Iranians under royal dictatorship tended to describe their people in pessimistic terms. Mossadeq was granted decisional latitude to risk battle with imperial giants. The Shah had the decisional latitude to accept defeats and setbacks (as in the Kurdish conflict in Iraq in 1975) but seemed to avoid publicizing even minor episodes in which casualties could result.

My own reading of the evidence, particularly that of the Shah's foreign policy, leads me to the conclusion that grandeur was the foremost motive giving direction to his domestic and foreign policies. But it was a grandeur blended of nation, dynasty, and self that was ultimately intensely personal. Loyalty, which is usually associated with a tendency to be nationalistic, does not seem to have characterized the Shah's behavior. On the contrary, he seems neither to have given loyalty nor to have expected it from his subordinates or from his people, nor does he appear to have had any real friends. The case of Hassan Arsenjani is instructive in this regard. Arsenjani in the mid-1950's was one of the Shah's regular visitors and, by Arsenjani's own account,[62] was in this period the author of the Shah's policy of de facto alliance with Israel—a policy Arsenjani advocated on simple balance-of-power grounds. But in the abortive Qarani *coup* attempt against the Shah in 1958, Arsenjani was deeply involved. He was arrested and for several weeks imprisoned. Only a few years later Arsenjani was back in the Amini cabinet as Minister of Agriculture and the primary proponent of land reform. When Amini resigned, Arsenjani remained as Minister of Agriculture even though he had spent

[62]Statement made in an interview with the author, July 1957.

much of his life in the service of Amini and Amini's relative, Qavam as Sultaneh. But when Arsenjani appeared to be receiving too much peasant gratitude, he was ordered to go to Rome as Iranian ambassador. Shortly thereafter he died and, although he had a history of heart disease, few Iranians believe his death was a natural one. The Shah appeared to assume disloyalty and to assert control by balancing talented men of ambition against one another.

The Shah's attitude toward the Iranian people paralleled his attitude toward individuals. They were children receiving the beneficence of a knowing and divinely inspired leader. But they were children viewed with little affection, an ungrateful lot who could not appreciate his services to them. His was an attitude of noblesse oblige.

Conclusion

Iran as a case study of nationalism suggests both the importance of nationalism as a behavioral determinant and its limitations. The Mossadeq era is an example of a period in which control was exercised primarily by manipulating the symbol of nation. It was not enough. Mossadeq's overthrow in 1953 as a consequence of a blundered, American-supported *coup* attempt would not have occurred had his internal position not been badly weakened. Many Iranians were willing to make any sacrifice for what they saw as the goal of national independence and dignity. But for many others the price was much too high.

The Shah, lacking the ability to manipulate national symbols successfully for important sections of his population, survived by a combination of coercion and an ability to satisfy the demands of important societal elements for material wealth and influence. But his inability to project an image of national leader was a prime source of vulnerability and limited severely his range of decisional options. When much of the population felt deep economic distress, the extent of the Shah's vulnerability was clearly revealed. The challenge to him was led by men who could manipulate with strong effect both national and Islamic symbols. Iran has entered a period of its history which will tell even more about nationalism, its power and its limitations.

INDEX